Ethiopia, the Unknown Land

ETHIOPIA, THE UNKNOWN LAND
A Cultural and Historical Guide

Stuart Munro-Hay

with photographs by
Pamela Taor

I.B. Tauris *Publishers*
LONDON • NEW YORK

Published in 2002 by I.B.Tauris & Co Ltd,
6 Salem Road, London W2 4BU
175 Fifth Avenue, New York NY 10010
www.ibtauris.com

In the United States of America and in Canada distributed by
St. Martin's Press, 175 Fifth Avenue, New York NY 10010

ISBN 1 86064 744 8

A full CIP record for this book is available from the British Library
A full CIP record for this book is available from the Library of Congress

Library of Congress catalog card: available

Set in Monotype Ehrhardt and Franklin Gothic Heavy by Ewan Smith, London
Printed and bound in Great Britain by MPG Books Ltd, Bodmin

CONTENTS

ILLUSTRATIONS

FOREWORD

Ethiopia occupied a special place in the cosmology of the ancient Greeks. According to Homer, the ancient gods often journeyed to the farthest reaches of the Hellenic world to enjoy the hospitality of a people who, unlike corrupt Mediterranean man and his gods, were renowned for their grace and virtue: the 'blameless Ethiopians'. Modern Ethiopia may be far removed in time and space from the Ethiopia of classical Western mythology, but like its legendary namesake, it too occupies a special position.

Recent research in paleo-anthropology has given rise to the belief that Ethiopia was one of the earliest homes of humanity. For it was in the Afar desert of eastern Ethiopia that the three-million-year-old skeleton of an upright-walking woman, *Australopithecus afarensis*, better known as 'Lucy', was discovered in 1974. Ethiopia's recorded history dawns in the millennium before Christ with the establishment of the Kingdom of Aksum, which attained a high level of civilisation. Indeed, in its heyday the Aksumite realm was probably the most powerful state between the Roman Empire and Persia. Aksum was converted to Christianity around AD 330, an incident that was to play a fundamental role in shaping the country's cultural heritage.

However, for the past quarter of a century, the name 'Ethiopia' has been a synonym for famine, fratricidal wars, and poverty in the eyes of the outside world. Thus it is with a sigh of deep relief that we Ethiopians welcome the publication of *Ethiopia, the Unknown Land: A Cultural and Historical Guide*, by Stuart Munro-Hay.

Dr Munro-Hay, a respected scholar of Ethiopian history and archaeology, has written outstanding books on Aksum, Aksumite numismatics and the Ethiopian Orthodox Church. His latest oeuvre is a major contribution to re-establishing Ethiopia's image as a country with a unique history and a formidable culture.

Lij Asfa-Wossen Asserate, PhD,
Chairman of the Board of Patrons, Society for the Preservation
and Promotion of Ethiopian Culture,
Frankfurt am Main

ACKNOWLEDGEMENTS

Many useful extras, particularly the excursus on the church hierarchy, were contributed by an Ethiopian friend, Ato Niftalem Kiros, himself of a distinguished ecclesiastical family at Aksum, in a series of long conversations and letters. To him, to his brother Gedion Kiros, to Negasi Tsehaye, Fitsum Gezahegn, Wondimu Yohannes, mayor of Aksum, Massresha Fentahun at Gondar, and other Ethiopians who have made my visits both pleasant and profitable, I express my deep appreciation.

To my friend and colleague Dr Bent Juel-Jensen, for his constant help and encouragement, to M. Jean Doresse, to Pamela and William Taor, who accompanied me on photographic tours, to Dr Rachel Ward of the Department of Oriental Antiquities, British Museum, who helped with the interpretation of an Arabic text, and to many others who have helped with information or ideas, I offer my grateful thanks. Rolf Gronblom kindly supplied the photographs of Harar.

Finally, for stepping in with the vital subvention that permitted the book to appear in this format, special thanks to my friends Endre Rösjö and William Taor.

S. C. Munro-Hay,
Château d'Auzac, Mézin, France

PREFACE

Woe to the land shadowing with wings, which is beyond the rivers of Ethiopia; that sendeth ambassadors by the sea, even in vessels of bulrushes upon the waters ... (Isaiah 18.1–2, King James version)

The Ethiopia of the 1990s was a country still recovering from the traumatic experience of two and a half decades of war, revolution, drought and famine, accompanied by human tragedy on an epic scale. In 1998, once again, Ethiopia found itself at war, this time with its neighbour and historical partner, Eritrea. At the same time famine warnings from the Ogaden region were growing more and more ominous. In 2000, peace talks with Eritrea began, but so far, it seems, they have remained inconclusive. United Nations forces are, however, in place until progress is made.

In the preface to the third edition of his book *The Ethiopians*, published in 1972, Edward Ullendorff commented that the impressionistic picture of the country that he drew then had not basically altered since he first saw Ethiopia and its people more than thirty years before. One cannot say that now – it is doubtful that one could properly say it even then, unless one limits one's description purely to external appearances in selected regions. Even while Ullendorff wrote, the first phase of the Eritrean independence movment was well under way. Two years afterwards, in 1974, the end of an era came with the deposition of Emperor Haile Sellassie. The seeds of these events had been sown long before. There had been the *Weyane* (rebellion) in Tigray in the early 1940s, an attempted coup in 1960, insurgency in Bale and Gojjam in the 1960s, and the increasing pace of resistance to Ethiopian rule in Eritrea. With the Ethiopian revolution the whole of the traditional way of life of the country was to alter radically.

1

Ethiopia under Haile Sellassie was a very poor country. There were grave problems, becoming more apparent as the reign continued. Agricultural productivity was diminishing year by year; drought and consequent famine existed in several regions. The imperial government was authoritarian and unyielding to change. Even though the emperor had once seemed to foreigners a leader open to reform and progress, and modernisation had continued, this was within the limits of his personal judgement of the country's capacity for acceptance. In certain urgent matters, such as land reform, vested interests supporting the imperial system could not be easily set aside. Progress was shelved. An attempted coup in 1960, with progressive aims, had already sounded an alarm that was largely ignored. Many saw the country as dominated by the Amhara section of the population to the exclusion of other groups. The Eritrean crisis posed further doubts. As the emperor grew old, despite his immense personal prestige internationally as a statesman the imperial government was seen increasingly as anachronistic. It was at this stage that the Ethiopian Revolution intervened.

Yet despite the sweeping changes, the abolition of the monarchy, the land reforms and other progressive aspects, revolutionary Ethiopia is remembered by many Ethiopians largely for its horrors. The quality of life of most Ethiopians sank to an even lower level than before. The country's GDP per capita in 1991 was US$120; even in 1997 it was only US$137; neighbouring Kenya rated $339, Egypt $614, and the United Kingdom $16,994. Few seem to have regretted the end of the government of the Workers' Party of Ethiopia in 1990, and the final collapse of President Mengistu Haile Maryam's regime with his flight in May 1991 to his safe haven in Mugabe's Zimbabwe.

Today, the revolutionary government may have disappeared, driven out by the liberation fighters of several regions, and life seems, on the surface, to have returned to something like normality. The country is again open to tourism – although the Eritrean problem has, until the announcement in August 2000 of the resumption of flights on Ethiopia's 'historical route' up to Aksum, discouraged most visitors. Yet the legacy of the great changes, and the great suffering, is still there. To the visitor of the 1990s, much of the external aspect might look the same as to the visitor of the early 1970s – indeed, the early photographs taken by the Deutsche Aksum-Expedition in 1906, for example, could in many cases be reproduced more or less exactly in modern scenes. Underneath, however, the immense task of reorganising, forgetting – or at least readjusting – and recovery is only beginning. The funeral of the murdered emperor in Addis Ababa late in 2000, twenty-five years after his death, was perhaps a sign of this happening. Social and political patterns have to be – and are being – rethought. Ethiopia still has very considerable internal problems. The present government may have begun to tackle them, but with the enormity of the task, and the scarcity of the means, progress can be only relatively measured.

The idea to write a book about the important historical sites of Ethiopia was the result of a British Museum tour of the country, for which I acted as lecturer, in January 1995, followed by photographic tours later with my friends William and Pam Taor, the most recent in November 2000. No one on the BM tour had been able to acquire a good up-to-date guidebook to the main sites, or even to Ethiopia in general. Even the books on the reading list were hard to get. The information is there, scattered in works chiefly in Latin, Ge'ez (Ethiopic), French, German, Italian, Portuguese and English; it merely needed to be collected and arranged.

As well as describing the historical sites as they are today from personal investigation, and noting current trends of scholarship in relation to them, I have also exploited documentation by early visitors, including extensive citations from mainly sixteenth- to nineteenth-century travellers' accounts. The Ge'ez chronicles provide another source, which presents a completely different perspective. I have often cited from these, too, because from them alone can we glimpse, if only dimly, something of the attitudes and reactions of the Ethiopians of medieval and Gondarine times to their own history – a glance into a world of ideas and behaviour radically different from our own. I have also added a brief general outline of Ethiopian history and society, and some appendices on the Church and on Ethiopian art, subjects important for understanding Ethiopia, but obscure enough for most visitors.

Travelling around post-revolutionary Ethiopia, listening to the opinions and reflections of some of those who joined the tour, and discussing events of the past and present in the country with them and with Ethiopian friends, it seems to me that a new idea of Ethiopia needs to be expressed. This is not my task here, in a book concerned primarily with the ancient sites and their history. It may even be impossible to do just now, when so much is still in a state of incertitude and flux. Nevertheless, it is worth emphasising that in the Ethiopia we visited after Mengistu we saw not Ullendorff's image of an ancient almost unchanged society being shepherded into the atomic age by a benevolent emperor, nor the later tragic reality, the Ethiopia of Mengistu's 'Red Terror', the famines and the civil wars – but a new, and perhaps more hopeful Ethiopia. The radical change to a federation on ethnic lines permits each constituent part to have its own say in its government, with no single element possessing too great an influence. On the other hand divisive factors within greater Ethiopia are inevitably emphasised, with who knows what consequences for the future. Public opinion, both within and without Ethiopia, is divided, and one can only await events. The war with Eritrea at a time when renewed famine had struck the Ogaden region created much discouragement among international observers.

This is the Ethiopia we see attempting – with what success we cannot yet divine – to move into the twenty-first century. There are many threads to the pattern: nationalistic groups supporting regional separatism, monarchists with a hankering for the relative stability and international respect of the reign of the last emperor, disgruntled ethnic groups who resent the prominence of Tigray figures in the government, and many other interests. Perhaps out of all this Ethiopia's people will succeed in finding the balance between its traditional values, and the progressive views necessary to ensure the country's development in the modern world.

Those who come from the West to visit the historic sites of Ethiopia will be introduced to another way of life, utterly different from their own. Even the bases are different. As a friend and colleague of mine in Ethiopian studies, Dr Bent Juel-Jensen, once wrote, in Ethiopia, time 'loses all meaning ... in a country where the clock shows six at twelve, and twelve at six, and where the calendar is eight years behind ours and there are thirteen months, twelve of thirty and one of five days, and the year begins in September'. If even such fundamental concepts differ – the Ethiopian calendar is still seven to eight years behind the Gregorian calendar, and the Millennium is years away yet – it is easy to imagine how the whole fabric of Ethiopian society is woven from a different stuff from that familiar to Westerners.

Searching among the available Western stock of ready-made concepts, the nearest many have come to a general descriptive term for Ethiopia is summed up in the words 'biblical' or 'medieval'. While it cannot be denied that some of the sights that permitted such impressions are still visible even today, these are emotive words. They signify no more than a modern author's dream of what constituted medieval or biblical society. The latter is particularly misleading, the typical 'biblical' concept being based largely on nineteenth-century Western Orientalist images of contemporary Arab society in the Holy Land, arguably having very little to do with the realities of Palestinian society in biblical times. As far as comparisons with Ethiopia are concerned, there is even less likelihood of any genuine level of similarity. More than two thousand years of extremely eventful history, and around two thousand kilometres in physical distance, intervene – let alone the differences between the ancient Near East, and the Horn of Africa, in customs and population.

From the reactions of the people I accompanied in Ethiopia, it was clear that some aspects of life there induced astonishment, sometimes even shock, while others delighted. I will not define these aspects; there are likely to be many different points of view. Nevertheless, it is amusing to observe how far apart impressions can be. Compare, for example, the frequent modern allusions to the 'graceful' or 'dignified' appearance of the ubiquitous shawl-like garment called the *shamma*, to Yohannes T'ovmacean's eighteenth-century practicality – he saw no more than a 'kind of bed-sheet which serves as a coat'. Recalling those words 'biblical' and 'medieval', one should not forget that the picturesque has another face as well. The donkey trotting to the market, the woman returning from the well with a water-pot on her back, the dignity of robed elders in conference, or the stately magnificence of the ceremonies of the church are part of one face of the 'medieval' coin; leprosy, polio, malnutrition, extreme poverty and rudimentary hygiene are an all-too-visible part of the other. Life expectancy in Ethiopia is about forty-five years for men, and forty-nine for women. As any tourist will see at first glance, most urban Ethiopians live in accommodation and in general condiditons that are quite unacceptable.

Despite such glimpses into reality, for the tourist the picture tends to be limited. Typical schedules explore the history of the country through the historical sites. Half a dozen main stopping-places, most transfers from city to city by aeroplane, hotels nearly always set apart in positions selected for the magnificent scenery or a good viewpoint over a town, Toyota Land Cruisers for site visits, an assiduous staff of couriers and guides – such programmes ensure that many facets of Ethiopia and its society and culture are kept very far away from visitors. There is an element of isolation and cocooning, of impressions at a certain distance. Nevertheless, the contacts that there are with Ethiopians, the indescribable splendour of the country, its fauna and flora, and not least the story of its magnificent past and the exploration of the remains still visible, produce, in general, a very positive reaction.

The scope of this book is deliberately selective. It follows the main lines of the 'historical route', which includes visits to the maximum possible number of the ancient sites of the country within the time limits and possibilities of travel set by the average 15-day tour. These are the places most visitors see.

Yeha temple and palace ruins represent the pre-Aksumite civilisation of the kingdom of D'mt or Di'amat, of which they are certainly the most prominent relics. The ruins of Aksum, obviously, are the embodiment of the long and splendid period when the rulers of this city controlled a large part of northern Ethiopia and spread their empire even overseas into other regions far beyond. The town also furnishes good examples of some later churches, Maryam Seyon cathedral especially, seat of the mysterious object called the 'Ark of the Covenant', but also Arbaat Ensesa church. At the feast of Timqat in January, the celebration of one of the great annual festivals of the church can be witnessed in the town. The remote Tigray monastery of Debra Damo, like Maryam Seyon cathedral and the church of Abba Pantalewon in Aksum, is forbidden to women. Nevertheless, it is remarkable enough to be included here; a monastic church that, though occasionally reconstructed, seems to have been used continuously from the post-Aksumite period until the present, and an architectural – and scenic – showpiece. The rock churches of Tigray are another remarkable phenomenon, worthy of a visit all to themselves, although here only a very limited account is given of the most easily accessible examples. Once one has started on the churches of Ethiopia outside this specific plan, it is tempting to go further than just the brief mention of certain selected examples. However, few of the remoter churches can be included in the average tour. I have limited my description to those most easily visited, and note the impressive and beautiful book produced by Georg Gerster for a fuller picture. I do, however, append a very brief note on some basic elements of Ethiopian art, and another on the church structure and hierarchy, to clarify the picture a little.

Lalibela, with its rock-cut churches, represents the quintessence of a period, although there are chronological uncertainties. It is also one of the most incredible sights on the entire continent of Africa. Here too it is worth stepping a little outside the immediate environs of the town to glance at the church and 'palace' of Yimrehana Krestos, the church a beautiful structure belonging to the same milieu as the Lalibela churches, but built instead of being cut from the rock. The same dual view applies to the imperial city of Gondar. The city and its churches and castles are one facet, but the surrounding sites nearer the lake, with the palaces and churches of Azazo, Old and New Gorgora, Guzara and others, contribute to a fuller understanding of Gondar's history. Zage (Zeghie) is a different environment, another glimpse of Ethiopia's great lake, with typical round churches beautifully decorated in traditional style. From a historical point of view, the sites on the islands of the lake itself ought to be included, but they are difficult of access, and tours do not visit them beyond sailing past Entons and Kebran on the way to Zage. Finally, stepping right outside highland Christian Ethiopia, Harar represents Ethiopia's most prominent Islamic city, whose rulers once briefly vied with the Christian kings of kings for the dominion of all Ethiopia. It is not the only trace of Islamic monuments in Ethiopia – recently French archaeologists and historians have been studying the remains of stone-built fourteenth-century mosques and associated structures in the former territory of the Muslim state of Ifat, northeast of Addis Ababa, and Arabic tombstones are known from other places – but it is the most substantial.

Yeha, Aksum, Lalibela, Harar, the Lake Tana sites and Gondar – each is the principal representative of a distinctive phase of Ethiopian civilisation over a period of some two thousand five hundred years. In this book I have chosen to tell the story in reverse, from the rich descriptions of the intrigue-filled court of Gondar, where individual characters stand out clearly, back through the chronicles and reports of foreign visitors to the far scarcer information for Aksum and Yeha. These are really the preserve of archaeologists, and if we can find a rare outside view to make them come alive beyond the more sober domain of scientific excavation we are very lucky. The single view of the Emperor Kaleb of Aksum, covered in gold, leaving his palace like a Byzantine eparch on a high chariot drawn by four elephants, with his musicians in train, or the rigid staring figure of the 'nigos' of Aksum in his almost episcopal garb painted in the caliph's palace at Qusayr Amra in the early eighth century, are tiny windows into a lost world. At Yeha, even more remote in time, we have only the imagination to assist us.

It is only fair to add that apart from following the 'historical route', there is much else one can do in Ethiopia. Some visitors may wish to add the vast area south of Addis Ababa to their itinerary. The now-restored stelae or tomb markers of Tiya, carved with swords and other symbols, just beyond the Awash in Soddo, the monuments of Wolayta Soddo further south towards Lake Abaya, or the strange bovids carved on the rock at Shebe in Sidamo are interesting to see, as also is the famous prehistoric site of Melka Konture, excavated by M. Chavaillon, on the Awash river, easily accessible from Addis. A river journey on the Awash between the different sites there is a delightful experience. Cave paintings can also be included; the site of Laga Oda in the Chercher massif some 30 km. west of Dire Dawa is one of the attractions of this genre. For simple relaxing, there is the splendid sight of the Rift Valley lakes, a combination of glorious scenery, bird-watching (there are huge flocks of water birds, including flamingos, and even an ostrich farm not far south of Addis Ababa near the lakes), and hot spring bathing if one goes on as far as Wondo Ganet near Shashemane. Even further south is another world, in Bale, Sidamo, Kafa and Gamu Gofa, of game parks and a totally different way of life among the Omotic and other peoples of the region. The history of some of these areas impinged briefly and rarely on that of the great states further north until relatively recently, and so is not detailed here. Local travel agencies organise tours to all these regions, and even specialist requirements, such as bird-watching, are catered for.

Conditions of Travel in Ethiopia

In the interests of visitors, a note is required about conditions of travel and the like. Travel in Ethiopia, so recently ravaged by war and famine, is neither really easy nor really comfortable (by modern Western standards). However, air and land transport facilities are constantly improving, and organised tours provide the best there are. Among the most reliable of the companies that provide these services is Experience Ethiopia Travel, centred in Addis Ababa (POB 9354: web site http://www.telecom.net.et./eet: email eet@telecom.net. et): they provide an excellent service, with experienced personnel, comfortable vehicles and up-to-date information.

Hotels and their level of service in Ethiopia come in for their share of criticism, particularly those run by the government hotel organisation. It can be rather unfair criticism, as the visitors from the cosseted West often cannot even begin to conceive the difficulties involved merely in providing the basics – electricity, water, a reasonable diet – but it is also true that certain hotels could profit from a change in management structure. Individual impressions, depending on the person and the place, vary widely, from glorious to ghastly.

In Gondar, the government hotel, the Goha, is the best in the town at the moment, though rather isolated from it. It is situated on an eminence looking over Gondar opposite the ridge with the castle compound. Qwesqwam palace, too, is just visible on the other side. The hotel terrace offers a superb general view over the whole valley in which the modern town lies, and its surrounding mountains. The former Itege Menen Hotel, now called the Terrara, is far more conveniently situated for exploration of the town, just opposite the church of Asasame Mikael in the imperial compound. Like Gondar itself, now decidedly down-at-heel, it has fallen far from its former condition, especially as far as the plumbing is concerned. A new small hotel nearby, however, the Belegez Pension, supplies clean small rooms with good bathrooms at 60 birr per night.

Bahar Dar has the usual government hotel, the Lake Tana, excellently situated with a garden on a spit of land projecting into the lake. It is one of the better government hotels in Ethiopia. Bahar Dar is well placed for visiting the remarkable Tissisat or Blue Nile Falls.

The main tourist resort at Harar, the Ras Hotel, is situated on the main road into the town in the Italian 'new town'. Most tourists, however, arrive at Dire Dawa, which is connected by air to other parts of Ethiopia, and stay in the Ras Hotel there, visiting Harar by vehicle on a one-day trip. There is a good road from Dire Dawa running through interesting hilly countryside and by-passing Lake Haramaya.

The little town of Lalibela has only two hotels, the Seven Olives right inside the town (or village) of Lalibela, and the more modern Lal Hotel some distance outside. The latter is the more comfortable, but the former does not require a long journey to see the churches; one can easily walk. The Seven Olives also has a delightful terrace and a pleasant round Ethiopian-style dining room. Both have the usual chronic problems with water and electricity.

Aksum has several hotels. The Yeha is beautifully situated, a typical government hotel set quite outside the real life of the town. The view from the terrace is delightful, with the stelae and Maryam Seyon church both visible. Inside, its decoration has been carefully prepared, concentrating on Aksumite themes; it is Aksum's best – and most expensive – hotel. Here tourists can get the best that is available, but they must remember that this is in a relatively modest market. The price in 1997 was $42 per person. The Aksum Touring Hotel belongs to the Tigray Development Association, and is situated in a pleasant garden near the centre of the town. Like the Yeha Hotel, it has chronic problems with water and electricity (even though it has a generator), and the usual bills in triplicate for even a cup of coffee. Prices are discriminatory, as is usual, between foreigners and Ethiopians, but here the price for foreigners, at $20 (125 birr), is a fairly staggering four times the price for Ethiopians (30 birr). Considering the services offered, the foreigners' price is far too elevated. A little further down the road, also with a pleasant courtyard surrounded by rooms to the rear is the Africa Hotel (manager Aklilu Berhane). This has the distinction of offering permanent water, a more 'Ethiopian' environment with many local people coming in to drink, chat and eat, and a modest price; 17 birr for Ethiopians, 50 birr – only three times the Ethiopian price – for foreigners. Another modest hotel – 10 birr for Ethiopians and 50 birr for foreigners, an even higher proportion of discriminatory price – is the Kaleb (Atse Kaleb), south of the main tarmac road, with a rear garden surrounded by rooms and little booths for dining or drinking; but here the foreigners' price is still a very low one. It is significant that the archaeologists who come to Aksum – who stay for longer periods than most tourists – have selected the last two hotels for reasons of economy and service in preference to the government and TDA ones.

Tourist shops abound in Aksum, and tourists are constantly pursued by people trying to sell crosses and so on in the street. The best place to buy is in the calmer atmosphere of a shop, where one has time for reflection and comparison. It is hard to select particular shops among the many in Aksum; I can only express an individual preference for shops whose owners and their families have become personal friends. Almost opposite the Post Office, on the way to the Stele Park, the small shop of Tsehaye Hagos sells a selection of typical Ethiopian objects, from statues to silver or brass crosses, fly-whisks to paintings, scrolls, sistra, and other things. Further away, opposite the Aksum Hotel, the larger and richer shop of Haile Mariam Zerue offers good-quality jewellery and crosses, and skilled carving and painting on traditional themes. Prices are higher, but the work is often of good quality.

Ethiopia is a country that definitely has to be seen – and it rewards its visitors richly. But all too often the hand of bureaucratic man can mar the impression given by the land and its history. Here I merely touch on a few themes that aroused vigorous complaint among those visitors I met and accompanied, so as to prepare others. These matters need to be aired. On the one hand the visitor knows what to expect, and on the other hand it is evident that if Ethiopia wants to build its vitally important tourist industry, changes, some radical, are imperative.

First, the airports. Constant searching of bags and individuals is *de rigeur*; no one can legitimately complain about this, as security is thus ensured. Nevertheless, it means long waits at all internal airports, and chaos at Addis Ababa, an old international airport quite unsuited to the new volume of passengers. Here, even such fundamentals as labelling of luggage conveyer-belts on mornings when several flights arrive together has not been achieved. A new airport is under construction, but meanwhile the old one sinks under neglect – at my last check-out in November 2000 the official told me that the computer, printer and weighing machine were all malfunctioning. What it will be like at the provincial airports with the new larger planes, and the new runways at Aksum, Gondar, and Lalibela permitting an enlarged intake of travellers, can only be imagined.

There is also another element to the searching. The arbitrary confiscation by a policeman – not an authorised antiquities expert – at Bahar Dar airport of an expensive cross purchased by one tourist in the group that I accompanied left an extremely unpleasant impression on the whole group concerned. Tourists are officially told – if they take the trouble to enquire – that gifts purchased in Ethiopia should be taken to a small office behind the National Museum in Addis Ababa, where they submit them to inspection by an 'expert', who issues a Ministry of Culture and Sports, National Museum, 'Clearance for Non-antiquities Gift Item' certificate. The process is tedious, inconvenient and not easy. Indeed, it borders on the ridiculous – one has to go to this office ready-armed with paper and adhesive tape, so the objects can be wrapped and stamped with the official seal. But at least there is a clear regulation, and everyone can understand the concern for the country's antiquities that prompted the arrangement. The Bahar Dar confiscation pre-empted a decision that should have come from the National Museum office. The valuable silver cross in question has not been seen since by its all-too-temporary owners, despite the certificate they had obtained with it from the shop at Aksum where it was purchased.

A similar procedure, at Aksum this time, aroused fury among a group of French tourists. This was the confiscation of the small attractively coloured stones, geodes and so on, collected as souvenirs. Children sell them as a small private enterprise initiative at Enda Kaleb. These are removed from the baggage during the strict search at Aksum airport; the reason given is 'for analysis'. The small mountain of stones there already indicates that such confiscations are numerous; analysis, of course, never takes place, as everyone knows perfectly well what these stones are.

Unfortunately for the children, and indeed for the souvenir and other shops, all this tends to discourage purchase of gifts and mementoes, even the most harmless-seeming, in Ethiopia. Even a couple of cheap brass crosses or the like, if lacking a receipt, can cause endless, completely unreasonable, trouble at Aksum. All in all, the civil aviation section responsible for this aspect of Ethiopian Airlines' security bears the responsibility, without question, of leaving many visitors, who have been delighted with other aspects of Ethiopia, with the worst possible impressions of the country. It is doubtless of no importance to them that these visitors pass on their airport horror stories – the intrusive searching of a woman passenger at Dire Dawa airport by a woman security official there was another incident. But under these circumstances, who can blame tourists if they thereafter regard Ethiopia with a jaundiced eye?

For those who love Ethiopia, and for many Ethiopians in the tourist industry who have to watch these scenes daily, such clumsiness and stupidity is a tragedy. Yet no one seems to have yet managed, by protesting letters or personal complaint, to achieve any change in the quality of the personnel or the procedures involved. If the benefits of tourism are to be exploited, the government needs speedily to install the necessary mechanisms to curtail these general blights on travel into and within Ethiopia.

Another discouraging aspect to spending money in the country is the currency regulations. Alone in the East African region, Ethiopia still retains currency forms, which the visitor must fill in on arrival, and which bedevil him – and others – until departure. At every stage, even to pay the most minor hotel drinks bill or the like in the government hotels, it must be produced, to prove that money was not changed on the black market. Then it must be produced at every bank where one changes money, and finally again at the airport on departure, to be checked with the remaining money. This, of course, is utterly impracticable, and is not done, making a mockery of the system. Provincial banks do not even ask for the forms when changing money. Another surprise for tourists not using tours (where the courier deals with such matters) is the $20 required as an airport tax; it is not acceptable in local currency.

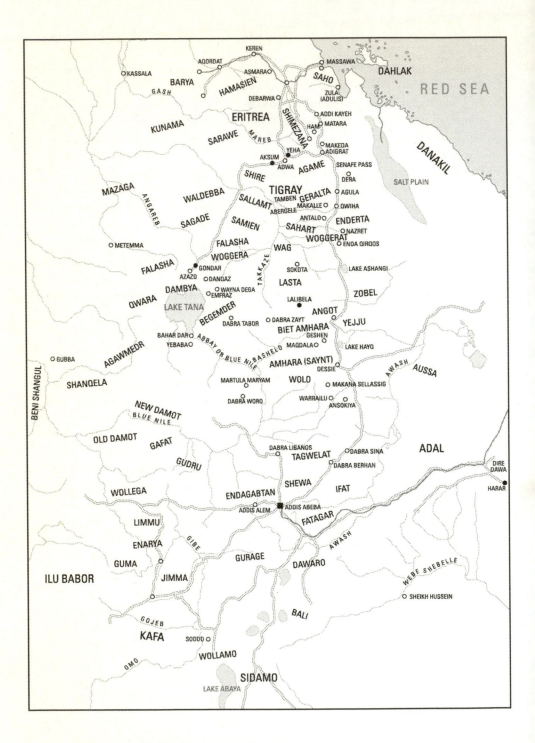

1. Map of Ethiopia showing the main provinces and cities, and important settlements. Adapted from J. Doresse, *L'empire du Prêtre-Jean*, 1957.

THE LAND, THE CHURCH AND THE TRAVELLERS

AN OUTLINE SURVEY OF ETHIOPIAN HISTORY

Ethiopia is a land utterly out of the common. It is like no other in its geography and geology, its fauna and flora, its people and their customs, and its long and fascinating history. Although it is not fashionable to say so among those who dream of African unity, Ethiopia has long preserved a sense of apartness, even from its closest African neighbours. Its long domination by a warlike Christian population in the highlands, amid the neighbouring Muslims and animists, its very ancient literate civilisation based on a Semitic-speaking ruling élite, and the very geography of the land itself have contributed to this element of exclusivity.

The topography of Ethiopia is remarkable. The Great Rift Valley, filled with many lakes, runs northeast to southwest across the country, dividing the formidable elevated blocks of the flanking highland regions. These form no mere flat tableland, but instead are themselves composed of numerous mountain ranges and plateaux much fissured with valleys. It is a tortured, lavish landscape of great beauty, splendid to contemplate, difficult to traverse. One understands why the Ethiopian monarchs over the ages needed to be constantly on the move – outside the rainy season, of course – if they wished to retain control over the disparate sections of this wild land.

The most prominent mountains are the Semien range, with Ras Dashan the highest peak (4,620 m.). East and west of this central highland core are lowlands, steppes and semi-desert regions. There are five main rivers. The Takaze in the north runs westwards to join the Blue Nile in the Sudan. The Abbay or Blue Nile itself rises west of Lake Tana, passes through the lake, and describes a huge curve round the province of Gojjam before falling down to join the White Nile at Khartoum. The Awash runs from the Addis Ababa region through the Great Rift Valley down towards Jibuti, the Omo flows into Lake Rudolf in Kenya, and the Shebele passes through the Ogaden to Somalia.

Modern Ethiopia has no coastline. The entire sea coast region belongs to Eritrea (the ports of Misiwa, commonly written Massawa, and Assab) or to Jibuti and Somalia, an element that encourages, or encouraged, a certain interdependence between Ethiopia and Eritrea. In ancient times, Aksum looked outwards from its Red Sea port of Adulis to India, the Yemen and to Egypt and Syria in the Roman/Byzantine world. Later the coast was to become dominated by Muslim states while the Ethiopian Christian empire re-formed in the lands washed by the Blue Nile and its tributaries. This contrast has been emphasised in my history of Ethiopia written with Roderick Grierson, *Red Sea, Blue Nile*. Sometimes the later polity could reach out to the sea at Massawa, but only as an incidental in an overwhelmingly landlocked history.

Various descriptive epithets have been applied to Ethiopia; 'the Roof of Africa' for its geographical situation; a 'Museum of Ethnography' for its multiplicity of peoples, sometimes interpreted rather as a 'Prison of Peoples' by those dissatisfied with central government; the 'Country of the Queen of Sheba' or the 'Land of Prester John' from the traditions about some of its legendary rulers. Edward Gibbon in his famous work *The Decline and Fall of the Roman Empire* granted Ethiopia a brief comment about its supposed isolation which has since been repeatedly quoted: 'Encompassed on all sides by the enemies of their religion, the Aethiopians slept near a thousand years, forgetful of the world, by whom they were forgotten.'

Such phrases, emphasising the dramatic and the exotic, offer a romantic and fragmentary fleeting impression of some aspects of Ethiopian history, culture and society. The reality is in fact infinitely more complex and infinitely more exciting, both in the Ethiopia of yesterday and in that of today. Even now, surprisingly little of that reality is known outside the country. Ethiopia may have reached the headlines and enjoyed wide media coverage at intervals over the last three decades. Yet this, limited largely to famine, politics and internecine conflict, has scarcely encouraged awareness of the country's history, traditions and social development. It seems that, the headlines having disappeared from the newspapers and the television news coverage having faded, many people still view today's Ethiopia frozen in the tragic image of its nadir in the 1980s.

If Ethiopia's geographical and scenic variety is impressive, it is also noteworthy for its flora and fauna, being the home of several species of animals and birds unique to the country. Its human population, too, is richly varied. Apart from the great communities such as the Amhara in the centre, the Tigray people in the north, and the Oromo in the south and centre, there are many hundreds of smaller groups, each with their own special characteristics of language and custom. Perhaps the best known – again from their media attraction in recent times – are the Falasha or Beta Israel, the so-called 'black Jews', many of whom were taken to Israel to start a new life in a strange land.

In outlining even the main trends of Ethiopia's history and culture, and particularly in a book devoted to the historical sites, many of these smaller groups must be ignored. Only certain significant developments among the majority groups can be traced. Even among these, too, when there is little or nothing surviving on the ground, there is relatively little representation here. During a great part of the history of the 'Solomonid' dynasty, until the construction of the lakeside castles and then Gondar, almost nothing was built that still survives. Major figures such as Emperors Amda Seyon or Zara Yaqob are well known from literary sources, but those churches or dwellings they erected do not exist today. The places they employed as 'capitals' – Tagwelat and Debra Berhan, for example – preserve nothing from their time.

Hominid Evolution, Prehistory

Ethiopia can claim to be the cradle of the human race, after the discovery at several sites there of the earliest hominid remains yet to be revealed by archaeology. Traces of ancient hominids had earlier been discovered in the far south, in the Omo valley region. Until very recently (1994) the oldest known branch of the human family tree was represented by fossil remains of a hominid found in 1974 at Hadar nearly 200 miles northeast of Addis Ababa. The famous partial skeleton dubbed Dinqinesh, or Lucy, a specimen of *Australopithecus afarensis*, is exhibited in the National Museum of Addis Ababa. *Australopithecus afarensis*, dated by several other finds to between 3 and 3.6 million years ago, has now been superseded by even older discoveries of hominid remains, named as a new species, *Australopithecus ramidus*. The remains of seventeen individuals – dental, cranial and arm-bone fragments only so far – were found at Aramis, on the left bank of the Awash river system as it flows north and east towards Jibuti, about 45 miles south of the Hadar region. These new finds take the record in Ethiopia back to 4.4 million years ago, and appear to confirm the estimates of molecular biologists engaged in genetic research that the divergence between man and the modern apes occurred some 4 to 6 million years ago. At that time, it appears, this desolate region of Ethiopia was rich woodland, filled with wildlife.

Recently announced (1996) is the discovery of very early stone tools – cobbles with sharpened edges – in deposits some 50 miles north of Aramis on the banks of the Gona river, in the Afar depression about 180 miles northeast of Addis Ababa. These tools are the earliest yet known, over 2.5 million years old according to dating from overlying volcanic tuff samples. They push back the date of tool-making in Ethiopia another 200,000 years before the tools found by the Leakeys at Olduvai Gorge in Tanzania. Broken animal bones were found with the tools. These tools, though found only five miles distant from the 'Lucy' site, could be from between one million to five hundred thousand years younger. Later Palaeolithic and Mesolithic stone industries have been discovered in a number of places in the south and in the central area, and prehistoric sites of more recent date are known all over the country.

The Gods' Land: Punt

Equally remarkable is Ethiopia's subsequent early history, whether legend or archaeologically confirmed fact. This phase may include, in the northern borderlands with the Sudan, the fabulous land of Punt (Pwene). Punt was known to the ancient Egyptians as a supplier of luxuries, especially incense, to the Pharaonic court. Incense is still collected from the stunted resin-bearing trees of certain areas of Tigray and Eritrea. The ancient Egyptians called this country, or at least the coastal part they knew of, Ta-neter, the Gods' Land. They regarded it as a mysterious and beneficent place. The most famous representation of Punt is on the carved reliefs of the great funerary temple of the female pharaoh, Hatshepsut (c. 1479–1457 BC), at Dayr al-Bahri near Luxor, where the people, and the typically African flora, fauna and dwellings of the coastal Puntites can be seen. Other tomb reliefs in Egypt show the people of Punt navigating on the Red Sea in curious flat raft-like boats equipped with sails, or the products of Punt, gold, incense, exotic animals and skins, being offered to the pharaoh. One inscription even makes it quite clear that the ancient Egyptians were aware of the fact that rain in Punt meant a rise in the Nile in Egypt. Stone tools, upright stone markers placed over graves – seemingly much older precursors of the famous stone stelae at Aksum – a pottery tradition, and other material represent the prehistoric peoples of this time on the Ethiopian plateau. There is also a certain amount of evidence from the Sudanese borderlands, in the Gash Delta and Barka regions, which might relate directly to Punt or its successors in the region.

The Kingdom of D'mt (Di'amat)

At an uncertain epoch, a new phenomenon entered Ethiopian history. Some time during the first half of the first millennium BC, perhaps as early as c. 800 BC, perhaps around 500 BC, a civilisation that shared certain cultural elements with South Arabian population groups arose on the Ethiopian plateau. This 'pre-Aksumite' civilisation developed in the Eritrean and Tigray

highlands, where a polity was established under rulers who referred to themselves as the kings or *mukarrib*s of Di'amat and Saba. The latter title indicates
something like 'federator', and in southern Arabia was assumed by the ruler
who currently held the primacy over a group of tribes linked by a covenant.
The pre-Aksumite people wrote their inscriptions in a script and language
closely similar to that found on ancient south Arabian inscriptions, and
evidently belonged to a common cultural background with peoples on the
other side of the Red Sea at the time.

Of the people of Di'amat we have only some remains – sparse but not
unspectacular, and witness to a high level of development. At Yeha the
impressive temple of the god Ilmuqah still stands, the best-preserved monument and most ancient building in the whole country. Other temples of more
modest architecture were excavated in the Hawalti-Melazo region a few miles
southeast of Aksum. Inscribed altars and some splendid stone sculptures
from this period are now on exhibition in the Addis Ababa museum. Tombs,
the ruins of a few secular buildings, and some of the equipment of life in the
form of pots, weapons, jewellery and other personal items also survive.

The First Ethiopian Empire

Aksum The Ethiopian uplands were destined, not long after this pre-
Aksumite period, to become the seat of one of the greatest – and perhaps still
the least publicised – of all Africa's ancient civilisations. This phase in
Ethiopia's history takes its name from the old capital city of the Ethiopians,
Aksum, a site now known to have been occupied from prehistoric times, with
a significant presence during the pre-Aksumite period as well. The people
called themselves, and were called by others, Aksumites. However, other names
that were later to take over as designations for the Aksumites were also
beginning to be employed at this time. Ancient south Arabian inscriptions,
and others in the old Ethiopic language called Ge'ez, refer to a section of the
population as 'Habashat'. From this word originated the general Arab name
for Ethiopians, Habash, and the old name used in Europe until the twentieth
century, Abyssinia. By the fourth century AD, the term Ethiopia appears. The
name derives from a Greek expression meaning 'burned faces'. It was formerly
used to designate the kingdom of Kush centred on Meroë in the Sudan, and
black Africa in general, and began to be employed by the Aksumite kings in
their Greek inscriptions to refer to their own country. The two terms Habashat
and Ethiopia are paralleled in a trilingual inscription of Ezana, the king who
converted to Christianity about EC 333, or AD 340. This is the first known use
of the name Ethiopia for a part of the present-day country of Ethiopia by
one of its own rulers; in general the land was called Aksum after its capital.

The importation of Christianity into the country during the reign of Ezana is recounted by a number of ecclesiastical historians, the earliest being Rufinus of Aquilea (c. AD 345–410). He tells the dramatic story of a certain Frumentius of Tyre in Phoenicia (see Chapter 2). After a long sojourn in Ethiopia, Frumentius was consecrated as bishop of Aksum by Athanasius, patriarch of Alexandria. This instituted the tradition, which entered ecclesiastical law, that the Alexandrian patriarchs should appoint the metropolitan bishops of Ethiopia. They were always foreigners, usually Egyptians. This institution lasted, incredibly enough, until the 1950s, when the first Ethiopian was appointed to the post. Only after this was the independent Ethiopian patriarchate of today established. Ethiopian traditional history does not preserve the name Ezana, but instead remembers two brothers, called Abreha and Asbeha, as the rulers of Ethiopia at the time of Frumentius.

From the middle of the fourth century until the present, the highland Christian civilisation, spreading from the north to the central region, has been the characteristic which differentiated the northern part of Ethiopia from its African neighbours. Only some of the states established in Nubia – Nobatia, Alodia and Makoria, and Dotawo later – shared Ethiopia's Christian faith and some similar artistic traditions from the sixth century until their eventual submersion by conquest into the Islamic world in mediaeval times.

Aksum maintained its hegemony over the Ethiopian highlands in the north from about the first to the seventh centuries AD. Internally, the economy, as in most ancient states, was basically agricultural and pastoral, as indeed it is today. There were no major industries, and what manufactures there were, such as pottery, served local needs and were not exported. The kingdom seems to have prospered, employing its own natural products – ivory, rhinoceros horn, animal skins, obsidian, monkeys, slaves – to develop a rich international trade network based on its Red Sea port of Adulis. Several different routes encouraged commerce with the outside world, the Nile and certain desert caravan routes in Sudan and Egypt, the Red Sea route for access to the Mediterranean and the Indian Ocean. Aksum long maintained an interest in the lands on the other side of the Red Sea, and at different times was able to dominate certain areas of southern Arabia. Several military expeditions in that direction are noted from the early third century AD onwards. The most famous illustration of this was in the sixth century, when King Kaleb of Aksum led a victorious campaign to the kingdom of Himyar, to punish the Jewish Arab King Yusuf Asar Yathar, who had persecuted Christians and disrupted international commerce.

Historical details about the Aksumite period are relatively meagre. Nevertheless, a certain amount of literary and archaeological material exists to give us at least a vague idea about life in Aksumite Ethiopia. A flourishing and prosperous civilisation is revealed by objects recovered from excavations in the country. Particularly noteworthy are the very individual characteristics in certain fields – for example, pottery, architecture and numismatics. The pre-Aksumite and Aksumite periods saw the spread of Semitic-speaking peoples in the highlands, supplanting or subordinating the native Kushitic-speaking Agaw and other groups. If one follows some newer and even more radical suggestions by certain linguists, it may be that Semitic languages themselves developed and diverged in Ethiopia, and were not an import there – although this does not, of course, nullify the suggested interaction between Aksumites and Agaw on the periphery of the region at a much later date. Under the Semitic-speaking Aksumites, the Agaw Zagwé rulers, and later the Amhara kings, the Christian religion and culture were to become dominant throughout the region, competing with Islam and local cults and languages to form a distinctive 'Habash' culture.

During a period of some seven hundred years, Aksum left its mark firmly on highland northern Ethiopia. Traces of some elements of the earlier southern Arabian influences persisted, linking Aksum, in a way that is not yet very clear, with old Di'amat. Aksum's adoption of Christianity, and doubtless certain other material and social aspects of Aksumite civilisation that we cannot now properly evaluate, were not abandoned even when the city itself eventually ceased to be the political centre of the land. They entered into the general cultural heritage of semiticised highland Ethiopia, even if new characteristics came to overlay or supplant them in due course. From every point of view the Aksumite period was a high point in Ethiopia's history.

Kubar: The post-Aksumite period Aksum seems to have prospered until perhaps the sixth century. At this stage, Persian power overthrew the dominance of the Ethiopian breakaway dynasty founded after a coup against King Kaleb's viceroy in the Yemen, while in the seventh century the extraordinary Arab conquests fired by the rise of Islam completely changed the regional map of both political and commercial activity. The markets of Egypt and Syria, and beyond them the whole Byzantine world, were closed to Ethiopia. Ethiopia lost what control it had over Red Sea routes, and was, in the end, gradually to lose its coastline as well. Ethiopia seems to have entered into a phase of relative isolation, although it maintained trade with certain Arab states, and was still recorded in Arab reports as a powerful and prosperous kingdom. A new capital is mentioned at this time, at a place called Kubar (Ku'bar).

The Ethiopian kingdom of this period maintained its Christian faith. Among the rare accounts that have come down to us, most are preserved in the *History of the Patriarchs of Alexandria*. They deal with the activities of the metropolitan bishops sent from Alexandria. In the tenth century several records touch on the distress of the Christian kingdom when a mysterious 'queen of the Banu al-Hamwiyya' is said to have ravaged the country, killing the reigning *hadani* or king, and destroying the churches. This incident seems to have been enshrined in Ethiopian tradition in the legends about a destructive queen called Gudit, whom the Ge'ez traditional historical texts claim destroyed Aksum and slew its ruler.

An Agaw interlude: The Zagwé dynasty Despite the depredations of this queen, the Ethiopian state survived, but by around 1137 the old dynasty seems to have come to an end. We depend for almost all information about this phase of Ethiopian history on meagre Ge'ez records dating probably not much farther back than the fourteenth or fifteenth centuries – and these, varying considerably in their information as they do, are patently unreliable. This traditional history tells how a new dynasty, which is referred to as the Zagwé, succeeded to the government. They seem to have been Agaw, Kushitic-speakers, deriving from the province of Bugna, in Lasta. Records in the *History of the Patriarchs* do in fact mention a usurping king in Ethiopia around the middle of the twelfth century.

In the Ge'ez manuscripts enticing tales are preserved 'legitimising' the Zagwé, suggesting that the first Zagwé king was the son-in-law of the last of the old imperial line, or that they had the same 'Solomonic' origins that later tradition was to attribute to the former Aksumite dynasty. Instead of descent from King Solomon of Israel through the Queen of Sheba, the Zagwé were supposed to derive from a companion (sister, friend or maid-servant) of the queen. Another legend, which the twelfth- to thirteenth-century writer Abu Salih, a contemporary of the Zagwé, recorded in his book about the churches and monasteries of Egypt, claims that they descended from the family of Moses and Aaron.

Several Zagwé kings were subsequently revered as saints. The historical content of their surviving *Lives*, written centuries later, is very small, and although it may preserve information derived to some extent both from older documentation and from oral tradition, it also delights overtly in the miraculous and the wonderful. But by combining it with information from a few copies of Zagwé land grants, and some rare notes from other sources, something of Zagwé Ethiopia can be perceived. None of the kings of this dynasty, save for King Lalibela, is known from contemporary sources. Lalibela, however, is mentioned by name in the Arabic *History of the Patriarchs of the Alexandrian Church* in an account of the problems that arose over the deposition of a bishop of Ethiopia in 1210. A certain amount of detail is provided that confirms to a certain extent the traditional history. The dynasty derived from Bugna, the king's name was Lalibela, the queen was Masqal Kebra, and there was a royal son called Yitbarak. The capital city during this period was called Adefa. This place, also known as Roha or Warawar, was later named Lalibela after this most famous of the Zagwé kings. It is he who is said to have caused the vast complex of rock-cut churches there to be hewn from the rock in imitation of the celestial Jerusalem.

The Zagwé kings did not rule over an impressive territorial area, even though they were recognised by the patriarchs of Alexandria as the sovereigns of Ethiopia. From Adefa (Roha) they seem to have maintained control over Lasta and Angot, with Tigray to the north, and perhaps some part of Begemder. At this time, even if there might have been some Christian settlements further south, the area of control of the Christian kingdom remained restricted. Other polities, such as the kingdom of Damot, dominated there. The situation in the south seems to have acted to the advantage of the coastal Muslims, whose power grew strong enough to establish states stretching even as far west as the lowland eastern fringe of Shewa. The same situation doubtless applied not just in the Zagwé period, but in the time of their immediate predecessors at 'Kubar' as well, since the chronicle of the sultanate of Shewa begins in pre-Zagwé times.

The Second Ethiopian Empire

The 'Solomonic restoration' A coup in about 1270 permitted an Amhara pretender to seize the throne. At a later stage, this coup was legitimised by the claim that the first monarch of the new line, Yekuno Amlak, was of 'Solomonic' origin, a descendant of the old Aksumite rulers. The southern dynasty was to claim that it originated from King Solomon of Israel and the Queen of Sheba through their son Menelik, legendary first emperor of Ethiopia. This dynasty lasted into the nineteenth century, and was linked even with the late Emperor Haile Sellassie's family.

The power centre of the new kingdom was situated in the Amhara (Welo, Wollo) and Shewa regions. Although occasional more permanent centres are mentioned, such as Maradi or Tagwelat under Emperor Amda Seyon, and Debra Berhan and others later, there seems to have been no real permanent capital. The court and the emperor were perpetually on the move, establishing the administration temporarily in each place as the need arose. The 'capital' appeared in the form of a great but rigidly disciplined city of tents during the campaigning season. During the rains, the emperors sheltered in some more permanent – but still cheap and easy to build – structures built in some favourite spots. This was an absolute necessity enforced by the terrain. During this season, the tortuous landscape of Ethiopia became utterly inhospitable to ordinary travel, let alone the mounting of any sort of extensive expedition. The tracks became seas of clinging mud, the mountain passes lethal slides, the rivers torrents that could not be crossed by the usual method of inflated skins, or clinging to ropes attached to trees on either side – there were no bridges. All one could do was stay put, waiting for the rains to diminish and the rivers to go down.

The founder of the new dynasty, Yekuno Amlak (1270–85), and his successor Yigba Seyon, may have consolidated their power over a good part of central and northern Ethiopia, but they seem to have run into a number of problems as well. Tigray was perhaps never properly under their control. It is interesting that Egyptian records hint that the patriarchate of Alexandria did not send bishops to these kings, despite pressing requests, perhaps because they regarded them as usurpers. The expedient was adopted of installing Syrian bishops instead of Egyptian ones. However, this issue seems to have been solved in due course, and Egyptian metropolitan bishops came again for many centuries.

Some of the later kings of the so-called Solomonic dynasty were remarkable rulers. Amda Seyon (1314–44) consolidated and extended the kingdom, forcing Tigray and many other regions to submit to the central power. He waged war on the eastern Muslim states in particular. A short chronicle describes some of Amda Seyon's wars with Muslim Ifat, a state based on the Red Sea coast but whose power reached inland as far as eastern Shewa. The local sultans paid tribute to Amda Seyon, but also frequently rebelled against him.

Succeeding rulers, particularly Sayfa Arad, Dawit I and Yeshaq, fought to maintain control over the eastern borders, as well as trying to equal Amda Seyon's exploit in reaching the sea coast in Eritrea. Yeshaq defeated both Ifat and the island sultanate of Dahlak, taking Massawa, and in the south advanced as far as the kingdoms of Enarya and Jinjero.

Emperor Zara Yaqob (1434–68) was a veritable dictator. His queen, Seyon Mogasa, was beaten to death as a result of the monarch's fury over a plot to dethrone him. His son Baeda Maryam was punished for mourning her demise. Zara Yaqob sought to control even his subjects' consciences. It was a time of a great deal of discussion of religious questions, combined with unhesitating brutality to those who refused to obey the decrees of the emperor concerning the faith. Pagan cults, witchcraft, indeed any dissent at all were to be stamped out. Nevertheless, Zara Yaqob made significant contributions to religious and cultural life, particularly with his massive programme for the promotion of the worship of Mary in the Ethiopian Church. Only a few churches (reputedly), manuscripts and manuscript paintings survive from this early period of the dynasty. Apart from the Ge'ez literary texts, chronicles and hagiographies – at once fascinating, informative and biased – there is little else available to describe the Ethiopia of this epoch. A few dynastic records concerning local Arab states, and reports of Arab historians, help to clarify the course of events on the eastern frontiers.

Zara Yaqob and his son Baeda Maryam controlled a substantial central Ethiopian state in relative tranquillity – although the former had to fight with Ahmad Badlay b. Sa'ad al-Din, ruler of the eastern Muslim successor state of Ifat, called Adal. Zara Yaqob defeated him in 1445, but Baeda Maryam in his turn suffered a defeat from Lada'e-Asman, successor of Badlay's son Mehmad. These emperors also gained access to the sea coast at Massawa. Baeda Maryam's son Eskender (1478–94) followed tradition in combating Adal, ultimately unsuccessfully.

The Amhara kings controlled their subjects by their patronage through a system of land tenure called *gult*. The term *rist* applied to hereditary land, while *gult* was land granted by the king to an office holder, but only so long as he retained that office. The benficiary possessed the right to exploit the workers on that land, taking a tribute of the crops and animals, while he paid to the king an agreed sum for his office. This placed the kings in a strong position *vis-à-vis* their local governors and officials, since they could reward good service with more land, or remove it at will by the simple appointment of a new benficiary. Destitutions of this nature were often implemented without warning, at whim, with the result that few *gult*-holders are likely to have bothered much to make any attempt to improve the land.

The period from Amda Seyon's reign onwards for some two hundred years was stable enough to permit a new burgeoning of arts and literature. Zara Yaqob himself was apparently the author of several religious works, and other kings (and queens) are recorded as composing works as well. Numerous churches were built, some of them apparently lavishly decorated and very richly endowed. Much of the development of this period, in terms of both territory and cultural heritage, was destined soon to be lost again in the wars with Adal and Harar. After this, any further territorial expansion was to remain modest until the time of Menelik II in the late nineteenth century.

The kingdom of 'Prester John' and the Portuguese   The 'Age of Discovery' brought a flood of information about Ethiopia to the outside world. In the early sixteenth century, the Portuguese were expanding their explorations, their commerce and their conquests in the East at a rapid rate. They knew, or thought they knew, of a mysterious Christian ruler in the East popularly called Prester John of the Indies. With this potentate, it might be possible to conclude an alliance that would allow them to destroy Mecca and oust Muslim merchants from the trade routes. Exactly who he was or where he was to be found long remained a mystery. But by the 1400s Italian,

Portuguese and other explorers were to identify a suitable candidate for Prester John in the 'Solomonic' king of kings of Ethiopia – even if emissaries of Zara Yaqob reported to Europe that the emperor himself found the name and attribution ridiculous. Portugal particularly was to cement fairly close relations with Ethiopia in the period to come.

A first Portuguese envoy, Pero da Covilhã (Pedro de Covilham), was sent in 1487 and arrived in 1493 in the reign of Eskender. Other envoys followed in 1508. A letter, written according to the advice of the regent for the child-emperor Lebna Dengel, Queen Eleni (Helena), was despatched to the Portuguese sovereign with an ambassador, Matthew, apparently an Armenian merchant, in 1509. By 1513 the man who was destined to be the first official Portuguese ambassador to Ethiopia, Duarte Galvão, could relay to Afonso de Albuquerque, conqueror of Goa and Melaka, his interpretation of the divine purpose behind the Portuguese discovery of Prester John:

> It seems to me now, as I have said to the king, that when the loss of Christianity by the coming of Muhammad occurred, it was commanded, by a mystery of God, that Prester John should remain in those regions, with his country and his people, in the faith and truth of Christ, to the end that when that other mystery of our navigation and arrival in those regions was accomplished, we would find there Christians and people with whom, more easily, we could put our hands on Muhammad and on Mecca, his main seat.

Ambassador Matthew reached Portugal only in 1514, to return with a Portuguese embassy in 1520. Duarte Galvão had meanwhile died, never having landed in Ethiopia, and Rodrigo de Lima was appointed ambassador in his stead. A report, *Carta das Novas que vieram a el Rey nosso Senhor do descobrimento do Preste Joham*, based on the accounts of the Portuguese governor in India and his deputy and describing the first contacts of the mission and the Portuguese fleet with the Ethiopian subjects of 'Prester John', was published in Lisbon in 1521. Speculation was rife: what would the realm of Prester John prove to be like?

Later the Portuguese humanist Damião de Gois was to attempt to explain why this foreigner, Matthew, was selected as ambassador of the ruler supposed to be one of the great monarchs of the world. A mere merchant-supplier to the Ethiopian court, he arrived with few gifts – although a piece of the True Cross aroused awe and exaltation among the Catholic Portuguese. Matthew's retinue was tiny, consisting of people of no great rank, who, moreover, bickered together and created embarrassing scandals for the ambassador. The reasons advanced by Gois were lack of the necessary linguistic skills among the great nobles of Prester John, and the lack of awareness in Ethiopia that Portugal had made so many great conquests in the East, which might have induced them to send some grave counsellor of the *negus*. In fact, the concept of sending plenipotentiaries to treat with other powers was foreign to the Ethiopian royal court, and Matthew was to the Ethiopians no more than a royal messenger.

The Ethiopian royal correspondence of the period refers to several propositions. The Ethiopians would revictual Portuguese ships. They would supply gold and fighting men. 'I will give a thousand times 100,000 drachms of gold, and as many fighting men, and moreover I will give wood, iron, and copper, to make and equip the fleet, and an infinite quantity of supplies,' wrote Lebna Dengel, at the same time requesting makers of firearms, masons and other craftsmen. Lebna Dengel wished for Portuguese forts to be built at Massawa and Dahlak. He suggested that the Portuguese royal chaplain Francisco Alvares (a member of the 1520 mission, who helped prepare the letters) be made lord and bishop of these places and of Zayla and the isles of the Red Sea. King Dom Manoel of Portugal wrote to Pope Leo X that Portuguese engineers were needed to deflect the Nile and destroy Egypt. Everyone, it seems, was in the grip of one fantasy or another. Concepts had become grandiose. With the aid of 'Prester John', Islam could be utterly rooted out, Mecca wiped from the face of the earth, and Jerusalem and the Holy Land returned to the Christians.

Alas for their hopes, the dreams of the Portuguese, like those of Lebna Dengel, were scarcely supported by reality. On the very edge of the civilised world, inward looking, technologically backward, with no monetary economy, no significant political associations abroad, a tenuous hold only on a fragment of the sea coast, and no fleet, what, really, had Ethiopia to offer? The country had no overseas trade either, except for that conducted by the Muslims. The Muslims, moreover, cut Ethiopia off from outside routes, while themselves maintaining connections with a much wider and more powerful world well supplied with firearms and shipping. Through the Muslim traders even news from abroad could be filtered and edited. At one time, to the embassy's alarm, Lebna Dengel was informed that the Portuguese had been driven from India. The Prester John whom the Portuguese found was very far in quality beneath the one they had sought and fantasised about for so long. As Aubin (1996) comments, after the failure of a Portuguese expedition to sack Jidda, the death on a baking island in the Red Sea of the disillusioned ambassador Duarte Galvão, prophet of the destruction of Islam, at least 'spared him from a no less bitter disillusion; that of discovering the reality concealed by the myth of Prester John'.

The Portuguese diplomatic mission that came to Ethiopia in 1520 in the reign of Lebna Dengel had little effective diplomatic result – except later, when Portuguese arms helped save the Christian Ethiopian monarchy in its hour of greatest need. But it heralded a new age for Ethiopian historiography. The royal chaplain Francisco Alvares compiled an important record of the embassy, combined with descriptions of places, people and customs that he saw in Ethiopia. His was the only account written while the mediaeval Habash kingdom was still more or less intact, though hardly at its zenith, before the Muslim incursions that destroyed much of the Christian kingdom's cultural heritage. It was, however, the first of a long series of such records over a hundred or so years, which opened up Ethiopia to the outside world as never before. The missionaries, many of them Portuguese Jesuits sent via Goa, compiled detailed notes on almost every facet of Ethiopian life. They wrote about its history, politics, society, religion, customs, fauna and flora, as well as sending home annual letters about the progress of the missions and the current state of affairs in the country.

The *verdadera informaçam das terras do Preste Joam das Indias* that Alvares offered was published only in 1540, shortly after his death, but his work, or perhaps even a fuller version of it, had already been seen in manuscript by others in India in the later 1520s. It confirmed the de-mythologising of Prester John that Portuguese policy had already taken fully into account with a suspension of active expansion in the East after the accession of King D. João III in 1521. After the Muslim onslaught in Ethiopia in the 1530s, there was anyway nothing left of the mirage of Prester John to cling to. Even so, another change in Portuguese policy permitted, with an expeditionary force led by Cristovão da Gama in 1541, a modest implementation of the old notion of a Portuguese–Ethiopian alliance.

The great rivals of the Christian king of kings in the Ethiopian highlands were the Muslim rulers of Adal, called the kings of Zayla. This region lay east of the Awash river and extended to the sea coast. It also included Harar. The Adali sultans were the successors of the sultans of Shewa and Ifat. Emperor Lebna Dengel, in 1516, had defeated the sultan and his *amir*, Mahfuz, in battle. Perhaps because of this victory and a certain confidence it engendered, there seemed to be no immediate need to cement a military pact with the Portuguese, beyond the suggestions the emperor included in his letters.

To Christian Ethiopia's misfortune, it was at just this time that the most competent of all Adal's military leaders seized the initiative. In a period of some fifteen years, from about 1526 to 1541, under the leadership of the *amir* and *Imam* Ahmad b. Ibrahim al-Ghazi, called Grañ (meaning the 'left-handed') of Harar, the Ethiopian Christian state was almost extinguished. Ethiopian and Arab sources tell the same story. *Imam* Ahmad resumed the Muslim offensive, scoring a great victory over the emperor's army at Shembera Kure (on the Awash River about 40 miles south-southeast of Addis Ababa) in 1529.

Subsequently the Muslim armies invaded and overran the greater part of Christian Ethiopia between 1531 and 1543. Emperor Lebna Dengel ended his life a fugitive in his own empire. The emperor, who had received the Portuguese embassy enthroned in his great pavilion hung with silks and brocades a few years earlier, became a fugitive, hunted from place to place until he died and was buried at Dabra Damo. The cultural centres of the land, the churches and monasteries, were sacked and burned, and a large part of the population abandoned their former faith and converted to Islam.

For a time, it seemed that the old Ethiopia, the Habash Christian state, was doomed. Rescue came through a joint effort by the new emperor, Galawdewos, and a Portuguese contingent of some four hundred men – small in numbers, but armed with modern weapons, and under the competent leadership of the governor-designate of Portuguese Melaka, Cristovão da Gama. Despite assistance from the pasha of Zabid, who sent Turkish support, Ahmad Grañ suffered defeats, even if he was, at one point, to capture and execute da Gama himself. Grañ was killed in battle in 1543. The emperor, too, was to die in 1559 at the hands of Grañ's successor *Amir* Nur of Harar, but the Muslims had lost the initiative. Harar was soon to lose all military power, though it continued to exist as the centre of Islam in the country and an important market.

Christian imperial rule could now be re-established over upland Ethiopia – but it was soon to be severely attenuated. With the eclipse of *Amir* Ahmad, both the Muslim states and the Christian kingdom had almost immediately to look to their defence against newcomers to the scene – the Cushitic-speaking Oromo peoples, often called by the derogatory designation Galla. The Oromo, relatives of the Somalis and a pastoralist people, began to migrate into Ethiopia in force from their former lands to the south. During the sixteenth and seventeenth centuries the Oromo penetrated into many different regions of the former Habash empire, entering the province of Bale and spreading rapidly (as recorded in 1593 by an Ethiopian monk, Bahrey, the first historian of the Oromo). The Oromo, who now form a major section of Ethiopia's population, rapidly became the chief enemies of the Christian state that still maintained itself in the north and centre. They attacked Harar as well, before coming to an accommodation with the city-state that was all that was left of the conquests of Ahmad Grañ and his nephew Nur.

The Oromo were to change the face of Ethiopia radically, especially as many of them converted to Islam. They caused a realignment of the empire by their conquest of many southern regions, inclining Minas, Sarsa Dengel and subsequent rulers to select camping places round Lake Tana rather than further south in Shewa as had long been the custom. Sarsa Dengel fought Oromo chiefs in Hadya, and managed to extract tribute from Enarya, but southward and eastward Ethiopian influence had vanished. Gradually, however, as time passed, and the Oromo settled after their conquests, a *modus vivendi* was achieved. In the end marriages with Oromo chiefly families meant that some of the Solomonic emperors themselves, and many of the great provincial families, became part Oromo by descent.

Meanwhile, in the north the Ottoman Turks seized Egypt in 1517, establishing in 1557 their imperial province of Habesh based on possession of the port of Ethiopia, Massawa. At different times they were able to make considerable incursions into Ethiopia, establishing themselves also at Debarwa. Emperor Minas fought them, and Sarsa Dengel was able to defeat an alliance between Yeshaq, his rebellious *bahrnagash*, or governor of the sea coast region, and the Turks. He seized and demolished the Turkish fortress at Debarwa in 1577.

For about one hundred years after their opportune entry (for the Christians) into Ethiopian affairs under Galawdewos, the Portuguese remained in Ethiopia. The papacy appointed patriarchs to the country, parallel with the Alexandrian-appointed *abun*s who headed the traditional Orthodox church. Jesuit missionaries, largely Portuguese – although one of the best of them, Pero Pais (or Pedro Paez), was Spanish – attempted to convert the country to Catholicism. Unfortunately, religious differences and a certain arrogance of behaviour on the part of some of the Jesuits led to conflict. Early during this 'Portuguese period', Emperor Galawdewos felt it incumbent on himself to compose a 'Confession' or testament to his faith, explaining his people's attitude to certain elements in their religion, such as the prohibition of pork, and the practice of circumcision. The Spanish bishop Andre de Oviedo had the temerity, in the name of the absent Latin patriarch Nuñez Barreto, who had remained in Goa, to launch an excommunication of those who upheld the Alexandrian church. This gesture, not surprisingly, greatly irritated the emperor. Galawdewos was killed in battle with the Hararis shortly afterwards, but his brother Emperor Minas (1559–63) kept the foreigners away from the centre of influence, banishing the Spanish prelate from court. Minas' successor Sarsa Dengel employed the Portuguese for his buildings but was not inclined to their religion.

Religious questions led to the deposition and death of Emperor Za-Dengel (1603), who had accepted Catholicism under Pais' influence. Eventually, increasing troubles in reaction to the activities of Afonso Mendez (Mendes), the new Catholic patriarch, led to the abdication of Emperor Susneyos, who had also embraced Catholicism. The accession in 1632 of his son Fasiladas, a supporter of the Ethiopian Orthodox Church despite constraint to accept Catholicism in his father's reign, removed all chances of a Catholic conversion of Ethiopia. The Jesuits were in 1633 first exiled to Fremona, or Maigwagwa, their centre (at Endiet-Nebersh, c. 6 km. northwest of Adwa according to Anfray 1988: 11) in Tigray founded in 1557, then definitively expelled. Hatred of them remained so intense that the emperor even wrote to the Muslim authorities at Massawa and elsewhere to arrange for the detention and execution of any foreign priests who might attempt to enter the country, an arrangement that seems to have been fulfilled to the letter.

The writings of the Jesuits – together with the assistance of a learned Ethiopian monk at Rome, Gorgoreyos – also contributed significantly to the works of a seventeenth-century German scholar, Job Ludolf. He never visited Ethiopia, and his mentor Gorgoreyos was drowned when he attempted the return journey, but his linguistic and historical work was the foundation of Ethiopian studies in Europe. Another remarkable character, James Bruce of Kinnaird, a Scot, actually lived at the court of Gondar for some years in the 1770s. He later published an important work describing many aspects of the country, and in addition formed a core collection of manuscripts in Ge'ez, which he brought back with him. As European interest in Africa developed, many others followed in the nineteenth century. The country and its people gradually became better known to the outside world (see Chapter 3).

We have already noted the Ethiopian traditional histories, chronicles and other works containing historical information. Among these are king lists, often differing radically. They survive only in late copies, but purport to show the descent of the rulers from the Queen of Sheba and King Solomon of Israel, or even from Adam. Much of their content is patently legendary. The royal chronicles, which exist for the reigns of many 'Solomonid' rulers, are very informative, though rather limited in scope to royal matters – the affairs of the court and king, wars, religious questions and the like. There are no chronicles for the Zagwé kings. The writings that refer to them are fourteenth- or fifteenth-century hagiographical works – little more than miracle-filled hymns of praise to the saintly kings of the dynasty, containing hardly any reliable historical material. On the other hand, in the Ge'ez *gadlat*, the hagiographies or lives of Ethiopian saints as a whole, we have an extraordinarily valuable archive of documentation of social and economic evidence, not to mention religious opinions, for the period from the fourteenth and fifteenth centuries onwards. Together with the lists of metropolitan bishops, and the land charters often copied into manuscripts, these literary sources represent an Ethiopian 'official' history, which can be supplemented by other indigenous writings including the important Arabic chronicles from Harar and other neighbouring Muslim states. In some regions of the north and centre, oral traditions have been collected that enhance the picture. More recently, oral traditions from certain southern peoples have been added too, helping to clarify to some extent the development of their history.

The rise and fall of Gondar Fasiladas' expulsion of the Portuguese Jesuits contributed to a new isolation of the country. European influence largely departed, although there were still descendants of the Portuguese settlers who had been granted land by the different emperors after Galawdewos, and who had married Ethiopian women and raised families. Nevertheless, a few foreign travellers did come during the seventeenth century. A doctor Poncet arrived from France to treat Iyasu I, who as a result corresponded with Louis XIV. The Bohemian Remedius Prutky came in the reign of Iyasu II, and the Scotsman James Bruce was in Gondar in the time of Tekla Haymanot II, Empress Mentewab, and *Ras* Mikael Sehul.

By this time, the country had a new centre. This phase of Ethiopian history is generally known as the Gondar period, because from the middle of the seventeenth century a new element entered the Ethiopian scene. After the expulsion of the Jesuits, the emperors from Fasiladas onwards began to build themselves stone castles at Gondar, just north of the great Lake of Dambya, or Lake Tana (Tsana), whose islands had long been a refuge for monks and are still full of churches and monasteries. Here at Gondar emperor after emperor resided, and the place began to take on some of the characteristics of a true capital city. The towered and battlemented castles of Gondar, which bear the names of many of the most famous Ethiopian emperors and empresses of the time, Fasiladas, Yohannes I, Iyasu I, Bakaffa and his wife Mentewab, still stand, with some of the forty-four churches that local tradition claims eventually embellished the city. Government still did not become truly centralised. Most emperors, as their chronicles reveal, spent a good part of each year on campaign in the different regions of their empire. They dwelt, like the former rulers, in a great movable city of tents, or in other favoured residences such as Aringo and Yebaba.

Zemana mesafint, the 'era of the princes' In the eighteenth century the power of the central monarchy began to decline. Assassinations and bitter struggles for power undermined the monarchy. Imperial Gondar slowly fell into decay as great provincial lords, deploying more powerful military means than the emperors themselves possessed, became capable of manipulating the succession in favour of their own puppet kings. The curious custom of exiling all princes of the dynasty to an *amba*, or flat-topped mountain, to prevent them from plotting against the current ruler, provided a reservoir of princes with the required Solomonic blood for these lords to draw on for each new attempt to seize power. After the assassination of Emperor Iyasu I in 1706, and that of Tekla Haymanot I in 1708, followed by the usurpation of Yostos and the poisoning of Dawit II, the monarchy grew more and more unstable. Bakaffa's exhibition of naked strength against the nobles was a last gesture.

Subsequent further weakening of central control under the later Gondarine rulers, particularly from about 1769 after the murder of Emperor Iyoas, allowed the country to fragment, although the theory of the 'Solomonic throne' remained intact. Certain regional lords, with the high military titles of *ras* or *dejazmach*, ruled in Tigray, Begemder and Gojjam. They supported different 'Solomonid' emperors in order to raise themselves to supreme power. The loss of the imperial power resulted in constant civil wars – the so-called *mesafint* era, ending in the mid-nineteenth century with feeble kings dwelling at Gondar, completely at the mercy of the great provincial lords. Some of these 'kings of kings' lived in such poverty amid the ruins of the palaces of Gondar that there was scarcely enough money to bury them decently. Only the magic of their Solomonic descent, or perhaps rather the need for the great chiefs to have someone under their control who could make them imperial *ras*, or supreme commander, kept the system going.

It was at this time – when *Ras* Walda Sellase was ruler of Tigray – that Henry Salt, Nathaniel Pearce and William Coffin came to Ethiopia, under the patronage of Lord Valentia. Other European travellers followed, French, Italian or German, and once again reliable information about Ethiopia and its ancient sites began to spread abroad. An important area of stability that interested European governments was the eastern Shewan province of Manz, where a family claiming Solomonic descent seized control of a district almost cut off from the rest of the Christian kingdom by the Welo Galla. As the century progressed a series of capable rulers was able to enlarge this small province into the substantial and stable kingdom of Shewa. In the end, this dynasty was to reach the imperial throne itself in the person of Emperor Menelik II.

The Third Ethiopian Empire

Tewodros II In the mid-nineteenth century the interloper Kasa cut through the old imperial traditions and the more recent authority of the provincial lords alike. A remarkable character by any standards, against continual opposition and frustration he created a new, if ultimately disastrous, form of government. His rise to power eliminated most of the rival elements, and re-established a stronger and more united Ethiopia. He was crowned as Emperor Tewodros II (1855–68). The genealogists duly found a Solomonic background for him, with a claim to descent from Fasiladas' daughter Sabla Wangel. With his reign a central monarchy was once more established in large parts of highland Ethiopia. Tewodros even subdued Shewa, which had maintained its separate and semi-independent existence under rulers reputedly descended from Lebna Dengel. Attempts at modernisation were inaugurated. Even the frustrating of the emperor's ambitions, his strange and increasingly un-predictable behaviour, and his disastrous clash with the British, which led to the Maqdala expedition in 1868 and Tewodros' suicide, did not completely undo his work. This reign, culminating in the British expedition to Maqdala, saw a foreign army entering Ethiopia, successfully fulfilling its mission, and – astonishingly – retiring again once the conflict was over.

Yohannes IV and Menelik II The British retreat resulted, after a short struggle between two powerful rivals for the throne, in the reign of the victor, the former *dejazmach* of Tigray, Kassa. He took the throne as Emperor Yohannes IV; his Solomonic descent was traced through the eldest child of Sabla Wangel, daughter of Yohannes I's daughter Amlakawit. In his time, and throughout the subsequent reign of Menelik II, the emperors' policies were aimed at retaining, with increasing difficulty, the independence of Ethiopia. Egyptian expansionist aims in the Eritrean Bogos area constituted a major problem for Yohannes IV, and this brought him at times into not overly successful contact with British diplomacy. The Egyptians seized Harar in the south. Yohannes managed to control the powerful tributary kingdom of Shewa, but was compelled to recognise Menelik of Shewa as the next imperial heir. In addition, the colonial ambitions of Italy set a sinister pattern for the future. The Italians were able to acquire the Red Sea port of Assab in 1869, and seized the more northerly port of Massawa in 1885. Yohannes died, as did his one-time visitor (and detractor) General Charles Gordon, fighting the powerful militant Islamic state founded by the Mahdi in Sudan.

Menelik II of Shewa succeeded Yohannes in 1889, and was crowned at Entotto near Addis Ababa as King of Kings of Ethiopia. The need for peace to establish himself more firmly on his new throne placed him in a weak position *vis-à-vis* the Italians, who proclaimed their first African colony, Eritrea, in 1890. Further pressures resulted in the battle of Adwa (1896), in which the Italians, who had claimed a protectorate over the whole of Ethiopia, were humiliatingly defeated. This was a turning point. Ethiopia, uniquely in Africa, succeeded in retaining its sovereignty in the face of the European 'scramble' for possession of the continent. It is true that Menelik lost control of parts of Eritrea. In return, he launched a massive programme of colonial expansion in the south, destroying the independence of such kingdoms as Jinjero and Kafa, and seizing Harar from the last of the *amir*s when the Egyptians departed.

The enormously enlarged Ethiopian empire that Menelik's conquests real-ised is the Ethiopia of today. It was quite unlike anything that had existed before. Even the greatest of the mediaeval emperors had been able only to impose tribute, and some token Christianity, on certain southern regions, but now a much stronger and more centralised Amhara-dominated state had become ruler over a vast congeries of minor peoples. The history of these regions, however, scarcely enters into the account of Ethiopia's historical sites.

Menelik II (1889–1913) and his wife Empress Taytu, a woman of very strong character and no lover of foreign influences, steered a political course designed to maintain Ethiopian independence. Nevertheless, they took what advantage they could of what the modern world had to offer. With the help of selected foreign advisers, Menelik began to modernise the country. A new capital was founded at Addis Ababa, the 'New Flower'. As the reign continued, despite major political storms such as the war with Italy, modern facets began to appear. Railways and roads were built, and banks, schools and hospitals appeared. A post and telegraph system and a coinage were instituted. There was, of course, resistance to some elements of change, but by and large Ethiopia was set on the path it would follow under its next major leader, Emperor Haile Sellassie.

Ras Tafari, Haile Sellassie   After the reign of Lij Iyasu, who was deposed and imprisoned after a short period, Menelik's daughter Zawditu succeeded as empress. The pace of change increased under the regent *Ras* Tafari, son of *Ras* Makonnen, a relative of Menelik's who had been governor of Harar. *Ras* Tafari – who was to give his name to the Rasta movement in Jamaica and elsewhere – had already gained experience in government, and had travelled extensively in Europe. On the empress's death in 1930 he was crowned as Emperor Haile Sellassie.

Haile Sellassie seems to have been forward-looking in many ways, transforming his empire into a modern bureaucratic state. But he was still a traditional Ethiopian emperor to the extent that he was determined to retain power in his own hands, and to decree the pace and manner of change himself. He promoted education, took steps to eradicate slavery and implement land reforms, and oversaw developments in the army and in transport and communications. He instituted certain reforms in the government. A constitution was granted and ministries were established. His attempt to design a progressive independent Ethiopia was interrupted in 1935 by the invasion by Italy under Mussolini's government. Ethiopia was defeated, but the country was never completely subjugated. When Italy entered the European war on Hitler's side, the short-lived Italian empire was doomed. British and Ethiopian troops were able to liberate the country in 1941.

Despite some difficulties with the British and with some local resistance groups, Haile Sellassie was soon re-established on his throne. The status of Italy's former colony of Eritrea was debated internationally, resulting in the decision to federate the ex-colony with Ethiopia. The federation, maintained for a certain time, gave way eventually to complete unity with Ethiopia. On the surface, this might have seemed a victory for the emperor's policies, but it was to herald the beginning of an Eritrean–Ethiopian conflict that has still not come to an end. There were other dissatisfied elements in the country too, impatient with the emperor's insistence that his was the guiding hand, that he was the deciding judge for every reform. During a state visit by Haile Sellassie to Brazil, the imperial bodyguard staged an abortive coup that installed the crown prince as ruler. Despite its swift suppression, it was the writing on the wall. As the emperor grew older, military and student discontent increased. Reforms slowed. Troubles in Eritrea and other regions developed. Drought, together with extensive crop failure and famine, exacerbated the problems. In 1974, the emperor was deposed by the military, and the monarchy was terminated.

The Ethiopian Revolution

With the revolution, radical changes burst upon the people. Land was confiscated from great landlords and the church. Industry was nationalised. The entire traditional ruling class vanished from the seats of power, to execution, prison or exile. A military man of no particular skill in government, Mengistu Haile Maryam, emerged as the most powerful figure in the regime. The ex-emperor was murdered. Students were sent out into the country to 're-educate' the rural population, peasants' associations and co-operatives were formed and a new socialist order was proclaimed. Some reduction was observed in 'amharisation' of education and government. However, as time went on, the changes went hand in hand with an authoritarianism no less than that of the emperor. The brutality of the 1977 'Red Terror' followed, with increasing agrarian problems, famine on a major scale in 1983–84, and escalating internal (Eritrea, Tigray, Oromia) and external (Somalia) military conflict, which consumed a large part of the annual budget. Unpopular policies, such as the resettlement and villagisation programmes supposedly instituted to relieve famine-devastated districts, and to permit provision of modern services, tore the fabric even of family and regional life apart. The separatist groups grew more influential, and, particularly in Tigray and Eritrea, began to erode the dominance of Mengistu's government, which with the collapse of the Soviet Union lost an important source of military aid. In 1991 it was an alliance of these groups that was able to defeat Mengistu's forces and to end what must have been one of the most miserable periods in Ethiopia's long history.

Post-revolutionary Ethiopia

The government that replaced Mengistu's regime remained a provisional one – the Transitional Government of Ethiopia – with a president who chaired a Council of Representatives with eighty-seven seats divided among some of the many political and ethnic groups in the country. The parties sharing the government were numerous: the Ethiopian People's Revolutionary Democratic Front, with its coalition member organisations the Tigray People's Liberation Front (whose leader was President Meles Zenawi), the Ethiopian People's Democratic Movement, the Oromo People's Democratic Organisation and the Ethiopian Democratic Officers' Revolutionary Movement. There were also a number of smaller parties such as the Ethiopian Democratic Coalition, with regional representatives of the Afar, Benishangul, Burji, Gambela, Gurage, Harai, Isa and Gurgura, Kambata, Kefa, Wolayta, Somali and Yem Liberation or People's Democratic Fronts, as well as some Oromo parties. There were many opposition parties, generally regional, the largest being the Oromo Liberation Front, which ceased to be represented in the Council. The Prime Minister was Tamirat Layne, with some twenty other ministers derived from a number of groups (including Tigray, Amhara, Oromo, Hadiya, Afar, Somali and Harar), and a similar number of vice-ministers.

Federal Ethiopia, 1996

The shape of Ethiopia crystallised into a new form when the Provisional Government gave way to the Federal Democratic Republic of Ethiopia. The elections of August–September 1995 brought in new people to represent a new order. The country is now divided into regions, based on ethnic lines. These are as follows:

1.	Tigray	8.	Kambata and Hadiya
2.	Afar	9.	Sidama
3.	Amhara	10.	Gamu Gofa
4.	Oromia	11.	Kafa
5.	Somali	12.	Gambela
6.	Benishangul	13.	Harar
7.	Gurage	14.	Addis Ababa

Regions 7–11 formed the Southern Region, under a Southern Peoples' Administrative Region, presided over by Abata Kishu (Sidama). The country's president was an Oromo, Dr Nagasa Gidada, with Meles Zenawi (from Adwa) as prime minister. Tamirat Layne (Gondar Amhara) became vice-prime

minister with the Defence portfolio as well, and Dr Kasu Ilala (Gurage) was appointed vice-prime minister for economic affairs only. A bicameral parliament was instituted. The higher house was named the Council of Representatives, the lower the Federation Council. Under this new system, the idea seems to be to achieve a truly federal state, with each region participating, but not dominated – an ancient cause for resentment – by any other ethnic group.

Manifestations of the new dispensation were quickly visible. For example, in Oromia the regional black, white and red flag imprinted with an acacia tree is frequently seen, and the language is now written in the Somali style with the Latin alphabet. (At Shashemane, once a place where many northerners were resettled, I saw an amusing manifestation of this in the name of a bar called Miinii Aksuum.) Property confiscated from individuals under the former regime could now be reclaimed. Even the late emperor, exhumed from his clandestine burial by Mengistu after his murder, was granted temporary burial in Ba'ata church, the mausoleum of Menelik, Taytu and Zawditu. More recently, although a government statement excoriating his rule was issued at the same time, Haile Sellassie's family were permitted to offer him a final funeral in November 2000 in Sellassie cathedral, where he had prepared his own tomb and that of his empress, *Itege* Menen.

Positive though the outlook is in some ways, the shape of the Ethiopia of the future is still uncertain. Perhaps modern Ethiopians can bring out of the disasters of the recent past something more encouraging – just as the message of woe to the older Ethiopia, *'the land shadowing with wings'*, cited at the head of the Preface to this book, is tempered to a prouder image by more recent translations:

> Country of whirring wings beyond the rivers of Cush, who send ambassadors by sea, in papyrus skiffs over the waters. Go, swift messengers to a people tall and bronzed, to a nation always feared, a people mighty and masterful, in the country criss-crossed with rivers. (Jerusalem Bible)

> Terre, où retentit le cliquetis des armes, au-delà des fleuves de l'Ethiopie! Toi qui envoies sur mer des messagers, dans des navires de jonc voguant à la surface des eaux! Allez, messagers rapides, vers la nation forte et vigoreuse, vers ce peuple redoutable depuis qu'il existe, nation puissant et qui écrase tout, et dont le pays est coupé par des fleuves. (Gideon Bible, French translation)

Ethiopia Today

Ethiopia today is a country of some 1,200,000 square km., with a population of about 56 million, increasing by about 3 per cent annually. The population of the capital, Addis Ababa, is about 3.5 million. Ethiopia remains one of the world's poorest countries.

About one hundred different ethnic groups are recognised, sharing some seventy languages. The country is divided into twelve major regions following ethnic patterns – the largest groups being Oromo, Amhara, Tigray and Somali. These regions are subdivided into *woreda*s, or local administrative units. The Christian and Muslim religions are followed by approximately equal numbers of adherents, with by far the majority of the former belonging to the Ethiopian Orthodox Church. In broad terms, the northern and central highlands form the Christian region, while the eastern area is primarily Muslim. Some 2 per cent of the population subscribe to other beliefs.

Agriculture is the principal economic activity, with stock-rearing on such a scale as to give Ethiopia the largest livestock population in Africa – apparently some 24 million head. Coffee is an important crop, and the main export, pulses, oilseeds, cereals, potatoes, sugar cane and vegetables, are also cultivated. Industry is not very widespread, but there are cement, textile, food-processing and oil-refining plants. The potential for tourism at the historical sites that illustrate Ethiopia's dramatic history, as this book will show, is one of Ethiopia's great assets for the future.

Three climatic zones are traditionally recognised by the Ethiopians. These are *kwolla* (below 1,800 m. and with a hot tropical climate, 26 degrees C or more), *woina dega* (from 1,800 to 2,400 m. with a sub-tropical climate and temperatures averaging 22 degrees C), and the highland area, *dega* (above 2,400 m. and with an average temperature of 16 degrees C). The cultivators' year commences in March with the little rains, which ideally will soften the ground for ploughing. These rains sometimes fail. From June to September is the main rainy season, prolonged somewhat in the southern region. An extremely important crop in the highlands is a grass called *teff* (*Eragrostis teff*), which produces very small grains that are used for the preparation of one of Ethiopia's dietary staples, the pancake called *injera*. This is eaten with a number of different meat or vegetable accompaniments; especially delicious is the sauce of onions, meat or vegetables combined with chillies and other mixed spices (*berbere*), called *wot*. In the warmer south, the staple is the false banana (*ensete*).

THE ETHIOPIAN CHURCH

Church buildings, perched on precipitous hilltops, or cut deep into the rock, offer some of the most dramatic sights in Ethiopia. Of great variety and often of impressive workmanship in comparison to surviving domestic architecture, they constitute an important part of Ethiopia's heritage today. The Ethiopian Orthodox Church that they represent is the most ancient institution surviving in the country after the fall of the monarchy in 1974. For visitors to the historical sites of Ethiopia, the churches and the ceremonies that surround them are among the most striking features of the highland northern and central Ethiopians' way of life.

To some extent even today, the lives of all Ethiopians of the Christian highlands are marked by the rites, ceremonies and beliefs that intimately connect them to the Church. A fascinating collection of notes on all the main aspects of life from birth and baptism to death and burial was compiled from records of conversations with Amhara people by C. H. Walker in his book *The Abyssinian at Home* (1933), and few of these lack constant reference to the Church. Accordingly, although the post-1974 regime, with its deliberate reduction of the Church's influence, affected this situation to some degree, I provide here these notes on the Ethiopian Orthodox Church's history and its functions.

The appointment of Frumentius of Tyre as bishop of Aksum by Athanasius, patriarch of Alexandria, around AD 340, has already been described, with its resulting tradition by which (almost) all the metropolitan bishops (or *abun*s) at the head of the Ethiopian Church were Alexandrian appointees until the mid-twentieth century. Frumentius' story, as related by Rufinus of Aquilea, a near contemporary of the events, is an extraordinary one. He and a relative, Aedesius, were taken as children by a kinsman, a philosopher called Meropius, to India. On returning from India, their ship touched at an Ethiopian port, but, a Romano-Ethiopian treaty having been at that moment broken, all on the ship were slain except for the two youths.

> The philosopher's ship was boarded; all with himself were put to the sword. The boys were found studying under a tree and preparing their lessons, and, preserved by the mercy of the barbarians, were taken to the king. He made one of them, Aedesius, his cupbearer. Frumentius, whom he had perceived to be sagacious and prudent, he made his treasurer and secretary.

Later, on the king's death, the queen, regent for a minor son, asked Frumentius to assist her in ruling the land. Despite their having been granted their freedom, he and Aedesius stayed. Frumentius took the opportunity to propagate the Christian faith, with the result that, when he finally left the country to return to the Roman world, there was already a nascent Church.

> Frumentius went to Alexandria, saying that it was not right to hide the work of God. He laid the whole affair before the bishop [Athanasius, patriarch of Alexandria] and urged him to look for some worthy man to send as bishop over the many Christians already congregated and the churches built on barbarian soil. Then Athanasius ... declared in a council of the priests 'What other man shall we find in whom the spirit of God is as in thee, who can accomplish these things?' And he consecrated him, and bade him return in the grace of God whence he had come.

Athanasius' consecration of Frumentius to this post officially founded the Ethiopian Church. This story is told by a contemporary historian, Rufinus of Aquilea, who claims to have heard it in person from Aedesius, who later became a priest in Tyre.

Christianity evidently took root, in court circles at least, in King Ezana's time. The king's coins and inscriptions employed pagan symbolism or phraseology at first, changing later to Christian. It is thus fairly certain that the unnamed kings of Rufinus' account were Ezana and his father Ella Amida, who seems to be identifiable as the king called Ousanas on his coins – the usual problem posed by Ethiopian rulers' use of several names. In addition, a letter written about AD 356 by the Roman emperor Constantius II about Frumentius himself is addressed to the brothers 'Aizanas and Sazanas', and Ezana is known from some of his pagan inscriptions to have had a brother called Sazana. However, later Ethiopian records do not preserve the names Ezana or Sazana known from the earlier inscriptions; only the twin names 'Abreha and Asbeha' are found in Ge'ez accounts of the conversion of the country.

How quickly the new faith spread from this 'conversion from above' among the people themselves is unknown, but Ethiopian records tell us that in the fifth and sixth centuries numerous foreign missionaries, particularly the famous 'Nine Saints', came and established themselves in the Aksumite countryside. Their names are to be heard still in church dedications and local tales: Za-Mikael Aregawi, Liqanos or Mata'a, Pantalewon, Guba, Afse, Garima, Yemata, Alef and Sehma. These monks or hermits, even if the records pertaining to them date from nearly a thousand years later, and are not to be taken at face value, seem to continue a memory of a secondary Christian impetus that spread the faith into regions more distant from the capital, and doubtless also reached to a different level of society.

For centuries the bishops – exiles for life in a country strange to them – continued to come from Egypt, and the Ethiopian Orthodox Church developed to become one of the characteristic features of highland Ethiopia. The record is very sparse (see Munro-Hay 1997 for an account from the fourth to the fourteenth centuries). But whenever we hear of Ethiopia, it is still a Christian land, with its bishops still deriving from Alexandria. Only twice, in the thirteenth century, do the records mention people of other nationalities being consecrated to the Ethiopian bishopric; once an Ethiopian nobleman was consecrated by the patriarch of Antioch, and later Syrian bishops are mentioned. Both these occurrences are noted as being illegal; they were only brief interruptions in the long sequence of Alexandrian-appointed Egyptian monks who became metropolitan bishops of Ethiopia. A further bizarre episode was the claim by João Bermudes, who came to Ethiopia with the 1520 Portuguese embassy, to be not only the bishop of Ethiopia, but also patriarch of Alexandria.

The Ethiopian Church naturally followed the Coptic Church of Egypt in its doctrinal decisions, most importantly in 451, when the Eastern churches refused to accept the decrees of the Council of Chalcedon. This schism has never been healed, and the Coptic, Ethiopian, Syrian, Armenian and other Churches still follow the monophysite (one nature) interpretation of Christ's nature, contrasting with the diophysite (dual nature) interpretation followed by the Catholic Church.

The Ethiopian Church undoubtedly instituted its own local hierarchy apart from these foreign bishops – whose chief function was the ordination of priests – but we hear very little of it in early times. Occasionally some assistant bishops are recorded. The chief figures in the native Church hierarchy in later times consisted of the *echege*, or head of the monks, who was the prior of the famous monastery of Debra Libanos, the highest-ranking ecclesiastic after the *abun*, the Egyptian metropolitan bishop. He was the real leader of the church, and at his investiture the emperor placed his own crown briefly on the *echege*'s head. The third in rank was the *aqabe-sa'at*, 'Guardian of the

Hour', earlier an office in the hands of the abbots of Debra Estifanos at Hayq (the first *aqabe-sa'at* of Debra Estifanos was apparently Abba Za-Iyasus in the reign of Amda Seyon, 1270–85) and later more or less a palace chaplain. These ecclesiastics (whose offices and titles are now redundant), with the abbots of some of the greater monasteries and some of the chief priests, supervised the day-to-day running of the Church, whose legal head could not even speak the local language. Some ecclesiastical titles are known to have an old pedigree. A number of abbots of the monastery of Debra Libanos of Shimezana held the title *aqabe-sa'at* in the time of King Lalibela in the early thirteenth century, according to information from land charters, and other monastic leaders bore the title *nebura'ed*, signifying one whose office was conferred by the laying-on of hands.

Apart from familiar offices, metropolitans (generally called *abun, liqa-pappasat, pappas*) and other bishops (*episqopos*), abbots or priors (*mamher*) and deacons (*diyaqon*), the title *qese gabaz seyon*, indicating a provost of a church dedicated in the name of Zion, is known from these charters. *Qala-pappas*, interpreter for the *abun* or metropolitan bishop, *qas-hasani*, the royal chaplain, and *liqa diyaqonat*, archdeacon, are further titles attested in land charters attributed to King Lalibela (these charters generally list ecclesiastical or court officials in office at the time of their granting). *Abba*, father, is a general title bestowed on many monks and other revered holy men. A certain Nablis, with the vague title of *aleqa* (master, or administrator of a church), is traditionally supposed to have been a teacher of sacred poetry and songs (*qene, zema*) and religious literature in King Lalibela's time, also performing in the choir at Aksum; all these activities are still practised at Maryam Seyon cathedral in Aksum and in many other places.

I owe to the efforts of Ato Niftalem Kiros, son of the late *liqa mezemiran* Kiros of Aksum, who spent considerable time researching the obscurer points, much of the information on which the following account of the structure of the Ethiopian Church hierarchy is based. Part of this refers to Aksum in particular, but it is more or less universally applied on a lesser scale elsewhere.

The Church Hierarchy

PATRIARCH, RISA LIQANE PAPASAT   The patriarch is the head of the Ethiopian Orthodox Church. He is elected by the Holy Synod, of which he becomes the chairman. In times past the head of the church was a metropolitan or archbishop, generally an Egyptian monk, consecrated by the patriarch of Alexandria as the chief bishop for the Ethiopians. But in the 1950s the first Ethiopian, *Abuna* Basilios, was chosen for this post, and the next incumbent was elevated to the rank and style of patriarch. The church is now autocephalous, though an honorary attachment to Alexandria is recognised. In former times the metropolitan bishop or *abun* occupied a curious position; they were often unable to communicate with their flock save through interpreters (*qala pappas*), and lived as exiles for life in Ethiopia. They were sometimes persuaded to reject or support candidature for the monarchy, and they were the chief ecclesiastical actors in the ceremony of the royal coronations at Aksum, although in most of the coronation ceremonies outside the holy city the crown was placed on the king's head by a court priest, the *saraj masare*. Their chief significance for the church was the ordination of priests. The patriarchal functions nowadays incorporate those formerly performed by the *echege*, head of the monks. The present patriarch is *Abuna* Pawlos, Patriarch of the Ethiopian Orthodox Tawahado Beta Krestyan, as the Church is officially known. He has adopted titles that associate him directly with the two great centres of church influence, *echege* of the See of Tekla Haymanot in reference to Debra Libanos, and head of the priests of Aksum. For more information on the early Ethiopian 'metropolitan bishops' see Munro–Hay 1997.

LIQA PAPPAS   A *liqa pappas* is member of the Synod, often a regional Church leader or a monastic leader ordained by the patriarch. His title indicates that he is an archbishop, chief of the *pappasat* (see below).

PAPPAS   This word has the same derivation as 'pope'. In Ethiopia the *pappasat* or bishops are regional church leaders or monastic leaders, ordained by the patriarch and in turn ordaining priests and deacons. There is also the office of *episqopos*, held by an ecclesiastic ranking below a full bishop, who acts as his vicar and fulfils some of his functions.

The following are the officials in charge of the administration, church services, and choir at Aksum today.

NEBURA'ED   The title indicates one appointed by laying hands upon him. This important official is usually nominated by the Church and in the past was appointed by the king. Originally there were many *nebura'ed*, monastic leaders, but in later Solomonid times, after the fifteenth century, the term gradually came to be applied only to the head of the Church in the holy city of Aksum. Later, Emperor Menelik II created a second *nebura'ed* in the south at Addis Alem, about 55 km. from Addis Ababa. The *nebura'ed* is in charge of the civil administration and the church leadership, nominating ecclesiastical functionaries, and assigning *liqa kahenat* (see below) to newly built churches. Among his insignia are a golden anklet on his right leg and golden shoes (a pair belonging to the *nebura'ed* Gabra Masqal in the time of Emperor Haile Sellassie are kept in the Maryam Seyon treasury; such external splendours, shared only with the holder of the now-defunct title *liqa Aksum*, have vanished with the revolution, as also has the *nebura'ed*'s magnificent house, destined now to become a cultural centre). The *nebura'ed* is assisted by an official entitled *aina mahaber*, the 'eye' of the congregation (priests, choir and administration), who is a sort of secretary of the *nebura'ed* and spokesman for the congregation. The present *nebura'ed* is called Belai Marasa.

QESE GABAZ   The *qese gabaz* is a sort of provost or high priest, in charge of church services. He is nominated by the Church and formerly was appointed by the king. He assigns the four *afa qese gabaz* (see below), one for each week every month. He is responsible for all the prayer services of the Church throughout the year; in addition to the diurnal services, the Ethiopian Church has a number of nocturnal services, especially on the occasion of great festivals such as Easter, or *Timqat* (Epiphany, when the commemoration of the baptism of Christ is celebrated). The title *gabaz* in Walker's glossary is translated 'Sacristan'; the term refers to a treasurer, the 'guardian of the goods of the *tabot*' (the stone or wooden altar tablet).

AFA NEBURA'ED   This official, literally the 'voice' or spokesman for the *nebura'ed*, is in charge of the choir. He is appointed by the Church elders. He is the highest choirmaster, leading the choir on important occasions, and has to be a competent interpreter of the Bible and the liturgy, chants, and so on.

LIQA LEBAS (KELEBAS)   There were formerly two officials with this title – literally Master of the Robes – who dispensed the correct vestments appropriate to the different ecclesiastical ranks. They also acted as ushers whenever the *nebura'ed* received important guests, such as the king or the patriarch.

KERE GETA   This was formerly an official appointed by the king's vassals and ratified by the Church to administer justice to the people.

The *qese gabaz*, *afa nebura'ed*, *liqa lebas* and *kere geta* are of equal rank, though the *qese gabaz* and *kere geta* tend to be rather more prominent than the others.

MERE GETA   These are two officials who stand right and left of the *afa nebura'ed* as leaders of the church choir, leading the songs, hymns and *qene*. Walker translates the name as 'guide master'; he may be the same as the *aleqa*. To clarify the order of the choir, Walker's informant (Walker 1933: 110–11) explains:

> Along the western wall of the choir they will stand thus, beginning from the right or south – the Right Master [*kegn geta*], the Guide Master [*mere geta*], the *Alaqa* [administrator or head], the *Ré'isa Dabir* (archimandrite), and the Left

Master [*gra geta*] – while the *dabtaras* will stand in front … The *Alaqa* himself, being the Guide Master, will know the *qalam* [tune] perfectly, and after he has chanted the others receive from him. Also the Left and Right Masters alternately bring their part to an end according to the *qalam*, and the *dabtaras* pick them up responding.

MEGABI   Literally, 'feeder'; the holder of this office is equal to the *mere geta*, though the *mere geta* has a certain extra prominence. The *megabi* is also a leader of the church choir, though that office is assumed by the *afa nebura'ed* or *mere geta*s on important feasts. He 'feeds' – encourages, teaches and corrects – young choir members, as well as leading the change from one chant to another. The name *megabi* also refers to the treasurer in a *gedem* ('wilderness' or monastery). He assigns monks to the services and daily work, and distributes the rations.

LIQA MEZEMIRAN   This is the office of choirmaster, leader of the choir next to the *mere geta*s. On most normal occasions he leads the choir, but on occasions of special solemnity, or when a more complex chant is required, the *mere geta* or even *afa nebura'ed* will lead.

KEGN GETA AND GRA GETA   The 'masters of the right and left' are members of the choir, leading the sections of the choir standing towards the right and left of the congregation. They are appointed by the *aleqa* or equivalent (administrator).

Church dignitaries or elders of the Church   Generally these are persons who have acquired great experience in the church liturgy, songs, hymns, church calendar, and so on, but without the higher knowledge of the *afa nebura'ed*, *liqa tebebt* or *mere geta*. They could be appointed, on a superior level, by king or bishops, or on a lower level by an *aleqa*, *qese gabaz* or *nebura'ed*, perhaps during the celebration of some special occasion. Sometimes in Gondarine times, such persons were the heads of important churches such as Asasame Mika'el, Debra Berhan Selassie or Qwesqwam.

MALE'AKA SAHAY   The 'angel' or messenger of the Sun.

MALE'AKA GHENET   Messenger of Paradise.

LIQA MAIMIRAN   Chief of the knowledgeable.

LIQA HIRUIAN   Chief of the chosen.

LIQA BERHANAT   Chief of the lights.

LIQA TIGUHAN   Chief of the awoken, or those who actively participate in the church services.

RE'SA DABIR Elder of the Church (literally, head of the mountain).

MALE'AKA SIBHAT Messenger of praise.

MALE'AKA SELAM Messenger of peace.

MALE'AKA MEHRET Messenger of mercy.

MECHENE There are two of these officials, not priests, one responsible to the *afa nebura'ed*, serving with the choir under his charge or that of the *liqa tebebt* or *mere geta*, the other involved in the church services under the *qese gabaz*. They act as ushers and chamberlains, and are in charge of such requisites for the services as sistra (musical instruments), prayer-sticks, drums, and so on, according to the position and responsibility of each choir member. Sometimes they are also referred to as *re'sa dabir* ('archimandrite' in Walker's glossary).

THE CHOIR Anyone cognisant of the church liturgy may be a lay member of the church choir. The choir's part in Ethiopian Church liturgy is a very important one, as the members – who need not all be priests – are required to have a high level of knowledge of the hymns and chants, to be able to narrate new *qene* immediately, suitable to the occasion and conforming to the poetic rules. They are considered much more learned than priests, who serve much the same liturgy daily with changes of anaphora according to the occasion. They are, of course, aware of exactly what takes place in the sanctuary, but cannot enter it if they are not ordained. Some members of the choir are involved voluntarily, with no benefit from the Church, merely acting as part of the choir in praise of God. The twofold division of the services between *kahen* or priests and *mahalet*, choristers or *dabtara*, is a feature of the Ethiopian Church.

Returning to the officials not part of the choir, but in charge under the *qese gabaz* (see above) of the church services:

AFA QESE GABAZ These are four priestly officials responsible to the *qese gabaz*, working by weekly shift as leaders of the church service.

LIQA KAHENAT This title means 'chief of the priests', an equal of the four *afa qese gabaz*. He would be appointed as chief priest to some other church outside Aksum, Addis Alem, Gondar, and so on, when new churches were founded. He is also known as *afa mammir* (Walker 1933: 109), 'a learned man and a teacher ... who is set in each province to guard the justice of [the metropolitan]'. Nowadays he is a servant of the Church, less concerned with the evangelisation of new regions, but leading the morning mass in the sanctuary.

LIQA DIYAQONAT   This official is the 'chief of the deacons', responsible to the *afa qese gabaz* and *liqa kahenat*. He assigns the deacons to their shifts according to their ability. As the highest-ranking priest, he may be head of the secular clergy of a province (though not the monastic clergy). Some *liqa diyaqonat* are not priests. He possesses judiciary and disciplinary functions. Other holders of the title are servants in churches such as Maryam Seyon, Maryam Addis Alem, and others. They are also involved in evangelisation, church construction, preparation of priests and deacons for ordination, and baptise new converts and babies.

DIYAQON   The word is the same as 'deacon', a minor ecclesiastical function-ary ordained (like priests) by a *pappas*. They serve in the sanctuary; some later choose to go in one or other of the directions available for further careers in the Church, either to the priesthood, or to choir positions. Three deacons are required, with two priests, for the saying of mass, and in a large church with perhaps twelve deacons will work in weekly shifts of three. One keeps the key and opens the church, holding the book during the service, a second holds the cross, and the third acts as 'raker of embers' assisting the second priest who swings the censer (Walker 1933: 107). The *qese gabaz*, *afa qese gabaz*, *liqa kahenat* and deacons are all privileged to enter the sanctuary, wrap and unwrap the *tabot*, carry it in processions (not the deacons), set penitence for those who confess, offer the cross for kissing, and pray for intercession for the people's welfare. They are involved with the overnight services, and the public worship at the morning service.

These titles and functions of the hierarchy at Aksum are not universally applicable, there being some slight differences at, for example, Addis Ababa and Debra Berhan. In Addis Ababa, the office equivalent to *afa nebura'ed* is *liqa tebebt*, and that equivalent to *qese gabaz* is *aleqa* (the administrator of a church). The *megabi* is entitled instead *aggafari*, which can be translated as chamberlain; he performs such tasks as supervising entry into a church, or preceding the deacons and priests carrying the host to a dying man for absolution.

To sum up, the national Church is headed by:

Patriarch
Liqa papas
Papas

In Aksum, the hierarchy is as follows:

Nebura'ed

(Choir)	(Ordained priests and deacons in charge of church services)	(Special officials)
Afa nebura'ed	*Qese gabaz*	*Kere geta kelebas*
Mere geta megabi	*Afa qese gabaz*	*Liqa kahenat*
Liqa mezemiran	*Liqa diyaqonat*	
Kegn geta gra geta	*Mechene*	
Male'aka sahay	*Diyaqon*	
Male'aka ghenet		
Liqa maimaran		
Liqa hiruian		
Liqa berhanat		
Liqa tiguhan		
Re'sa dabir		
Male'aka sibhat		
Male'aka selam		
Male'aka mihret		
Mechene		

A few other officials with specialised offices are the *qomos*, a canon or church official who settles disputes among the clergy; the *memher*, a title designating a master or teacher; and the *afa mamhir*, the prior or head of a monastery.

To the foreign observer there are a number of curious, even startling, aspects about the Ethiopian Church, its personnel, and its ceremonies, some of which differentiate it from all other Christian churches. Even the Alexandrian patriarchate accepted that in Ethiopia, although the patriarch of Alexandria was the head of the Church, certain special elements existed, and arrangements were made to accommodate them.

Older churches in Ethiopia, and some more modern ones in certain districts such as Tigray, were oblong in shape, while in many districts in the country since medieval times the custom has been to build round ones. Early churches – not surprisingly given the Mediterranean influences to be expected at the time – seem to have been basilical, generally with a central nave, two side aisles divided off from the nave by columns, and an apse at the altar, or east, end. All Ethiopian churches nowadays conform to the basic requirement of three separate areas. The outer is the *qene mahlet*, where the choir sings the hymns and chants led by the *afa nebura'ed*, *mere geta*s or *liqa tebebt*. Next, divided from the *qene mahlet* by a wall pierced by entrances called *'amda* *warq*, 'pillar of gold', is the *qeddest*, where the administration of communion occurs. The innermost area, central in a round church, at the east end in an oblong one, shut off by doors or curtains to all but priests and deacons (and, in the past, to the king), is the *maqdas*, or *qeddesta qeddusan*, the Holy of Holies, where the *tabot* or altar tablet is kept. Usually there is an outer court, walled, with a gatehouse, sometimes a building called the *daga salam*, 'gate of peace', in which certain ceremonies take place, and other structures called *bet lahm*, where the eucharistic bread is prepared, and *'eqa bet*, treasury. At the entrance to churches, shoes are removed; the area within is seen as being carpeted and covered by angels, protectors of the church and the people. (See the description in Chapter 5 of Debra Berhan Sellassie, Gondar, for a graphic representation of the throngs of angels watching over a church from above.)

In Ethiopia, it is not church buildings that are considered consecrated, but the *tabot*, which is dedicated to the saint whose name the church bears. It is, nowadays at least, envisaged as a replica or representation of the Ark of the Covenant – or, perhaps, more strictly, the tablet of the law – which is supposed to reside in a special shrine at Aksum (for information on the complex symbolism involved, see Grierson and Munro-Hay 1999). In a church, there may also be subsidiary *tabot*s with other dedications apart from the eponymous one. The *tabot* is a flat tablet or plaque, usually of wood inscribed with the dedication, a cross, and sometimes with a certain amount of carved decoration; there are a number in the British Museum in London that were brought back from the 1868 Maqdala expedition.

According to one of C. H. Walker's informants 'the tabot itself is a mystery, and he who fashions it is a learned man, a Qomos [canon] or priest or monk … every tabot must be blessed by Abbun [the metropolitan, now the patriarch] in his house in Addis Ababa, where none are present save only the Qomos and the priests, since the laity may not enter at such a time'. The *tabot* – or, strictly speaking, the *sellat* or tablet representing the *sellata hegg*, tablet of the law of Moses – is usually housed in or on a cupboard-like canopied altar called the *manbara tabot*, which is the main piece of furniture in the *maqdas* or Holy of Holies of the church, the interior part where only the officiating priests are admitted. Three *manbara tabot* in the rock-hewn church of Golgotha in Lalibela are part of the living rock. Walker wrote that the *tabot* was kept in a container or basket called *masoba warq* or 'golden basket', where it lay covered with some costly silk or brocade wrapping, but this basket is in fact used for the communion bread. It is said to represent Mary, while the bread within represents Christ. The *tabot* is placed, always wrapped, on the *manbara tabot*, and upon it the paten and cup are placed. The liturgy is celebrated over the *tabot*. On festival days, such as *Timqat*, the celebration of the baptism of Christ in the Jordan, the *tabot* is taken out, wrapped in brocade or velvet 'like the mantle of Christ', and carried on the head of a priest in procession. The *tabot* and its priestly escort are shaded by ceremonial parasols, an African feature, and often comprising an important part of the regalia of African monarchs, including those of Ethiopia. Processional crosses, of varying size and elaboration, and a very characteristic Ethiopian art form already seen developing on Aksumite coins, are also carried before and around the *tabot*.

Churches are of two types, *gedem* (monastery) or *debr* (mountain, referring to an ordinary church). Aksum, formerly a *gedem*, also became a *debr* as other activities in the town increased, although it remains exceptional, and women are not admitted into its precincts. In a *gedem*, the morning service is conducted by monks and hermits. In all cases, two priests and three deacons are required to conduct services.

Timqat is one of the high festivals in the ecclesiastical calendar of Ethiopia, and was one that roused European disapproval in the past. It celebrates the baptism of Christ, but was regarded by the Jesuits and others as a re-baptism, something that, like circumcision and the celebration of the Jewish sabbath, or baptism after forty or eighty days for male and female infants, or married priests, they could not countenance. The ceremonies are conducted with great pomp, the *tabot*s of the churches being carried out in procession to a place near water – in Aksum today, to the church of Aregawi at Enda Abba Mata'a beside the Mai Shum reservoir. Here a tent is set up in which, all night long, the members of the church choirs chant the hymns and other texts appropriate to the occasion. The next day, the whole concourse of people and ecclesiastics go to the water, which is blessed. Then the water is either scattered over the people, or they themselves go down into it. This latter proceeding particularly scandalised the foreigners. Alvares not only disapproved of baptising more than once – not understanding that the *Timqata Krestos*, Baptism of Christ, ceremony was merely a commemoration, not an annual re-baptism – but was also shocked by the nakedness and mixing of the sexes involved:

> In the tank stood the old priest, the Prester's [Lebna Dengel's] chaplain ... and he was naked as when his mother bore him (and quite dead with cold, because there was a very sharp frost), standing in the water up to his shoulders or nearly so, for so deep was the tank that those who were to be baptized entered by the steps, naked, with their backs to the Prester, and when they came out again they showed him their fronts, the women as well as the men.

Being placed at the other end of the tank, Alvares adds, he saw backs when the Prester saw fronts and vice versa.

Another unusual feature of the Ethiopian Church is the use of musical instruments, particularly the *sanasil*, or sistrum, a kind of rattle of ancient

Egyptian origin strung with wires supporting discs of metal, and an assortment of drums (*kaboro*) at certain services. At times, trumpets and stringed instruments are also employed. During the sometimes immensely long ceremonies, a special group of lay clerics, cantors, or 'canons' after Alvares, called *dabtara*, sway in time to the music, or even take certain synchronised steps in a sort of ritual dance, *aqwaqwam*; at the same time they wave long prayer-sticks or crutches (*maqwamia*) often distinguished by a metal head with a double volute, like an Ionic column – employed as a support under the shoulder during the long services – and incline their sistra to right and left, marking the rhythm. The prayer-stick only is used to mark the rhythm during Lent, when sistra and drums are not employed. One interpretation of the symbolism of these instruments is that the sistrum inclining from side to side evokes the beating of Christ, the sound of the *maqwamia* striking the ground recalls his flogging, and the drum the sound of the slapping of his face.

The music of the chants the *dabtara* intone is said to have been originally divulged to a sixth-century deacon, Yared. He had great difficulty as a young man in remembering his lessons, until one day, like Robert the Bruce with his spider, he learned persistence from watching a caterpillar repeatedly trying to climb a tree. One incident in his life may often be seen in traditional Ethiopian paintings. When he went to sing before the reigning king of Aksum, Gabra Masqal, son of Kaleb, both singer and listener were so entranced that neither noticed that the spear on which the king leaned had pierced the foot of Yared.

The *dabtara* – variously described as cantor, precentor or scribe – are those who, while not entering the priesthood, nevertheless make a special study of the complex liturgy of the Ethiopian Church, combining studies of *qene* poetry, the several modes of musical chant attributed to Yared, and an extensive ecclesiastical literature. They are the learned repositories of the sacred literature. At many services and ceremonies they can be seen, with prayer-stick and sistrum, wearing a white turban and wrapped in the typical Ethiopian toga-like garment called the *shamma* in Amharic, which often has a wide striped border of scarlet or some other colour. The choir members in general are often described as *dabtara*. Early European commentators on the Ethiopian Church found these 'dancing' *dabtara* scandalous, having little understanding of the old established rituals of the Church. A messenger from Tsar Ivan the Terrible, Visili Posniakov, who had come to Jerusalem in 1558 to see the patriarch, was most indignant:

> The heretics demeaned themselves as though they were demented in the church
> … the Ethiops walked around the Holy Sepulchre with four large drums. They
> struck them as they walked, jumping and dancing like clowns. Some of them

advanced jumping backwards. We were astounded that Divine Mercy endured all these goings on while a man could hardly stand the sight of such deviltry in such a place. (Jesman 1969)

The Ethiopians saw the matter quite differently. The *dabtaras*' ceremonial movements are often compared to the actions of King David, when he danced for joy before the Ark of the Covenant (2 Samuel 6), and the clapping, singing and music (or, after Lobo, the 'tumult that is more of an enormous cacophony than church music') is justified not only in the same verses but also by such texts as Psalm 47, mentioned by Lobo in this context: 'Clap your hands, all you people, cry out with joy to God.'

To terminate this account of the Ethiopian Church, I include here in translation a brief chapter by an early seventeenth-century writer that summarises the sort of opinions Europeans of the time had about the Ethiopians and their Church. I have selected the Sieur de Villamont's account of his *Voyages*, on which he departed in 1588, to illustrate one impression of Ethiopia that had seeped through from the works of the ecclesiastics, Alvares and others, whose missions to Ethiopia had begun to arouse interest during the century. In addition, Villamont was able to add some of his own observations of the Ethiopian community in Jerusalem. I choose this particular work largely because I have never seen his comments on Ethiopia recorded elsewhere, and because I happen to have a copy of his 1605 book in my library. Also, Villamont is not so disapproving as either the Jesuits, who regarded the Ethiopian Church from their own narrow 'professional' point of view, and found it horribly deficient, or later Protestant clergymen such as Gobat, who filled a book with accounts of the long lectures about their errors to which he treated his unfortunate hosts.

Jacques de Villamont did not go further than Egypt, but in Jerusalem he was able to meet Ethiopian monks. True to his time, he concentrated in comments about Ethiopia, typically labelled 'Opinions et erreurs des Abyssins et leurs coustumes', on religious matters, though by no means exclusively. But despite their 'errors' he seems in general to have rather approved:

There are other schismatics ... occupying the Holy Sepulchre, such as the Abyssinians, Maronites, Copts ... The Abyssinians are from Ethiopia, otherwise called Abbasia, or Kush by the ancients, as St Jerome says. It is a part of Africa, forming the largest part of it because of its wide extent. Their king is called by them Negus, and in Persian language is called Prester John or Catholic, which Prester John was formerly in Tartary until he was chased thence by Genghis Khan and other Tartar kings, as you can see in Nicolas the Venetian [Niccolo de' Conti]. He is nevertheless today one of the great kings of the East and among the most powerful in Africa, his kingdom extending from the borders of

Egypt until the Indies; and this king has more than forty kingdoms under him.
In the time of Clement VII, the King of Abyssinia who was called David [Lebna
Dengel] subjected himself to the Holy Apostolic See, and later he had a successor
called Claudius [Galawdewos] … who remained some time unsure which path
to take, but all the time fearing the Portuguese; but the present king of Abyssinia
(his name is unknown to me) in about the year 1582 [Sarsa Dengel], gave
obedience to the sovereign Pontiff of Rome Sixtus IV [this must refer to Sixtus
V, 1585–90] through his embassy, and with all humility asked to be informed
about the ceremonies, customs and ordinances of the Roman Church. These
Abyssinians (whom we also improperly call Indians) are mostly black, or of olive
colour. They are very determined to hear Mass and visit the holy places. They
pray to God with devotion and prolixity, as also their priests say and celebrate
the divine service with great reverence and with long and beautiful ceremonies.
It seems they love poverty, leading a somewhat austere and necessitous life,
although they do not lack means. They use vestments of different colours, and
both men and women bind their heads with cloth of different colours, and all
usually go barefoot. Moreover they observe Judaic or Saracen circumcision; and
like the Jacobites … they circumcise their children and imprint them like them,
by a brand or hot iron with the sign of the cross, sometimes on the forehead,
sometimes on the nose, sometimes on the cheeks, sometimes on other places on
the body, asserting the same reasons as the Jacobites.

(Villamont earlier noted about the Jacobites 'viuans pesle mesle', as he puts
it, 'among the Turks, Persians and Tartars … in Nubia … and a good part
of Ethiopia and the upper Indies', that they held that this branding 'delivers
their children from original sin, following John the Baptist's statement when
he baptised Christ "I baptise you in the Holy Spirit and Fire."' Tattooing –
not branding – is still very commonly seen in Ethiopia, the chief image being
a cross in blue on the chin or forehead.)
   Villamont continues:

And when one remonstrates with them that they are acting contrary to the
ordinances of the Roman Church, to which their King and they themselves
have submitted and sworn to give obedience, they ingenuously confess that
they are wrong, and desire that circumcision be discarded, and baptism be
received by all their country as it is by the Latins. Further, the Abyssinian
priests consecrate with leavened bread in the Greek way, and communicate
their *corbon* [qwerban, Eucharist] or sacrament under both kinds, and both small
and great receive it. Children take the sacrament of confirmation, not from the
bishops' hands, but from simple priests. It is a fine thing to see the Abyssinians
at Mass on the day and solemnity of some great feast, for you will see them all
together rejoicing and singing at full force, jumping in the air, turning around,

seven or eight here, nine or ten there, making so much noise that you could not hear God thunder. They chant sometimes, dance and rejoice in this way for a whole night, even the night of Easter or the Resurrection of our Lord, when they do not stop singing until it is day. There are among them some so active at this singing and nocturnal dance that the next morning they are all exhausted and weary and some fall ill. The Abyssinians understand Arabic, Saracen and Turkish well, but for the divine service liturgy and prayers they use the Abyssinian language, or Ethiopian, which is close to Hebrew and Arabic. They write like us, from left to right, not like the Hebrews, Arabs, Syrians and Chaldeans, from right to left. The Abyssinians received the Catholic faith by means of the eunuch of Queen Candace, baptised by saint Philip, and the town of Chaxumo [Aksum] was the first which received baptism and where Queen Candace was baptised. This is a tradition which they have among their writings, as Francesco Alvarez reports. Their chief and first Bishop, whom they obey like the Pope, is called *Abun*, as if in our language, our father. Further, the Prester John acts in a truly Christian way, as only exceptionally does he make war on the Christian kings his neighbours, but usually one finds him campaigning against neighbouring Muslim kings, against whom he fights hard, and because of his subjects' continual martial exercise they are reputed the most warlike of Africa.

Some Notes on Ethiopian Religious Painting

Brightly coloured narrative paintings of biblical and hagiographical stories on the walls is one of the characteristic features of Ethiopian churches. It helped to illustrate the texts read from the Bible, in a fashion the illiterate could readily understand. Church wall-painting has a long history in the country. Two of the prophet Muhammad's wives, Umm Habiba and Umm Salama, both of whom were in exile in Ethiopia in the 620s with their former husbands, are quoted as having mentioned the paintings in the church of Mary, presumably at Aksum, then the capital; Muhammad, however, disapproved of such things. He merely commented: 'These are the people who, when a saint among them dieth, build over his tomb a place of worship, and adorn it with their pictures; in the eyes of the Lord, the worst part of all creation.' Nevertheless, the Ethiopians continued to use paintings, as in medieval European churches, both in books and on walls, 'to adorn and to instruct' as Buxton (1970) neatly phrases it. The quality, naturally, varies from place to place. Even if there is a large cultural gap between the different styles of painting to which foreign visitors are accustomed, and the formal style, broadly in the Byzantine tradition, of Ethiopian paintings, the visitor can expect much more than what the ever-critical James Bruce found: 'a daubing much inferior to the worst of our sign painters'.

From Aksumite times onwards, doubtless, the traditions of Ethiopian painting developed, seemingly with some Coptic, Armenian and Syrian influences on the style and the choice of compositions. This has often caused it to be defined as 'Byzantine', and indeed Ethiopian painting does belong broadly within the trend of church art in the oriental Christian world. Very little has survived that might be early. We may hope that perhaps one day paintings like those found in Nubia at Faras and other places might turn up in archaeological excavations, but the highland Ethiopian climate, with its two rainy seasons – lesser rains may fall between March and May, heavier rains from late June to early September – is not so suitable for preservation of such materials as plaster and wood as the Nubian desert climate.

A few paintings on parchment in manuscript gospel books seem to be the earliest actual survivors of the Ethiopian painting tradition, and though on a different medium, the style and choice of subjects is essentially similar to wall-paintings. Some of these date from the thirteenth to the fifteenth centuries. The earliest so far known seem to be the Abba Garima Gospels, from the monastery of that name near Adwa, which have been variously dated to the eleventh, or possibly even to the ninth, century. Wall-paintings some centuries old survive in some of the rock-hewn churches, those in Beta Maryam at Lalibela being – perhaps – attributable to the thirteenth century, with whole sets surviving in other places such as Yadibba Maryam in Daunt, Abba Yemata near Guh, and the nearby Abba Daniel at Qorqor (see Gerster 1970: 79–84, pls. 34–43 for a commentary and some excellent pictures). Often rich geometrical designs occur, as well as figurative painting.

An extraordinary feature of the Portuguese period in Ethiopia is that the iconography of a number of sacred scenes common in the West was adopted by the Ethiopian painters even despite the expulsion of the Catholics, and the hatred evinced for them. When the Ethiopian monk Tasfa Seyon, for example, went to Rome in the 1530s and supervised the printing of religious books in Ge'ez, they were illustrated in European style, and some of these might have found their way to Ethiopia and influenced local art forms. Nathaniel Pearce related how some of the illustrated books of this period were found in a monastery long after, and destroyed, although some of the monks were apparently sad to see such lovely pictures discarded. The basic composition of some of the European pictures, Ethiopianised, became part of the stock seventeenth-century and later painting themes in the country. A number of these themes have been studied, and the originals identified, among them depictions of the Virgin and Child, Christ with the crown of thorns, and several gospel illustrations deriving ultimately from Dürer's engravings via an Arabic gospel book published in Rome in 1590.

For the Gondar period, two styles can be distinguished. The first Gondarine style can be described (Buxton 1970) as 'mainly an art of outline drawing'. When carefully done this simplicity bestows on it an air of elegance and refinement. Early Gondarine art retains a rather 'medieval' air, with little modelling of the human form, and often very little in the way of background. Where architectural scenes were required, the inspiration is very obviously the castles of Fasiladas and his successors at Gondar.

The second Gondarine period, especially associated with the reign of Iyasu II and the Empress Mentewab, includes richly filled backgrounds, often in several colours, and some attempts at perspective and modelling. Clothing is often very richly decorated, and there is a fondness for realistic local detail, which bestows on the paintings a great charm. Basketwork or other small objects of everyday use are of Ethiopian style, biblical armies carry muskets, and buildings such as the palace of King Herod are unmistakably Gondarine in their architecture. In both of these styles a Western influence can be detected, emerging ultimately from the Portuguese presence, which brought, as noted above, some new stylistic elements into play without destroying the older oriental traditions.

One notable characteristic of Ethiopian painting is the depiction of occasional profile heads. These usually indicate someone not favourably re-garded in scriptural report, such as Herod or Herodias; Jews and Muslims automatically qualify for this iconographical segregation, just as they qualified for physical segregation in Gondar under Emperor Yohannes I and others.

Two interesting medical observations relevant to the local style of the paintings were remarked on during a tour of Ethiopia that I undertook with William Taor. He noted that goitre was very prevalent in Ethiopia owing to the lack of iodine in the water, and that this was often depicted in the paintings in the form of several curved lines on the neck, and also that the protuberant eyes of many of the figures in paintings was to be observed in modern Ethiopians suffering from exophthalmos.

Paintings might be found almost anywhere in the churches, some cave churches like Jammadu Maryam near Lalibela even being painted on the outside, and others, such as Yimrehana Krestos near Lalibela, exhibiting richly painted ceilings. Beta Maryam at Lalibela was also richly decorated using both carving and painting. The commonest situation for later painting is on the inside walls of rectangular churches such as Debra Berhan Sellassie in Gondar, or on the outer walls of the square sanctuary or *maqdas*, and on the round drum supporting the roof above the *maqdas*, in the centre of round churches such as Debra Sina at Gorgora and many others. There is some painting direct on stone or plaster, but many churches are decorated by painted panels of cloth, which are glued to the walls and can be removed and replaced if necessary. Unfortunately, neglect, and the relatively swift decay of

roofs made of reeds and straw, has often resulted in the fairly speedy oblitera-
tion of many such paintings.

Wall-paintings are theoretically placed according to a set of rules governing
their relative positions in a larger scheme, though this is sometimes altered or
even ignored. For example, the entrance to the maqdas or Holy of Holies
usually has on the outside one or two guardian archangels, generally wielding
a sword, painted on the wooden doors. Commonly, to the right, on the wall
there is a Virgin and Child, protected by the archangels Michael and Gabriel
with drawn swords. To the left is usually depicted St George on a white horse
killing the dragon. Other themes were depicted where suitable. One of C. H.
Walker's informants commented: 'Women are evil, and therefore inside the
women's entrance to the church [the south door – to the right when facing
the sanctuary] may be seen a picture of the Satans with the Devil, their
Emperor. A man lighting suddenly upon these will go forth in gloom and
sadness as he ponders over the work of the devil.' (For details of complete sets
of paintings, see descriptions of Debra Berhan Sellassie and Abba Antonios
churches, Gondar (Chapter 5) and Debra Sina, Gorgora (Chapter 6.))

Some Ethiopian Saints and other Religious Imagery

Many wall-paintings, usefully enough, are labelled, so that anyone literate
could quickly discover the meaning, if it were not immediately obvious from
the iconography. For foreigners, the most difficult pictures to identify are
those of native Ethiopian saints, whose symbolism is scarcely known outside
the country.

Among the most frequently represented is St Tekla Haymanot, who morti-
fied himself by standing on one leg in a cell the walls of which bristled with
sharp points to prevent him from sleeping. A bird fed him with one seed per
annum. Eventually, the other leg atrophied and fell off, so that God rewarded
him with triple sets of wings.

Abba Gabra Manfas Qiddus is another frequently depicted local saint, one
of the most venerated in Ethiopia. He was apparently an Egyptian by origin,
a hermit who was miraculously transported to Ethiopia, where he became the
founder of a monastery at Zuqwala, a high mountain (2,870 m.) with a crater
lake on top, near Addis Ababa on the Debra Zeit road. He dwelt there for
forty years. He wandered in the deserts, and preached peace to the beasts,
and so is generally shown covered in hair (or dressed in animal skins) with
wild animals lying or standing around him. He once succoured a bird by
allowing it to drink the water from his eye, and this incident too is frequently
shown in paintings. Abuna Samuel, a monk who lived near the Takaze river,
is also a popular figure. He was assisted by a lion, and is sometimes shown

in paintings riding it. Finally, as noted above, Yared, the supposed founder of the Ethiopian ecclesiastical chant, can often be seen in paintings depicted as a *dabtara* equipped with his crutch and sistrum, standing chanting before King Gabra Masqal, son of King Kaleb. The king leans forward, fascinated, as the chant develops, and the royal spear accidentally pierces the foot of the singer unobserved by either king or saint.

A theme often occupying an important place in manuscripts or wall-paintings – over the sanctuary door – is the Trinity represented as three equal beings, generally three old men. This style of representation for the Trinity was forbidden in Europe after the prohibition of Benedict XIV in a *Constitution* of October 1, 1745 (Chojnacki 1983: 101–2), but is still current in Ethiopia. It seems, however, that it was not known in Ethiopian art until after the arrival in the country around 1480 of an Italian artist, Nicolo Brancaleone of Venice. He has left a few pictures which can still be identified as his work. The Trinity in this form is described very clearly in 1521, in the *Carta das Novas*, the record of the arrival of the Portuguese embassy, at the monastery of Debra Bizen in Eritrea:

> a square wooden picture, which had three figures all of one measure of equality and age, as they are ab eterno. And in each of the corners, to wit, in the bottom right-hand one, was a lion, and above, an eagle, and in the other, an ox, and above, the figure of a man, whence he knew it was the Trinity, and the four Evangelists who affirmed it; for Ezekiel saw them in those shapes, as he says in the first chapter, and likewise Saint John in the fourth chapter of the Apocalypse.

Another very frequent symbolical theme is this use of the four living creatures of John's vision in Revelation, which he beheld surrounding the throne of God. They had the heads of a man, an eagle, a lion and a bull, and were winged. Similarly, Ezekiel saw in a vision four winged creatures each with the face of a man, a lion, a bull and an eagle, surrounded by four wheels. The four living creatures generally accompany God the Father, the Ancient of Days, or the Trinity as described above, or sometimes a figure of Christ.

A crucified Christ on a wooden *manbara tabot*, or altar table (Grierson 1993: 138) from Lasta is surrounded by four circles inscribed with the words *arbaat ensesa*, 'the four animals'. The Ethiopian *Senkessar*, or Synaxarium, which provides readings about saints or holy persons for every day of the year, interprets the four beasts as 'the Wheels of God that bear His Divine Throne'. These same four beasts also occur as symbols for the four Evangelists: the lion of St Mark, the eagle of St John, the angel of St Matthew and the ox of St Luke.

3

FOREIGN TRAVELLERS IN ETHIOPIA

In this book, I have made frequent use of citations from visitors ancient and modern who have described life in Ethiopia over the centuries. These foreigners, who travelled in the country for various reasons and returned home to publish accounts of what they saw, have bequeathed to us an enormous amount of information about Ethiopia. Many of them described not only the current political, economic, religious and social circumstances of their time, but also added vital details about the historical sites. As always with such documents, one must remember that the strangers may have observed badly, remembered details incorrectly long after the event, had some grudge to express, or merely written lightly and carelessly. But in sum, these travellers' records form a key archive for many aspects of Ethiopian history.

Brief accounts of Aksum and the Aksumite sphere of interest occur in the so-called *Periplus of the Erythraean Sea*, a sort of guidebook in Greek to the commercial potential of the whole region bordering the Red Sea and Indian Ocean in the first century AD. In the *Naturalis Historia* of Gaius Plinius Secundus (Pliny) of about the same date, the Aksumite port of Adulis and its exports is mentioned, while in Claudius Ptolemaeus' *Geographia*, written in the mid-second century, it is noted that the royal palace was at Aksum. Aksumite expansion is implicit in the country's inclusion in the *Kephalaia* of Mani in the later third century as constituting one of the four kingdoms of the world.

Kosmas Indikopleustes ('voyager to India') is the name given to a sixth-century merchant, later a monk, possibly an Alexandrian, who travelled in Ethiopia during the reign of Kaleb, *negus* of Aksum. He was interested in proving that the world was flat, modelled after the tabernacle of Moses, but outside that absorbing theme he also included a number of brief statements about Kaleb's capital city and kingdom. His great achievement for posterity was the copying, at the request of the governor of Adulis, Asbas, the famous inscription called the *Monumentum Adulitanum* – an account of a campaign by an unnamed Aksumite king, which constitutes little less than a gazetteer of the Aksumite region. Only later manuscripts of Kosmas' work survive. Some even include illustrations: local animals, Aksumites on a journey, and the *Monumentum Adulitanum*, an inscribed stone throne.

A little later in the sixth century a Byzantine ambassador, Nonnosus, visited Kaleb's Aksum. He was accustomed to the great cities of the Eastern Roman empire, Constantinople, Alexandria and Antioch, but still described Aksum as 'a considerable city, as if it were the metropolis of all Ethiopia'.

In the next century, exiled Muslims fled to Ethiopia and put themselves under the protection of the Ethiopian king, between 615 and 628. Several tales about events in Ethiopia have survived in the Arabic histories of the life of the prophet Muhammad. In one case, two of the women who were to marry Muhammad were later reported by the writer Tabari, collecting the traditions or *hadith* of Islam, to have mentioned the cathedral of Aksum and its paintings.

This sparse information – except for a few Arab geographers' accounts and some lines in the *History of the Patriarchs of the Alexandrian Church* – is all we have until the early thirteenth century. At that period, some notes concerning Ethiopia, particularly Adefa (Roha, later Lalibela), the Zagwé capital, appear in the *History of the Patriarchs*, and in a book by Abu Salih about Egyptian churches and monasteries. A little later some medieval documents, pilgrim's reports, and the itineraries collected by Alessandro Zorzi between 1470 and 1524 supply some more information about Aksum and other places.

Then comes the astonishingly rich variety of reports from the Portuguese visitors, missionaries and soldiers, who entered Ethiopia from about 1480 onwards. They continued to come at intervals until their eventual expulsion from the court and final departure in 1632–33. Some of these visitors wrote superb accounts of Ethiopia as they saw it, and left very valuable information about the historical sites. First, and foremost in interest, was Francisco Alvares (Alvarez), chaplain to the mission led by Dom Rodrigo de Lima in 1520. His descriptions of Yeha, Aksum, Yimrehana Krestos and Lalibela were not to be equalled for a long time, and in addition preceded the destruction wrought in the country by *Amir* Ahmad Grañ in the 1530s. Alvares' book, published in 1540, was the main source for information about Lalibela until the later nineteenth century; in the Italian version by Ramusio even printed plans of the churches were included. (In my book *Aksum. An African Civilisation of*

Late Antiquity: 22, following Doresse, the title page of Alvares' 1540 book was described as showing Prester John 'with all the trappings of a contemporary European monarch'. I subsequently noticed the *quinas* on the standard behind the main figure, who must therefore be a Portuguese – presumably, as he holds a sceptre, the king of Portugal himself. The building behind has a coat of arms with a ship over the door. It seems to represent a scene in Portugal rather than in Ethiopia.)

Other visitors followed, such as Miguel de Castanhoso, a soldier who accompanied a Portuguese force to help fight *Amir* Ahmad in 1541–43. He included a few notes about Debra Damo and Lalibela. At the same time we have the strange figure of João Bermudes, the ex-surgeon who later claimed to have been made patriarch of Ethiopia by the *abun* himself – who certainly had no authority to do this – on his deathbed, and to have had this appointment confirmed by the Pope in Rome with the additional title of patriarch of Alexandria. He accompanied the Portuguese expedition, and supplied in his published report a very brief note about Lalibela. In the next century came Péro Pais, who arrived in 1603 and died in Ethiopia in 1622, Manoel de Almeida and Emmanuel Barradas, both of whom were in the country between 1624 and 1633, and the Patriarch Afonso Mendez, who came with the priest Jerónimo Lobo in 1625 and remained on Ethiopian soil until 1635. Balthasar Tellez (Telles), a friend and colleague of Lobo, published in 1660 a summary of the travels of the Jesuits in Ethiopia, quoting voluminously from their – then unpublished – works. All of these ecclesiastics left some notes about Aksum.

In Europe, from the 1640s, Job (Hiob) Ludolf, a German scholar, began to study Ethiopian language and history. With the help of a learned Ethiopian who had been at Emperor Fasiladas' court, called Gorgoreyos (Gregory), then living at Rome, Ludolf was able to produce various grammars and histories. Included were some few comments derived from published works or from Gorgoreyos about the historical sites. Ludolf himself never travelled to Ethiopia, and Gorgoreyos was drowned on his return journey.

Foreign visitors to Ethiopia, or at least those who recorded anything, were extremely rare after the expulsion of the Jesuits in 1632. An exception was the Yemeni ambassador Hasan b. Ahmad al-Haymi, sent by his master *Imam* al-Muayyad billah in 1648. He was the first we know of to describe Gondar, then only recently founded by Emperor Fasiladas. Several other sources mention Gondar as the Ethiopian capital, including French travellers to India such as Thévenot and Bernier. Murad, the merchant and factor who traded and acted as envoy for several emperors, confirmed this when in the 1690s he answered in Batavia some questions about Ethiopia drawn up by Ludolf. One Frenchman, the chemist or physician Charles Jacques Poncet, actually managed to penetrate into Ethiopia. He journeyed from Cairo to Gondar in 1699, describing the capital as he saw it in the time of Emperor Iyasu I. In 1751 the Bohemian priest Remedius Prutky was in Ethiopia with his colleague Martin Lang.

During 1764–66 Yohannes T'ovmacean, an Armenian, came to Gondar, where he became treasurer to *Itege* (queen consort, empress) Mentewab, an office that sounds more impressive than it was in reality. T'ovmacean had mixed feelings about his experiences, as his text quickly indicates (Nersessian and Pankhurst 1982). At Digsa, he records, when he first arrived there from Massawa, he 'gave thanks to God for having saved him from the Infidel Mahometans. He did the same on his return from Abyssinia, when this same T'ovmacean sacrificed two sheep at Digsa, this time for having been saved from the Abyssinians.' T'ovmacean's story is honest and amusing. He was a little at sea at times, but recounts his reactions very directly. He was, for example, horrified when in return for his gifts to *Itege* Mentewab and King Iyoas, only a few animals and chickens were delivered – accompanied by a large crowd, with 'singing and drumming' – at his house in the palace compound (which contained five rooms bare of all but 'a small carpet'). He briefly described 'Saba' (Aksum), and some of its monuments, and the mysterious 'tablet of Moses' kept there, which he actually saw. Adwa, he noted, was known as the 'city of Be'ela Mika'el. It is named after Mika'el (Sehul), a stern and merciless man for all the people of the town who commit crimes have the responsible part of their body severed.'

T'ovmacean was soon to be followed by one of the great travellers to Ethiopia, the Scotsman James Bruce. Bruce's contribution to Ethiopian studies was enormous, not only as an eye-witness to the bloody 'reign' of *Ras* Mikael Sehul and as an intimate – a respected servant is the impression he himself gives – of the imperial family of the time, but as a collector of manuscripts and a compiler of history. Bruce's character had its strange points, and he had some bees in his bonnet about Ethiopian history and geography, but on the whole his contribution was tremendous, ranking next after the Jesuits and Ludolf/Gorgoreyos among the monuments of Ethiopian historiography. Bruce contributed too to the study of Ethiopia's important historical sites. He visited and described Aksum, albeit idiosyncratically, and dwelt for some time at Gondar. Unfortunately, he missed both Yeha and Lalibela. His famous book *Travels to Discover the Source of the Nile* was not published until 1790.

Next came Henry Salt, first as a member of Lord Valentia's 1805 mission to explore the Red Sea for commercial ends, then again in 1809–10 as an envoy of the British government. Theoretically, he was accredited to the by-then-defunct 'imperial court' at Gondar, which he did not reach. Not only did Salt himself write extensively on Aksum (in Lord Valentia's *Voyages and*

Travels of 1809, III, and in his own *Voyage to Abyssinia*, published in 1814), but in his party he brought two other Englishmen who would also leave some notes about Aksum and Gondar, Nathaniel Pearce and William Coffin. Pearce stayed behind in 1805, remaining in Ethiopia as a retainer of *Ras* Wolde Sellassie of Tigray until the *ras*'s death, later departing the country in 1818. Coffin came with Salt on his second visit in 1810, staying on with Pearce, in whose book his account of a journey to Gondar was included.

There were, of course, numerous mid-nineteenth-century foreign visitors to Ethiopia who left nothing of note for our purposes here, although they wrote on many other aspects of the country. A few, like the British consul Walter Plowden, gave only the briefest attention to the ancient ruins of Aksum, chiefly as a contrast to the miserable state of affairs in Ethiopia in his own time. Plowden was there in 1848, but his book was not published until twenty years later, posthumously. Some missions simply went to Shewa, then virtually a separate kingdom from the dominions of the 'King of Kings' and his *ras* at Gondar, and in a more hopeful condition for European trade ventures.

Other visitors wrote largely on different themes, flora and fauna, geography, or political or religious conditions, but did occasionally contribute a few useful comments about the ancient sites of Ethiopia, or the country's decaying capital, Gondar. Samuel Gobat, for example, later Anglican bishop of Jerusalem (where, despite his opinion of their beliefs, he was generously to support the Abyssinian monks in their problems over their property in the Holy Land) travelled to Gondar in 1830. He was not, as Ullendorff thought, 'the first European to do so since the days of Bruce', but the next after Coffin. He left Ethiopia in 1832 and published an account of his journey in 1834. The naturalist Eduard Rüppell, in Ethiopia between 1832 and 1834, seems to have been the first to acquire Aksumite coins, and to publish and comment on them (1838–40), as well as on other aspects of the ancient city. He also visited Gondar. Two Frenchmen, Ed. Combes and M. Tamisier, travelled via Massawa, Adwa, Debra Damo (where Coffin was then in refuge), and Aksum, where they observed very little, and then south to Debra Tabor and Angolala, the capital of Shewa, in 1835. They visited Ankober and Tegulat, then continued on to Gojjam and via Emfraz to Gondar. Here too they recorded little, being more concerned with the Saint-Simonian principles of improvement for the deprived classes, and the search for the 'female Messiah'. They returned via Tigray in 1836. The German traveller A. von Katte also passed through Aksum in this year. These visitors published their accounts in 1838. A Piedmontese Lazarist father, Giuseppe Sapeto, was also in Ethiopia in 1838, journeying from Egypt in the company of two Basque–Irish travellers, Antoine and Arnauld d'Abbadie, who remained in Ethiopia until 1843. Sapeto's notes on Aksum were published by Monneret de Villard in 1938 from a manuscript in private hands.

Arnauld d'Abbadie, like Pearce before him, became a retainer of an Ethiopian lord. He travelled considerably in Ethiopia, as well as living for some time at Gondar. It is fascinating to observe through their writings how these Europeans, living a way of life no longer possible in their own countries, became fired with admiration and loyalty for their Ethiopian lords. A French expedition under Théophile Lefebvre in 1839–43 studied many aspects of Ethiopian life and culture. The expedition was stationed both in Aksum and in Gondar, publishing the results of its survey in 1845–51 – a major study, and beautifully illustrated by the artist Vignaud. Two more Frenchmen, Pierre Victor Adolphe Ferret and Joseph Germain Galinier, were in Aksum in 1840–1. They published an account of the standing stele at Aksum in 1844 and of their travels, which included Gondar, in 1847.

In a different part of the country, indeed in a part completely independent of Ethiopia at the time, Richard Burton in 1855 was exploring the area between Zayla and Berbera, and Harar, which city he was the first European to enter (in disguise as an Arab merchant). He spent ten days there, the main theme of his book *First Footsteps in East Africa*, published in 1856.

Guillaume Lejean, French consul at Gondar in Emperor Tewodros' time, journeyed in Ethiopia in 1862–64, and published in 1872 some notes about Aksumite inscriptions he had seen ten years earlier. He offered only a brief account of Aksum, 'too often described by travellers that I need to weary my readers with sage dissertations on its church or above all its obelisks'. He also bought a few Aksumite coins. Another German naturalist, Theodor von Heuglin, and his companion Dr W. Steudner were in Aksum in 1861 and by the next year both had published descriptions of what they saw, von Heuglin producing a fuller version in 1868. In 1868 the German explorer Gerhard Rohlfs too was at Aksum. Rohlfs returned in 1881 as an envoy of his country to Emperor Yohannes IV, visiting Gondar and Lalibela during his stay. He published accounts of his visits in 1870 and 1883.

An unusual visitor was Father Timothy (Dimothéos Sapritchian), a priest sent by the patriarch of Jerusalem in the company of the Armenian bishop Isaac de Kharper. The bishop's mission was to see the Emperor Tewodros and try to liberate the British prisoners held at his fortress at Maqdala. In 1869 Dimothéos claimed to have seen the 'Ark' or tablet of the law in Aksum cathedral. He describes it in his book published in 1871. Achille Raffray, an entomologist, and later French vice-consul, followed in 1874, describing Aksum and Lalibela in an 1876 publication, in which his sketches were produced as engravings by L. Breton. The Lalibela churches were beautifully illustrated too by Gabriel Simon, a cavalry officer, in his 1885 book.

From this time there were many Europeans in Ethiopia, some of whom left descriptions of the ancient sites and Gondar, often with engravings (for example, Cardinal Guglielmo Massaia (Massaja), Elisée Reclus, in his general history of Africa, and Theophilus Waldmeier, one of Emperor Tewodros' foreign craftsmen – see Pankhurst and Ingrams, *Ethiopia Engraved*, for some of the illustrations mentioned above). J. Theodore Bent and his wife travelled to Ethiopia in 1893, publishing an agreeably written account of their travels with descriptions of the antiquities of Yeha and Aksum in 1896. Finally, the most important record of all for Yeha and Aksum was the 1906 visit of Enno Littmann, Daniel Krencker and others as part of the Deutsche Aksum-Expedition (DAE). Their remarkable four-volume 1913 publication is still a treasure house of information on many aspects of life in Tigray even today.

THE HISTORICAL SITES
OF ETHIOPIA

4

GONDAR

General Survey and History: Foreign Visitors

To read the royal chronicles of the emperors of Ethiopia during the Gondarine period is to be transported into another world and time. Kings descended from Solomon and the Queen of Sheba ride forth in procession from their city of Gondar under the shadow of an icon of Christ wearing the crown of thorns. Seated on a portable throne of purple and silver, the emperor surveys the heaps of sliced-off genitalia of his enemies as the soldiers bring them in for the counting. The stuffed skin of a rebel, flayed alive, is hung on a tree in front of the palace, the same tree that formerly bore the hanged corpse of a murderous queen. The dogs and hyenas squabble at night over the bloody fragments of traitors in the Addebabai, the great marketplace of the imperial capital.

There are other scenes, too, noble or terrible. An emperor visits his princely relatives, condemned to spend their entire lives on an inaccessible mountain to keep his own throne intact – he offers them a banquet. Synod after synod is held in the palace to settle the minutiae of Christ's nature, and one of the disputing parties is massacred wholesale by the soldiers of the emperor. The veil covering the sacred features of the King of Kings is whisked aside by a thornbush, and the governor of the district and his son must die at the end of a rope, hanged on that same tree for their negligence. High on his tower in Gondar, the emperor witnesses a theft in the marketplace below. The criminal is dragged up the tower and the emperor orders him to be thrown down from it. Gondar is bathed in blood, the scene of endless maiming, blinding, beheading and hanging. Yet this period when Gondar became the capital of Ethiopia is not in the remote medieval past. It began just after 1632 and continued, more or less, to 1855 when Emperor Tewodros II (Theodore) succeeded in making himself King of Kings of Ethiopia.

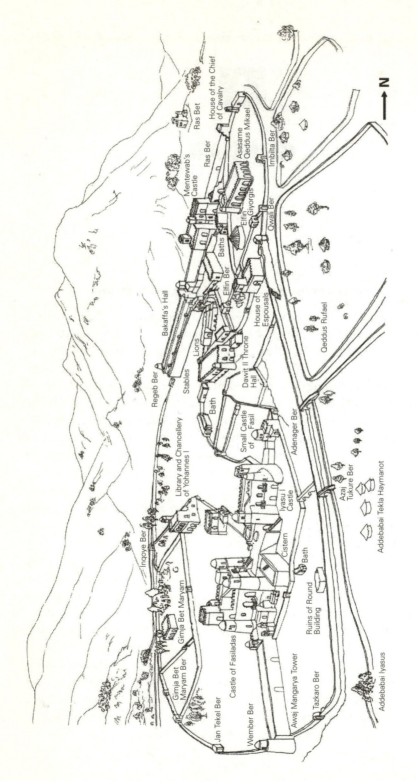

Jan Tekel Ber

Inqoye Ber

Gimja Bet
Maryam Ber

Gimja Bet Maryam

Wember Ber

Castle of Fasiladas

Addebabai Iyasus

Awaj Mangarya Tower

Tazkaro Ber

Ruins of Round
Building

Bath

Cistern

Iyasu I
Castle

Library and Chancellery
of Yohannes I

Bath

Stables

Small Castle
of Fasil

Dawit II Throne
Hall

Adenager Ber

Azaj
Tukure Ber

Addebabai Tekla Haymanot

Lions

Regeb Ber

Bakaffa's Hall

Baths

Elfin Ber

House of
Espousals

Qeddus Rufael

Mentewab's
Castle

Ras Bet

Ras Ber

Asasame
Qeddus Mikael

Elfin
Giyorgis

Qwali Ber

Imbilta Ber

House of the Chief
of Cavalry

N

2. The buildings, walls and gates of the imperial compound, Gondar, adapted from a sketch by E. Zacchia published by A. Monti della Corte, *Castelli di Gondar*, 1938. A major structure missing from this plan lay behind the Castle of Fasiladas. Only fragments of it now remain. The present church of Gimja Bet Maryam is round.

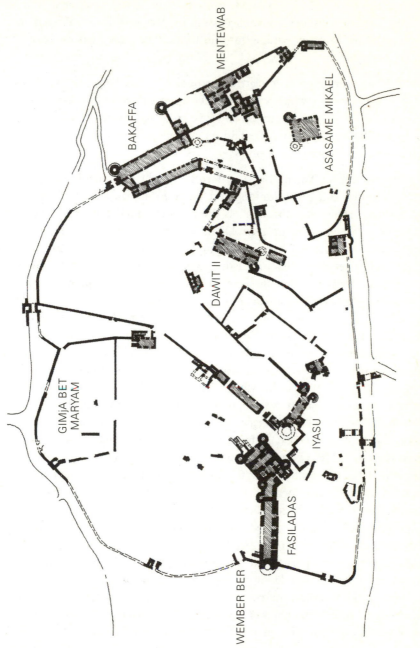

3. Plan of the buildings in the imperial compound, Gondar. From the *Guida*, 1938: 354.

BAKAFFA

MENTEWAB

ASASAME MIKAEL

DAWIT II

GIMjA BET
MARYAM

IYASU

WEMBER BER

FASILADAS

Gondar emerged in troubled times. In 1632, Prince Fasiladas (often called Fasil), *dejazmach* of Semien, visited his father, the newly converted Roman Catholic Emperor Susneyos, just as he was preparing to leave his residence at Danqaz. 'Lord king,' he said, according to the abbreviated chronicle of the Ethiopian emperors:

> behold how everything is desolate and troubled by this belief of the Franks, that we know not, of which we have never heard tell, and which is not in the books of our fathers. We fear you and love your face; we are united with you voice and heart. Pray God as the faith of Alexandria prescribes, that he might give you victory over your enemies.

The emperor left for Wayna Dega, where he fought the rebellious *seyum* of Wag, killing him and other leaders, and many Ethiopian soldiers: 'the king exterminated his numerous troops', as the royal chronicle tells us. In 1542 at Wayna Dega, the Muslim invader Ahmad Grañ had been wounded, to die shortly afterwards, and Christian Ethiopia had been saved from foreign domination. Ninety years later an Ethiopian monarch again had the victory, but this time it was his own subjects who had perished. Emperor Susneyos grieved, and proclaimed: 'Let this [Alexandrian] faith be restored and let my son Fasil reign. As for me I am weak, I have committed errors, I am ill.'

Emperor Fasiladas, who reigned under the title Sultan Sagad or Alam Sagad, succeeded to the throne of a country in turmoil, induced by popular protest against Susneyos' acceptance of the Roman Catholic faith. The Portuguese Catholic patriarch, Afonso Mendez, had attempted with unwise precipitation to overhaul religious practices ingrained by centuries of use, and hallowed by their long preservation against Islamic incursions. The new emperor took prompt steps. Almost immediately an orthodox metropolitan bishop arrived, and 'the Frank Afonsu returned to his own country'. In reality, Patriarch Mendez retreated only to Portugal's viceroyalty of India in Goa, where he devoted his efforts to trying to stir up trouble for the Ethiopian monarch in the form of Catholicism accompanied by the sword.

According to the records, Fasiladas requested the Funj king of Sinnar in the Sudan, the ruler of Mocha (Mukha) across the Red Sea in Yemen, the *pasha* of the Sudanese port of Suakin (Sawakin) and the Egyptian authorities in Cairo not to allow 'Franks' or Europeans to pass their territories towards Ethiopia. Catholics inside the country were persecuted. Missionaries caught attempting to enter Ethiopia were put to death. Patriarch Mendez and the Roman Church did not relax their efforts. One can read in *Etiopia Francescana* the numerous letters and minutes filed over many years proposing military expeditions to Massawa, or dealing with the sending of new missionaries or money to those still there, even with the election of a bishop, and his successors when he died. More missionaries were sent, to die of fevers or at the hands of the Muslims, or to languish in misery on that inhospitable coast. There is a great deal of material about the attitude of various *pasha*s of Sawakin. Rather naively – in fact, fatally – letters were even written to Fasiladas himself asking permission to enter his country.

It is fascinating to see how often these records note with honesty the hatred there was for the Catholics in Ethiopia – a hatred returned in lively fashion by the Catholic priests as far as Fasiladas was concerned. The emperor who had 'saved' Ethiopia from Catholicism was savagely castigated by Father Torquato Parisiani in a 'brief relation of the miserable state in which Ethiopia is at present' in 1649. This report is devoted to a description of the deaths of three Franciscan priests at Sawakin the year before. It sums up Fasiladas' character in the worst possible way: 'Sultan Segued Faççilades, a man of the most brutish habits, of coarse intellect, a changeable spirit, an inconstant will, a degenerate and cowardly heart, friend of wickedness, enemy of the truth, filled with hatred of all virtue and with a rooted and perverse hatred of the Holy Catholic faith.' Torquato also relayed a tale about the king's sending to Yemen for a Muslim doctor to instruct him in Islam, something surely utterly improbable for any Ethiopian emperor at that time, and for Fasiladas in particular. It was, however, the very same error that led to the arrival of al-Haymi, a Yemeni *qadi* who came as ambassador from the *imam* of Yemen. If anything, his presence at Gondar seemed to add confirmation to the rumours.

From Sawakin, on 1 May 1647, one of the missionaries, shortly to be executed, had written: 'The king has nearly been destroyed by the Galla people.' This was wishful thinking, even if the depredations of the Oromo had been terrible. Fasiladas and orthodox Christian Ethiopia survived, and, it seems, even prospered in a small way. Some small fragments of what had been lost under Grañ seem to have begun to filter back. The first castle at Gondar is a symbol in stone of this recovery. In the end, the city of Gondar that this emperor founded was to represent a complete change from the past.

Although the chronicle of Galawdewos had earlier proclaimed a permanent royal residence in Waj, it was to have no future:

> Galawdewos, full of goodness and commiseration ... to gather together in one place all those who were scattered and to reunite in one place all those who had been deprived of their property ... built a town in one of the districts of Waj, and abandoned the custom of the Kings of Ethiopia who travelled from place to place until their last sleep, until the day of their last rest. (Pankhurst 1967: 74)

But with the establishment of Gondar, the peripatetic court of the emperors really did begin, very gradually, to fix itself in one spot. In the end, it was to stay there until it became moribund. Castles and other buildings were constructed, and eventually there emerged a 'capital' rather than just another among many royal occasional residences.

The place was destined to be, for Emperor Lebna Dengel years before had been visited in a vision by the Virgin and the Archangel Raguel. They announced that a capital blessed by heaven would be built in a place whose name began with the letter G, or the syllable Go (see Pankhurst 1982: 117ff for variations and expansions of the legend: legends, stories of the saints, and the like are living things in Ethiopia, always changing, updating, or shifting in emphasis as things alter on the political scene). Emperor Fasiladas appears to have been the real founder of Gondar, although some sort of village evidently existed there before – a church dedicated to St Tekla Haymanot had been built at the spot by Fasiladas' father Susneyos. James Bruce noted that 'this town was only an obscure village till the time of Susneus'. When in 1635 or so Fasiladas selected for the site of his new castle the lovely valley of Gondar, guarded by mountains on three sides but open to the south towards Lake Tana not too far distant, he probably did not imagine the place's future as a major Ethiopian city.

There was already a history of lakeside residences and others a little to the north of Lake Tana. Emperor Za Dengel (1603–04) had built 'very high houses' at a place called Ondeguê by the Spanish Jesuit Péro Pais (Wandge, on the southwestern shore of the lake). Pais visited the emperor there and was received in audience in 'the highest of the houses overlooking the lake and wide and beautiful fields'. Here another of these patient Ethiopian emperors was lectured about the errors of his religion. One of the buildings had a raised 'varanda', but it remains uncertain if this was really a multistorey structure or merely a flat-roofed building with a terrace set on a high vantage-point. The houses at Wandge were protected by two enclosures, and were designed for residence in the rainy season. Fasiladas' father Susneyos, and Emperor Sarsa Dengel before him, had built fortress-like palaces at other places beginning with G, Guzara (Guba'e) and Gorgora in the same lakeside region. But these were palaces of a single reign, only occasionally used afterwards, without the necessary extras that would make Gondar into something more permanent.

What were these extra factors? Trade must have been a significant, even a key, element in Gondar's success. The site lay on routes that connected the commerce of many of the lost provinces of the former empire of the Kings of Kings of Ethiopia, from Enarya in the south, to Massawa on the northern coast. Gondar looked – to its misfortune at times – westwards towards the Sudan, the kingdom of the Funj sultans centred at Sinnar, and so to the Nile trade. To the east, it traded as far as Yemen, where it linked into the international commerce directed towards Europe. Coffee from the south of Ethiopia went via Yemen to the Western world.

Environment was another significant factor. Gondar had practical advantages. It was accessible to abundant woodland and possessed ample water supplied by two streams, the Qaha and the Angarab (although there was a disadvantage in the lack of water sources on the high ground). The rich plains of Dambya around the northern part of the lake and the province of Woggera just to the north supplied Gondar with foodstuffs, both crops and cattle. Occasionally, it is true, the closing off of these regions in times of civil strife would cause famine, but that risk was run by any city.

A good view of the irregular patchwork of the fields in Dambya, lying between Gondar and the lake, can be seen on arrival at the airport near Azazo. The hot flat plain is seamed with river beds running slowly down to the lake side. Further north, where the hills begin, the scenery is dramatic and beautiful, with dazzling views over range after range of mountains towards the Sudan and Semien. Near Gondar, it is now largely eucalyptus country, but with considerable stands of older trees surviving. The fields of maize, wheat, millet and teff mount the stony hillsides, divided off sometimes merely by hedges, sometimes by stone terracing. In the hills, the sound of running water over the rocky stream beds permeates the air, and where there are no fields, wild sweet pea, wild thyme, red-hot pokers, small clover plants, daisies, variegated thistles and many other plants flourish. Above, the kites and vultures soar on the updraughts. Chilada baboons can also be seen in several places among these hills.

There are different opinions as to Gondar's situation from the point of view of health. Some regard the place as less exposed to malarial and other fevers than the lakeside palaces and camping places, others (such as Jean Doresse in his summary of Gondarine life *La vie quotidienne des éthiopiens chrétiens aux XVIIe and XVIIIe siècles*) suggest that it was not so healthy as some other Ethiopian cities, not being in so elevated a position.

It is worth noting that the Ethiopia of Fasiladas' time was a shrunken empire, and Gondar was reasonably placed for access in all directions. It was more or less central to what remained of the Ethiopian Christian kingdom, especially as regards the important provinces of Tigray and Gojjam, although the customary camping spots of the peripatetic court and some of the royal residences had often lain considerably further south and east. Tagwelat in eastern Shewa was a royal residence in Amda Seyon's time, and Zara Yaqob too stayed there at times; he was also fond of Debra Berhan in the same region, and made it his retreat for many years. Entotto and Yarar further south, where Addis Ababa was to be built later, had also been royal residences, and Barara is mentioned often in old itineraries. Galawdewos built a new capital in Waj. Minas and especially Sarsa Dengel seem to have initiated the move away from the Oromo or Galla towards Lake Tana. Gondar represented a strategic retreat in the face of the reality of the Oromo invasions.

The chronicles tell how Fasiladas dwelt at first at Libo, in the direction of Wahni, and other places. It must have been from here that in the third year of his reign the king fled before the rebel Malkea Krestos, taking the crown with him: 'the rebel entered the palace, sat upon the throne, and set a diadem on his head in place of the crown'. But, in the fourth year, when Metropolitan Marqos arrived, 1635–36, 'the prince fixed his residence at Gondar'. In between expeditions here and there, to Gojjam especially, to fight the Galla, to Begemder, to Lasta, the king began to spend long periods in the new city. In the seventh year, the eleventh year, the fourteenth to the nineteenth years, the twenty-second year, the twenty-fourth to thirty-second years, the chronicles reveal, 'the king did not leave his city', or 'returned to his residence'. In the thirty-fourth year, Fasiladas 'caused the books of the Franks to be burned', and in the next year he died. His passing drew from a chronicler a tribute as far as possible different from the bitter analysis of Fr. Torquato:

On 8th Teqemt, a Sunday, at three o'clock, when the shadow measured 3 feet, began the illness of our king Alam Sagad, as comes to all men. A great weight of sorrow weighed upon all the dignitaries, and particularly on blattengeta Malkea Krestos. He passed two days and nights forgetful of eating; on Monday and Tuesday he distributed gold and silver to the poor, and precious vestments to the church; he did good to those in despair, depriving himself of food and clothing, smashing the drums of silver and the daggers of gold and cutting up the casing to make church vessels. All this with tears and sighs, weeping and rolling on the ground with prayers and supplications in the church; for all the world believed that the sky and earth should tremble, that the land would be shaken and the enemy make himself master on the day of the death of our king Alam Sagad, knowing that he had re-established everything by his good deeds more numerous than the sands of the seashore, by his counsel strong like the mountains and hills ...

On Tuesday, after 3 o'clock, when the shadow measured 4 feet, he died ... Alas, his mouth with its gentle discourse has become mute, likewise his perfumed tongue from which the grace of words ever flowed through his lips. Weep and groan over this green plant, faded! His eyes were more joyous than wine, his teeth white like milk, as the Testament says. His figure resembled a palm tree, and his form was like the cedars of the Lord; the branches of his wisdom extended to the sea; his wisdom and counsel flourished to the rivers. What shall we say? What has been, has been! O flower of the kingdom with a sweet odour! Have you been destroyed like all other creatures? Behold accomplished here the words of the prophet who said; 'What man lives, who shall not see death?'

The fact that Fasiladas' long and seemingly fairly stable reign consolidated Gondar as a royal residence was emphasised when his son Yohannes I (1667–82), Alaf Sagad, from whose chronicle the above extract comes, also built at Gondar. Two attractive buildings, which still survive, may have been erected at his command. It should be emphasised that many of the buildings at Gondar are of very uncertain attribution. The chronicles might mention that a palace or church was built under such and such a monarch, but identifying it on the ground with a particular ruin at Gondar is never easy. Local legend, in fact, is the key to most attributions, and even then there is the question of possible destruction, rebuilding and reconstruction.

Emperor Yohannes, like his father and his son, preferred segregation for Muslims and Jews, and although edicts of 1668 and 1678 allowed them to continue to live in Gondar, they dwelt henceforth in separate quarters of the town. Al-Haymi had already remarked that the Muslims dwelt in 'special closed ghettos' even in the first decades of Gondar's existence. Like his father, Yohannes I still spent a great deal of his time out of Gondar, employing Yebaba, south of the lake near Bahar Dar (where a castle called Aroge Gemb is later mentioned in the chronicles of the *zemana mesafint*; Blundell 1922: 211), and Aringo east of the lake, as his summer capitals. At Aringo and Yebaba now remain only the enclosure walls with towers, with at Aringo a unique structure in Gondarine architecture, locally called *af-mekurabia*, possibly a granary (? Anfray 1988: 18, 20). Aringo and Yebaba remained in favour through several subsequent reigns, the Frenchman Charles Jacques Poncet stating in Iyasu I's reign that 'the palace of Arringon is no less magnificent than that of Gondar'.

There were obvious difficulties in provisioning a single large capital city. In the chronicle of Emperor Tewodros attributed to the *dabtara* Zanab, a memory of this was evoked when a priest in 1856 counselled a return to former practices: 'Remain four months in Gondar and eat up Aramachaho, Sagade, Walqayt and Tegré, then for four months establish yourself at Aringo, and eat up Begemder, Lasta, Yajju, Warra Himano, Wallo and Sawa, and then for four months make your residence at Yebaba, to eat up Macha, Agaw Meder, Damot and Gojjam as was done in the past' (Moreno 1942: 166–7). The term used was no joke – it was claimed by Andrea Corsali in the early sixteenth century that after an imperial sojourn in a given spot there could be no return for ten years, so utterly ravaged were the local resources.

Despite the summer campaigning, and the other residences, from Yohannes' time onwards Gondar was firmly established as the chief royal residence. In his chronicle it is recorded that Yohannes 'arrived at his dwelling for the rainy season, that is, Gondar'. Later, the emperor fell ill at Aringo, but 'came, suffering as he was from his sickness, into his fort of Gwondar, which his father king Fasiladas had built' (BM. ms. Orient. 660 after Budge, *The Book of the Saints of the Ethiopian Church*, I: lxxiii). The chronicles often repeat the itinerary, with its day-by-day camping places, between these favoured royal residences: Aringo, Hamad Bar, Qaroda, Enferaz, Waynarab, Menzero, Sadda, Gondar. Nevertheless, the use of the new centre was chiefly for the rainy season. When the weather was more clement, most kings still went on long and frequent tours of inspection, or conducted military campaigns and royal hunts, all over the kingdom. They were often absent from the city, residing in tents or in other royal residences. But when a third emperor, Iyasu I (1682–1706), Adyam Sagad, who also resided at times at Yebaba and Aringo, continued the building at Gondar, the imperial city could be regarded as firmly established. The emperor went regularly to and from his city of Gondar, to wars, to synods, to visit the churches on islands in the lake. There, Shaqla Manzo became a favourite resort with a palace, church and fortifications in the Gondarine style.

The habit of passing the rainy season at Gondar became so fixed, a chronicler notes, that when in 1697 Iyasu I decided to spend it at Yebaba to deter the Galla (Oromo) people from crossing the Abbay (Blue Nile), his followers were unhappy, as 'they were accustomed to pass the rains at Gondar'. The signal for the moment of the royal departure from Gondar is often cited in the chronicles – the herald would order the people of Gondar to bring in the horses and mules needed for the vast procession. Sometimes the immense list of necessaries that were transported in the train of the emperors is detailed minutely in the text.

Some records about the way of life in Gondar come from the chronicles, but, naturally enough, much is taken for granted by those secretaries or chroniclers, *azaj* and *sahafe te'azaz*, who wrote the records. They were familiar with Gondarine ways, and did not feel the need to enlarge with too many details. It is only from foreigners' descriptions that we can gain a fuller picture – that, too, inadequate enough. With the expulsion of the Jesuits after the disasters of the patriarchate of Afonso Mendez, and the defensive measures against any repetition taken by Fasiladas, foreign visitors to Ethiopia became very rare. Little outside the imperial chronicles themselves remains to relate the city's development. There are, however, occasional glimpses; from al-Haymi, Poncet, Bruce, Coffin, Gobat and d'Abbadie some sketchy idea of Gondar can be gained. Poncet, whose odd description of 'pyramidal and triangular needles' in 'Heleni' (see Chapter 10) does not really convey much of the true nature of the Aksumite stelae, was to describe Iyasu's court in

1700 in a way that carries more conviction. Moreover, it is complemented by the official chronicles.

The first report about Gondar was that of an envoy from Yemen, Hasan bin Ahmad al-Haymi. He visited it in 1648. He described a town of 'nests of grass' or typical conical-roofed huts, a few larger mud houses, and the 'stately edifice' the emperor was then building.

> We went to the King's stronghold and climbed a high building, a stately edifice which ranks among the most wonderful of wonderful buildings and among the most beautiful of exceptional wonders, constructed of stone and lime. And there is in that town, indeed in the whole of Abyssinia, no other but it (as it is of very pleasing appearance and handsome design), because all other dwellings in these localities are only nests of grass. The builder of the edifice was an Indian, and the characteristics of his design correspond to the methods of his country. And this stronghold, which partakes of the characteristics of the King's house, is situated beside the town and at the highest point there; and it comprises many courtyards and long halls. Around these quarters are some other buildings made of earth, stretching in length, breadth and height to an extent which no eye has beheld in any other building [these presumably represent the offices and quarters of the court, on the model of the travelling camp]. And these apartments are furnished as the King is wont to stay there, and there is in each apartment manifold Byzantine beds and Italian mattresses, which are embellished with gold, and magnificent sofas which are studded with precious stones and gems. And these palaces are unsurpassed as a wonder for the visitor and as a pride for this unbeliever king.

Al-Haymi continued, describing the splendid dress, the gold-encrusted swords, the brocades, the jewels glittering against the black skin of the courtiers assembled at the audience.

When Emperor Fasiladas, Alam Sagad, died in 1667, the *blattengeta* Malkea Krestos and all the dignitaries selected the *abeto* (prince) Yohannes as his successor. The chronicler opens the account of his reign with all the hyperbole of his trade:

> In the name of the Father, Son and Holy Spirit, one God. We begin to write the history, sweeter than honey or sugar, more desirable than gold or topaz, inviting the mouth to tell and the ear to hear, the history of the great and honoured King of Kings Alaf Sagad, by the Grace of God, called by the name of John the Evangelist, and of whom the faith and the works justify the identity of name.

Already Gondar was the scene for the great ceremonies of the court. The dignitaries 'entered the *Bet Afras* [the House of Horses, the guard barracks of the palace] where Yohannes was, and they brought him and made him mount the great tower' of his father's palace – the first such exhibition of a new king at Gondar. When the officials, nobles, governors, the dignitaries bearing the titles of *liq, liqa dabtara, sehafe te'zaz, aqabe sa'at, liqa ma'meran, echege, qes hase, azaj,* the four *liqa member* and the other judges had gathered, Yohannes sat on the 'royal throne of David and Solomon'. The official entitled *saraj masare* crowned him and decked him in the royal white robe. Then the dignitaries and the *azaj* or judges went out to the open space of the Addebabai, and caused the flutes and trumpets to be sounded, while a herald proclaimed the new king. So the ritual was established that would usher in the other Gondarine reigns.

Yohannes' Gondar was already, it seems, a substantial place. His chronicle mentions a new palace (see below), and also a 'hippodrome' – presumably an exercise ground for horses within the enclosure. A certain Bishop Yohannes, from Armenia, came to Gondar with an 'inestimable pearl, and very precious', a bone of St Ewostatewos, the Ethiopian saint who had long ago departed from Ethiopia for Egypt, and gone on to die in Armenia. He also brought a letter from the patriarch of Alexandria. Yohannes I summoned a synod of ecclesiastics to meet 'in the third enclosure, which is the hippodrome', according to Guidi's translation. The bone was accepted.

After Yohannes' death and Iyasu I's succession, the new king promptly had the *tabot* or altar tablet of Tekla Haymanot consecrated. He 'introduced it into the house of (*Grazmach*) Tequre', according to his chronicle, beside the spot where he founded the church of Tekla Haymanot. Emperor Iyasu so honoured and exalted the name of this saint that he constructed a 'rainbow', or arched bridge, which led from the imperial compound over the road outside to the church of Tekla Haymanot to the east of the castles. *Grazmach* Tequre had been a high official at the court of Yohannes I, accompanying *Abeto* Iyasu himself on one mission, and figured among the dignitaries present when Iyasu was proclaimed king. He died on the thirtieth of the month of Nahase, in the sixth year of Iyasu I, but his name is still commemorated by the now partially ruined 'rainbow' bridge the emperor built near his house.

Charles Jacques Poncet, visiting Emperor Iyasu's Gondar in 1700, has left us his impressions:

> Altho' the extent of the town be of three or four leagues, yet it has not the beauty of ours; nor can it have, because the houses are only of one storey, and there are no shops. This does not hinder but that they have a great trade. All the merchants meet in a wide, spacious place to treat of their affairs ... Everyone has his own proper place, where he exposes upon mats what he has to sell.

This open space was the Addebabai. As far as the palace was concerned,

Poncet found it 'great and spacious, and the situation very fine. It is in the middle of the town, upon a rising which overlooks the country round about; 'Tis about a league in compass. The walls are of freestone, flank'd with towers, on which are rais'd great crosses of stone [an extra that Bruce thought had, among other things in Poncet's description, 'been superadded afterwards', although perhaps it is not impossible that, as on the churches, crosses had once risen above the towers. In the chronicle of Emperor Zara Yaqob it is remarked that the king had a cross set up over the royal dwelling for the first time when he built his palace at Dabra Berhan.]. There are four imperial chapels within the enclosure of the palace.' Poncet estimated that 'there are about a hundred churches in the town of Gondar', and mentioned that 'the Patriarch … dwells in a fair palace near the Patriarchal church'.

Poncet was lodged in the palace grounds, where he had an 'apartment prepar'd for me, near to that of one of the Emperour's children'. He noted that there were 'some houses at Gondar built after the European fashion; but the greatest part resemble a funnel with the mouth downwards', a reasonable description of the round mud and branch houses covered with conical straw roofs that were typical of Ethiopia until the arrival of the ugly but more lasting corrugated iron roofing. A letter from the French consul in Egypt, M. de Maillet, cited by Le Grand in 1728, asserts that Poncet had complained about the typical Ethiopian dwelling given him at first, and was reassigned a house 'built after the European manner by the Portuguese'. The king, Poncet wrote, 'came almost every day to visit me, thro' a little gallery which had communication with his apartment'.

On 10 August 1700 Poncet was received in public audience. His description of the occasion revives for a moment a slight impression of one of the great empty halls of Gondar – perhaps the main hall in the Fasil Gemb – as it was in its heyday, with its furnishings and crowds of courtiers.

> They waited on me at my chamber, and, having conducted me thro' more than twenty apartments, I enter'd into a hall, where the Emperour was seated upon his throne. It was a sort of couch, cover'd with a carpet of red damask flower'd with gold. There were round about great cushions wrought with gold. This throne, of which the feet were massy silver [gold in the French original], was plac'd at the bottom of a hall, in an alcove cover'd with a dome all shining with gold and azure. The Emperour was cloath'd with a vest of silk, embroider'd with gold and with very long sleeves. The scarf with which he was girt was embroider'd after the same manner. He was bareheaded and his hair braided very neatly. A great emerald glitter'd on his forehead and added majesty to him. He was alone in the alcove I mention'd; seated upon his couch, with his legs across, after the manner of the orientals. The great lords were on each side of him, standing in their ranks.

Poncet also witnessed a church service attended by the king, on the day of the Feast of the Assumption. He describes the lavish procession and the pomp of an imperial visit. The great court of the palace was filled with twelve thousand men (or so he estimated) drawn up in ranks. The emperor was received at the palace gate by two princes carrying a magnificent canopy. Musicians went before, ministers followed, and even the crown was carried out. The 'patriarch' (metropolitan bishop) waited at the entrance of the chapel, named as Tensa Christos, the church of the Resurrection of Christ. It may have been Addebabai Iyasus or Tekla Haymanot church, since the emperor had to go out of the palace gate to reach it. On the return to the palace the crown, escorted by the High Treasurer and a band of fusiliers, was replaced in the treasury, while the emperor went into the great hall and 'seated himself on a throne rais'd very high'. He was offered mead and orange peel in a golden cup before listening to petitions. More information is supplied about ceremonies and customs, but very little of interest about the palace or city.

It was Poncet who, in 1700, influenced Emperor Iyasu to write to Louis XIV. A copy of the letter, which mentions Poncet by name, survives in the archives of the Ministère des Affaires Etrangères in Paris. It opens with the words: 'May the letter of Adiam Saghed, Emperor of the World, Servitor of a single God in Three Persons, King of the Kings of the World, reach your Majesty.' The letter discourses at great length about the emperor's faith, and his reliance on the Trinity. One can easily see the reflection of the faith of the man who whenever he could 'went up to Debra Berhan to celebrate the feast of the Trinity, according to the custom of the kingdom'.

Doubts were later cast by learned savants in France about Poncet's visit. One key fact in the accusations against him was that he claimed that Gondar was the Ethiopian capital. The assumption was that because the Jesuits had made no mention of it – Aksum was the traditional famous city of the Ethiopians – Poncet must have made his story up. Evidently the fame of Gondar's castles had not greatly spread with the virtual blockage of European visitors during the last sixty-five years. Even so, at least two French travellers in the East, Thévenot and Bernier (see Grierson and Munro-Hay 2002) had long since reported in the published accounts of their travels that Gondar was the Ethiopian capital, even if they had not been able to visit it. Bruce considered that 'Gondar was not built till the end of the reign of Hannes I ... about the year 1680', which might imply that it had until then been regarded as another occasional imperial residence such as Guzara (Guba'e, c. 30 miles southeast of Gondar) Ayba (c. 7 m. east of Gondar), Danqaz (c. 10 m. southeast of Gondar), Gorgora (c. 25 m. south of Gondar) and many others.

James Bruce supported Poncet's bona fide. He thoroughly enjoyed getting his literary teeth into others' errors – although he went too far in castigating, in several pages of sustained argument, that 'grovelling fanatic priest' Jerónimo Lobo for his geographical ignorance in misplacing Aksum, when in fact Lobo was discussing Qishn – which he spelled Caxume – in Arabia. (Richard Burton, too, made a similar error when, in his *First Footsteps in East Africa*, he stated that in 1541 Christovão da Gama 'landing at Massawa ... slew Nur the governor and sent his head to Gondar, where the *Iteghe* Sabel Wenghel received it as an omen of good fortune'. This was a century before Gondar's foundation, and the poor empress, far from dwelling in an imperial city, had been cooped up on the top of the inaccessible mountain of Debra Damo in Tigray for several years while the Muslim forces ravaged the land.)

The chronicle of Iyasu I notes that in the Year of the World 7175 (1682), Emperor Yohannes I, in the last days of his reign, came to Gondar. He had been taken ill at Aringo; by the time he reached Enferaz his malady had worsened. The emperor vowed that if God gave him the strength, he would return to Gondar. He distributed alms in huge quantities, breaking up even the crown to bestow gifts on the churches. Yohannes recovered enough to make the three-day journey by mule, and 'remained 10 days in the great new house, built (decorated?) with ivory with an ebony throne. It was Walda Giyorgis, gifted with intelligence, who built it, that same year'. The emperor died on 15th Hamle.

What was the 'great new house'? Pankhurst (1982: 126) suggests that it was the (rather small) Chancery, a building supposedly erected in Yohannes' reign (see below). The man called Walda or Wolde Giyorgis is presumed to have been an Ethiopian, but this is by no means certain. He could perhaps have been a foreigner, or half-foreigner, who had been given an Ethiopian name, a common enough practice. Although Pankhurst notes that the foreigners had been 'largely expelled' by this time, the truth is much more nuanced. The expulsion probably applied much more to the religious, than to persons of Portuguese origin who had been long settled in the land. From de Covilhã's time until Fasiladas' reign – one hundred and fifty years – these people were part of the landscape. For example, the abbreviated chronicle notes that Fasiladas' daughter Walatta Mangest, who died in the seventh year of Bakaffa's reign, had married 'Fasil the Frank'. The chronicle of Yohannes I confirms that *afrenj* (Franks, Europeans in general) who had converted to orthodoxy might remain in the city if they wished.

Whatever his origin, Walda Giyorgis was to surpass himself in the next reign. In 1685, he completed Iyasu's palace at Gondar; unless he in fact merely decorated Fasiladas' already existing castle, or, alternatively, this palace of Iyasu's was the same as the 'great house' in which Yohannes I had spent the last ten days of his life in 1682, now completed in his son's name. Whichever of the buildings it was, the result, in the typical high phraseology of the chroniclers, was vaunted as being 'more beautiful than the house of Solomon'. The palace was 'built with ivory'; presumably meaning that it was decorated with ivory ornaments. Gilded and jewel-encrusted ceilings glittered above. The walls and foundations were, improbably enough, of 'chalcedony', while 'on the surface of the walls and ceiling, palm trees had been painted; on all the windows were mirrors, pleasing to the eye, seven cubits long ... In the middle of the square ran the water of a handsome canal' (Guidi 1903, 1905: 89).

Perhaps it really was beautiful. Traces of painted rosette decoration remain in the neglected ruins of Susneyos' palace at Danqaz, for example. We are told, in the 1702 entry in his chronicle, that Emperor Iyasu also possessed a palanquin or portable throne made of pine and ivory, with palms and flowers represented on it inside and out, numerous large mirrors and two cushions. Above was a baldaquin of ivory and pine, with five golden *sandaq* standards. Iyasu's magnificent seat was a far cry from the throne of the last emperor of this line, Sahela Dengel (1832–40, 1841–55), who received Arnauld d'Abbadie reclining on a ceremonial divan with crumbling inlay, surrounded by servants in rags (see below).

Iyasu may also have built some of the lesser structures in the compound. Not all were permanent – his chronicle mentions that when in 1693 he emerged from his retreat for the month of Nahase, 'he entered the great tent of the *addarash*', which, adds Guidi, served as a tribunal. *Addarash* was the name later generally given to a royal reception hall; it is mentioned, for example, in the chronicle of Bakaffa. Dawit II appointed his uncle *Fitwrari* Agne to be *bajerond* or chamberlain of the *addarash*, and Kombe, ex-*dejazmach* of Damot, was made *azaj* of the *addarash* in Iyasu II's reign. *Addarash*, sometimes a tent, might then be a generic term for any of the other reception halls we find noted by other names, *zofan bet*, *anbasa bet*, and so on.

The chronicle of Iyasu I records that in his twenty-third year (1704) an earthquake shook Gondar. Houses collapsed, and a tower of the palace, called Jan Tekel, fell and crushed many people. The abbreviated chronicle sets this in the twenty-second year, on the first day of Maskaram: 'On this day there were great troubles among the people of Gondar, because of a violent hurricane called taro, which overturned the houses of the people of the capital and that of the king, destroyed the tower of Jan Tekel and killed many who had taken refuge there.' Doresse, who identifies Jan Tekel as the 'donjon du château de Fâsilidas', attributes to Bruce the information that the Fasil Gemb tower fell in 1704 – but as we shall see, all that Bruce actually says of the 'square tower' in his description is that 'part of the tower' was 'demolished and laid in ruins, and part of it let fall for want of repair'. It may be that the Jan Tekel tower was not actually an integral part of the castle of Fasil as we see it today, but belonged to one of the other buildings whose ruins indicate that very substantial structures once stood nearby. Close by the castle of Fasiladas one can see the remains of what seems to have been a hall of impressive size; a gateway with the usual red stone capitals and arch, with some decorative niches inside, a single pier for a side doorway (?), and the springing of another immense arch on the side facing towards the Jan Tekel Ber. Perhaps this building once supported the tower called Jan Tekel? As we shall see later, the name is associated with the palace by the title of certain officials of the interior of the palace, *jan tekel damsash* for example, but also with one of the *makkababya* or imperial compound gates called Jan Tekel Ber. Even today, the huge *warka* or fig tree that spreads its low and enormously wide boughs in a small garden or park just outside the imperial compound at the corner near the Jan Tekel Ber, the Wember Ber, and Addebabai Iyasus church, is called the *jan tekel warka*. It, or perhaps an ancestor in the same spot, earned a sinister reputation as the gibbet where those who dared to oppose the kings of Gondar met their end.

The open space, the *addebabai*, outside the palace was often the setting for important events. The abbreviated chronicle (as well as James Bruce in his historical account) describes the extraordinary scene in the Addebabai when Emperor Tewoflos (1708–11) condemned Queen Malakotawit, widow of his brother Iyasu I, and one of those who had conspired in his murder, to be hanged from a tree there. The queen, the only woman of her rank ever known to suffer such a punishment in Ethiopian history, was taken out and hanged with her brother Pawlos. Another brother, Dermen, who had pierced Iyasu with his sword, was put to death in the same way. Other conspirators were shot or hacked to death with a cutlass. The very same day that Emperor Tewoflos punished Queen Malakotawit and the murderers of Iyasu I, he celebrated the commemoration of his brother at Debra Berhan Sellassie church, with the drums beating. Later he gave a feast in the house called the *molale gemb*. This name crops up occasionally, being listed among the halls in which Emperor Bakaffa also held feasts, and where a great banquet was given in Iyasu II's time to celebrate the dedication of the church of Ewostateows.

Not long after the collapse of the tower of Jan Tekel, we hear the name again. At the end of the reign of the usurper Yostos (1716), certain soldiers anxious not to see Fasil, his son, perpetuate his illegal rule, cleared the *makkababya* or imperial compound and shut the gates at Jan Tekel and Sarasemba Ber. They emerged to slay some dignitaries who had just been to visit the dying Yostos. The guards later went to the treasury and took out the kettle-drum to announce the accession of Dawit II. After Dawit II was poisoned in 1721, Jan Tekel and Sarasemba Ber were again closed, barricaded and obstructed by soldiers under *Bajerond* Kucho, with the crown also under their guard. At the same time a council met under *Ras* Giyorgis to deal with the succession. They elected a prince, but when they sent soldiers to proclaim him as usual in the Addebabai, the troops in the vestibule of the palace instead proclaimed a rival, Bakaffa.

Do these references apply to a restored Jan Tekel tower after the collapse of 1704? Pankhurst (1982: 145, 147) assumes that in both these cases it was gates of these names in the *makkababya* that were shut, and this seems to be correct. The Jan Tekel Ber, with the Wember Ber and the Tazkaro Ber, was directly associated with the older castles of the compound. The name Sarasemba too is followed by the designation *ber*, or gate (see below for a list of the gates – perhaps this was an older name for the Wember Ber). In 1685, while Jan Tekel tower presumably still stood, during one of the interminable councils held to try to settle the question of the unction of Christ, Iyasu I sat on a dais erected near the Jan Tekel gate, while the metropolitan and the *echege* took their places on the *awaj mangarya* tower (Guidi, *Annales du roi Iyasu*: 92). This must have been another tower near enough the Jan Tekel gate to allow participation in the council; it seems in fact to be the tower attached to the next gate, Wember Ber, the Gate of the Judges. The tower was used for making proclamations in subsequent reigns.

In later references, whenever Jan Tekel is mentioned, it appears to be the gate that is in question. Early in Iyasu II's reign, for the Feast of the Cross, the clergy of the *se'el bet*, or royal oratory, came to the Tadla tower in the palace and took out the fragment of the Holy Cross: 'they went out by Jan Tekel to the Addebabai with all the dignitaries clad in mourning garments', and installed the relic in the tent of the *se'el bet*, which was erected in the middle of the Addebabai. The name Jan Tekel survived. Once again, over seventy years later in 1794, during fighting at the palace between the king's men and *Balambaras* Asrat, the Jan Tekel (gate and associated buildings?) is reported to have been burned.

The term *sarasemba* designates a royal official, one of a number of door-keepers of the palace according to Pais (1945–46, Vol. I, Ch. IV). The *sarasemba azaj* is marked fifteenth in precedence among the royal officials (named in the order they were to be consulted on juridical questions, the lowest first) in a list in the royal chronicle of Iyasu I in 1690. The 'Preface to the History of Abyssinia' in Bruce's book mentions this official as 'the judge of the Ozoros or Nobles'. Apparently the name derives from lands 'assigned to the office for their support'. In this context one might recall that Ebnat Sarasemba, defined as land reserved by the rulers for the needs of the court, was given in Iyasu II's time to Debra Sahay church at Qwesqwam.

The list in Iyasu I's chronicle (p. 152) names the officials as follows, in inverse order of importance, according to the record of the *Nagara Wag*, the 'Book of Customary Institutions':

* *shalaqa* of the *dal-shefra* troops (the commandant of the royal bodyguard)
* *shalaqa* of the troops in the city (military governor of Gondar)
* *tej azaj* (royal butler, in charge of the making of the royal *tej*, or mead)
* *liqa maqwas* (the king's double in war and (against the evil eye) in ceremonies; Bruce also identifies him as *hasgwe*)
* *ba'ala hambal ras*, *balambaras*, (master of the horse)
* *bajerond* of the *anbasa bet* (chamberlain of the 'House of Lions')
* *bajerond* of the *zofan bet* (chamberlain of the Throne Hall)
* *nagadras*, who has the right to a seat and cushion (head of the merchants)
* *fitawari* (general of the van guard)
* *grazmach* (general of the right)
* *qañazmach* (general of the left)
* *teqaqen blattenoch geta* (assistant chamberlains)
* *jandaraba azaj* (chief of the eunuchs)
* *sarasemba azaj* (a judge with jurisdiction over the nobles)
* four *azaj* of the right and left (supreme judges)
* two *sahafe te'azaz* (royal secretaries)
* *west azaj, raq masare, sasargwe* or *saraj masare* (or *eraq masari, alafa azaj*; major domo and governor of the king's house, also a judge)
* *pasha*, for he is *dejazmach* (officer over the Muslim musketeers)

Here follow the titles of governors of the great provinces of Ethiopia:

* *sahafe lahm* of Damot (Damot ranking first for *shewa* or militia)
* *nagash* of Gojjam, the chief of chiefs
* *sahafe lahm* of Amhara (literally, superintendent of the cattle)
* *azmach* of Begemder, chief of clergy, archpriest of Warwar
* *Semien aggafari* (ruler of Semien, a title sometimes taken by royalty)
* *Tigray makwennen* (ruler of the imporant northern province)

Finally, the greatest offices of all:

* *aqabe sa'at* ('guardian of the hour', a high-ranking court cleric, third in rank in the Church after the *abun* and the *echege*)
* *talalaq blattenoch geta* (grand chamberlains, senechals)
* two *ras bitwoded/behtwadad*

At an earlier period the *bahrnagash*, ruler of the maritime province with his seat at Debarwa, was the third in rank. This office had fallen in standing by

Iyasu's time, though it is still mentioned, for example, by the Bohemian priest Remedius Prutky, who arrived in Iyasu II's reign. Some other lists place the *nebura'ed* or governor of Aksum directly after the *aqabe sa'at* (Pétridès 1964: 207), but this seems to have been when the title was held by the incumbent *makwennen* or governor of Tigray.

The Gondarine emperors succeeded one after the other, embellishing the castles and churches, building new ones, until the compound as we see it today was completed. But it was not then as it is now. There were more buildings, now collapsed and fallen into ruin. Some of these were substantial. We must imagine the whole area seething with activity, with innumerable tents and temporary buildings filling up the now empty courts. Early in the morning, the ritual surrounding the Solomonid emperor began, whether in the camp or in the city. The *saraj masare* and his assistant grooms would crack their whips at dawn, 'worse than twenty French postilions', as the signal to rise (and to chase away the hyenas, Bruce adds). The ordinance of the royal house recorded in the *Ser'ata Mangest*, the book of the laws and institutions of the kingdom, stipulates that the *bajerond* of the *zofan bet*, and the *taqaqen blattengeta* should clear the hall, and see to the carpets and hangings, informing the *pasha*, so that he might keep the people away. He in turn would inform the *jan tekel damsash* and the *west damsash*. These were two officials of the interior of the palace, who are often noted together, employed about the person of the king. When he was moving from place to place, their task was to keep the people at a distance. (There is a legend about this. Long before, the king lists inform us, when Ayzor had become king in Aksum, he had ruled only for half a day. So handsome was he that a vast concourse of people came to admire him, and he was suffocated. After that, a barrier was always kept between the king and his people.) The officials next informed the *ras* of the *bet ansa* – a corps of guards who, with the *best egre*, carried the impedimenta of the royal chapels while on the march, and were also employed in lopping off the limbs of those condemned to such punishments – so that no one might enter the door. The *taqaqen blattengeta* and the *bajerond* of the *anbasa bet* did the same at the *anbasa bet*. The two halls were now ready for royal audiences. Gradually, at Gondar, a complex city and court life succeeded – or rather ran parallel to – the old custom of constant campaigning from a capital of tents. Urban activity flourished as Gondar grew larger and older.

In the past, too, and even today, the churches of the imperial compound contributed emphatically to the life of the palace quarter. The morning service, with the drums and chants echoing from the church of Elfiñ Giyorgis, and people clustering round the church and that of Asasame Mikael to kiss the gateposts or door-jambs, nowadays bestows an evocative glimpse of the buildings of the imperial compound in use. The silence and emptiness of the courts today offers an entirely false impression of the Gondarine castles.

A Muslim suburb, Islambet or Islamge, developed at Gondar as trade increased (see Chapter 5). Two ecclesiastical suburbs, Abuna Bet (north) and Echege Bet (south and west), reflected the presence of the Ethiopian Church, which now had its new centre here in Gondar too. Bruce noted that the house of the *abun*, the Egyptian metropolitan bishop, lay in the suburb near the brook of St Raphael in the northeast quarter of Gondar. The *abun*s possessed a country residence, too, at Janda to the south. The *echege*s were later to take over the Jesuits' former fief at Azazo. With this important ecclesiastical presence – including the staff serving the forty-four churches that local legend holds were eventually built at Gondar – there were enough rowdy elements participating in the ecclesiastical councils as religious controversy burgeoned sometimes seriously to disturb the peace of the city.

Bakaffa's chronicler – perhaps not surprisingly given the stern character attributed to this emperor – refers to Gondar as 'the city of peace'. By and large, a stable throne in a more-or-less permanent capital encouraged the development of the activities of peace. There was a flowering of arts and literature, trade and industry. Gondarine artists, encouraged by the patronage of emperors and empresses, particularly Mentewab, produced splendid manuscripts on parchment, with fine illustrations. A first and second Gondarine style can be distinguished. Larger paintings on cloth, or even true fresco painting, partook of the same traditions. The Ethiopian Jews, Beta-Israel or Falasha, who lived near Gondar in their own quarter called Falasha Bet, became involved in many of the city's local industries, such as pottery, blacksmithing, thatch- and cane-work, and building. Trade, too, flourished. Gondar became an important market for agricultural products from its surrounding area, as well as a long-range luxury market and caravan centre for goods passing to and from Adwa and Massawa, and the Sudan, or to the south to Enarya, Kafa or Jinjero. There were bi-weekly markets in the city. Arnauld d'Abbadie mentions only a weekly one, but that was 'the most important in Ethiopia, attracting caravans from all parts of the interior'. Rüppell observed that the market in the main open space south of the castles was held on Mondays.

Fire must often have been a problem with the relatively closely packed wood and thatch houses of the majority of the population. The chronicle of Iyasu I mentions that in April 1696 a fire 'broke out in the house of a prostitute, and burned all the houses of the town in the Gra Bet (the Left suburb) of Gondar'. The abbreviated chronicle notes the destruction of the churches of St George and of Abuna Tekla Haymanot. In 1700 fire at Gondar burned Gemjabet Maryam church, the king's house called Bet Tazkaro (House of Funeral Commemorations), and a house of the queen, as well as some town houses. In 1716, the usurper Yostos, falling ill, suspected witchcraft. Retiring to a tent pitched outside Gondar, he had his apartments fumigated with gunpowder. This dangerous procedure resulted in the burning of another of the palace buildings. The church of St Mikael was burned in May 1726, together with many houses.

Emperor Bakaffa's chronicle notes that he entered the central tower (or the interior of the tower, *makala makhfad*) to be proclaimed by the clergy and dignitaries. They anointed him, and crowned him with the usual recitation of Psalm 20 (21).4: 'You have set upon his head the crown of precious stones.' In 1723 the emperor Bakaffa 'sat on the royal throne in the Ma'kalay Gemb' (the same as *makhal* or central *gemb* or palace, meaning probably a tower in the Fasil Gemb). Here he married the beautiful Awalda Negest, himself crowning her there as *itege* after the *mashafa taklil* or marriage service had been read. She then went on foot, crowned, to the Queen's House, preceded by trumpets, to take her place on the throne and participate in the banquet. Her moment of glory was brief. She fell ill that same night, and died a few days later. She was buried at Debra Berhan Sellassie church.

Prutky, curiously enough, visiting Gondar in the reign of Bakaffa's son Iyasu II, believed that Bakaffa himself was the founder of Gondar; he 'chose for his capital a more spacious site [than 'Mt Thabor' near Siré] which today is called Gondar city and which was built by him before his death'. Bakaffa and Mentewab do seem to have decided to begin building in a completely different part of the plateau, beyond the Zofan Bet of Dawit II, but this was no more than a northern enlargement of the already substantial complex that had been there before, and continued to be used. Other less massive buildings might already have existed there before Bakaffa's own construction work began; the whole area between the now-blocked Elfiñ Ber in the west wall of the Asasame Mikael church compound, Dawit's throne hall, and the palaces of Bakaffa and Mentewab is filled with ruins. Among these is a small two-story structure with a vaulted roof pierced with holes, perhaps a bath house of some sort (the *Guida* designates it a *bagno turco*), a 'lion house' now equipped with bars, some sunken pits or cisterns, and some substantial traces of walls.

On one occasion in Bakaffa's reign, rumour interpreted the emperor's long stay incommunicado inside the palace to mean that he had died. The guard was called out by *Blattengeta* Kucho. To calm the tumult, Bakaffa then appeared, riding in procession to Debra Berhan Sellassie. The great officials scrambled to await him outside, falling prostrate before his horse. Later, the emperor summoned all the dignitaries before him to the *warq saqala*. There, seated on the throne and wearing the royal robes, he demanded through the *azaj* of the interior of the palace: 'Why have you troubled my capital?' Kucho and others, apparently fourteen people, were judged and condemned. They were dragged forth, their throats cut, and their bodies abandoned in the square. Later the bodies, naked, were thrown aside for the wild animals to devour. In certain Gondarine reigns, Yostos, Bakaffa, the generally bloody business of ruling in Ethiopia seems to be even more emphasised. Many officials also suffered having their eyes put out.

Iyasu II's chronicle offers an account of Gondar as an established capital city, the residence of the emperor and his mother almost to the exclusion of other places. Aringo and Yebaba are mentioned far less often. The chronicle names many of the apartments in the palace and even describes their use, especially at the great moments of crisis such as the death of an emperor and the succession of a new one. When Bakaffa 'knew that his hour had arrived', he brought Princess Yolyana, Mentewab's grandmother, with the empress herself and Iyasu into the royal apartment called the *mazaga bet*. His illness was kept secret between a very few officials who dwelt with him in the *masari*, the inner apartments. After the emperor's death, the chronicle of Iyasu II tells us, *Grazmach* Niqolawos brought Iyasu and the empress, with Arkaledes and Yolyana, into the *masari*. He assembled the dignitaries in the *ashawa*, apparently an open courtyard in the palace grounds; it was there that Bakaffa used to exercise his horse. Particularly conspicuous among the officials were two ecclesiastics, Mammo, the *saraj masare*, who would crown the chosen successor, and the *qas hase*, Elfeyos, who would bless him. The *ras* then announced that the late king wished his son Iyasu to be his heir. The great officers in secrecy led Iyasu, the empress and her grandmother out of the *masari* 'by the way of Shashana' into the Mannagasha Gemb. (Shashana was an area in the king's house or compound, where a large tent was erected for a church council in Iyasu I's reign, perhaps the same spot where the Hadas Shashana hall of Bakaffa was later constructed? If this were the case, the *masari* might have been, at that time, in the buildings attributed today to Mentewab herself.) The *saraj masare* was summoned, and the chamberlains entitled *aggafari* and *asallafi* opened the doors of the Makhal Gemb, the central palace, probably part of the Fasil Gemb. The *qas hase*, the royal chaplain, was also summoned. He found Iyasu seated at the foot of the throne, mourning his father. The *bajerond* Abreham appeared with the crown, while the *saraj masare* Mammo installed the new king on the throne; numerous psalms were then recited before Mammo placed the crown on Iyasu's head, falling prostrate before the throne with the dignitaries when this was accomplished. Outside, the great drum *deb anbasa* was taken to the *awaj mangarya* or proclamation tower, where one of the officials called *jan tekel* and the herald proclaimed the death of Bakaffa and the enthronement of his son.

The coronation of the emperor's mother, Mentewab, presumably necessary to confirm her position as regent, was announced at a reception in the Makhal Gemb, and took place shortly afterwards. Later, the queen, wearing the crown and golden shoes, left the Mannagasha Gemb on a mule decorated with a golden collar. She approached the Sarasemba Ber while the court chantresses called *darababet* and *ite agrod* sang: 'Now the sun that was hidden has risen.' The empress crossed the Addebabai to the sound of trumpets and gunfire, guarded by her brother, the *Asallafi* Walda Leul. She entered a chamber or tent called *saqala* or *adanager*, where she offered a banquet to the dignitaries. She later returned to the apartments in the palace called *masari* over the *qasta damana*, the poetically named 'rainbow' bridge. Over this bridge, too, the perfumed body of Bakaffa had been carried on an ivory litter covered with rich brocades, from the *elfiñ* or royal apartments to the church of Tekla Haymanot, where it was buried. As part of the funeral ceremonies, the dignitaries in the *ashawa* brought out an effigy of the deceased king, setting the royal robes on a mule. A procession of musketeers, sword and shield-bearers and dignitaries moved to the *makkababya*, surveyed by the new emperor from his station high above on the wall of the Makhal Gemb.

Remedius Prutky and two companions, Martin Lang of Bohemia and Anthony of Aleppo, were at Gondar in 1751, towards the end of Iyasu II's twenty-five-year reign. Mounted on mules sent to them by the king, they were conducted to Gondar, 'which is situated on the slope of a high mountain' (Arrowsmith-Brown 1991: 91ff). The emperor was then 'staying with his court at a place called Kaha about one hour from Gondar'. Prutky notes that the old writers assert that Aksum was once the royal city, but 'I call Gondar the royal city'. After a night's rest the foreigners were conducted to Qaha, where they found the imperial court:

> The residence at Kaha lies between two mountains, with a stream of clear water flowing beside it and set about with a variety of tall trees, a pleasant and pretty location where it is always summer. A wall three fathoms high surrounds it, and within the circuit of the walls are at least ten houses, each set with its own wall, so that one cannot pass from one house to another without opening the doors, which are always kept closed. No one can know in which of these pavilions the Emperor is to be found, nor is it permitted for anyone to enter without previous notice and the announcement of the visitor's name.

Prutky, for whom the Ethiopian character consisted almost entirely of defects, later noted the absolute simplicity of these 'pavilions ... small and entirely detached from each other, constructed without elegance, without dignity, almost without craftsmanship'. He later employs exactly the same words to describe ordinary Ethiopian houses, though he does mention that in the imperial pavilions (whether at Qaha or Gondar is unclear), 'the interior is decorated to the height of the walls in glowing red colours in a wonderful though crude taste'. Prutky and his companions were received in a chamber where the emperor sat on a couch spread with gold cloth. Iyasu II questioned the visitors on those characteristic enduring Ethiopian themes: where are the tablets of Moses? Sheba, Queen of Abyssinia? Later he enquired about Europe. The missionaries found themselves virtual prisoners in the security-conscious imperial residence until, the emperor returning to Gondar, they too were permitted to leave. They were lodged in 'that part of the royal palace once the abode of the emperor's father' (Bakaffa, whom Prutky believed was the original builder of Gondar itself).

But Prutky nowhere describes the stone-built palaces he must surely have seen, even in ruin, except to mention them obliquely when he tells how Iyasu as a young man was brought after the death of his father 'secretly to royal Gondar, and prudently guarded ... within the palace, which had been built in the past by the Portuguese and was well fortified'. He describes the revolt of 1732, noting that the

> palace's construction was of immense ingenuity and strength, of squared stone and cement, and in default of artillery they could force neither the wall nor the gates: the palace is the most magnificent building in the whole Empire, the best suited to the protection of the Emperors, and even though it is now in Ethiopian fashion split up, within its walls, into nine separate habitations, yet it remains difficult to storm however great a besieging force.

Prutky otherwise only refers to mud-daubed walls, thatched circular buildings, and a few oblong ones 'like the cottages of European peasants' as making up the palaces, though he does remark on Iyasu's penchant for pebble pavements and the discomfort these caused to one who was not used to them. Prutky wrote:

> To the visitor to Abyssinia it is a wonderful sight to see for the first time the dwellings of the Emperor and, even more, those of the ministers and great lords, all of them circular in construction, and all thatched with straw the better to withstand the tremendous rainfall.

In the Gondar of Iyasu II Prutky found little to charm him; there was 'no beauty, no splendour, no precious stones or other magnificence'.

James Bruce, writing of the rebellion against Iyasu II, when the palace compound was besieged, offers some account of the castles and their sur-roundings – presumably as he saw it in the 1770s, but dating the information back to the 1730s according to what he had heard or read. The *abun* and *echege* went to an open place in front of the palace called 'Dippabye', which was, Bruce notes elsewhere, the way Addebabai was locally pronounced, to declare Emperor Iyasu II, the *Itege* Mentewab his mother, and their supporters accursed. Later these ecclesiastics had publicly to recant at Dippabye after the collapse of the rebellion. The chronicle of Iyasu II refers to the place where the anathema was pronounced as the Shafari Meda. Several days of effort by the rebels failed to carry the gates and strong walls, although 'on that side of the palace called Adenaga [i.e. by the Gate of the Spinners], the rebels had lodged themselves so near as to set part of it on fire'.

Bruce then describes the state of the structure as he remembered it.

The king's house in Gondar stands in the middle of a square court [this is how the irregular compound, certainly not square, is shown too on Bruce's plan of the battle of 'Sabraxos'] which may be fully an English mile in circumference. In the midst of it is a square tower, in which there are many noble apartments [Fasiladas' castle]. A strong double wall surrounds it, and this is joined by a platform roof; loop holes, and conveniences for discharging missile weapons, are disposed all around it. The whole tower and wall is built of stone and lime; but part of the tower being demolished and laid in ruins, and part of it let fall for want of repair, small apartments, or houses of one storey, have been built in different parts of the area, or square, according to the fancy of the prince then reigning; and these go now by the names of the ancient apartments in the palace, which are fallen down. These houses are composed of the frail materials of the country, wood and clay, thatched with straw, though, in the inside, they are all magnificently lined. They likewise have magnificent names.

Then, a far cry from Prutky's lament for the lack of magnificence, Bruce adds: 'These people, barbarous as they are, have always a great taste for magnificence and expence. All around them was silver, gold and brocade.'

Continuing with his description of the revolt at Gondar, Bruce tells us that 'the next night the soldiers ... with fiery arrows ... set one of these houses, called 'Werk Sacala,' within the square, in flames'. A sally drove off the rebels 'setting on fire the houses that were near the palace, till part was entirely burnt to the ground. The next night, an attempt was made upon the gate to blow it up with gunpowder.'

On the 25th December they burned a new house in the town built by the king, called Riggobee Bet [House of the Pigeons, presumably referring to a site near the Gate of the Pigeons, possibly the small structure next to Bakaffa's large hall] ... The next night there was another great fire in the king's house; Zeffan Bet [Dawit II's throne hall?], and another large building, were destroyed by the rebels, as was the church of St. Raphael. Gondar looked like a town that had been taken by the enemy.

Iyasu's chronicle describes the same events in some detail. The dignitaries who remained loyal prepared to defend the *makkababya* when the news came that the rebels' nominee emperor, Hezeqyas, had reached the river Qaha. The chronicle supplies a very long list of those who supported the rebels, and those who stayed with the sovereigns in this hour of crisis, offering an unusually full survey both of the palace, and of the officials of the administration. Naturally, many of the loyal dignitaries had little choice. They were relatives of the empress regent, whose defeat would also entail their own certain downfall. The *Blattengeta* Efrem and *Qañazmach* Senye guarded several of the gates; the Jan Tekel Ber – an attempt was made to blow it up with gunpowder – the Sarasemba Ber, the Madab Bet Ber, and the Gemja Bet Ber. The *madab bet* is noted as having an upper storey, from which the defenders could shoot down on the rebels. *Blattengeta* Walda Leul guarded the Regeb Ber, in which was the House of the Table or royal dining chamber, and the Tazkaro Ber (with its viaduct bridge or *qasta damana*, which was destroyed in the fighting), occupying also the *tazkaro bet*. *Dejazmach* Arkaledes held the Kualhi Ber and the Asasame Qeddus Mikael Ber, or, in another version of the chronicle, the Akal Ber. Others held the *adenager*, and the *qasta damana* or viaduct bridge leading to St Rafael church. Shalaqa Lencho was stationed at the *warq saqala*, in the *adenager*, and Guncha in the *shashana*. In the *eqabet gemb* (called in another version the *eqabet ber*) were *bajerond* Mammo and others. The *abeto* Zena Gabre'el occupied the *anbasa bet*, and the *aykal gemb* was under the charge of *Balambaras* Aykal and others. According to the alternative version of the chronicle, the *anbasa ber* was occupied by *Azaj* Fesa. In the *danqaz gemb* the *Ligaba* Walda Sellus was posted with his associates. The second version of Iyasu's chronicle notes an Abuna Tekla Haymanot Ber, under the guard of *Balambaras* Adaru and Aykal. It could, then, indicate the building elsewhere called the *aykal gemb*, near the church of Tekla Haymanot and its bridge? The attachés of the *zofan bet* remained in the royal apartments, ready to sound the trumpets, to beat the *deb anbasa* drum, and to carry the standards. The *azaj* of the *elfiñ*, the *azaj* of the *addarash*, and officials connected to the *anbasa bet* and the *rasge bet* were also in attendance.

The 'great royal house, the addarash', was burned on 21 Tahsas. From it, the staff of the *zofan bet* managed to extract the great throne with the *warq wember*, or golden throne, and the carpet, and take them into the (Fasil?) *gemb*. Rafael church was also burned.

Iyasu II, victorious, was given the opportunity by the conflagrations caused by this revolt, and by the lucky arrival of a number of craftsmen of Greek origin, to indulge in a flurry of building and interior furnishing. Bruce describes how 'he had built a large and costly church at Koscam [Qwesqwam], and he was still engaged in a more expensive work, in the building of a palace at Gondar. He was also rebuilding his house at Roggobee-Ber (the north end of the compound near Bakaffa's hall), which had been demolished by the rebels.' He mentions the emperor's further building activities at Azazo (see below), and then describes the work at Gondar.

> Besides all these occupations, he was deeply engaged in ornamenting his palace at Gondar ... he finished his presence-chamber in a manner truly admirable. The skirting, which in our country is generally of wood, was finished with ivory four feet from the ground. Over this were three rows of mirrors from Venice, all joined together, and fixed in frames of copper, or cornices gilt with gold. The roof, in gaiety and taste, corresponded perfectly with the magnificent finishing of the room; it was the work of the Falasha, and consisted of painted cane, split and disposed in Mosaic figures, which produces a gayer effect than it is possible to conceive. This chamber, indeed, was never perfectly finished, from a want of mirrors. The king died, taste decayed; the artists were neglected ... part of the mirrors fell down; part remained till my time; and I was present when the last of them were destroyed ...
>
> The king had begun another chamber of equal expence, consisting of plates of ivory, with stars of all colours stained in each plate at proper distances. This, too, was going to ruins [when Bruce saw it some twenty years later in 1770–71]; little had been done in it but the alcove in which he sat, and little of it was seen, as the throne and person of the king concealed it.

The Gondar that Bruce saw had also recently suffered another fire in March 1769, when more palaces, churches and houses were destroyed.

We learn a little later in Bruce's description that a 'daroo-tree before the palace' was used for executions by hanging – the famous *jan tekel warka*. Justice tended to be swift. The moment the king had given the order, the criminal was taken straight out and hanged from this *warka* or sycamore fig tree (which suffered some hasty pruning in Iyasu II's reign to prevent it offering shelter to the rebels). It was here that Queen Malakotawit had been hanged with some of the conspirators who had slain Emperor Tewoflos' brother, Iyasu I. The tree was destined to bear some strange fruit at times. When Bruce describes his arrival at Gondar in the time of Emperor Tekla Haymanot II he notes; 'amidst the king's and the Ras's baggage, came a man bearing the stuffed skin of [Wachaqa, a rebel whom Ras Mikael had had flayed alive] upon a pole, which he hung upon a branch of the tree before the king's palace appropriated for public executions'. Abba Salama, the *aqabe-sa'at* or 'guardian of the hour', a very high-ranking ecclesiastic who had rebelled against Tekla Haymanot II, was also hanged there in full ecclesiastical robes. It was not always hanging that was the punishment meted out. When Hezeqyas, son of prince Yaqob, rebelled against Bakaffa the soldiers who had supported him were executed; 'the blood ran like water on the public square'. As we have seen, this was not uncommon during the reign of Bakaffa, whose Oromo name, adopted it seems when he was in hiding among them, indicates inflexibility; it is often translated as 'The Inexorable'.

Like his father, Iyasu II too died at Gondar. The king had been spending time at Qaha, but returned to the palace when he fell ill. He died in the *masqal gemb*, the Palace of the Cross, about which nothing else is known. During the swift and secret preparations for the accession of Iyoas, messages were sent to certain dignitaries who were in attendance in the *baqlo bet*, another part of the labyrinthine palace complex about which nothing seems to be recorded but the name.

As time went on a gradual change came over Gondar and the monarchy. The walls of Gondar became a trap, even though the emperors still issued forth almost every year on campaigns, and maintained several other residences. Eventually even this almost ceased. During the reigns of two minors, Iyasu II and Iyoas, there were few major campaigns beyond those needed for general maintenance of order and disciplining of any regions that failed to offer tribute. Iyasu's campaign to Sinnar was a disaster. With their majority these kings did sometimes venture forth, but they always returned to Gondar after the campaigning season. By the time of Iyoas and his successors, it was usually some great king-making *ras* who dragged an emperor with him on his campaigns. From a royal residence for the rains, Gondar rose to the status of capital city of the emperors, only to become, in the end, their prison. The control of the emperors grew feebler. The great feudatories, entitled *ras* (more or less equivalent to dukes) or *dejazmach*, who ruled the important provinces, waxed ever stronger.

Problems had been apparent earlier. First Emperor Iyasu I, then his son Tekla Haymanot I were murdered, and after the brief reign of Iyasu's brother Tewoflos the usurper Yostos seized power. His 'Solomonic' successor Dawit II was poisoned. Instability increased. Emperor Bakaffa, son and brother of murdered emperors, was supremely cautious. He halted the decay of the imperial power for a while, emphasising the role of the Oromo in court and camp, and wreaking havoc amongst the courtiers. But the decline of the monarchy resumed after him despite the efforts of Iyasu II (1730–55) and his mother the Empress Mentewab (Mentuab et var., died 1773) supported by a powerful family clique from Qwara.

Prutky frequently mentions this or that governor's attitude to the central monarchy, at least as he interpreted it, in 1752, towards the end of the reign of Iyasu II. The *nayb* or governor at Arckicko (Arqiqo, Hargigo) altered his unpleasant attitude towards the visitors when a letter from the emperor arrived. He is defined as an official who performed 'the duties of governor for both the Turkish and the Ethiopian emperors simultaneously'. Respect for the emperor's letters gained Prutky and his companions welcome from the *dejazmach* governing Debarwa (apparently the 'Bahr Nagasch' of Hamasien, ruling from Debarwa, to whom Prutky refers later in his book). In contrast, the governor of 'the city of Serai', possibly Addi Baro in Sarawe, was 'disobedient to his Emperor', as was also the ruler of Tigray at Siré. He had 'refused over many years to appear in Gondar before the Emperor, for whom he cared little and obeyed less'. Returning via 'Serai' later Prutky commented that 'for the first time ... during this exacting journey the production of the Emperor's letters afforded us a good reception', but only because the governor 'was a youth whose father had been held in prison in Gondar for a whole year, for sedition'. They had worse luck this time at Debarwa, the *bahrnagash* being then resident at Tadazecka (Sa'azzaga?). He had left 'seven substitute governors, differing from the devil only in bodily appearance', who ignored the emperor's letters. They declared, Prutky informs us: 'We are a long way from Gondar, and cannot hear the emperor's voice; in this town it is we who are the kings.'.

Prutky sums up the condition of the empire at this period, mentioning that once the emperors held an undoubtedly great power, but 'the greater part of that power has now departed, and ... day by day the Abyssinian Empire is sinking further and further into decay'. This was sublimely ignored, as usual, by the royal chroniclers and secretaries. Prutky perused with amazement the letter that Iyasu sent to greet them at Massawa, full of empty, sonorous, phrases:

> the Emperor of Emperors, acknowledged by the Christian and Turkish emperors as the successor to the Lord of the world, his gerent both for things secular and for things sacred, established ruler over the business of created creatures, through whom God administers justice to man and rules human affairs aright, and brings light to lands and to provinces ... strong in counsel, of perfect prudence ... benefactor of mankind ... promoting justice, goodness, and benefits ... fount of liberty ... so high lifted up that all the kings wished to imitate him but none were able to attain to him.

The high-sounding titles rolled on, 'so many ... that they outnumber the very stars themselves, and the multitude and density of the clouds', while the provinces departed.

One need not perhaps add that Iyasu II's chronicler also dwelt more or less exclusively on the rosier aspects of almost the last reign of any reality in Gondar: 'The book of the history of the king of kings Iyasu', he wrote, 'is astonishing like the Advent [of Christ], majestic like the cloud of the night; for his friends he was like drops of honey, to his enemies bitter as the juice of absinthe … may God give me strength and vigour to be able to write all the wonders of King Iyasu and Queen Mentewab.' He relates how after the death of Iyasu in 1755, when the body had been wrapped in a winding-sheet, it was removed from the palace by the door leading to the *makhal ashawa* or central court, opposite the *medr gemb* – a chamber noted in Bakaffa's chronicle as a court room. The body was conveyed, unknown to his mourning mother, over the viaduct or bridge, the rainbow, built by Iyasu I, to the church of Abuna Tekla Haymanot. There the corpse of Iyasu the Little was laid in the tomb of his father. *Ras* Wadage, his constant companion on campaign, mused, as had the friends of Alexander the Great when they gazed into his coffin: 'O you who once scattered gold, behold you are shut today in a coffin.'

After the mourning, when the effigy of the dead king had been prepared in the *ashawa*, his mule Wambade and the horses Lola and Salda were caparisoned. A great procession of dignitaries, with parasols, drums and standards, moved out to the *makkababya*, where the empress-mother recited a long funeral oration. Not long afterwards, the dead emperor's half-Oromo son Iyoas 'was led up to the top of the tower which is called Mannagesha; he was made to sit upon a lofty throne of gold and was clothed in the royal robes'. His accession was announced from the *awaj mangarya* tower. He reigned until 1769, at first under his grandmother's regency. Mannagesha Gemb, like Makhal Gemb, seems to be one of the names given to Fasiladas' castle, used primarily for certain state functions, *mannagasha* indicating a place where a king is crowned, such as the Mannagasha Court at Maryam Seyon church at Aksum.

Another account, in Iyoas' chronicle, tells of his anointing and crowning by Metropolitan Yohannes – instead of the *saraj masare* as was usual – in the building called the *ajale gemb*. The *Nagadras* Gergis on this occasion brought the crown. Yohannes anointed both crown and emperor with the *meron* unguent, the holy oil. He then set the crown on Iyoas' head, reciting the usual psalm 'you have set upon his head the crown of precious stones'. There followed a bizarre scene when Empress Mentewab sent for gold from the king's house to distribute for the commemoration of Iyasu II's funeral. Iyasu had indeed 'scattered gold'; only 20 (or in another version 80) golden dinars could be found, 'Iyasu having squandered his riches, in giving to everybody'.

From the description in Iyoas' chronicle, it seems that while the coronation was enacted in the *ajale gemb*, spectators in a structure called the *wesate gemb* could also participate in the proceedings. The chronicler notes that until the moment when the bishop removed the crown from Iyoas' head, he had not shifted restlessly on the throne, though only a child. Someone cited an apposite proverb, at which those who were in the *wesate gemb* and outside rejoiced. The *ajale gemb* was also employed on the occasion of a banquet given to those who had participated in an expedition against the Agaw early in Iyoas' reign, and another building, the *haddis bet* or 'new house', was used in 1760 for an audience attended by the court dignitaries. However, the name itself was not new; an *addis gemb* was the name given to the part of the palace where Iyasu II and his favourites and servitors sought refuge during the siege of the palace early in his reign.

It was during the regency of Mentewab for Iyoas that the Armenian jeweller T'ovmacean, who was for a while to preside over the meagrely furnished Ethiopian treasury, came to Gondar. He says very little indeed about the town or its buildings, merely noting a few incidentals. Summoned to court, T'ovmacean 'entered the reception hall where the Queen was waiting, sitting with her grandson the King on a bed covered with a carpet in the presence of many princes and high dignitaries'. At a later Christmas feast he noted that the Queen and her grandson sat 'on a high decorated platform'. He mentions also that

> there is at the palace a large open space where during celebrations they let lions free with a few bulls. The royal dignitaries and populace stand around and watch how the lion after a great struggle kills the bull which it takes by the throat, and sucks its blood, after which the animal sinks to the ground and the victor begins to tear it up.

Another Armenian then at court found this performance disgusting, and volunteered to combat the lion himself, killing it with his knife, for which the *itege* gave him 50 *warq* of gold.

The outbreak of disputes in 1766 between rival factions at court, the Oromo (related to Iyoas' Oromo mother Bersabeh) and Qwara (related to Empress Mentewab), encouraged Iyoas and his grandmother to appoint Mikael Sehul of Tigray to the supreme military rank of *ras*. He succeeded so well that the emperor became cautious, and tried to send Mikael back to Tigray. In the end, Bakaffa and Mentewab's grandson was murdered by his too-powerful servant in 1769. More of the palace was burned at this time, including the archives: 'The books of the kings which were destroyed when the Beta Mangest was burned by the wrath of Ras Mikael, heavy in anger,' laments one text. A nobleman, *Dejazmach* Haylu Eshete, was later in 1785 to try to replace the missing works by searching through surviving manuscripts and compiling a 'Compendium of History'.

The internal situation in Ethiopia reached such a pitch of disorder that the period has been given the designation *zemana mesafint*, the 'era of the princes' or judges, by comparison to that time recorded in the Bible, 'when there was no king in Israel; every man did that which was right in his eyes'. To make the contrast clear, there were in the eighty-six years of the *zemana mesafint* after Iyoas' death, 1769–1855, twenty-six reigns of nineteen 'emperors', or rather, as several visitors were more realistically to call them, 'kings of Gondar'. In the previous eighty-six years, 1683–1769, there were eight reigns of eight emperors, and in the following eighty-six years, 1855–1941, seven reigns of seven emperors plus the interim of the Italian occupation. The *Guida* not unjustly sums up the period as one of '*intricatissime guerre civili*', accompanied by massacres, burnings and raids, betrayals, intrigues and cruelty.

Iyoas was succeeded by Yohannes II, an old man, son of Iyasu I. A small but significant indication of the state into which the monarchy had fallen – if we can believe Bruce in the matter – was the *ras*'s cynical treatment of this emperor. Yohannes had one hand missing, cut off as a punishment for rebellion in his brother Bakaffa's time. When there was protest at this, no emperor being supposed to have any bodily defects (the reason for such mutilations in the first place was to prevent the possibility of those thus treated aspiring to accession) the *ras* merely replied that he himself would support the emperor on to his horse. When Yohannes refused to go on campaign, only wishing to return to the prison-mountain of Wahni and his prayers, *Ras* Mikael is said (by Bruce, who arrived in the country not long after) to have had him poisoned – although one chronicle states that 'he died in peace' after his reign of five months and seven days. It was his son Tekla Haymanot II who succeeded to this dangerous tutelage.

A chronicler of the *zamana mesafint* wrote openly of the might of *ras* Mikael Sehul of Tigray in comparison to the emperor himself – the history of his 'Lord Mika'el Chief of the Dignitaries, and Power of the Negus' (Blundell 1922: 217). The chronicler relates how in 1763 the deposed king of Sinnar, Badi IV, went to visit Mikael Sehul, and then went on to Gondar. The king and the queen (Iyoas and Mentewab) wanted to meet him at Qwesqwam:

> On hearing this the Chief of the Captains Walda Le'ul replied to them 'Do not go out from Quesquam, lest Badi the King may see the fewness of your troops, with the same eyes that he has seen the multitude of the troops of the Governor Mika'el, and despise you.'

It was in Tekla Haymanot II's time that James Bruce lived in Gondar for a while, leaving for us a strange, intimate glimpse of the Gondar monarchy in the days of the waning of its power. Bruce first glimpsed the town from about ten miles away: 'The king's palace (at least the tower of it) is distinctly seen, but none of the other houses, which are covered by the multitude of wanzey-trees, growing in the town, so that it appears one thick, black wood.' Bruce provided a general description of the suburbs:

> Below the town, on the S. W. at the conflux of the Angrab and Kahha, is the

Mohametan town. These rivers inclose the town on its N. and S. sides, and join on the W. On the S. E. part of it is the church of Debra-berhan. On the N. E. is Kedus Gabriel. Two suburbs above Kedus Gabriel, is Anta Naggar, the hill, where, till Yasous's time, the Tigre, in consequence of a proclamation, were obliged to halt, and not allowed to enter Gondar.

According to Bruce, about ten thousand families lived there in time of peace, in clay houses with thatched cone roofs. He estimated it as '2¾ miles, perhaps 3, at its greatest length, and nowhere above a mile broad'. The king's house he describes as 'on the west end of the town', or, again, 'the palace is in the centre'. It was

formerly a structure of considerable consequence; it was a square building, flanked with square towers [a description that actually fits none of the round-towered castles]; it was formerly four stories high, and from the top of it, had a magnificent view of all the country southward to the Lake Tzana. Great part of this house is now in ruins, having been burnt at different times; but there is still ample lodging in the two lowest floors of it, the audience-chamber being above one hundred and twenty feet long.

As well as describing the palace, Bruce notes the characteristics of the compound wall:

The palace, and all its contiguous buildings, are surrounded by a substantial stone-wall thirty feet high, with battlements upon the outer wall, and a parapet roof between the outer and inner, forming a gallery, by which you can go along the whole and look into the street. There appears to have never been any embrasures for cannon, and the four sides of this wall are above an English mile and a half in length.

Solomon Woredekal, in a report on the restoration of Gondar (*Annales d'Ethiopie* 13, 1985), reduces this rather, to 3 m. high and 800 m. long.

Bruce also presents occasional scenes from palace life. The king when in the council chamber 'sits in a kind of balcony, with lattice windows and curtains before him', the 'shekshek'. He occasionally spoke through a hole in the side of it to his spokesman the *qal ase*, or 'voice of the king'. This balcony, or a similar one, is doubtless that often described in the chronicles of Iyasu and of Iyoas, when the rulers held audience in the *makata* of the *masari*. This was apparently a balustraded part of the hall of the inner apartments that kept the royal party concealed. Outside, the dignitaries remained in the *ashawa*, an open area. Empress Mentewab and Iyasu II often held audience in the *makata* of the *masari*, confirming appointments and destitutions from office, sometimes doing so also in the *addarash*. In Iyoas' reign it is recorded that *Dejazmach* Warañña, seated in the *ashawa* of the *saqsaq*, rose to mourn the dead Emperor Iyasu II. Again, the next day, empress and emperor held audience in the *makata* of the *masari*, the dignitaries being in the *makhal ashawa*.

Makata and *saqsaq* – seemingly two distinct descriptions – indicate in the first case a balcony, and in the second the grille or trellis, in the reception chamber, the *masari*. Here the sovereigns could sit in privacy, while their spokesman conveyed messages out into the court where the officials attended. This seems to have been an innovation of the period, the monarchs now distancing themselves not just from the populace in general, but even from the officials who surrounded them in the palace. The seclusion perhaps grew more pronounced because the ruler was an empress-regent, even less inclined to appear in public than previous emperors had been. In later times it became a tradition, and was continued by Tekla Haymanot II.

When Tekla Haymanot II went to church daily, Bruce informs us, guards stood at every avenue or door through which he would pass: 'He rides up stairs into the presence-chamber on a mule, and lights immediately on the carpet before his throne; and I have sometimes seen great indecencies committed by the said mule in the presence-chamber, upon a Persian carpet.' A 'Badjerund' (*bajerond*, steward) was 'keeper of that apartment in the palace called the Lion's House'. This official, the 'Bazirwand of the Anbasa Bet', appears in the list of officials in Iyasu I's time as number twenty-three in precedence. Bruce also mentions a keeper of the banqueting house or *Zofan Bet*, noted in the list as 'Bazirwand of the Zefan Bet' (throne room), twenty-second in precedence. Both these structures also had corps of guards attached to them. This is illustrated in the chronicle of Iyasu II, when the emperor and his mother requested 'all the dignitaries, the soldiers, the clergy, the *liq* of the tribunal, the shield-bearers, the fusiliers, the *zefan bet* and the *anbasa bet*, and all the corps of troops who were at the royal palace', to swear loyalty before the *Kwerata Reesu*, the icon of Christ with the crown of thorns. Other palace guards were known as jan tekel, and the chronicle of Iyoas adds the gemja bet troops to a similar list as well.

Bruce provides some information about the throne, noting that

> the kings of Abyssinia sat upon a gold throne, which is a large, convenient, oblong, square seat, like a small bed-stead, covered with Persian carpets, damask, and cloth of gold, with steps leading up to it. It is still richly gilded; but the many revolutions and wars have much abridged their ancient magnificence. The portable throne was a gold stool, like that curule stool, or chair, used by the Romans … It was, in the Begemder war, changed to a very beautiful one of the same form inlaid with gold.

Just before the three battles of Sarbakusa, which were to finish Mikael Sehul's dominance and substitute *Ras* Gusho of Amhara as the king's master, the rebels again approached Gondar: 'The king often ascended to the top of the tower of his palace, the only one to which there remains a stair, and there contemplated, with the greatest displeasure, the burning of his rich villages in Dembea.' In fact, Bruce adds, the same fate nearly came to Gondar itself. *Ras* Mikael claimed that a vision from Michael the Archangel had come to him advising him 'to set fire to the town of Gondar, and burn it to the ground, otherwise his good fortune was to leave him there for ever'. The king, however, declared 'that he would rather stay in Gondar, and fall by the hands of his enemies, then either conquer them, or escape from them, by the commission of so enormous a crime'; a sentiment that earned him the friendship of the people.

The final view Bruce gives us of this sad king was when he had returned to Gondar after the defeat of *Ras* Mikael, and was residing, almost alone, in the palace, in a city without government.

A body of Galla ... stole privately into the town, and plundered several houses. They came next into the king's palace, and into the presence-chamber, where he was sitting alone in an alcove, while, just by his side, but out of sight and without the alcove, I and two of his servants were sitting on the floor. This room, in the time of Yasous and the Iteghe (the days of luxury and splendour of the Abyssinian court), had been magnificently hung with mirrors, brought at great expence from Venice, by way of Arabia and the Red Sea; these were very neatly fixed in copper-gilt frames by some Greek workers from Cairo; but the mirrors were now mostly broken by various accidents, especially when the palace was set on fire, in Joas's time, upon Michael's coming from the campaign of Begemder. These savages, though they certainly saw the king at the other end of the room, attached themselves to the glass nearest the door, which was a large oblong one; and after they had made many grimaces, and a variety of antics before it, one of them struck it just in the middle, with the butt-end of his lance, and broke it in shivers, which fell tinkling on the floor. Some of these pieces they took up, but in the end they were mostly reduced to powder, with repeated strokes of their lances. There were three glasses in the alcove where the king sat, as also one in the wings on each side, without the alcove; under the king's right hand we three were sitting, and the Galla were engaged with a mirror near the door, at the other end of the room, on the left side, so there was but one more glass to break before they arrived at those in the alcove, where the king was sitting.

Fortunately at this moment some armed Gondarines arrived. 'The Galla ... ran out to the great hall of the king's chamber, called Aderasha, when one of these soldiers of Gondar shut the door of the room where the king sat.' The intruders were overpowered and sent off for punishment. It was in an *addarash saqala*, or great reception hall, that in happier times Iyoas's grandfather Emperor Bakaffa, well in control of his nobles after his firm curbing of their aspirations, had received the gold, carpets, guns and horses sent as tribute by his provincial governors.

Bruce grants us a few other glimpses of the Gondar palaces of his day, by which we can see that portions of the palace complex remained in some sort of order, if neglected. For example, at one point in the wars when Gusho of Amhara was captured, he was 'confined ... a close prisoner, and in irons, in a high, damp, uninhabited tower of the king's house'.

The great feudal lords who soon divided the decaying empire into private fiefs still needed, or at least still employed, the old theory of the Solomonic principate to support their pretensions. They accordingly made use of the ready supply of captive imperial puppets exiled to the *amba* or steep-sided mountain of Wahni northeast of Gondar. There, theoretically, all male children of kings of the 'Solomonid' family were interned so as to offer no threat to the throne (although in fact the system began to fall into desuetude at this period, several ex-emperors remaining at large elsewhere, though 'bound in fetters', as a chronicler notes). The imperial idea remained valid, celebrated by the records with an increasing sense of unreality. So could the chronicler Alaqa Gebru write of Tekla Giyorgis, a puppet emperor who acceded to the throne five separate times between 1779 and 1800 at the behest of the 'princes':

> the story of the reign of the honoured Anointed, whose eyes are as the morning star, and whose countenance is shining and beneficent, whose stature is like an exalted angel, and his valour like the terrible Samson, his mind pure as the mind of the Creator, his wisdom great as the wisdom of Solomon, his dominion extensive like that of Alexander, the King of Kings Takla Giyorgis, whose throne name was Feqr Sagad.

Indeed, Tekla Giyorgis is remembered as the last emperor who was able, occasionally, to take an action on his own initiative, even though he was nicknamed *fesame mangest*, 'end of government', or perhaps rather 'end of the monarchy' (Shiferew Bekele 1990: 52). But despite the hyperbole, the truth seems to be, as David Mathew (1947) expresses it, that 'the later sovereigns of that house sank through a decreasingly gilded idleness beneath the rule of governors'. Tekla Giyorgis himself saw the way matters were going, if the chronicler truly records his answer in 1795 to messengers sent to fetch him: 'If I come back, shall I be an image and a puppet?' The answer was evident enough. Such a state of insecurity at the top of Ethiopian society did nothing to improve the lot of those below. All Ethiopia suffered from the depredations of civil wars.

Just before Tekla Giyorgis lost his throne temporarily in 1794, there was further damage to the palaces, or at least to the temporary structures built among the ruins. The chronicle states that the emperor having fled from Gondar 'since he had not had rations, and nothing to drink ... Balambaras Aserat came up with a force to drive out the men from the King's walls, and he set fire to the Royal Takal [hut] and broke down the Negus' wall'. The city suffered again when Tekla Giyorgis attempted to capture it in Solomon II's 'reign' (1777–79). *Balambaras* Asrat set fire to the Jan Tekel (gatehouse?) and caused further damage to the wall at the end of the reign of Hezeqyas (1789-94). Soon after this Gondar had a brief moment of holiday when Baeda Maryam II was crowned King of Kings: 'the Abun and the Echage came to the centre of the Royal Castle (*gemb*), and placed the crown which was of fine gems on his head, and there was dancing at Gondar and pedlars, and dancing girls'. But when King Solomon III was driven out in 1797, *Balambaras* Asrat surrounded Gondar. He 'knocked down the walls of the house and burnt the property of the Negus Takla Giyorgis, and only did not enter (break through) owing to want of strength, and the defence of the King's retainers'. The ordinary wood and thatch houses of the town doubtless suffered, however, when Asrat 'put *Negus* Solomon to flight, and sacked Gondar'.

Behind the elegant measured phrases of the chronicles, the shabby reality grew worse and worse. Visitors such as Pearce and Gobat tell of 'emperors' huddled in the few dilapidated but still habitable rooms in the decayed palaces of Gondar. They had no money, no soldiers, and no hope of improving their lot. At their deaths they could not leave enough money or goods even to pay for their burials. The chronicler laments the lot of the kings in 1801, the year in which Tekla Haymanot III, Demetros and Egwala Seyon were pushed and pulled like puppets on and off the throne. Tekla Giyorgis was in exile in Waldebba: 'and the kings moreover that were bound in fetters were Atse Yonas in the land of Lasta, and Atse Solomon in Tigré, and Atse Ba'eda Maryam in the land of Semen'. In January 1813 Pearce summed up 'the kings now living in Abyssinia' – Tekla Giyorgis, still in Waldebba, Hezeqyas (1789–84) in Gondar, Egwala Seyon (1801–18) then on the throne in Gondar, Yonas (1797–98) in Gojjam, Iyoas (presumably not Iyoas II, who died in 1821, but perhaps meaning Iyasu III, 1784–88, or yet another Iyasu who reigned briefly in 1788) in Gondar and Baeda Maryam II (1795) in Semien. In April 1813 two of them, Iyoas and Yonas died, 'both very poor, without leaving sufficient even to purchase a coffin to receive their remains' or for the appropriate ceremonies of remembrance. Pearce was at Aksum when Tekla Giyorgis died in 1818:

> he was buried in the church-yard of Marian Sean, at Axum, being a great
> holiday for [several saints], on which account great ceremony was used over his

grave. He was buried without a coffin, the times being so disturbed, that people could not be procured to cut down a tree to make him one, nor had the house he lived in any better than cane doors; so that a coffin could not be procured.

It was not only the foreigners who were conscious that much was wrong with Ethiopia's government. When Egwala Seyon (Gwalu) was enthroned by *Ras* Gugsa in defiance of *Ras* Walda Sellassie of Tigray and King Tekla Giyorgis, the chronicler bemoaned that

> he took his oath to and made king Abeto Gwalu, son of Atse Hezeqyas, by the hand of his underling; and there was no one to say, 'How is it that the kingdom has become contemptible to striplings and slaves? How is it that the kingdom is the image of a worthless flower that children pluck in the autumn rains?' I indeed lament as I ponder over the kingdom, for I was present in that day, its trial and tribulation.

It has been suggested that a better translation in such passages would read 'monarchy', for 'kingdom', because the Yejju Oromo lords of Gugsa's line did in fact maintain a kind of state or 'masfenate' for sixty-seven years between 1786 and 1853 (Shiferew Bekele 1990). Nevertheless, the gist is clear enough: 'If I lament over the oppression of the Kings, it is because masters have become servants, and servants masters ... "Gold shall be as dross, and brass be esteemed of higher worth."' When Egwala Seyon or Gwalu died, Pearce wrote simply that 'Itsa Guarlu, king of Gondar ... died'. The title fairly encompasses the real power of Gwalu, 'King of the Universe', as he is named in a painting at Debra Berhan Sellassie church.

In 1814 another Englishman, William Coffin, visited Gondar. He left a description of the city in its ever-advancing decay. Coffin had been one of Lord Valentia's servants (Pearce was the other) who returned with Salt on the 1809–10 expedition. The British Foreign Office, still forty years out of date with Bruce, thought in terms of Salt using 'his utmost exertion to reach the Court of Gondar and deliver His Majesty's letters and presents to the Emperor of Abyssinia in person'. This did not happen, and the presents were, in the end, given to *Ras* Walda (Wolde) Sellassie, with whom Pearce had stayed after the 1805 visit, and with whom Coffin remained as well on Salt's departure.

Coffin, in due course, made the trip Salt could not manage, and observed for himself what had happened to Gondar. On approaching the town he noted one of the old 'Portuguese' bridges, constructed in Fasiladas' time. A priest told him there were several of them, called by the name *Fasil dilde*. He mentioned seven in all. Some can still be seen today (Anfray 1988 lists them, and describes their present condition). Coffin learned that the reigning king Egwala Seyon or Gwalu had fled to one of the sanctuary islands in Lake Tana with what property he had. He may have been happy enough to go, for, as Coffin attested, *Ras* Gugsa, the Oromo governor of Gojjam, kept him 'shut up, more like a prisoner at large than a king'.

Coffin's description of Gondar was as follows:

I could only see part of the east side of the town, where I was stationed, but from a hill about a quarter of a mile from our camp I could survey the whole. The king's house, called Itsa Gamb (king's tower), stood in the middle on a height, and looked more like a Portuguese church than a royal palace. The king does not live in it, nor has he for many years past; the doors are all broken down, and the whole is very much out of repair, though within the walls Itsa Guarlu [Hase or Ase (king) Egwala Seyon] had built several decent apartments, besides the one he lived in when here. According to the Abyssinian way of building, the town is scattered about over a vast tract of land, in general high with small hillocks; every part takes its name from either the church, market, or people, that occupy the ground. Chegge Bate [Echege Bet] is a large piece of ground, spacious enough to build a town upon, from which no one, if even guilty of murder, can be taken, it being the residence of the chegge or head-bishop of Abyssinia [the echege, abbot of Debra Libanos, and chief of the monks]; the Abuna's premises have the same respect paid to them. The part of the town occupied by Mahomedans, though many Christians are intermixed with them, is called Salem Ga [Islamge]. Ardervaohi [Addebabai] is the name of the main public road, that leads to the king's house, where they hold the market; the same road leads to the wock-gavier, [gold market] where they exchange gold for salt ... If Gondar were built in a regular manner after the mode of building in Europe, one eighth of the ground would be sufficient for its population. The houses are all thatched, but, on account of the badness of the clay, they are obliged to thatch their walls likewise, to prevent their being washed down by the rain ...

The whole town is lined with wanztra trees, which hide the houses from the view; one part especially, and the only part I have been in, which was by night, is so thickly covered with these trees that you cannot see a house before you get within the trees that surround it. This part of the town goes by the name of Turkouch Minder, which name arose from the Sennar troops having been quartered there, when in the service of the king [Iyasu I].

The wanza trees are still there, but now augmented with foreign imports, eucalyptus and jacaranda.

Coffin summarised the goods from the neighbourhood available in Gondar; wine, brandy, butter, pepper, greens, wood, corn, cattle and fish. Scarcely four hundred Jews were in Gondar – they had a prayer house at Derfecher Keder Merret (Kidane Mehret church at Dafacha across the Angareb near

Gondar). Coffin mentioned that there were many priests, maintained by the land belonging to each church. Qwesqwam (Debra Sahay) was then the mother church (see below). He noted: 'the priests are of the opinion that their city is very grand and they even call it ... the city of forty-four churches'. He adds that 'nearly one half of the forty-four churches have fallen down', carefully cautioning against anyone's imagining that they were 'on a par with St Paul's, or Westminster Abbey'.

In 1830 Gobat, later to become Anglican bishop of Jerusalem, visited 'the Emperor Guigar, who bears, however, nothing more than the name of royalty', successor of Iyoas II.

> He resides in a small circular house, built by Joas, on the ruins of a part of the palace that was erected by the Portuguese ... He then directed a servant to show me the different apartments of the palace. It must have been once a fine edifice, and although now in ruins, it is far superior to anything I had expected to see in Abyssinia. Three chambers or halls, and several smaller rooms, still remain in a tolerable state of preservation, though they have lain so long unoccupied that they present a very disagreeable appearance ... The king occupies but a single room. This is decently furnished for this country, and divided by a white curtain. After I had completed my examination of the mansion, he asked me if I had ever seen so superb an edifice. 'Yes', said I, 'I think I may have seen some in my own country that might bear a comparison with it'. 'What!' he exclaimed with surprise, 'are there indeed men at the present day who are capable of executing such magnificent works?'

Gigar, noted Gobat, unlike his brother Iyoas who was 'efficiently sustained by Ras Googsa, who was his firm support, or rather his superior ... has no Ras; he lives upon the contributions of the grandees of his dominions, who furnish him with whatever their generosity prompts them to bestow'; evidently, little enough. This tale of 'King of Kings' Gigar, son of Hezeqyas, son of Iyasu II, son of Bakaffa, son of Iyasu I, son of Yohannes I, son of Fasiladas, founder of Gondar, sums up the speed and the nature of the rise and fall of the city.

Two years later, in 1832, a new emperor, Sahela Dengel, established by *Ras* Ali, received Eduard Rüppell in a miserable house on the north side of the old palace. The Saint-Simonians, Edmond Combes and Maurice Tamisier, visiting in early 1836, were preoccupied with their own ideas, and seem to have remarked only that the town was severely damaged by constant warfare, with a much reduced population. They did, however, find one substantial library of books there translated from Arabic and Indian works, as well as noting that it was a 'town of pleasures' with many prostitutes. Later, in 1846, Combes, by then apparently an ex-Saint-Simonian, was to reminisce gloomily about Ethiopia and Africa in general:

The Abyssinians, who embraced Christianity, an eminently progressive religion, inhabit huts, their kings go barefoot and they have only huts for churches. Unable to rise to the height of Christianity they have lowered Christianity to their own stature.

Then, doubtless in memory of what he had seen in the Gondar region, he continued:

This people was, however, visited by the Jesuits and by the Portuguese who built them palaces; they erected churches and constructed bridges on the rivers; but after their departure, the bridges, churches and palaces fell down, and there remains nothing but the ruins of all these great works. (English translation taken from Pankhurst 1969: 221)

Arnauld d'Abbadie and his brother Antoine arrived in Gondar in 1838. Antoine soon departed for France to collect various instruments, and to deliver letters to the king of France and queen of England seeking help against a possible Egyptian invasion. In his excellent account of his sojourn in Ethiopia, Arnauld d'Abbadie describes minutely his life in the country, his impressions, reactions, changes of mind and associations with many Ethiopians from emperor to slave. The Gondar of the *zemana mesafint* he brings alive as no other writer does, save perhaps Bruce in occasional passages.

D'Abbadie estimated the population of Gondar as comprising 11,000 to 13,000 persons, enlarged by one-third again in times of trouble when people came in for protection from outside the town. An official bearing the title *kantiba* (governor) was in charge of the policing of the town. D'Abbadie, like Prutky and others before him, attributed the building of the palace, then surrounded by ruins, to the Portuguese:

It consists of an agglomeration of buildings without symmetry, some topped with battlemented platforms, others with domes or vaults; round about is a wide irregular enclosure formed by a crenellated wall, with walkway, loopholed and with towers at a distance from each other; the principal building has as its façade a large high square tower, which dominates all this group. Only a section of the gable wall of the banquet and audience hall remains, in the middle of which the arched bay of the high entrance doorway stands out against the sky. The baths, the stoves are broken in; the women's rooms shelter only night birds; the treasury, the stores, the kitchens, the stables, the apartments where, it is said, the emperors retired with their familiars to rest from the rigid etiquette of the court, all is uninhabitable, and no one in the country is even capable of making the mortar to repair the damage caused by time. A former prison, and the large hall of justice are the only well-preserved parts. An old man of Gondar said, when narrating to me anecdotes about the emperors; 'God wished that among the ruins, the prison and the hall of justice should remain standing, to witness to the iniquitous violence of our imperial family.'

D'Abbadie on his visit to the emperor was led by an attendant into the hall of justice by an external staircase through a 'sort of Guard Room, from which he introduced us into the hall of justice, a vast bare rectangular room, at the end of which, crouched on a canopied bed, was the Ats, or Emperor, Sahala Dinguil [Sahela Dengel, 1832–40, 1841–55]'. The emperor lay on an Indian couch, still exhibiting the remains of rich marquetry work in ivory and mother-of-pearl. It was covered with a narrow and worn Turkish carpet that allowed part of the stuffing to be seen. 'Four little pages in rags, a deformed eunuch and two old men stood immobile with lowered eyes on each side of the shoddy throne.' D'Abbadie mused on the fate of 'this imperial family, which, daily, like a statue overturned from its pedestal, sinks more into the dust of time'.

Turning to the churches of Gondar, d'Abbadie noted nineteen; the total of forty-four, he thought, included those of the nearly abandoned eastern suburbs. He commented that the best preserved parts of the city were

> to the south, not far from the palace, the quarter called the echege's and the Salamge or Muslim quarter, situated at the foot of the hill within the Angareb and Kaha; nearby is a place where an important market for mules and horses is held. To the southeast, the Dinguiagu quarter (land of stones), occupied by Christian merchants; beside is another large irregular place full of stones where an important weekly market is held. To the north, and at the foot of Tigray-Mutchoaya [Tigre Meceha] mountain, the quarter of the Abun ... partly separated from the town by a deep ravine; and near the palace, the house of the ras bitwodded or Grand Constable, a pretty castle in ruins, surmounted by a tower. To the east, the Bata quarter. To the northwest, over the Kaha, on the edge of a little plain, the shady suburb of Kouskouam, where one sees the pretty ruins of the church, the house, and the large tower built with mortar, about 1720, by the Itege Mintwab.

Later he adds that the *abun*'s quarter, like Bata (Be'ata) church, enjoyed the right of asylum, but that it was little respected if the prelate was absent. If he were there, a fluid population of refugees, priests and students was present also.

D'Abbadie thought that the *echege*'s high-walled quarter was the most populous, 'in some ways the heart of the town. It owes its importance to its right of asylum which is nearly always respected.' He describes the quarter's mixed population, including numerous high-ranking persons who stayed there when in Gondar. The emperor, he adds, 'deprived of all power and all authority, lives abandoned in the isolation of his palace' save when on rare occasions he judged, as a last court of appeal, some special case in the hall of justice. D'Abbadie later provides – an interesting and significant comparison – an account of his reception by *Ras* Ali, Sahela Dengel's *ras*, at Debra Tabor, a 'mini court' seething with activity, with soldiers, chiefs and generals paying respects to their lord.

Gondar, as well as being an important market, was in the late 1830s an industrial centre, although

> the simplicity of the Ethiopians' needs only renders necessary a limited number of trades: weavers, all Muslims, welders (corroyers), leather workers, makers of harness and other equipment for horses, blacksmiths and spear-, sword- and knife-makers; saddlers, sandal makers, book-binders, clerks, copyists and preparers of parchment; makers of sheaths and all those who sew leather; goldsmiths, casters and workers in copper; embroiderers of panels for the saddles of mules or the amulets borne by women, men and horses, and also those who embroider in coloured silk the long robes of the women, their capes, and those of the priests; shield makers, carpenters, turners, stock makers for guns, makers of drinking horns, women who make basketwork in straw and those who make 'bouza' beer, mead and brandy for retail sale. Pottery is made by Falasha or Jewish women, and their husbands build in mud mixed with straw.

D'Abbadie mentions too that there were always certain celebrated teachers of grammar, law and theology with their pupils, who begged for their living or made parasols from reeds, or hired themselves out for temporary tasks. He describes the scenes of daily life at Gondar, a city that he personally found, though dilapidated and run down, charming in many ways.

In contrast, d'Abbadie quoted *Dejazmach* Birro of Dambya's opinion of Gondar: 'un ramassis de vils marchands, de grandes dames au rabais, d'ecclésiastiques faux savants et de clercs séditieux'. In order 'to breathe a purer air' the *dejazmach* led d'Abbadie to see his ancestress Mentewab's dwelling at Qwesqwam. They managed to climb up to the top of the tower by the dilapidated staircase; the *dejazmach*, elated, enquired: 'Am I not a fortunate man to be able to claim such palaces as having belonged to my ancestors?'

From 1839 to 1843 the members of the Lefebvre expedition were travelling in Ethiopia. In the *Atlas* volume of their report, Pl. 8 illustrated Koskouam, Dabal Guemb, 'Palais du Ras Ouelda Loule' – this building is also illustrated in Pl. 9, where one can see that the name indicated the Fasil Gemb. *Ras* Walda Le'ul was a brother of Empress Mentewab, who sped through the lower ranks to this pinnacle at record speed. He was employed to lead numerous expeditions and more or less headed the government during the reign of Iyasu II and at the beginning of the reign of Iyoas. The *dabal gemb* seems rather to be identified as the *zofan bet* of Dawit II (see below), though there was also a *beta dabal* at Gondar in Iyasu I's time.

When Lefebvre's expedition was in Ethiopia, *Ras* Ali of Begemder was the ruler of the Gondar region, with his 'capital' at Debra Tabor. His defeat by Kasa, later Emperor Tewodros II, caused further destruction to the palaces of Gondar. The mother of Ali, Menen, had married the briefly usurping Emperor Yohannes III (1840–41) and thus gained the title *Itege* Menen – which d'Abbadie noted that no one used except in her presence. With her husband, she had dwelt in the ruins enjoying, as d'Abbadie also commented, being empress there. Furious at her son's humiliation, she is supposed to have pulled down part of the royal palace so that no one else might live in it.

So things continued until finally in 1864, then again in 1866, came Tewodros. He was not from the old Solomonic line, although a pedigree was produced to conform with that requirement, nor did he have any desire to retain the capital at Gondar. He chose, rather, Debra Tabor and Maqdala, although his chronicle tells us that on occasion, as in the month of Hamle 1856, he came to the *gemb* in Gondar and stayed for the rainy season. In that year good news was brought to him at Gondar of a victory in Gojjam. But he sacked Gondar. The churches were systematically plundered. It was largely their plundered treasures and books that the British later seized as loot at Maqdala in 1868 after Tewodros' decline and suicide, ensuring the preservation of many of the books in the British Library and at Windsor. Indeed, one chronicle seems to attribute the coming of 'the people of Jerusalem, that is the English' to Tewodros' destruction of Gondar, 'mother of cities', and the burning of its churches (Guidi 1926: 417). The people of Gondar were driven out, and then the torches were set to burn Gondar down. (Foster, editor of Poncet's account, wrote incorrectly that Gondar was 'destroyed by Menelik in 1866'.)

Nevertheless, something of the old city remained. After Tewodros' defeat, when *Wagshum* Gobeze declared himself emperor as Tekla Giyorgis II, he granted money and lands to the churches of Gondar to help them recover from Tewodros' depredations. He was deeply mourned there after his defeat and death. As far as the castles are concerned, the ruins shown in an engraving by Waldmeier published in 1886 are still impressive – the buildings attributed to Fasiladas, Iyasu I, Bakaffa and Mentewab can be distinguished, as well as the walls and gates. In 1888 Azazo and what was left of Gondar with, supposedly, forty-two of its churches was burned again by the Mahdist army, who scattered the army of King Tekla Haymanot of Gojjam, sent by Yohannes

IV to defend Dambya and Gondar. Only a few churches, Medhane Alem, and Debra Berhan Sellassie, protected, a legend relates, by bees, remained intact. Still, however, the burnings mainly concerned the churches and houses of wood, reeds and straw. The stone palaces still stand, dilapidated even after restoration.

Doresse cites a poem, attributed to the lawyer Kefle Yohannes, who died in 1853; whoever really wrote it, it shows the despair of a citizen for the fate of a once great city:

O Gondar, of the beautiful buildings,
Gondar, hope of the poor as well as the great,
Gondar the inimitable, to which nothing can compare,
Gondar, who, maternal, satisfies all desires,
Gondar, where no fevers come,
Gondar of the lovely name; land of pleasure and delight.

O Gondar, house of Iyasu and the esteemed Bakaffa;
Gondar, fairer than the City of David, the land of Salem,
You who should have kept your splendour forever,
Why have you, who did not deserve it, been destroyed like Sodom?

Gondar Today

The town is situated at about 2,270 m. above sea level in the province of the same name, of which it is the capital – in former times the region around Gondar and the eastern part of the lake was called Begemder. The main road from the north via Adwa and Aksum continues on from Gondar southwards to Bahar Dar and Addis Ababa.

Much of the imperial city, the Fasil Gibbi, was restored by the Italians, who occupied Gondar on 1 April 1936 – a circumstance that sometimes makes it difficult to be certain about the original form of the buildings. Government offices were installed in the structures that remained more or less intact; the *ras gemb* was restored, and became a vice-regal residence. In May 1938 restorations began in the Fasil Gemb, the internal and external stairs and some balconies being replaced. Work was also done at the Bath of Fasiladas and its pavilion. Today, again, the Fasil Gemb is under restoration; the castles of Bakaffa and Mentewab are now supported by steel girders.

Fasil Gibbi, the imperial compound Within the huge circuit of the walls, embracing some 70,000 sq. m. on the ridge or plateau above Gondar, the remaining palaces and pavilions of the imperial court stand now amid trees and open grassy spaces. They are undoubtedly imposing, but sad and battered-looking. Many are partially ruined despite the Italian restoration of some decades ago and some subsequent work since. There is great archaeological potential here after some three hundred and seventy years of the city's existence. Some structures known to have once existed from the chronicles and other accounts can no longer be traced. Others, we know, were built of perishable materials. Certainly the rich interior furnishings, the divans, carpets, silks and tapestries, as well as the ivory wainscoting and Venetian mirrors that ornamented the walls, and the decorative coloured canework ceilings, have all gone.

Even so, peopled by the imagination with the individuals whose characters come over to us with force in some of the chronicles and traditional tales, and even more so in the accounts of writers such as Poncet and Bruce, the old castles take on a new life. The main difficulty is to know what the original use of the different structures was, from among the splendid, resounding names preserved by the chronicles. The accounts of foreign visitors scarcely help. They generally simply refer to the castle, or tower, or palace of the king, without any hint as to which of the many buildings they mean.

Bruce wrote that 'the level plain on the top of the hill was chosen by Faciladas and Hannes [Yohannes I] for the site of a palace, having a large space of ground about it, in imitation of the royal manner of encamping'. The 'Preface to the History of Abyssinia' inserted in Bruce's book adds that 'the respective parts of a camp were long visible in Gondar, which was chosen by Facilidas for the winter station of his court'. This may be true, but the plan of the camps was not followed beyond very general lines, though even now the ensemble is referred to as the *katama*, signifying the imperial camp and headquarters. In 1696, the merchant Murad, interviewed in Batavia, called the assemblage by this name (Chattama). Chattama, the Armenian merchant reported, was a big unwalled town 'situated on the mountain Gonder, where the emperor has for his use and pleasure a big walled palace consisting of more than a hundred and twenty large buildings, besides pleasant gardens and plantations' (Van Donzel 1979; Pankhurst 1982: 95, 133).

The great walled enclosure was called *makkababya*, a name applied much earlier in Baeda Maryam's chronicle, written in his son Eskender's reign, to the imperial camp. In front of this site (that is, to the south) was the open space called Addebabai (or Ashoa by Bruce, 'a public place where the troops assemble, and gun-powder is sold, and where public executions are made'. *Ashawa* does indicate an open space, but in the chronicles it appears always to be inside the palace walls. In 1716, for example, Dawit II assembled a synod in the *ashawa* to discuss the question of the three Capuchin friars who had been permitted to enter Ethiopia by Yostos. They were summoned to appear, and admitted that they followed the 'belief of Leo and the council of Chalcedon'. After condemnation, they were taken and stoned to death in the lower town together with a child of six who accompanied them. The dignitaries also met together 'in the house of the king, in the *ashawa*', to hear Bakaffa's bequest of the throne to Iyasu II in 1730, while Iyasu II himself kept some of the monkeys he captured in the *ashawa*.)

In 1692, when Iyasu I campaigned against the Shangalla people, the bodies and cut-off genitalia of the enemy were presented to Iyasu in the gory fashion of the time at Horat by the Mareb river. They formed 'an enormous heap, and the Addababay and the Makkababaya of the king's palace could not contain them', as the chronicler triumphantly wrote. It was in the Addebabai that the people gathered to hear proclamations. Bruce witnessed a proclamation delivered to the sound of the *nagarit* or royal drum, called 'the lion', beaten at the king's gate (Jan Tekel Ber). There was a proclamation tower here, Awaj Mangarya (*awaj* was the title of the royal herald), employed in Iyasu I's and Bakaffa's reigns, for example, for religious assemblies before the public. In the Addebabai public whippings, punishments and executions took place, and it seems also to be the same as that 'large waste space on each side of the palace, where the market is kept'. Emperor Tekla Haymanot II once witnessed a theft taking place here from his vantage point on the only tower to which a staircase then remained, and had the culprit brought up to him, ordering him to be thrown down from the tower. Bruce and some others about the king dissuaded him from this summary justice.

One assessment of the building of the castles comes from David Mathew: 'The actual building of this new capital would be the work of men who had been nourished in the Abyssino-Portuguese tradition, but it would seem reasonable to deduce that the concept was at least in great part Ethiopian.' This was true in a sense. By the time Gondar was built, there were already castles and palaces enough to have allowed that concept some shape, but it is evident that, ultimately, the origin of these structures was a foreign one that had arrived in Ethiopia after the mid-sixteenth century. This was a time when Turks and Portuguese were resident in the country, and Indians as well. It seems that Manoel Magro, the man who in 1624 noted that the necessary rock for making a strong mortar was present in Ethiopia, was an Indian by origin. His discovery at Azazo permitted the building of strong-walled edifices, which allowed the Gondar style of architecture to develop rapidly and successfully.

By the time Gondar was being built, there were two types of relatively recent stone-built precursors available in Ethiopia as examples. One was the stone castle or palace such as is noted in the chronicles, Galawdewos' Golden House in Waj, or Guzara (Gub'ae) under Sarsa Dengel, though this castle may not necessarily have been of the same design as the structure that is there today. The other was quite different, the purely Portuguese architecture of the Jesuit churches, such as those built at Gorgora, Danqaz, or Martula Maryam, reconstructed on the ruins of an older church at Enebesse.

As early as the late seventeenth century, as de Maillet's note about the house Poncet was allotted in Gondar reveals, certain Gondarine buildings were being attributed to the Portuguese, possibly correctly in the sense that Portuguese or half-Portuguese workmen may have had a hand in their construction. But the Gondar castles followed an individual style, rather than the exported Portuguese style, although there may have been some technical input from the latter. Nevertheless, Prutky, Gobat, d'Abbadie and others generally attributed the building of the Gondar castles directly to the Portuguese. James Bruce mentioned his belief, in conformity with that of al-Haymi quoted above, that 'the Palace itself [he refers to Fasiladas' castle] was built by masons from India, and by such Abyssinians as had been instructed in architecture' – of course, 'masons from India' might mean from Portuguese India, but not necessarily so. One of the Abyssinian masons might have been the Walda Giyorgis, who built for both Yohannes I and Iyasu I; although, as we have seen, it is not impossible that he was a foreigner or part-foreigner employing an Ethiopian name.

Whatever the case, the Gondar architects did not invent the architectural style from nothing. As we have noted, earlier kings had the chance to exploit foreign architects and workmen. Empress Eleni and others had employed Egyptians to build stone churches like that at Enebesse. Galawdewos had built a palace of stone, the *beta warq* or Golden House, in Waj, including a stone tower decorated with gold and silver encrusted stone figures. This work was attributed by his chronicle to Frank and Egyptian engineers and Syrian and Armenian artists. He also created a building employing white columns brought from Adal for his hawks, and a pavilion in a beautiful garden. Sarsa Dengel, for whom Guzara was first built, demolished the Turkish fort at Debarwa, another possible source for ideas and techniques.

As to the reason behind these constructions, LaVerle Berry seems to sum up the psychological aspect well: 'Their appearance coincides with what was almost certainly a conscious effort to restore the majesty and invincibility of a kingly office badly shaken by wars and invasion' (Berry 1989: 124). They were testaments to the royal power and glory of the Solomonids. Indeed, there may have been rather more to it than that. As we shall see, Susneyos had had palaces and churches built for him by the Jesuits, buildings whose descriptions and whose existing remains indicate that the emperor had lived and worshipped with a certain grandeur, in painted and decorated, sculpted and carved stone residences and churches, often of more than one storey, endowed with a certain dignity, presence and luxury. Fasiladas, a Catholic convert himself in his father's time, had seen and lived with all this as the heir to the empire. His own prestige must have commanded him to try, at least, to equal – without the Jesuits, but not without those who had been to some extent imbued with their knowledge, ideas and techniques – what his father had accomplished.

This was doubtless combined with a desire to ensure royal privacy, but as in the *katama* or royal camps, it was perhaps mainly symbolic. Evidently the hedges or palisades of the camps, with their guarded gates, were far inferior to the walls and battlements at Gondar, but even the latter were not really capable of sustaining a major seige. When they were called upon to do so, as in Iyasu II's time, the weakness of the 'rainbow bridges' and other elements was manifest, even though the defences were, in fact, just strong enough to allow the defenders to hold out until help came.

As time went on Fasiladas' original compound grew larger and fuller, as the building of palaces and churches continued. A first wall, encompassing the castles of Fasiladas, Yohannes and Iyasu, was enlarged to include those of Dawit II, Bakaffa and Mentewab. What may be traces of this wall, with other substantial ruined structures, are visible in the southern half of the compound, stretching north of the small building with a round two-storey tower attributed to Fasiladas, and south of Dawit II's *zofan bet*. Bruce notes that a succession of kings built apartments by the side of the main palace 'of clay only, in the manner and fashion of their own country'. Some of these were doubtless those we find referred to as royal dwellings or 'palaces'. It may be that some of the luxurious apartments built by Iyasu II were housed in such impermanent structures, although it seems, from the tale Bruce told of its final destruction, that his mirrored hall was installed in the main castle of Fasiladas. Apart from such splendid if insubstantial dwellings, and more permanent archive and treasury buildings, there would also have been a host of minor service structures, doubtless constructed using less permanent materials than the larger castles. Among these we might envision kitchens, bakehouses, breweries, servants' and officials' quarters, the barracks of the royal guards, stables, storehouses of all kinds, and other minor buildings, indeed a small self-contained city, built in different parts of the immense grounds.

The compound eventually had twelve gates, erected at different times and sometimes known by several different names according to the chronicles and to different modern writers:

Fit Ber or Jan Tekel Ber (also called Gate of Giarra Grande (*Guida*), Gate of the Guard, Imperial Gate). This is one of the southern gates leading to Addebabai, where proclamations of accessions and other events were made by sounding the kettle drums. *Fit* means 'in front of', 'before'. Today the Jan

1. Zara Yaqob in his zeal for Christianity commanded that his subjects be tattooed on the forehead with the words 'Father, Son and Holy Spirit', and on the right and left hands with 'I deny the Devil', and 'I am a servant of Mary'. Today, a blue cross, and sometimes a necklace, are deemed sufficient.

2. The endless mountain peaks of Lasta stretch away, fold after fold, into the distance. By perilous mule tracks along the edge of these precipices the road leads on to Yimrehana Krestos church.

3. Sunset on the shores of one of Africa's great lakes, Lake Tana, or the Sea of Dambya, the inland sea set high among the mountains of central Ethiopia.

4. Although today the vegetation of Tigray province is relatively sparse, the statuesque *qwolqwal* or *euphorbia candelabra* trees stand dramatically out of the bare hillsides.

. The spectacular beauty of the *qwolqwal*, called for obvious reasons *euphorbia candelabra*, in flower near the ancient Ethiopian capital, Aksum.

6. The long mule ride from Lalibela to Yimrehana Krestos in Lasta province is relieved both by the dramatic beauty of the mountain scenery, and the attractive wild flora of the wayside.

7. Evocative of the Egypt of the pharoahs, or of Lake Titicaca in the Andes, the *tankwa* or reed boat of Lake Tana still ply between the monasteries of Lake Tana, and the peninsula of Zage

8. Below Lake Tana the Blue Nile begins its long journey to the sea, the river cascading down a great curving cliff face. The waterfall, called by the Ethiopians Tis-esat ('Smoke of Fire'), creates an eternal mist, often sparkling with a rainbow, that nurtures the abundant vegetation.

9. The characteristic tomb of an Oromo Muslim, in the countryside near Addis Ababa.

10. When an emperor died in Gondar, unrest and disturbances often fell on the city until his successor, robed in white and wearing the 'crown of precious gems', was displayed before the people on one of the high balconies of the castle of Fasiladas.

11. The 'most beautiful of exceptional wonders', the Yemeni ambassador called it. Splendid even in partial ruin, the towers of the Fasil Gimb at Gondar dominate the rest of the palaces and churches in the imperial compound.

12. It was the Portuguese Jesuits, apparently, who first created a roofed water cistern for Emperor Susneyos at Danqaz. After their expulsion, Emperor Fasiladas had this similar cistern built beside his new castle at Gondar.

13. Attributed to Emperor Yohannes the Just, this building may have been a royal library, the 'Beta Mangest', or House of the Kingdom, repository of the chronicles of the kings.

14. Imposing arches, and the vestiges of walls, are all that now remain of a huge hall with two-storey towers that once stood beside the Fasil Gemb at Gondar. It may have been a reception hall, or a hall for feasting for the monarch's retainers.

15. Perhaps the most attractive of the buildings still standing at Gondar, the so-called Chancellery of Emperor Yohannes impresses not because of its size, but by its elegance and delicate decorative touches.

16. The huge roofless hall or *zofan bet* attributed to Dawit II may once have held 'the great throne with the *warq wember*, or golden throne'. Decorated with rich carpets and hangings, it was the cene of royal receptions until burned in the seige of 1733.

17. One of the *qasta damana,* the arched 'rainbow' bridges that led in secrecy and security from the imperial city over the roadway outside to the neighbouring churches.

18. In Gondar, both in the imperial city and outside, are several buildings with small domed chambers, often called Doro Bet, 'House of Hens', by modern Gondarines. In fact, these buildings seem to have been Turkish bathhouses, their domed roofs pierced with holes to allow the steam to escape slowly.

19. Attributed to Empress Mentewab or her son Iyasu II, lovers of architecture and the arts, this elegant castle was the swan-song of the imperial period. Later emperors merely camped in the collapsing ruins of what Iyasu's ancestors had created

CHURCHES IN THE IMPERIAL COMPOUND

20. Broken and clumsily repaired, its inscription barely legible, the tomb of the British Consul Walter Plowden, killed in Ethiopia in 1860, stands in the courtyard of Gimjabet Maryam church at Gondar.

21. King Egwala Seyon prostrates himself and lays down his crown in humility before the cross of Christ, in the early 19th century painting in the church of Debra Berhan Sellassie – the 'Mountain of the Light of the Trinity' – at Gondar.

QWESQWAM PALACE AND THE CHURCH OF SEHAY MARYAM

22. A charming retreat from the cares of the world, the domed and balconied house of the abbots at Qwesqwam is placed strategically between the church and the empress Mentewab's palace and oratory.

23. One of the doorways at Empress Mentewab's great twin-towered reception hall at her palace in 'Upper Gondar', Qwesqwam.

SITES NEAR LAKE TANA

24. At Azazo, a favourite retreat of the emperors near Lake Tana, and the seat of the *echege* or abbot of Debra Libanos monastery, a fortified compound with a two-story tower house protects the church of Tekla Haymanot.

25. Lonely and mysterious, the strange high dome of Bahri Gemb dominates the ruins of the church and its compound.

26. Beautifully situated, the ruins of the royal palace at Old Gorgora evoke the new luxury of Portuguese architecture enjoyed by Emperor Susneyos, and the brief flowering of the Catholic faith in Ethiopia.

27. Simple outside, but a blaze of glorious coloured paintings within, the church of Debra Sina, Mount Sinai, at Gorgora is a classic example of a traditional round Ethiopian church.

28. Painted on the wall of the sanctuary of the church of Debra Sina, Gorgora, beside Lake Tana, the Virgin and the infant Jesus. Above, the round drum over the square sanctuary supports the roof.

29. The Gondarine emperors delighted to visit the monasteries of Lake Tana, bestowing on them gifts of elaborate votive crowns, beautiful books, or rich garments. These crowns are in the treasury of Beta Giyorgis church, Zage.

30. Crowned and richly robed, King Tekla Haymanot of Gojjam is painted surrounded by his courtiers and soldiers in the church of Kidane Mehret, the 'Covenant of Mercy', at Zage.

31. Painted in the church dedicated to him at Zage, Batra Maryam, the 'Stick of Mary', reputed discoverer of coffee and a hop-like plant for making beer and mead.

HARAR

32. Beside the Shewa or Victory Gate
(Bab al-Nasri) at Harar, one of the
markets that have for centuries formed the
lifeblood of this city of commerce.

33. A gate in the wall of the old city
of Harar. Every night, Sir Richard
Burton reported, the keys of the
gates of Harar were taken to the
Amir himself, and the city was
sealed until dawn.

34. Symbolic of Harar's role as the chief city of Islam in Ethiopia over many centuries, the gate and minaret of one of Harar's mosques.

35. Harar may have a decayed appearance externally, with its ancient collapsing *jugal* or enclosure wall, and dusty narrow streets, but the inside of the *divan*, or sitting room, of a traditional old Harari house is richly decorated with plates and typical Harari basketwork.

Tekel Ber is no more than a broken arch, now blocked. There are, however, traces of a second story.

Wember Ber (Gate of the Judges). This lies to the east of the Jan Tekel Ber. The Wember Ber, too, is now blocked. Beside it stand the ruins of a round tower, presumably the *awaj mangarya* tower, formerly at least two storeys high. Inside, this tower communicates with a long and very narrow building, with arched entrances on the east side, which joins on to the south wall of Fasiladas' castle.

Tazkaro Ber (Gate of Funeral Commemoration). Further east round the compound wall, just before the wall turns north, the Tazkaro Ber opens into an area now cut off from the imperial compound by an interior wall. It formerly had an attached bridge, destroyed in the fighting in Iyasu II's time.

Azaj Tequre Ber (Gate – bridge – of Chamberlain Tequre). The *Guida* refers to it as the *Porta del Ciambellano*. Access to the Azaj Tequre Ber is by an inner part of the bridge within the compound, borne on arches, and starting from a double wall abutting on to a rather primitive round structure, perhaps a later *tukul*, near the complex of ruins that lies beside the cistern beside Fasiladas' castle, and Iyasu I's castle. The bridge then turns parallel to the outer wall for a space (this part is now ruined), before turning again at right angles, crossing the road outside the compound. It once communicated with Addebabai Tekla Haymanot church over the road outside the imperial compound. It and the other 'rainbow' bridges are said to have been built by Iyasu I.

Adenager Ber (Gate – bridge – of the Spinners). This gate led by a bridge over the road outside the straight east wall of the compound, to the church of St Rafael in the weavers' quarter of the town. Interestingly, although there is now little trace of the double wall mentioned by Bruce, the area between the Azaj Tequre Ber and the Adenager Ber does preserve something similar. Here is a double wall, with an entrance arch on the inner side facing Iyasu's castle. The Adenager Ber is reached by a staircase from inside the double wall. Apart from these bridges, no other 'parapet roof' on the wall, as Bruce describes it, is now visible. Further traces of a double wall seem to be visible also north of the Adenager Ber, near the ruined building called the House of Espousals, or Qwali Bet, where there is also a half-round 'tower' in the wall.

Qwali Ber (Kohl Gate, Gate of the Queen's Attendants). This gate, beside the modern entrance leading to Elfiñ Giyorgis church, is an arched two-storey gateway, now blocked.

Imbilta Ber (Gate of the Musicians/flute players). The Imbilta Ber led into the compound of Asasame Mikael church.

Elfiñ Ber (Gate of the Privy Chamber). This gate is on the inside of the Asasame Mikael compound, leading on to the complex of ruined structures north of Dawit's throne hall. It is now blocked. The name Elfiñ Ber is sometimes translated as 'Gate of the Secret Chamber', but romantic though this sounds, the name of the gate seems to mean nothing more mysterious than that it gave access to the *elfiñ*, the private apartments.

Ras Ber (Gate of the Ras, or Chief) or *Qwarenyoch Ber* (Gate of the Qwara people, referring to *Itege* Mentewab's Qwara ancestry). The gate is still in use. It now leads into a quiet garden, often filled with people sitting reading. The garden is bounded by the so-called House of the Commander of Cavalry, the 'Turkish Bath', and the south and east façades of Mentewab's palace, the ground floor of which is nowadays used as the Gondar Public Library.

Ergeb Ber, or Regeb Ber (Gate of the Pigeons) or *Kechin Ashawa Ber* (interpreted as Gate of the 'Expert Farmers' or Gate of the Gifts. The word *ashawa*, however, usually indicates an open area inside the palace walls). This gate, beside the round tower of Bakaffa's castle, is a simple arched entrance (now blocked) in a small square one-storey gatehouse.

Inqoye Ber (Gate of Princess Inqoye or Enqwaye, the mother of Empress Mentewab). This is the present entrance into the imperial compound, where the 50 birr tickets for each visit (including Fasiladas Bath) are on sale. Outside the gate is a broken arch, perhaps the trace of another bridge to the exterior.

Gemjabet Maryam Ber (Gate of the Treasury of Mary). This gate leads to the compound around the church of Gimjabet Maryam.

Balderas Ber (Gate of the Commander of Cavalry). This is another gate not included among the twelve generally enumerated. It is situated at the northeastern corner of the compound. The gate is part of the House of the Commander of the Cavalry, but today another adjacent entranceway leads between it and another small building with a round cupola into the compound of Asasame Qeddus Mikael church. The Sarasemba Ber is also sometimes mentioned. It was perhaps another name for the Wember Ber. Madab Bet Ber, mentioned in the story of the rebellion against Iyasu II, might refer to the *madab*, or stone seat in the *zofan bet*. Asasame Qeddus Mikael Ber, or Akal Ber, also mentioned in a text on the same subject, is doubtless the Imbilta Ber.

For a dream-like invocation of the old Gondar of the emperors, David Mathew's book is well worth reading. He has much to say of the ritualistic, formal and measured hieratic life he conceives the Ethiopian sovereigns led, enclosed in their imperial compound, increasingly isolated from reality by ceremonial and the mystique of the 'Solomonic Throne'. In part, this is a dream interpreting another dream, the measured, praise-filled and heavily biblical lines of the royal chronicles. These were written, in a language few by that time could understand, by learned royal clerks, sons of similar court officials, in praise of kings at the foot of whose thrones they themselves lived. What happened in Israel over two millennia before was as real to them as what was happening today. Sennacherib, Goliath, Samson, Gideon are almost as often mentioned as the criminals and heroes of Ethiopia themselves. Through this charming but distorting mirror, Mathew attempts to comprehend how the Ethiopians regarded the phenomenon of Gondar. He sums it up: 'In one way Gondar was singularly solid, a series of stone palaces unparalleled for thousands of miles. Viewed from another angle it must have seemed the cardboard capital of an unreal empire.'

Fasil Gemb, castle of Fasiladas The first and most imposing of the Gondar edifices was the five-towered castle of Fasiladas, a massive solid-looking building constructed of unsquared dark stone and mortar, with cut stone arches of red tufa from Qwesqwam above the windows and doors. At the south end, a square battlemented turret rose above the four round corner towers, each of which, with its slight batter in the walls, was surmounted by a cupola. The square tower was built directly adjoining the southwest corner tower. This four-storey tower, c. 32 m. high (approximately the same height as the great fallen stele at Aksum) remained the dominating structure of the whole complex of buildings, and from its flat roof opened an arch leading to a balcony overlooking the countryside to the west. Inside the square tower was the staircase. Opposite it to the northwest a smaller 'saddle' roofed chamber – a chapel with a vaulted roof – rose above the main entrance. On the ground floor, too, there were four entrances. As with the similar castle at Guzara (see below) defence does not seem to have been the prime object.

Apparently construction began around 1635/6. The castle was seen and much admired by the Yemeni ambassador to Gondar, Hassan b. Ahmad al-Haymi, in 1648, though it might have taken longer to complete in all its details. As we have seen, he reported that the builder was an Indian.

The main body of the building consists of a two-storey block measuring about 25 by 25 m. It was approached by an external staircase and landing on the north (northwest) side at first floor level, and another staircase on the northeast side. Within, spacious halls with high ceilings and large arched windows open into each other. The interior was ornamented with shaped wall niches, and alcoves outlined in the dark red Qwesqwam tufa, or decorative devices such as the Star of David. Doors and other wooden elements, now gone, may well have been decoratively carved. The castle was used by many subsequent emperors for state functions, and it may have been this castle that Iyasu II refurbished so lavishly. Doresse asks: 'was it this palace or that of Iyasu the Great that was the scene of the assassination of Tekla Haymanot II, where in the tumult that followed, as recorded in the chronicle, the huge mirrors were smashed to pieces?' The incident has already been related above, but it had no such fatal conclusion as the assassination of the king.

The corner towers were three-storeyed, linked by battlemented parapets. Wooden balconies enhanced the building's external appearance, and were employed for certain state appearances; one on the west side was reached by an arched outlet through the battlements from the roof. Tekla Haymanot I, when he learned that his father Iyasu I, then at Barkanta, had sent for him, feared to be imprisoned at Wahni and replaced by Dawit, his brother. He therefore allowed himself to be proclaimed from one of the balconies on the tower called *makhal gemb* in 1705; Iyasu II's coronation in 1730 seems to have taken place in the *makhal gemb*, which was in turn within the *mannagasha gemb*. Emperor Iyoas was proclaimed from *mannagasha gemb* – it seems that the *makhal gemb*, 'which is the Mannagasha', as Iyasu's chronicle elsewhere puts it, might be the specific name of the high square tower within the castle of Fasil.

There were guard barracks to one side of the castle, and, to the east, reached by steps between the castles of Fasiladas and Iyasu I, lay a large structure with a (now collapsed) vaulted roof and stone steps leading down inside. This is variously described as a bath house, or cistern, or fish pond. Water was channelled to this from the east side of the building. Enclosed and roofed as it was, it was most probably a cistern, dug to relieve the problem of the absence of a source on the castle plateau. It seems that such vaulted cisterns derived from the architecture of the Jesuits. They built one at Fremona, their centre in Tigray under the earlier emperors Minas and Sarsa Dengel, and copied it at Danqaz, where the cistern survives almost intact. There was another beside the Catholic church and patriarchal residence of Mendes, at Debsan east of the lake near Guzara and Emfraz.

South from the castle there extends a ruined structure with a half round tower in its west wall, and a very long but narrow hall. It terminates in a round tower in the compound wall itself by the Gate of the Judges. This was probably the tower known as Awaj Mangarya, where the herald made proclamations. The tower is now partly fallen.

Northeast of Iyasu's castle is another tiny castle – no more than a little round pepper-pot tower with some fallen attachments – also said to have been built by Fasiladas. If so, the castle of Iyasu I must later have been inserted between the two. This castle, where the king is supposed to have dwelt while the larger building was being completed, may be the one sometimes called the *enqulal gemb*, or 'Egg Castle', from its domed tower (Pankhurst 1982: 123. Pankhurst (p. 153) also employs this name when describing how Mentewab and Iyasu II climbed up to watch a military procession following the *tabot* of Iyasus of Qaha, for the tower 'at the top of the Fasiladas castle', although that is not a round domed tower, but square with a flat roof). Between the enclosure wall and the *Fasil gemb* are many other ruins, including the foundations of what was probably a round *tukul*, rather than a round church. Just possibly, this could be the ruins of the residence of Iyoas II and Gigar, described by Gobat. There is also a small bath house with domed and vaulted rooms, some pierced with holes; similar to the two so-called 'doro bet', or House of Hens, near the Bath of Fasiladas. On the other side of the *Fasil gemb*, near the buildings attributed to Sadik Yohannes (see below) are more substantial traces, including the imposing arched doorway to a now-vanished structure. These seem to be the remains of a huge hall for feasting, c. 39 by 14 m., with arches in red tufa, and with some decorative motifs built into the walls, which could perhaps, since the structure is completely ruined, be associated with the Jan Tekel tower. Much more of it survived in the middle of the last century, as can be seen in a photograph in Mathew (1947, opp. p. 38), including a second storey over one of the arches with a round-arched window in the usual Gondar style. Even earlier, in the nineteenth century, this same structure appears to be described by d'Abbadie as a banqueting and audience hall.

Library and chancellery of Sadik Yohannes Emperor Yohannes 'the Just' built, or is said to have built, two attractive small edifices to the northwest of his father's castle. There appears to be some uncertainty about the identification of them. The nearest (the so-called chancellery after Doresse, identified as the library by Pankhurst, Lindahl and Mathew, and by Doresse also in an ETO pamphlet) is also called the *fekr gemb*, or 'love castle'. This identification is uncertain, though it is known that a *fekr* (*feqr*) *gemb* already existed in 1707 at the beginning of the reign of Tekla Haymanot I, when it was used for a synod. In Iyasu II and Iyoas's reigns Gef'omu, Galasyos and Tekla Abib were created successively *azaj* of the *feqr gemb*.

The first of these two structures, the so-called 'library', is an elegant small square two-storey building with a battlemented parapet decorated with open-work red stone filling on the balustrade. On the ground floor are three rooms, the largest divided lengthways by an arcade. An exterior stairway provides access to the upper part. The façade facing Fasiladas' castle has two tall arched doorways on the ground floor, and a row of smaller windows with typical Gondar-style frames in red tufa on the first floor. It has been plastered with yellowish stucco over the grey stone, and is decorated with some carved cross motifs over the doors and windows. The façade facing towards the chancellery shows an irregular arrangement of doorways and windows, with a staircase leading up to the first floor. Mathew comments that this building has motifs of stucco in the interior possibly derived from Hispano–Moorish models; these are in the form of false windows. The structure is connected by a range of now-ruined buildings with the castles of Fasiladas and Iyasu I (see below). It was roofless and crumbling earlier this century, as old photographs show, but has now been restored. It is in the angle between this building and the castle of Fasiladas that the large ruined arched doorway stands, with a few other fragments of walls, the remains of some vanished building.

Northwest of the 'library' (perhaps, if correctly named, the *beta mangest*, a store place for the state archives?), and built at an angle to it, is another small but elegant building also of two storeys, with tall high-arched doorways on the ground floor with double red stone capitals. There are also arched upper windows on the first floor. This is the so-called 'chancellery'. Traces of beams indicate that once a wooden balcony gave south onto the space separating it from the castle of Fasiladas. A little two-storey tower, which apparently once had a small cupola on top, rises above the battlemented roof. The interior staircase in this tower is still in relatively good condition, but a round tower attached to the northeast corner has collapsed. An exterior staircase was also provided rising on the north and west sides to offer an excellent view over part of Gondar. The building is now empty and ruined, but has been restored to reasonable condition (for its earlier state see the photograph in Doresse 1959: 138). Mathew states that this building (which he calls the chancery) 'had an atrium carried on arches; we find shallow pilasters for the first time'. The sign on it today calls it, confusingly, the library of Fasil.

As we have noted, an Ethiopian (?) called Walda Giyorgis, who was later to build for Iyasu I, constructed at least part of the buildings erected for Yohannes I. Perhaps he was responsible for one or both of these two structures, if they really date to Yohannes' reign.

Castle of Iyasu I; Castle of the Saddle   A smaller (24 by 14 m.) but still imposing castle was (apparently) constructed by Yohannes' son and successor Iyasu I, called the Great, directly beside his grandfather Fasiladas' larger edifice, slightly to the northeast. The resemblance between the two is close, and indeed the smaller castle is often considered as a mere adjunct to the larger one. Iyasu's castle is a rectangular two-storey building with a battlemented square tower, now fallen, but conjectured to have been crowned with a cupola at the southwest end. A very unusual feature is the round tower with a curving red stone exterior staircase of twenty-six steps mounting round it up to the first floor at the north end of the building. It also provides admittance into a first floor chamber in the northwest tower, which is crowned by a vaulted or 'saddle' roofed chapel, explaining the name sometimes given to this edifice – the Castle of the Saddle. The towers are linked by battlemented parapets. In the walls, at both ground and first floor levels, are tall window or doorway openings with arches of red stone springing from double capitals. Inside, there is a vestibule leading by an arched doorway into a spacious main room. The walls are pierced with rows of slots indicating where the beams to take the first floor, and the roof beams, were inserted. This castle was bombed during the British drive to force the Italians out of Ethiopia during the Second World War.

This may be the castle at Gondar called Geseñña in Iyasu's chronicle. It was described as 'the Geseñña, of admirable construction; for the roof was of mirrors and crystal ('fendjal', perhaps porcelain inlay?); it was square, with doors at its corners, and on the top seven sandaq' – seven flags (Budge), or seven gilded globes surmounted by crosses (Doresse) – *sandaq* means standard. On the feast of the Cross in 1703, after the dances in the *beta dabal* (see below) Emperor Iyasu sat here while a feast was prepared for the clergy:

> He commanded that the tent of Gimja be raised at the door, and in that house [apparently the Geseñña mentioned just before] he set up a dining table for the clergy with honour, and in the tent, for the dignitaries ... Later, he set up yet another table in the middle of the square, from the tent to the door of the house called haykal, and from another of its doors which is towards the east, until the enclosure which is near the church of St. George, and from the third door which is towards the south until the enclosure of the anqatsa argab (the gate of pigeons), and from the fourth door until the enclosure which is near the beta tazkaro [the House of Funeral Commemorations].

This description is a little confusing, but it clearly indicates that Geseñña was in Gondar. Mathew mistakenly envisages Geseñña as the summer palace that Iyasu maintained on an island in Lake Tana. He describes dramatically how Iyasu 'was stabbed by the queen's officers, and finally shot with muskets by two Mohammedan soldiers. He fell dead on the divan in his summer palace, his broken body mirrored in the ceiling of glass and porcelain.' The chronicles record that Iyasu was murdered on the island of Shaqla Manzo, where his palace and other buildings, of typical Gondarine style, still exist in a ruined state.

Possibly part of Iyasu's castle comprised the state apartments where, his chronicle records, he retired to fast every year in the month of Nahase: 'The king distanced himself from all the people of the city, and entered into the private part of his inner apartments, or elfeñ, which is situated near the part of his private apartment called aday, to observe the fast of the month of nahase'. Iyasu had another (?) set of private apartments, mentioned in his chronicle as the place where the office of metropolitan was handed over to Bishop Marqos in September 1689: 'in his private apartments of the Hashawa'. Is this the *masari*, opening onto the *ashawa*?

Adjoining the castle by a staircase is another substantial block of buildings, still intact, with a two-storey gate dividing them through which one can pass from the open area northwest of Iyasu's castle, to that in front of Fasiladas' castle. These buildings, which preserve several arched entranceways, are also linked to the so-called *feqr gemb* attributed to Emperor Yohannes, and to the complex of ruins between Iyasu's and Fasiladas' castles. Stairs still lead up from the ground to the roof, whence one can look across more ruins to the northeast towards Dawit II's Zofan Bet. Below are some small vaulted rooms.

Throne Hall ('House of Song') of Dawit II   Emperor Dawit II (1716–21), son of Iyasu I and successor to the usurper Yostos (1711–16), is said to have built the spacious throne hall some way to the north of the cluster of buildings erected by his predecessors. The building atributed to Dawit II is often called the 'House of Song', apparently through an error, *zafan bet* for *zofan bet* (*zofan* indicating the low divan used at this time in Ethiopia, in eastern fashion, as a throne). Following this error, Mathew refers to the building romantically as the 'Pavilion of Gladness', and the *Guida* designates it *Casa del Canto*.

This building lay, it seems, in its own walled compound, only traces of which now remain among the other ruins in this area. During the troubles caused by Emperor Bakaffa's long invisibility inside the palace, when people began to think he was dead, it is stated in the abbreviated chronicle that the governor of Gondar, *Blattengeta* Kucho, had 'walled round the audience chamber', possibly erecting a defensive wall around this building of Dawit's. It is difficult to be sure which structure is meant, since more than one hall was used as an audience chamber or throne hall. In Bruce's book, the 'Preface to the History of Abyssinia' (written not by Bruce himself, but by his editor, Alexander Murray), listing the royal servants, mentions 'The Bajerund of the Zefan bet, or grand presence chamber, who keeps the crown, and oversees the decoration of the royal apartments'. The preparations made for the *zofan bet* and the *anbasa bet*, cited above from the *Ser'ata Mangest*, make it clear that these two halls were indeed 'presence chambers' for royal receptions. Bakaffa on one occasion held the ceremony of installation of Mammo, son of Gabra Krestos, as *Tigray makwennen*, in the Zofan Bet. Other ceremonies that took place in the presence chambers were more bizarre. In 1726 Bakaffa gave audience 'with great majesty', and the brave men of Amhara and Begemder 'threw down the genitalia of the uncircumcised' before him, *Dejazmach* Wadaje also sent similar trophies, some loaded onto a horse, others carried on a litter by two young men. After viewing the trophies, the king announced the appointment of Hellawe Krestos as *dejazmach* of Semien.

A substantial one-storey building with a round tower at the southeast corner, Dawit II's hall still survives in a roofless state in the centre of the compound. There are traces of a smaller ruined round tower at the northeast corner, beside a small square building now completely ruined. Attached to the northwest corner, at an angle, are traces of a square tower, most of which has collapsed. The usual arched windows and doorways provided light and access to the vestibule and single long hall within. This imposing hall may have been the 'Zeffan Bet' which, according to Bruce, was burned during the rebellion against Iyasu II. The walls could easily have remained standing while the roof and interior fittings burned.

Jean Doresse, in an ETO brochure, called this structure 'Debbal-Guémb', the name Lefebvre bestows instead on the Fasil Gemb. Such a *dabal bet* is mentioned in the chronicles, even before Dawit II's reign. Thus in 1698, Dawit's father Iyasu I celebrated the Feast of the Glorious Cross for eight consecutive days in the *dabal bet*, a name which Guidi explains as 'l'apartement de l'assemblée'. The emperor permitted all the dignitaries to enter into his private apartments to entertain them in the *dabal bet* for this period. In 1703, after the celebrations for the Holy Cross in the Addebabai, the king went to watch the soldiers dancing in the *beta dabal*. An assembly of dignitaries was also held there. The next day the king remained in the *geseñña*.

Not surprisingly, if it was a throne hall, there was already a Zofan Bet in existence before Dawit II built his. In the chronicle of Iyasu I, Dawit's father, it is recorded that the king gave judgement in litigation between the *pasha* (11th in precedence) and the *bajerond* of the *zofan bet* (22nd in precedence). The matter in question concerned court procedure – the way the charge of chamberlain should be filled in the king's house from the *madab* (a stone seat at the entry), when the king was present in the *zofan bet*. It was resolved by the decision that the *pasha* was in charge from dawn to dusk, and the *bajerond* from dusk to dawn. It seems from the use of the two different designations in Iyasu's chronicle that the *dabal bet* and the *zofan bet* were, at least then, two different structures.

In Iyasu II's chronicle, in a none-too-clear passage, the empress and Iyasu II summon the *liq* and the *azaj* to the *dabal bet gemb*. But later, the rebel soldiers are recorded as seizing 'robes of brocade, carpets and swords … leaving only the gemb, since it was impossible for them [to carry it off]'.

Might this indicate that in Iyasu II's time the *dabal bet* was an impermanent structure, a tent for the storage of precious objects?

Smaller buildings There were many minor buildings in the palace compound. It is difficult, or impossible, to identify them with any particular ruin today. Many such structures were doubtless constructed of perishable materials, others were tents. The use of different structures changed, too, over the years.

The House of Espousals (*qwali gemb*, or *qwali bet*, House of Kohl) by the Qwali (Kualhi) gate, east of Dawit's throne hall, is said to have been built by Fasiladas (Pankhurst 1982: 123) or by Dawit II for use during royal weddings. It is a two-story structure with a square tower, now ruined, but once not inelegant. Another name, and another purpose, suggested for the building was the *duqet gemb*, or Flour Building.

The ceremonies for the celebration of royal marriages are described in the *Ser'ata Mangest*. These were important occasions, since it was the children of the princesses who formed the core of the higher echelons of the government. They could not succeed to the throne (the usurpation of Yostos was the sole exception) and so were not condemned to be shut up on an *amba* for the rest of their lives like the direct male descendants of kings. A princess who was to be married would be seated in the king's presence, on a Sunday, ornamented with golden jewellery, clad in white silk, and wearing a coronet. The husband would arrive, dressed in a caftan, and take his wife away to the place arranged by the king to the sound of flutes and drums. For a bride who was the daughter of the emperor, the house would be decorated with various hangings of cloth called *tasawre*, *arwe* and *sora*, and carpets were laid down. The husband would enter, and after ten days be received by the king and given a robe of honour.

Fasiladas is also supposed to have erected a two-towered structure called *waraqat gemb*, an archive or secretariat (Pankhurst 1982: 123–4, citing Ghiorghis Mellesa's account of the legends of Gondar). Perhaps the *waraqat gemb* is actually identical with the small castle of Fasiladas, or with Yohannes I's 'library'. Evidently a *bet afras* or stable already existed when Yohannes I succeeded to the throne, since his chronicle states that he was fetched from it.

North of Dawit II's throne-hall is a complex of buildings including the so-called *anbasa bet*, or House of Lions, an exotic-sounding name that recalls the fact that the emperors often took chained lions with them on their expeditions. Although there must have been some structure where the beasts were accommodated, it seems that this name *anbasa bet* actually referred to the imperial private apartments. The vaulted and barred arched structure still exhibited as a lion house could perhaps have been a menagerie, attached to the private apartments. To the south of the *zofan bet* is a compound with buildings also sometimes identified as a menagerie, with a small house for the keeper of the wild beasts nearby. The so-called *Casa del Belluario* (*Guida*) south of Dawit's hall is a small structure consisting of several little rooms. One longer one is barrel vaulted, and two other very small ones have their vaults pieced with little holes, like the possible bath houses elsewhere in the compound and to the south on the hillside near the Bath of Fasiladas. Outside, there are three open vaults.

Bruce stated that the *anbasa bet* was where the coronation was performed, and the regalia kept. From the details of its preparation supplied by the *Ser'ata Mangest*, it seems that it acted as some kind of presence chamber as well. The 'lion' of the name therefore perhaps symbolises royalty, the emperor being 'the Lion of the Tribe of Judah'. When listing the royal household officers, Murray's 'Preface' in Bruce's book adds, after the title 'The Bajerund of the Lion's House', that four lions accompanied the royal camp, and that they were kept near the common prison. It also states that in the tented camps the lions were chained 'in a place called Anbasa-bet', adding, in reference to Aksum, that 'the Anbasa-bet is still distinguished in the ruins of that city' (see below for Francisco Alvares' mention of this structure in Aksum). In the plan of the royal tented camp supplied by Taddesse Tamrat in his book *Church and State in Ethiopia, 1270–1527*, the lions' cage is marked to the west of the royal tents between the 'Church of Justice' and the 'Church of the Market Square'. However, although the plan of the camp has a very broad resemblance to the later plan of Gondar, in the sense of a royal enclosure with a gate, a *saqala* tent, churches, the *abun*'s tent, queen's tents, a Gemja Maryam gate and so on, other names of the gates and the tents differ to a large degree and the city was apparently not designed to follow the plan of the camp in detail. Or, if it were at one time intended to resemble the camp, it was later to develop in a very different way.

Other lesser buildings in the imperial compound were the *warq saqala*, the gold house (or tent) and the *gemja bet*, identified as a treasury or brocade house, the wardrobe. *Warq saqala* is often translated to mean treasury. Bruce mentions that the 'Werk Sacala' was one of the buildings burned in Iyasu II's time in the revolt and siege of the imperial citadel. In Bakaffa's chronicle it figures as a place for festive banquets, on one occasion under the supervision of the *Azaj* Iyose, 'to whom this secret regarding the private apartments had been confided'. It is also mentioned as an audience hall, 'the central house, the Warq Saqala, which is surrounded on one side by the Addarash and the other by the Rasge bet'. It was in 'this sweet-smelling house', the Warq Saqala, when the tables had been prepared, that *Sahafe Te'azaz* Sinoda was ordered to read aloud the chronicle he had written of Bakaffa's reign, and to add it to those of his grandfather and father, Yohannes and Iyasu. Bakaffa is also recorded as having (re?)built a church dedicated to Mary 'near his royal house Rasge and the Addarash Saqala, and renewed the enclosure that had fallen into ruin'.

In the above-mentioned 'Preface' in Bruce's book the Warq Saqala is regarded also as a place for the sitting of a court of justice. When describing the royal regiments it is noted that their names derived from the place where they were stationed: 'Thus one regiment is called Gimja-bet, because it was stationed at the treasury-house; another, Werk-sacala, because placed near the court of justice ... Zefan-bet, the regiment of the banqueting house; and so on according to the names of the royal apartments.'

Alvares noted that each church tent in the camp was accompanied by a vestment store, and another tent for the 'fire and the corn for making the Corbon', the *qwerban* or host. These were the equivalent of the *eqa bet* and *beta lahm* in normal churches. In front of the church tents were other tents 'big, long and fully extended as though they were halls. They call these Balagamias. In them they keep the Prester's clothes, belongings and treasures.' These were the *gemja bet*, presided over by a *ba'ala gemja*. As the 'Preface' to Bruce's book noted, they were supplied with corps of guards. Most of these guards, Alvares tells us, were eunuchs.

Describing the royal camp, the 'Preface' to Bruce's work (following Alvares) mentions that the 'Saccala', with seats for twelve judges, was a large square tent located 'two shots of a cross bow from the eastern gate of the king's inclosure'. Alvares described the royal camp, with its palisade (*jagual* or *jagol* in Amharic), 'within which were many tents pitched, and a big long house of one story thatched with straw, in which they said the Prester sometimes stayed'. This would, according to his editors, have been the *saqala*. Alvares, however, also notes that the 'tent of justice' was 'a long tent ... which they call cacalla ... in it are thirteen plain chairs of iron and leather, and one of these is very high ... The ... judges do not sit in them; these chairs are only for ceremony, and they sit on the ground.'

The *saqala* as it is described in the *Ser'ata Mangest* was certainly a court-room, whether it was in the imperial city or in the camp. It is mentioned many times. If a princess brought an accusation her guard (*wa'ali*) went to the *saqala*; if it were a princess who was the accused, her *raq masare* appeared on her behalf in the *saqala* before the *azaj*, the judges. One of the two *behtwaded*, or in his absence the *blattengeta*, and the *azaj*, sat in the tribunal of the *saqala*. When the king held an audience of justice, the judges of the right and left in the *saqala* intoned certain chants of Yared: 'On the day of retribution, on the day of Judgement, on the day of the Lord, what shall we say to the soul, when the mother cannot save her son, and the earth gives up what is deposited in it?' with the response 'Better that a man have mercy on the poor, and perform good deeds'. This was repeated thrice. The text was expounded by high-ranking ecclesiastics, the *seraj masare* and the *liqa dabtara*. No one summoned to justice could be seated, not even a *behtwaded* or a *dejazmach*. Only the sick, women or church dignitaries, or the *nebura'ed* of Aksum by a special dispensation, were granted this privilege.

The *saqala* is mentioned, too, in the chronicle of Baeda Maryam (1468–78). Not long after he had succeeded to the throne he went to his father's capital of Debra Berhan for the feast of the Cross, where he revealed himself unveiled to the people and visited the churches. He went to the *saqala*, and then processed round the fire lit for the festival. Later, building the church called Atronsa Egzietna Maryam, the king sat beneath an olive tree watching from within a veil as the trees were cut and the land prepared. Then a large *saqala* was erected, ornamented with silk, into which the *tabot* of Maryam was introduced. *Saqala* in this text, written in the early sixteenth century, seems to mean simply a royal or ecclesiastical building, of the sort illustrated by the contemporary account of Alvares, and later in the eighteenth century accounts of Bakaffa's receptions in the *addarash saqala*.

When Baeda Maryam had performed the ceremonies at the feast of the Cross, he returned to his dwelling (or chamber, *serh*; the *saqala*?) and ordered that the treasures in the *nazret bet*, the *mangest bet*, the *barakat bet* and the *gadal bet* be sent to Gasambe in Shewa for security. All these structures were presumably storage buildings, or tents, in Debra Berhan, and similar structures were to be found in royal encampments and in Gondar. In Zara Yaqob's chronicle it is specified that 'the revenues, the beautiful objects, and the things which were useful were kept in the Nazret Bet; things which were not of use were put in the Barakat Bet'. It would be intriguing to know what exactly met the necessary criteria for storage in the *barakat bet*, the House of Blessings. Silks and other cloths were kept in the *mangest bet*, which was also used as a prison in Baeda Maryam's time, and later. Alvares notes that in the camp of Lebna Dengel, in front of the 'cacalla', 'there are two tents or houses like prisons, which are called *manguez bet*'. It could also be an archive of sorts. When *Ras* Mikael burned the *mangest bet* at Gondar, the books of the kings stored there were destroyed.

The *rasge bet* is also often mentioned in chronicles, and in the *Ser'ata Mangest*. It may have been, as Pankhurst suggests, not a precursor of the *ras gemb* outside the walls (described below), but one of the many smaller structures within the *makkababya*. Emperor Iyasu received dignitaries there in 1698 to listen to the accused in an inept-sounding case of high treason, and Emperor Bakaffa would sometimes feast there (see below). He also used it as a judgement hall when the case of the rebel Elfyos was heard in 1729. When a new *echege* was enthroned, the king would present him with new garments of office in the *rasge bet*. The king sat in the *dabana* (a round tent) – perhaps this applied only in the camp, and not at Gondar, or was the *rasge bet* always a tent at this time? – while the new *echege* was enthroned before him. So important was the office that the king crowned the *echege* with his own crown. Then, the investiture over, he escorted him to the door, as a sign of great honour. The *echege* departed on a royal mule to the sound of flutes and, another sign of the highest honour, *deb anbasa*, the great royal drum, was beaten. A new *aqabe sa'at*, too, was presented with robes, his face veiled with muslin, in the *rasge bet*. He was then seated on a throne, but in this case the king was not present, and the *aqabe sa'at* was escorted away by the magistrates.

Castle of Bakaffa   Along one part of the compound wall in the northwest, forming part of the compound wall and overlooking the open space outside, Emperor Asma Giyorgis, who bore the personal name of Bakaffa or the 'Inexorable', built (or is said to have built) a vast hall for feasts with a round tower at the east end. The emperor's generosity in feasting his people is recorded in his chronicle:

> Behold his constant habit. Dinner time arrived, the king stayed seated on a decorated throne. Then the king's table was prepared in an apartment; the Rasge bet, or the Danqaz Gimb, or the Warq Saqala, or the central Warq Saqala, or the Molale Gimb, or in the Hadas Shashena which he built in this month (August–September 1725) and which has paintings inside and out. Before him, the table azmatch was laid.

Azmach, 'the General' was apparently a table of such imposing dimensions that it earned a personal name.

It seems that all these structures must have been at Gondar, the Danqaz palace having been built over a century before and apparently not used since Susneyos' time. As we have seen, among the places put into readiness for defence in Iyasu II's time was the *danqaz gemb*, listed among the other Gondar palaces. However, since on one occasion the *shalaqa* Tekla Haymanot was created 'azaj of Qaha, of the danqaz gemb', according to Iyasu II's chronicle, it is perhaps not inconceivable that *danqaz gemb* was a name for one of the structures near the river, perhaps even the structure we now call the Bath of Fasiladas? In Iyasu II's time the rebel Tasfa Mammo was incarcerated in the Danqaz Gemb by *Shalaqa* Tekla Haymanot. Other (?) structures at Qaha are mentioned when Iyasu II stayed at Qaha in 1745. He slept in the *la'lay bet*, the upper or high house, and certain Balaw with their camels remained in the *manquit gemb*, received there by *Azaj* Tekla Haymanot.

Bakaffa's huge single-storey battlemented building has now been re-roofed in concrete. It consists of a single enormous room – banqueting hall, in all probability – oriented east–west, with three high red stone arched entrances on the south side, and windows on the north side. The north wall of the castle forms the wall of the imperial compound itself at this point. At the east end, where the compound wall turns north, there is another smaller attached building, a small and elegant castle with arched red stone windows and balcony on its west wall, and an arched gate below. On the first floor, facing north, are four red stone arches, two of them windows. A further round tower forms part of the compound wall to the north. The long hall attributed to Bakaffa is joined to the west by a smaller transverse structure with four doorways of red Qwesqwam stone, one in each wall. This vestibule links the long hall with another long wing opposite, thus enclosing on three sides a long trapezoidal courtyard. This subordinate wing with many plain arched doorways along its inner (courtyard) side seems to have been a *faras bet* or stable block for the emperor's horses and mules. (There was a corps of guard named *faras bet*, and a quarter of the city was called Faras in Iyasu II's time.) All the buildings are battlemented, with a string-course laid at a slightly lower level than the battlements. The ensemble presents today a sombre, massive appearance, but perhaps in its heyday, plastered and painted, it might have had a lighter air.

Possibly the long hall of Bakaffa was the hall called Hadas Shashana in the chronicles? Pankhurst prefers identification with a second structure noted in the chronicle, built by Bakaffa in 1726 near the *rasge* and the *addarash saqala*.

Bakaffa is the stuff of legend among the Gondarine kings, a sort of Harun al-Rashid of Ethiopia. Accordingly, the round tower of the long hall that flanks the Ergeb (Regev) Ber, the Gate of the Pigeons, is said to be where this emperor invoked the Devil, and surveyed the stars.

Castle of Empress Mentewab   The latest of the castles – if we believe the usual attributions for the structures at Gondar – was built by Empress Mentewab, wife of Bakaffa, or perhaps built for her by her son Iyasu II. After Bakaffa's death *Itege* Mentewab acted as regent for her son Iyasu II and later for her grandson Iyoas, and so long remained a prominent figure at Gondar. The castle lies next to and north of the long hall attributed to her husband right at the north end of the compound.

A very elegant castle of two stories, it may have been the last substantial structure built at Gondar, constructed about 1750 before the empress retired outside the city to her new palace at Qwesqwam. The western façade – the original part, most of the rest having been reconstructed by the Italians – has three arched doors on the ground floor, and three arched windows on the floor above with a long wooden balcony. Above is a square tower with a balconied window, and a further balcony at roof level. As usual on these castles, external string-courses mark the floor levels within. The main building and the tower are battlemented, and another small square corner tower to the east is topped with a cupola. The castle has a certain delicacy, when compared with those of Fasiladas, Iyasu I, or Bakaffa. There is some decorative work, consisting of blind arches and sculpted crosses, in the wall, just as at Qwesqwam. Triple-layer arches are employed over the doors and windows. Access to the upper floor is by a walkway from the level of the park on the south, or by a monumental staircase descending on the east side to the lower level. Access to the exterior is by the court of the Ras Ber, in which is the battlemented two-storey House of the Commander of the Cavalry. This, essentially a gatehouse with an external staircase and an arched gateway, is the northern-most stucture of the compound, facing the *ras gemb* (Palace of the Ras) outside the compound.

The interior of 'Mentewab's palace' has now been restored for use as offices. Doresse adds that when Bruce saw this castle the interior was still furnished. He is supposed to have noted great chests of cedar wood, and, in between the window bays, brackets evidently intended for wall mirrors that never arrived – I cannot trace this reference in Bruce.

As noted above, a building constructed nearby, a little to the south of the palace, is said to have been a bath house. Traces of flues can be seen in the walls, and the vault is pierced with holes, doubtless for steam to escape. The small rooms apparently formed a variety of Turkish bath, prescribed as a useful treatment for certain illnesses. From here a staircase descends to the lower garden and ground floor of the castle attributed to Mentewab. There is also a house supposedly the dwelling of a former servant of the empress, an Armenian – possibly that of T'ovmacean himself or his predecessor?

Ras Gemb, or Castle of Mikael Sehul Symbolising the power of the great *ras* of Tigray, Mikael Sehul, husband of Princess Aster or Esther, Empress Mentewab's daughter by her second husband Iyasu, this small but strong and well-built castle stands at a discreet but easily accessible distance overlooking the imperial compound from the north. Its position reflects the tutelage of the great *ras*es over the puppet emperors of the *zamana mesafint*. The Ras Gemb could, perhaps, date from Fasiladas' time (Pankhurst 1982: 124). It may be the official residence associated with the great office of *behtwaded*, called the 'house of the government of the *behtwadad*'. Alterna-tively, the castle was perhaps built at the time when Iyasu I for the first time created an imperial *ras*, a sort of commander-in-chief and governor of Gondar. Such a building – perhaps it was at this time the *rasge bet* inside the com-pound? – is mentioned in the chronicle of Bakaffa, when Tasfa Iyasus was made *bitwoded*, and entered 'into the house and rank' of the former *bitwoded* Eraqlis. It was to this title that Emperor Iyoas raised Mikael Sehul. The *Ser'ata Mangest* records that the duties of the two officers of this rank, of the Right and Left, were in the one case to lead the imperial forces in battle, while the other remained 'guarding the kingdom' and presiding over justice in the *saqala*. The two *behtwaded* acted, in modern terms, more or less as field marshal and prime minister.

Even though he did not build it, this castle is intimately associated with Mikael Sehul, who apparently lived in it when resident at Gondar. Bruce visited him here in 1770–71. Here, in 1769, as the *ras* sat on the balcony, an Armenian is supposed to have shot at him from the neighbouring imperial compound, from a window opening directly towards the *ras*'s house. If this is true, and the *ras*'s house was actually this one, the shot must have come from the direction of Mentewab's castle or one of its auxiliary structures, or perhaps from the small building adjoining Bakaffa's castle. Given the distance and the angle it is almost impossible to imagine that a gun of that time could have shot so far or so accurately. An early photograph (Pankhurst and Gérard 1996: 89) clearly shows the distance between the castle of Bakaffa and Mentewab, and the Ras Gimb intervening area at that time was completely unencumbered. Perhaps the *ras* was then residing in another building in the palace complex. The *ras* was unharmed, but his dwarf, who was fanning him, was killed. This incident – instigated by Emperor Iyoas, according to a page later questioned by *Ras* Mikael – was the culminating point of the developing distrust between the ruler and the great vassal he had summoned to help him. The result was Iyoas' murder the very night of the page's confession, and the installation of an aged and unwilling prince, hastily brought from Wahni, as Emperor Yohannes II. This assassination ushered in the *zemana mesafint*.

The *ras gemb* is basically a square two-storey block with two round corner towers to the west built with the characteristic slight batter of Gondarine round towers. One has a saddle roof, the other a round dome. A two-storey battlemented tower with wooden balconies rises above the castle's flat crenellated roof. Red stone arched doors and windows, balconies, string courses, and cupolas on the round towers soften the castle's appearance. There was an external staircase, as so frequently in these Gondarine structures. It appears to have been almost a total ruin before the restorations of the mid-century, when it was put into order to serve as a vice-regal residence for the Italians during the occupation (1935–41). Subsequently it was used by Emperor Haile Sellassie when he visited the town. A picture of it as it was in 1947 is included in Mathew's book (after p. 54), erroneously labelled as Fasiladas' castle.

Bath of Fasiladas   Northwest of the castles, in the Qaha valley a little over halfway to Qwesqwam, is the small structure traditionally called the Bath of Fasiladas. Some have suggested that it was actually built by Iyasu II, but Doresse considered that it dated back to the origins of Gondar, being built on the spot where legend says that Fasiladas, while hunting buffalo, came across a hermit who exhorted him to found a city here, in this place whose name began with G. This seems not improbable. Charles Jacques Poncet, residing in Gondar briefly in 1700 during Iyasu I's reign, mentions that during the Epiphany ceremony, when the people bathe in memory of Jesus' baptism, 'the Emperor goes with all his court to Kaa; which is a palace not far from Gondar, where there is a magnificent bason of water which serves for that pious ceremony'. Doubtless this was the Bath of Fasiladas, in the Qaha valley, existing well before the time of Iyasu II. Nowadays there is a large sports stadium next to the pavilion. Even so, the place still has an extraordinary charm. An irregular-shaped walled compound with a two-storey gate-house, six pepper-pot guard towers, and a two-storey stable building, shaded with olive and other trees, shields the pavilion from view.

Inside the walled compound a large basin, c. 50 by 30 m., has been excavated to form a pool, walled round and with broad surrounding steps forming a terrace. Particularly attractive is the way in which the roots of some of the splendid trees in the inner compound have flowed over the walls, offering the same impression of mixed stone and sinuous roots as can be seen on some of the jungle-invaded terraces at Angkor Wat in Cambodia. Small steps lead down into the pool from the surrounding terrace. From the front, an arched bridge leads over the water to a two-storey pavilion built on solid arched supports standing in the pool itself.

The façade consists of a central entrance door from the bridge, flanked by two windows, all arched with red stone and with white stone jambs. Above the doorway is a wooden balcony with a similar doorway, and another doorway to the left opens from the upper storey onto the roof parapet. At the rear there is a long balcony with window and doorway at the lower level, over-looking the lake, and a smaller balcony at the upper level. All these windows and doors are also ornamented with red stone arches and white jambs. Stairs inside lead to the upper story, really no more than a small tower, battlemented as usual. Further external stairs ascend to the roof.

In this attractive building, the ceremonies of Timqat or Epiphany are held in mid-January, and it is probably for this reason that the pavilion was constructed originally. However, it must also have furnished a marvellously tranquil temporary retreat for the emperors, away from the cares of state, yet easily accessible from Gondar. Bruce writes that Emperor Tekla Haymanot II came to the Qaha (Kaha) to celebrate Epiphany, setting up his tents there and

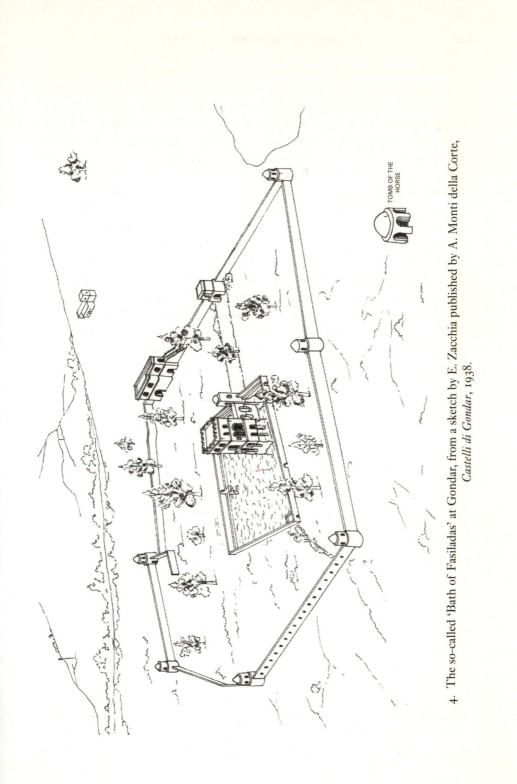

TOMB OF THE HORSE

4. The so-called 'Bath of Fasiladas' at Gondar, from a sketch by E. Zacchia published by A. Monti della Corte, *Castelli di Gondar*, 1938.

receiving state visitors. He drew in the 'King's palace on the river Kaha' on his map, and this is probably the same as the Bath of Fasiladas, although he indicates it a little to the northeast of the castles. Bruce's map, however, if turned a little to adjust the directions, actually fits quite well with the reality. In the time of Solomon II (1769–79), according to Doresse (ETO brochure), the pavilion was transformed into a church dedicated to St Fasiladas.

Outside the compound to the northeast stands a circular pavilion of plastered masonry, merely a cupola supported on arches. It is popularly called the 'Tomb of the Horse', but may have actually served as a royal reviewing stand for musterings of troops. Sylvia Pankhurst tells the story of Suviel, or Zubel, the horse supposedly buried under it. He belonged to Iyasu II (or, according to Doresse, to 'Iyasou le Grand', Iyasu I; or, according to the *Guida*, Yohannes I). During a campaign to Sinnar the horse was captured. He refused his fodder, and was too fierce to ride, so the king of Sinnar decided to kill him. However, an Ethiopian prince (the young Iyasu I in disguise in the *Guida*'s version) was able to master him, and fleeing away escaped back to Ethiopia. On reaching home, exhausted, Suviel dropped dead, and was buried under this pavilion by his grieving master.

Between the Bath of Fasiladas and the imperial compound, to the left as one leaves the former, on the right hand side of the road, is another stone building of the same period as the palaces, oddly named the House of Hens (*doro bet*). Like others in the city, including a near neighbour by Qaha Iyasus church (see below), and three buildings already described in the imperial compound, it is a low structure with several small vaulted rooms with round roof openings. At one end there are the ruins of a two-storey tower with an arched window on the first floor. A side room has a doorway with a squared 'arch' composed of three red stones. There is exactly the same sort of doorway in a similar bath house on the island of Entons, in Lake Tana, a place where Emperor Iyasu I, perhaps suffering again from the skin disease that Poncet had treated earlier, went several times in 1705 to bathe in a *beta belané*, or bath house (Dombrowski 1983: 237–9). The building is sometimes described as a place for rearing the birds destined for the royal table, or, alternatively, considering its isolated position, as a steam bath for the cure of contagious diseases (Doresse, ETO brochure). It certainly resembles in some respects the other supposed bath houses; an imperial chicken-house seems somewhat unlikely.

Churches in the Imperial Compound Emperor Fasiladas is said to have built seven churches at Gondar (see below for five of them). It is said, not implausibly in view of the extreme religiosity of many of the emperors, that they liked to be able to see a church from every window of their palaces. In addition, the church tents used on campaign were probably disposed around the castles. These were as follows: Jesus of the Camp, instituted by Amda Seyon; the Shield of Salvation chapel of Sayfa Arad; the two chapels which housed the enormously revered fragment of the True Cross, and the Kwerata Reesu (an icon of Christ with the crown of thorns), the first established in Dawit II's time; and the chapel of Mary the Virgin, first established by Zara Yaqob.

Gemjabet Maryam (Treasury of Mary) This church lies west of the buildings of Yohannes I in a separate compound included within the outer wall of the main compound. It was originally constructed by Emperor Fasiladas, possibly to house the *tabot* of the camp church of Mary noted above, which in Sarsa Dengel's chronicle is also called Gemja Bet Maryam. It is indicated in the *Guida* as only a fragmentary ruin, but now there is a restored structure on the site, a round church of the usual type. It is occasionally noted in the chronicles as a burial place; the *Azaj* Fasil was buried there in 1767, for example.

The church possesses some nineteenth-century paintings. A picture of the Virgin supposedly painted using the tears of Emperor Yohannes the Just is kept here in the sanctuary. There is also a processional picture of St Mary with the emperors Fasiladas and Iyasu I, the former holding a pearl said to have passed down from emperor to emperor as a symbol of sovereignty. In the compound behind the church is the plain rectangular tomb with a cross carved on the top, where the British consul Walter Charles Metcalf Plowden, who was killed in the time of Emperor Tewodros II, is buried.

Arnauld d'Abbadie describes a church of 'Notre-Dame', adjacent to the enclosure of the imperial palace at Gondar:

> Exceptionally it is built using lime. Despite its Ethiopian style, its materials, the good proportions of its parts, indicate that it is the work of experienced workmen. It is said that an emperor had it constructed by Portuguese workers and enriched it with so much ornamentation that it was given the name, still popular, of the House of silk. Its splendour has disappeared since the fall of the empire; one can see, perfectly preserved, the interior paintings, representing all the events of the parricidal war that Rougoum (accursed) Tekla Haymanot conducted with his father Iyasu the Great ... one can see also the death of the parricide, assassinated while hunting a little after ascending the throne. The neighbouring quarter composing the parish is nearly entirely destroyed ... the dilapidated palace, empty and silent, standing amid its deserted courts, seems to spread its melancholy shade over this church.

Asasame Qeddus Mikael (St Michael the Gracious) Asasame Qeddus Mikael, or Debra Gannat church, stands in its own compound within the imperial compound, east of Bakaffa's hall. The Imbilta Ber originally gave access to this compound, now entered from the north by a gate beside the House of the Commander of the Cavalry. According to the abbreviated chronicle the church was dedicated by Emperor Dawit II in 1717. A church of St Mikael is recorded as being burned down in the fifth year of Bakaffa's reign, but it is not necessarily this one that is meant. Among many other court figures, *Bajerond* Asahel was buried here in 1748, in Iyasu II's reign, as was princess Emmaya in 1750.

Asasame Qeddus Mikael is an oblong building with three piers in each of the four side walls supporting the four double arches of each façade, each with a stone capital at the spring of the arch. A western portico facing the Elfiñ Ber is flanked by two round towers (one ruined) in the style of the Gondar castles. The portico, entered by a door beside the northwest tower, is now undergoing repairs. Two further round towers are today indicated by the remains of their bases by the northeastern and southeastern corners of the church; after destruction, the church was rebuilt, as with so many Gondar churches, in a more modest fashion, occupying only part of its original space. Modern pillars support part of the roof on three sides. The *maqdas*, in the square main part of the church, is also square. The superior of this church, in the fashion of the time in Gondar, was given the title *male'aka gannat*, 'angel of Paradise'.

Elfiñ (Ilfin) Giyorgis Directly south of Asasame Qeddus Mikael a small adjoining compound by the Qwali Ber encloses the little round church of Elfiñ Giyorgis, said to have been built originally by Fasiladas. The name is often translated as 'St George in my House', but seems to indicate rather 'the church of St George by the Elfiñ Ber', or 'by the *elfiñ* (imperial private apartments)'. The church was also sometimes called Makkababya Giyorgis, St George of the Enclosure. Today the compound enclosing this small round tin-roofed church is entered by a double gateway at the end of a small side alley running along beside the south wall of the Asasame Qeddus Mikael church compound.

Churches Associated with the Imperial Compound

ADDEBABAI IYASUS (CHURCH OF JESUS OF THE ADDEBABAI) Addebabai refers to the esplanade or open space in front of the imperial citadel. The Jesus church lay south of the castles and Addebabai Tekla Haymanot church, in the neighbourhood of the Tazkaro Ber or Gate of Funeral Commemorations. It is thought to have been founded by Fasiladas. The coronation of some of the kings after Fasiladas apparently took place here. The church was readily accessible through the Gate of Funeral Commemorations, and, as with the rest of the churches near the citadel, it was used for burials of notables. Walatta Yohannes, daughter of *Dejazmach* Yosef, and Princess Walatta Giyorgis, for example, were buried here in Iyasu II's reign.

A modern square church has been reconstructed on the site. A late nineteenth-century picture kept here depicts the Emperors Fasiladas and Iyasu I, as well as the Empress Mentewab, naked, hands lifted in the *orans* gesture of prayer, standing in a bath of icy water like the ancient ascetics.

ADDEBABAI TEKLA HAYMANOT   Emperor Susneyos, as already noted, had built a church of Tekla Haymanot in Gondar. Another church with the same dedication was that built by Iyasu I, Addebabai Tekla Haymanot:

> Iyasu the king built a beautiful church close to his palace (or, fortress) and he brought into it a tabot in the name of Takla Haymanot, the light of the world. And he appointed priests thereto to recite the Offices therein and to chant the psalms therein by day and by night; and he endowed them with an estate sufficient for their maintenance, and the name thereof was Balasa. (Budge, Book of the Saints, from BM. ms. Or. 660)

Iyasu's chronicle confirms this, adding that the *tabot* was brought into Tequre's house, where the church was constructed. The church lies just outside the wall of the castle compound to the southeast, and was once reached by the (still intact) 'rainbow' bridge of the Azaj Tequre Ber from the castle enclosure. A bone of St Tekla Haymanot with curative powers is said to be kept here. According to Bruce, Emperor Iyasu I gave 2,000 cattle to this church and to Yasous church (Addebabai Iyasus) as being nearest the palace, after a campaign in Damot. Emperor Bakaffa was buried here in 1730. Rüppell noted the church of Abuna Teqela Haimanot northeast of the 'grosse Platz' (Addebabai). When he was in Gondar, the royal chronicles were kept there. The *Guida* refers to the old church as a ruin, with an insignificant modern one beside it. Today a modern round church with a tin roof stands here, on a concrete plinth.

As already noted above, the chronicle of Iyasu I mentions that the churches in the Gra Bet (Left Suburb) of the town, Tekla Haymanot, St George of Damot and Iyasu were burned down in a fire, which broke out in the house of a prostitute, in April 1695.

5

GONDAR CHURCHES, QWESQWAM AND ISLAMBET

On the first Saturday of the month of Tahsas, 1725, the chronicler Sinoda tells us, Emperor Bakaffa left Sadda for Gondar. The clergy received him everywhere he went with 'agreeable psalmodies'. The chronicle relates how

> the first to receive him were the clergy of Azazo, the second those of Dafacha, the third Gimjabet, the fourth Iyasus, the fifth Abuna Takla Haymanot, the sixth, Qeddus Rafael, the seventh Dabra Berhan, the eighth Ledata, the ninth Abora, the tenth Qeddus Mikael which is in the royal apartments, the eleventh those of Medhane Alem, Qeddus Giyorgis, Abuna Gabra Manfas Qeddus, Arbate Ensesa, and Qeddus Gabr'el, all together, the twelfth those of Hamara Noh, the thirteenth Qeddus Mikael Tahtay (lower), the fourteenth those of Abba Ewostatewos. With such singing of psalm, while the women danced each in her place, the king entered his city, Gondar.

Thus, almost at the end of the high Gondarine age, we see the churches, eighteen of them, from Azazo to the imperial compound, in full function, greeting their greatest patron, the emperor, on his return to his capital.

Debra Berhan Sellassie

North-northeast of the imperial compound on a hill (2,239 m.) is the very attractive compound and church dedicated to the Trinity. It was originally built by Emperor Iyasu I (although Bruce, who situated it southeast rather than a little to the northeast of the palace area, wrote that it was founded by King Zara Yaqob long before the city was built; he was doubtless thinking of

Debra Berhan in Shewa, where Zara Yaqob established his residence).
Remarkable for having survived the destruction meted out to most of the old
churches of Gondar by Tewodros and by the Mahdi's army, Debra Berhan
Sellassie is of interest for both its architectural and its artistic attractions.

The chronicle of Iyasu I declares that in 1693 the king celebrated Epiphany
'in the river Qaha', and later celebrated the consecration of the *tabot* of the
church of Sellus Qeddus or Holy Trinity. Iyasu followed the *tabot* to Debra
Berhan

> with all the dignitaries, the *liq*, the clergy, *Abba* Marqos, metropolitan of
> Ethiopia, and *Abba* Tsaga Krestos, abbot of Debra Libanos, to the sound of
> flutes and drums, with jubilation, psalms, canticles … The king arrived at the
> door of the church and descended from his horse, carrying the *tabot* on his
> head he introduced it into the altar, where *Abba* Marqos, metropolitan of
> Ethiopia, consecrated it.

The drums accompanying the procession were carried on camels. The *tabot*
of the Holy Trinity was installed on an ivory-inlaid *manbara tabot* or altar
under a gilded canopy. Iyasu also hung two metal bells here, a very rare thing
in Ethiopia. They had been brought by his agent Murad as a gift from the
governor of the Dutch Indies at Batavia. Iyasu I also appointed one hundred
and fifty persons to the church's service, and granted a number of estates to
it. Two-thirds of the yield were destined for the clergy, one-third for the
poor. In 1698, Iyasu rode to Debra Berhan clad in a robe of purple, and
wearing a gold collar, which he gave to the clergy on leaving. The superior
of this abbey church bore the high-sounding title of *male'aka berhan*, 'angel
of light'. The title appears again and again in the chronicles in the lists of
those whose place was close about the kings on different occasions.

The church was damaged by fire after being struck by lightning in 1707.
The damage seems to have been quickly repaired, for in 1709 Emperor
Tewoflos is reported coming there, and frequently afterwards royal and noble
burials took place at Debra Berhan. It was to this church that Bakaffa rode
in state after rumours had begun to percolate that he was dead, so long had
he remained unseen within the palace. Bruce regarded it as the principal
church of the town. In 1771, he relates, after the battle of Sarbakusa, one of
the officers of *Ras* Mikael shut himself up in the church compound with
some four hundred men while negotiating his surrender. There was water
there, and there were strong walls.

Today there are two enclosures, the second entered by a two-storey gatehouse. If one goes round behind the walls and towers of the compound, one
finds a collection of round *tukul*s, where the students studying *qene* and
qeddase, poetry and the liturgy, live. Their 'village' overlooks the Angareb

river, which runs to the east of the church. The Angareb dam lies below, and across the river valley one can see Dafacha Kidane Mehret church.

The original church of Debra Berhan Sellassie, it appears, was round (Annequin 1976). This can be clearly seen today by the remains of the round plinth and the arc of pillar bases that surround the rear part of the present rectangular church. It is also noted in Iyasu's chronicle that the distance between the two sets of doors eastwest and northsouth was equal. It had twelve columns inside, painted with figures of the apostles (the pillars were regarded as representing them, as the book called *Ser'ata Beta Kristyan* informs us). The roof was supported by slats disposed like the spokes of a wheel.

To complete the certainty that the present church is not the original, Antoine d'Abbadie, who was in Gondar in 1838, mentioned that a certain *Alaqa* Fanta told him that the old 'Dabra Brihan' church had been destroyed by lightning. We may suppose that while the compound gates and walls might well date from the time of Iyasu I, the oblong building of today was constructed at some time in the eighteenth century, while the Gondar style of architecture still prevailed. It may be that one of the emperors, perhaps Tewoflos, rebuilt it after the 1707 fire, but we have no means of knowing if this restoration was in the original round form, or the present form. D'Abbadie was told that the church was later rebuilt by *Liq* Haylu – thus, it seems, in the time of Mentewab around the mid-century. The present church may, however, still contain the original *qeddest* or *maqdas* and other internal parts, since it seems that these lie in the centre of the area of the ruined circular church. Even if the roof and the columns of the older structure burned, the solid square core of the interior parts, built of strong stone, could easily have survived. As with Maryam Seyon church at Aksum, reconstruction of an older church while preserving some of the former interior arrangements as part of the new structure may explain the irregular pattern of the side doors and windows. Debra Berhan Sellassie church has eight doors altogether, two at the front, and three on the sides.

Further indications of a later date, for the decoration at least, are the pictures of a donor, King Egwala Seyon. One of these appears under the portrait of St Tekla Haymanot in this church. The king lies flat in the traditional pose for donors. His crown, removed out of respect, lies to one side. The king clutches the discarded leg of the saint. The text reads: 'How the King of the Universe, Egwala Seyon, sought his help.' The picture constitutes a splendid memorial for the hapless monarch, 'reigning' from 1801 to 1818, whom Coffin described as more or less a prisoner of *Ras* Gugsa.

The church is beautifully situated on a hill in the east of the city, in its own tree-shaded compound, walled and fortified with eleven towers with cupolas and a two-storey gatehouse. The towers, with their cupolas, were occupied by monks, who used the lower floor as sleeping quarters, and the upper floor, approached by a ladder, as prayer cells (as the present priest does today). The gate-house has a double arched entrance, the arches constructed with the purplish Qwesqwam tufa. A balconied upper floor is used today as a church school. There is battlemented flat roof and a small tower with a cupola on top. Some old wooden brackets, with rudimentary carved decoration, are stored in one of the two entrances. On the inner side by the entrance arches are three crosses carved in stone. Also forming part of the fortified enclosure is the 'drum room', a small vaulted building occupied today by a baptistery and a chapel for the monks. There is an arched gate here, leading into the rear part of the compound, and there are several other remains of walls and gates in the compound. The *Guida* notes that the area was evidently once quite populated, judging from the ruins still visible then.

Debra Berhan church is rectangular with a more recent external colonnade beyond which can be seen the remains of the plinth and the bases of the columns of the former round structre. The *Guida* notes – in error? – that in 1938 the façade had three doors with arches, but it now has only two doors, with red stone capitals and arches. The style is a little like Maryam Seyon of Aksum, but now the battlements at the top of the walls and the former straw roof have been replaced by a new roof. Inside, the church is ablaze with colour from the magnificent sequence of paintings spread over every wall and even the ceiling and doors. The first room, the *qene mahlet*, in front of the doors leading to the *qeddest* where communion was administered, is beautifully decorated, the walls covered with paintings right up to the ceiling – although at a lower level the straw and mud mix covering the inside of the walls is visible. The ceiling itself, formed of wooden beams and transverse planks, displays one of the most famous graphic images of Ethiopia. Every beam is painted with alternate red, white or blue floral motifs contained in little oblong frames, while the planks between are painted with stylised angels or seraphim, reduced merely to heads with large eyes staring downwards, and blue and red wings covered with white dots. The faithful thus knew they were under the protection of the heavenly host while worshipping here. The decoration is appropriate, since the compilation called *Ser'ata Beta Kristyan*, or 'Rules of the Church', states that the roof-beams of a church represent the 'phalanx of angels'.

The wall-paintings are also very attractive, painted on to cloth that was glued to the mud-plastered walls. They were probably prepared by several different artists. They depict the life of Christ in various scenes on the right or southern wall. There are scenes from the life of Mary, the equestrian saints, George, Philotheus, Menas, Claudius, Theodore, Mercurius, Victorius, Sisinnios, Esteros and Fasiladas, and various other saints and, it is said, Iyasu

I himself, the original founder, on the left or northern wall. Mary, Queen of Heaven, dominates the west wall over the doors, together with various holy persons, kings, priests, and women, and Muhammad being led bound on a camel by the devil. Finally, the three persons of the Holy Trinity, and a crucifixion scene with another portrait of King Egwala Seyon below it, are placed over the doors leading to the *qeddest*. The doors themselves are painted, as is usual, with the archangels Gabriel and Michael guarding the entrance with their swords. The *qeddest* is also supplied with side doors opening to the outer colonnade; an external ladder mounts to a small room above the *qeddest*, from which, legend tells us, the king could watch the services. Behind it is the *maqdas* or *qeddesta qeddusan*, the Holy of Holies, with three windows visible at the back of the building.

The paintings in this church were accepted for long as being contemporary with Emperor Iyasu, the founder, himself. This is what one is told today when one visits the church, even to the extent that the pictures of Egwala Seyon, clearly labelled though they are with his name, are represented as the portraits of Iyasu I. Guy Annequin, however, observing that the paintings are distinctly related to the so-called Second Gondarine Style, known from dated manuscripts to have come into being around 1730–50, conducted a study of them, concluding that they date rather to c. 1820. The portraits of Egwala Seyon, 1801–18, seem to render this conclusive enough.

Hamara Noh (Noah's Ark), or Selestu Mit

In the second year of his reign, on 24 Hedar, according to the abbreviated chronicle, Emperor Tewoflos dedicated a sanctuary 'in the palace of Bitwoded Basle', to the 318 Orthodox Fathers of the Council of Nicea. It was called the sanctuary of Hamara Noh, or Selestu Mit ('three hundred', in allusion to the Fathers). In 1750 Iyasu II created Walda Rufa'el superior at Hamara Noh, and Tekla Haymanot II placed some priests there, who had assisted as guides during a campaign. Bruce refers to Hamara Noh as 'a large church belonging to the palace', and indicates its position south of the imperial compound (which seems to mean southeast). Rüppell recorded a church of Kyriacus at the southeast end of the 'grosse Platz', Addebabai, and this is still in existence. But there is no church now that bears the name Hamara Noh.

Abba Antonios (St Anthony)

This church is situated on a hill northwest of Gondar, beyond Qwesqwam, about half-an-hour's walk through a charming setting of hills, streams and fields of teff. It was once also part of a monastery. It was here that in 1716

Emperor Yostos was taken ill while supervising restoration work. A tent was erected for him, until in the evening he could be carried on a divan back through the hills to the palace. Emperor Yohannes I is said to have been the founder of the church of St Antonios.

The church contained paintings on cloth of some interest. The original paintings, which had points in common with those still existing in Debra Sina church at Gorgora (see Chapter 6) were found to be in a very bad condition and were taken to Paris with the Griaule Mission in 1933. They were replaced by copies by the French painter Gaston-Louis Roux, which had in turn, by 1956, almost disappeared (Staude 1959). Today, the little round church with its cement walls and orange doors seems almost abandoned in its tranquil country setting among the juniper trees of its compound. There are rough wooden columns supporting the roof round the outside.

The *maqdas* or *qeddesta qeddusan* (sanctuary) of the church is a cube of stone, with the usual three doors, very coarsely made, the main one to the west, two others on the north and south sides, and a window in the east wall. It contains a rough *manbara tabot*. A drum to support the roof above it was also originally covered with paintings. Although the most recent paintings have now completely disappeared, the original ones, or at least those which were not too badly damaged, are still preserved in the Musée de l'Homme in Paris.

The east wall was covered with paintings depicting the Four Just Kings (David, Solomon, Hezekiah and Josiah), prophets, saints, and a few biblical scenes – the sacrifice of Abraham, Daniel in the lions' den, and Susanna's arrest. The paintings on the south wall included a Last Judgement, scenes relating to the birth of Christ, the twelve apostles (eleven plus St Paul), and the Nine Saints. Interestingly, both Tekla Haymanot and Ewostatewos (Eustathius), founders of monastic orders whose followers at times were locked in bitter controversy over such matters as the observation of the Saturday sabbath, are also depicted.

On the west side – the most important, being directly over the sanctuary door – a magnificent scene was painted on the drum. God the Father is flanked by the twenty-four elders, with, below, the Covenant of Mercy (*kidane mehret*), the granting by Christ to his mother the right of intercession for sinners who have done at least one good action while invoking her name. Below, on the west wall of the sanctuary, the Virgin and Child and St George and the Dragon flank the door. Other scenes on this wall are Christ's descent into Limbo, Christ on the Cross, and the Flight into Egypt. There are also some scenes from the life of St Anthony himself.

The north wall showed paintings of equestrian saints and the martyrdoms of some of the great saints – John the Baptist, Peter and Paul, and the stoning of Stephen. Thus we have a schema: Old Testament themes to the east; the coming of Christ, and his apostles and saints to the south; redemption and the images of God, the Virgin and Child, and George, protector of Ethiopia, to the west; and finally, to the north, the martyrs for the faith.

Church of Medhane Alem (Saviour of the World)

Situated north of the imperial castles, not far west of the Ras Gemb, this is a circular edifice of typical Ethiopian type in a compound surrounded by juniper trees. The church is the seat of the bishop of Gondar. Originally it was constructed by Emperor Fasiladas. It was spared during the Mahdiyya invasion, to be restored later. The outside of the *maqdas* or sanctuary is (or was – access was impossible during my visit) richly painted with nineteenth-century paintings, some of which are founded on older work.

The paintings follow the classical arrangement to some extent. On the western wall of the sanctuary, over the doorway, appears the Trinity, with scenes of Christ's life below, and, flanking the doors painted with the arch-angels Michael and Raphael, the Crucifixion and Mary with the infant Jesus. To the left, the northern wall shows the Transfiguration at the top, and a selection of equestrian saints. To the right, the southern wall is devoted to Mary, Queen of Heaven, with attendant angels and others (including Muhammad in chains), and scenes from the life of Mary and of the Holy Family. Finally, on the eastern wall, the Ascension at the top dominates rows of scenes from the life of Jesus, with, in a central panel, the Virgin and Child.

Yohannes Wolde Nagwadgwad (John Son of Thunder)

A square building situated to the east of the Addebabai, this church of St John the Evangelist is said by the priest to have been built by *Atse* Tekla Haymanot around 1830, and restored in EC 1975. It seems that it was actually founded by Tekla Haymanot II, who ruled from 1769 to 1777, rather than by Tekla Haymanot III, 1800.

Qeddus Yohannes (St John)

The church dedicated to Qeddus Yohannes is situated west of the imperial compound beyond the valley of the Qaha. From behind the Bath of Fasiladas one takes a road that runs south parallel to the main road to Azazo, for about 1.5 km., almost outside Gondar. The setting is attractive, a semi-circular compound with a now ruined two-storey gatehouse with an arched entrance, and the remains of an arched window above. There are two domed Gondar-style towers in the enclosure wall.

Qeddus Yohannes was originally a round church. The ruins of this can still be clearly seen, with the traces of the positions of the twenty-four pillars that once supported the roof. All that now remains is the stone-built pedestal, with excavations inside it indicating where the priest, *Abba* Wolde Maryam, intends to rebuild a new church – a long-held ambition well worth supporting. Annexed to the church is a sacristy (adapted as a church in the 1930s, and still serving until the new church can be built). This is a delightful structure, a small but strong-looking Gondarine building, oblong with a round tower at each corner, like some of the palaces.

There is an old *eqa bet* or treasury in front, and a *qene mahlet*, *qeddest* and *maqdas* inside. The church was built originally, it is said, by *Ras* Walda Le'ul in Iyasu II's reign. In 1743 *Dejazmach* Arkaledes, another of Mentewab's relatives, was buried there. The chronicle of Iyasu II states that the church burned down in 1746. Nevertheless, in late 1747 the *Azaj* Tewodotos was buried there, and evidently the church was rebuilt during the reign of Iyasu II.

Qaha Iyasus Church and the 'Doro Bet'

Qaha Iyasus church is a little to the north and west of the Bath of Fasiladas, north of the road to Qwesqwam, above the river Qaha. As one climbs the road to the church, one passes a '*doro bet*', a so-called 'House of Hens', on the left some way up the hill. An arched entrance leads into a barrel vaulted room, followed by another arch leading to a larger room with a dome supported on squinches. The dome is pierced with three holes, to admit light – or, if this is, in fact, like the several other similar buildings in Gondar, a bath house, to let steam escape. Two other barrel-vaulted rooms and an open court are situated at the rear, and there is also what seems to be a place for a fire to heat water. Further ruins lie behind.

The church seems to have existed in Fasiladas' time, but the present priest claims that it was built one hundred and forty years before Fasiladas, and was not a royal foundation. The present edifice is a typical modern round church situated in a juniper-filled compound. There is a circular *qeddest* with very rustic arched doorways. The *Azaj* Dane and the *Asallafi* Qasala were among the dignitaries buried there in Iyasu II's reign, when the church also received the gift of lands at Menzeroq.

Abajale Tekla Haymanot

The church is situated a short distance to the northwest of the imperial compound. The name Abajale is supposed to refer to a village at this spot where horses were raised, but it seems not unlikely that the name Abba Jale could designate the founder; Ethiopian men of rank were quite often named with a 'horse-name' after their favourite war-horses. A church was built here apparently in the time of Emperor Fasiladas, and reconstructed by Iyasu I. Nowadays it is claimed that Tekla Haymanot II was the founder.

The church of Tekla Haymanot is, just as it was described in the *Guida*, a modern rectangular church. Some repair work here seems to have been undertaken by *Ras* Kassa Haylu. The ground plan is cross-shaped, with an octagonal sanctuary. An arched pillared colonnade is now being constructed around it.

Qeddus Abbo, Fit Abbo

Abbo is a customary abbreviation for the revered Ethiopian saint, *Abba* Gabra Manfas Qeddus. This was the oldest church in Gondar, first built by Emperor Fasiladas before he began the construction of his castles. The church, situated on a bluff with delightful views over the valley in the southern part of Gondar, was recorded by Bruce as 'the church of Aboo, in the way to Tedda'. In Iyasu's time, his chronicle records, there was a dramatic incident at Gondar when a certain Taklit killed an enemy, Hawarya, in the church of Gabra Manfas Qeddus.

The older church was demolished by the Mahdiyya forces in 1888. Now a new square church, with an open colonnaded *qeddest* lit from above, has replaced the original. Inside are pictures of the patrons who restored the church after the Mahdiyya destruction, *Dejazmach* Kifle Dadi (whose baptismal name was Kifle Hiwot) and his wife *Wozeyro* Tanagne Worq. In addition, the church has a large number of vigorous modern paintings around the *maqdas*, on the usual religious themes, with some other less familiar pictures, lively portraits of certain modern donors who have helped pay for the paintings.

Near this spot the bodies of three foreign Capuchin friars, Liberato de Wies, Michele da Zerba, and Samuele da Blumo, lay under the heaps of stones used to kill them in 1714. Tedda (Tadda, Sadda – frequently named in the chronicles as the first stop for the emperors on leaving Gondar southwards) Bruce marks as the 'burying place of the kings', noting that Yohannes I was buried there, and that there was a church of St George. (Yohannes' remains were later taken to the island of Mesraha in Lake Tana, where Iyasu I was also buried. Iyasu II's chronicle records that Yohannes founded the two convents of Sadda and Mesraha.)

Ledata Maryam (Church of the Nativity of Mary)

The Ledata church is situated on a hill above the Qaha river c. 1 km. south of Qeddus Yohannes church east of Gondar on the road to Azazo. Far across the valley, beyond the Muslim suburb of Addis Alem, Fit Abbo church is visible. A double-arched gatehouse leads into the walled enclosure (one arch is now blocked). There is a round two-storey tower to the left of the gate.

The abbreviated chronicle records that Emperor Yostos founded Ledata Maryam church in 1714. Despite his usurpation, he was buried there honourably 'with standards and drums, as is done for princes and also for the king'. In Iyasu II's reign several princesses and dignitaries are recorded as being buried there, and in Iyoas' time Fesa Gergis was appointed *alaqa* at Ledata Maryam. James Bruce noted that this church was used as an arms store in 1771 after the battle of Sarbakusa. Rüppell recorded Ledetat church as situated to the northwest of the Addebabai.

The ruined arcade of the former circular church stands within the walled and turreted enclosure. The capitals are of purple Qwesqwam stone. The modern church has been built within the older arcade, the latest restoration having been done by *Qes* Abbay in the time of Emperor Haile Sellassie.

Other Gondar Churches

Other churches are noted by Mathew, Pankhurst and others with very few further details. Some of these, whose names 'seem a corona for a God-protected dynasty' (Mathew 1947: 56), can still be identified today, others seem to have vanished. Some, such as Maryam Seyon, perhaps never existed. Many Gondar churches, like others elsewhere, include in their compounds the *beta lahm* (Bethlehem) for the making of the eucharistc bread, an *eqa bet* or treasury, and a number of family 'grave houses' or *meqabr bet*. At most Gondar churches, visitors, properly dressed, and willing to wait quietly until services are finished, are usually more than welcome. In some churches, such as Qeddus Yohannes, the priests are only too happy to explain the history of their church, and the projects they might have for the future. There are a few exceptions – Ba'ata Maryam, Abwara Giyorgis – where officious locals try to prevent entrance even into the compounds, but this is fortunately rare. Local information about the history of the churches can be reliable, but is very often not. Priests and deacons will supply the name of a founding king, but with a wrong date, or will describe a well-known event attached to a name (such as the murder by Tekla Haymanot I of Iyasu I) while attributing their church to Tekla Haymanot II. In Debra Berhan Sellasie church, as I have already mentioned, the picture of Egwala Seyon (1801–18) is said to be that of the famous founder of the church, Iyasu I (1682–1706), with the explanation, if pressed, that Egwala Seyon was the throne name of Iyasu (actually, Adyam Sagad).

Ewostatewos Eustathius, said to have been founded by Bakaffa. The abbreviated chronicle mentions that Dawit II, on 18 Maskaram of the third year of his reign, had the sanctuary of Abba Ewostatewos dedicated. It seems to have been rebuilt in Iyasu II's reign, c. 1736–37, if the account in his chronicle of the building of a church with this dedication by Arkaledes, the king's uncle, refers to the same place. The *tabot* of Ewostatewos, with others of Mikael and Sellassie, is apparently now kept in Debra Berhan Sellasie church.

Dafacha Kidane Mehret Covenant of Mercy, founded by Bakaffa at Dafacha just outside Gondar. Nahuda was named superior there by Iyasu II in 1754. Dafacha church is a small round structure built beside the ruined twenty-seven pillar arcade of an older and larger church (see Anfray 1988: 12, plan p. 28). Today it is not easy to visit, since the theft of one of the two *tabotat* dedicated to *kidane mehret*, the Covenant of Mercy, has rendered the local people very suspicious of strangers. LaVerle Berry kindly gave me some notes made after a visit in 1973, which attribute the presence of two *tabotat* to a prior foundation by Tewoflos and a later one by Bakaffa, who endowed it with lands in Dambya. The church was burned not by the Mahdists, but later, by a local forest fire. In 1973 the church was a ruin, but the walls still stood, enclosing, within the arcade and the walls of the *qeddest*, a square *maqdas* bearing a drum on triple-arched squinches. A two-storey gate tower leads into the compound.

Maryam Seyon Possibly refers to Gimjabet Maryam church, which had a *tabot* of Maryam Seyon.

Maryam Sihor Church southwest of Gondar.

Church of the Apostles of Deva This is the church of Dibabo (Diba-Abo) about 20 km. from Gondar.

Hawaryat Pankhurst notes that westward from the city is the circular church of Hawariat (the Apostles). The *Guida* situates it (Auriat) northeast of the imperial compound, west of Debra Berhan Sellassie. All that remained in 1938 was a fallen circular enclosure wall, and a mound of stones in which the square sanctuary could just be recognised, amid tall trees. It may originally have been built before the rise of Gondar as a capital city.

St Mary of the Gondar people This seems to refer to the church of Gemjabet Maryam, described above.

St Mikael of Aira Unidentifiable.

St Mikael of Belaggio This is the church of Bilajig Mikael, about 4 km. west of the Fasil Gibbi in Gondar. To reach the church one can either come via a track from Qwesqwam, or take the Azazo road, passing the Medical College and the Oil Depot. Opposite Fit Abbo church, right on the other side of the valley of the Qaha, a track leads up to the right. An hour's walk past beautiful hillside scenery leads to the grove of trees concealing the small unimpressive round church, which has a curious new wooden palisade around the outside. Here too a recent attempt to steal the *tabot* has left the locals suspicious of strangers. The priest attributes the origin of the church to an unknown monarch, *Atse* Ewostatewos!

Fit Qeddus Mikael The old church of St Michael. The *Guida* notes 'a poor church of Fit Micaèl'. Today there is only a modern round church at the site, although an old arched gateway still survives. Pankhurst (1982: 119ff) recounts an elaborate legend that claims that Fit Mikael was built by Emperor Fasiladas after an epidemic, in expiation for his entertainment of too many concubines. The emperor's conduct did not improve, and a plague of leopards and lions was sent. This was counteracted by the erection of another church, Fit Abbo (see above). Later Fasiladas married the sister of his wife, a 'princess of Rome', and, being upbraided by the monks, began a campaign of slaughter. Nine thousand and ninety-nine were killed; 'the baptism of blood with which Gondar was sanctified'. The legend goes on to say that Fasiladas' conscience troubled him after all this bloodshed. On the advice of a female hermit he built seven bridges, so that everyone who passed over them in safety might pray for him with the words 'God save the soul of Fasiladas!' Fit Qeddus Mikael church was burned down in 1726, according to the abbreviated chronicle.

St Simeon of Tzaamdi Possibly this name might indicate the church of Samuel southwest of Gondar, which was burned, the *tabot* being transferred to Asasame Mikael church as a *debal*. Or possibly it might be identified with the church of 'Tzemba' on the Angareb; Emperor Iyasu I in 1700 sent Poncet to 'Tzemba, a monastery situated upon the river Reb, half a league from Gondar'.

St George of Damot In Iyasu I's chronicle it is noted that among the churches burnt in 1695, in the Gra Bet suburb of Gondar, were those of Tekla Haymanot, St George of Damot and Iyasu.

St George of Uerangheb This is the church of Wrangeb Giyorgis, near Bilajig Mikael west of Gondar.

Avorra Ghiorgis The *Guida* notes this church west of the Qaha opposite Addis Alem. This is the church of Abwara or Abara Giyorgis, about 3 km.

south of central Gondar. To reach it, one takes the road behind the Bath of Fasiladas, passing Qeddus Yohannes church, and then taking a left turn into the valley about 1 km. further on. Fit Abbo church, and the suburb of Addis Alem, are visible to the west. Passing through a new suburb of small tin-roofed houses, in the valley, with a new mosque, one can walk across the swampy ground to the new square church of Abwara Giyorgis. The effort of getting there is not well rewarded, the local people being unwelcoming.

Church of the Four Saints This refers, probably, to the site of the former church of the Four Animals east of Gondar, marked on the *Guida* map as Arba-tenza. The church has now vanished, but people still go to the site, marked by a fig tree.

Cherqos The church of Cherqos (a saint who was martyred by being burned in a fire with his mother) is in the centre of Gondar, near the Saturday market, some distance southwest of the castle compound. It was founded by Tekla Haymanot II. The present church on the site is a square modern edifice.

Peter and Paul I have not been able to identify this church, said to have been founded by Tekla Haymanot II.

Qeddus Fasiladas It appears that this church, said to have been built in the reign of Solomon II, was actually nothing other than a re-use of the pavilion in the lake usually called the Bath of Fasiladas. The *tabot* is now apparently kept in the church of Qaha Iyasus.

St John of Guara Perhaps a foundation (Qeddus Yohannes?) of Gondarine times by one of the Qwara relatives of Empress Mentewab and 'Iyasu Qwar-eña', as Iyasu II is sometimes called.

Qeddus Rufael (St Raphael, the archangel). The chronicle of Emperor Bakaffa records that he founded a church of St Raphael in 1722, 'in the house of wozeyro Wallatta Rufael. He selected wise men among the priests, and put Abba Demetros at their head.' Situated to the east of the imperial compound, behind Addebabai Iyasus, the church was accessible from the imperial compound via the Adenager Ber bridge. Qeddus Rafael church was burned during the troubles in Iyasu II's reign, but was rebuilt. In 1753 Walda Rufael, former superior at Hamara Noh, was moved here, and then on to Debra Berhan in 1754. The present church is a new building, oblong but with a rounded form at the sanctuary end.

Qeddus Gabre'el (St Gabriel). This is a large new square church in north Gondar beyond the old Abuna Bet district. The original church here was supposedly constructed by Fasiladas. Here was buried Metropolitan Yohannes, who died in Iyoas' reign in 1761. *Abuna* Salama, the metropolitan who died a prisoner of Emperor Tewodros at Maqdala, had begged *Wagshum* Gobeze that he would see to his burial in one of two places, St Mark of Mai Guague, or St Gabriel at Gondar. His wish was in due course realised, his remains being taken to St Gabriel's and reburied.

Be'ata Maryam Bahata Maryam church is about 1 km. as the crow flies southwest of the imperial citadel, and was endowed by Emperor Tekla Haymanot II in 1775. The name refers to the entrance of Mary into the Temple in fulfilment of a vow of her parents if they were granted a child. In the book called *Ta'amer Maryam* (Miracles of Mary), and in other local legends about Mary in Ethiopia, there are many apocryphal tales about her life, one being that she was selected to weave the Temple veil. Arnauld d'Abbadie mentions that the 'Bata' quarter was named after this church, which had the right of asylum, and numerous clergy (around 1838). In troubled times the church became a repository for the local farmers' grain reserves. Rüppell too noted that to the southwest of Addebabai lay 'Bada' church, which he called the largest and most beautiful in Gondar. Today the church is merely a modern large round tin-roofed structure like so many others. It is being painted at the moment (again, like so many others) in the national Ethiopian colours. There is a good view from the compound (where visitors are not very welcome) over the Qaha valley. A curious feature is the round monument surmounted by a modern bell-tower approached by a long staircase of thirty-seven steps.

Debra Metmaq Maryam Metmaq means 'baptism', and the church was founded by Tekla Giyorgis at the end of the eighteenth century. It lies a little over 1 km. south of the Fasil Gibbi, north of Fit Abbo church. The present church, situated in a grove of juniper trees, is square, approached by a wide flight of stone steps. New concrete pillars indicate a project to extend the roof covering outwards to shield the area immediately around the church.

Abyezgi (Abba Abiesghi, *Guida*). Southwest of the imperial compound, this church was founded by a nobleman in the reign of Tekla Haymanot II. Today there is a round church of the usual type on the site. There is apparently also a *tabot* of Marqorewos here.

Egziabeher Ab Built by Yohannes IV, but destroyed by Mahdist forces, this church is said to have existed in the Muslim suburb on the site of a mosque built in Menelik II's time (Solomon Addis Getahun 1997: 4).

Woleka Ba'ata About three km. north of Gondar, on the Angareb river, is this small square church.

The above list embraces a total of forty or so churches that may be compared with the forty-four churches legend supposes to have been built at Gondar. There may be duplicates among the different records of the names, and some of them are not actually in Gondar. The phrase 'forty-four churches', however, may not be intended as a literal statement of fact – Ato Niftalem Kiros informs me that the use of this number can refer to an 'ideal representation'. One might say, for example, at Addis Ababa at the time of the *Timqat* procession, that 'the forty-four tabots have gone to the Jan Meda' – the field where the procession assembles – although there may well be more. Indeed, in Gondar today, with perhaps thirty-one churches functioning, there may be up to one hundred or more *tabotat*, churches having additional *tabotat* (known as *dabal*, extra or additional) consecrated in the name of saints other than those of the main dedication. On this theme, I was interested to note that my late friend and colleague, Ruth Plant, in her book *Architecture of the Tigre, Ethiopia*, recorded that Abreha and Asbeha were 'reputed to have founded 44 churches'. The number seems to have been considered a particularly honourable one. For example, in the chronicle of Iyasu I it is mentioned that the governor of Tigray had forty-four *nagarit* (drums) beaten before him when he travelled, and in a land charter of *Ras* Walda Sellassie and *Qese Gabaz* Za-Amanuel, around 1794, forty-four priests of the Tabernacle at Aksum are mentioned. We need not, therefore, take literally the attribution of forty-four churches in Gondar.

Qwesqwam Palace and the Church of Sahay Maryam

Just outside modern Gondar, some way to the northwest of the Bath of Fasiladas, stands Empress Mentewab's palace and reception hall, and the abbey of Qwesqwam, with the abbey church of Debra Sahay (the Mountain of the Sun). The superior, bearing the title *male'aka sahay*, 'angel of the Sun', was an important ecclesiastical official at the Gondarine court.

Qwesqwam takes its name from the Egyptian Qus Qam or Qusaqam, in middle Egypt south of Asyut, where the Holy Family, on their Flight to Egypt, are reputed to have stayed for a while. The setting is very beautiful, under the hill of Debra Sahay, with many *wanza* and other trees. The church was built in the spot where Iyasu I and/or Bakaffa had built a house, according to the chronicle of Iyasu II. Remote as it seems from everyday life in Gondar today, with the popular feast of Qwesqwam in November the whole compound comes alive again, people walking all the way from the city, as the chants and drums echo out over the countryside.

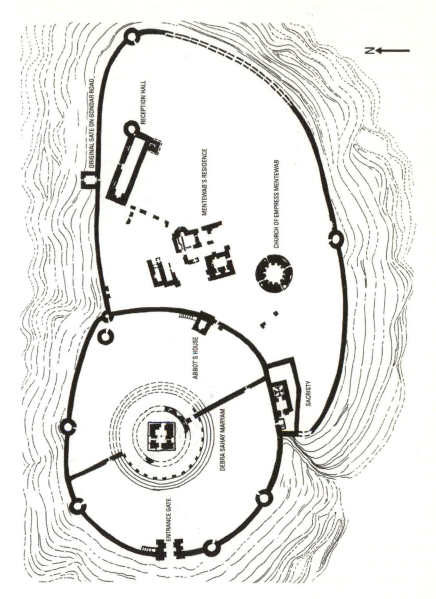

5. The palace and abbey complex at Qwesqwam, Gondar, adapted from the *Guida*, 1938: 361.

Empress Mentewab and James Bruce

The life story of Empress Mentewab is romantic and dramatic, part of the legend surrounding Emperor Bakaffa. At the same time, her story is one with the theme of the collapse of the Gondarine monarchy, over which she presided. The legend surrounding Mentewab's early life suits the idyllic atmosphere of her retirement palace at Qwesqwam. According to the story, Emperor Bakaffa, travelling incognito in the Qwara region west of Lake Tana, fell ill. He was taken into a house, where a beautiful girl cared for him. Her baptismal name was Walatta Giyorgis, but she was known then as Mentewab: 'How beautiful she is'. She was the daughter of a local official, but also a descendant of Emperor Minas through Enqoye (Enqwaye) her mother and Yolyana her grandmother. So impressed was Bakaffa by the girl, that he later sent for her and married her. Soon she gave birth to a son, one day to reign as Iyasu II. In time she was crowned empress or queen consort, *itege*.

Among the many tales about Emperor Bakaffa, it was said that he was uneasy about the fate of his descendants because of a prophecy. It was said that a certain Welatta Giyorgis, not a descendant of his, would rule in Ethiopia for thirty years. Anyone who bore the name was executed. Finally it was revealed that the name Welatta Giyorgis was Mentewab's original name bestowed at her christening. As to the question of her rule in Ethiopia, she had been elevated to the rank of *itege*, and was destined to be the legitimate regent for her son and grandson during their minorities. She later took the royal name Berhan Mogasa, presumably in reference, as was common, to the name of the reigning emperor, in this case her son Iyasu II, Adyam Sagad, or Berhan Sagad.

During her long period of influence while her son Iyasu II and her grandson Iyoas were on the throne, her Qwara family almost monopolised the great offices of state, causing resentment and conflict, particularly with the Oromo relatives of Iyoas. It was to end this that Mikael Sehul was called in, with fatal results for the empress's family. Some time after the assassination of her grandson Iyoas, Mentewab also meddled in state affairs during the reign of Tekla Haymanot II, assenting to the enthronement of the pitiable pretender Susneyos in 1770. As a result she was forced temporarily to flee Gondar and Qwesqwam.

After Bakaffa's death, the empress married a Qwara noble, a grandson of Iyasu I's called Iyasu, by whom she had three daughters. One was the famous Aster or Esther, who was so kind to Bruce during his time in Ethiopia. She was married to Mikael Sehul after the death of her first husband. Mentewab and Esther are some of the great characters of Ethiopian history brought to life for us through the writings of foreign visitors. James Bruce met the empress often and talked with her, cured her daughters and other relatives of sickness, and through this special relationship became quite close to Mentewab and her family.

Bruce described Qwesqwam, extraordinarily briefly for one who lived there at times:

> the palace of Koscam is situated upon the south side of Debra Tzai; the name signifies the Mountain of the Sun. The palace consists of a square tower of three storeys, with a flat parapet roof, or terrace, and battlements about it. The court of guard, or headquarters of the garrison of Koscam, is kept here; immediately below this is the principal gate, or entrance, towards Gondar. It is surrounded by a high outer wall, which may have been above an English mile of circumference. This outer precinct is all occupied by soldiers, labourers, and out-door servants; within this is another large court, inclosed by inner walls likewise; in this the apartments are but of one storey, appropriated to the principal officers, priests, and servants. In this also is the church, built by the present Iteghe herself, and reckoned the richest in Abyssinia. They have large crosses of gold for their processions, and kettle-drums of silver. The altar is all covered with gold plates, all the gift of their magnificent patroness ... The third, or inner court, is reserved for the queen's own apartments, and such of the noble women as are her attendants, that are unmarried and make up her court. Behind the palace, higher up the hill, are houses of people of quality, chiefly her own relations. Above these the mountain rises.

At another point Bruce mentions that

> Koscam is the richest church in Abyssinia; it is situated on the banks of the Kahha, below a ruinous palace, or house, of the king. There are about 40 houses in the village, all belonging to the principal Kuaragna, the party of the queen.

Debra Sahay Maryam

The round church of Maryam of Debra Sahay at Qwesqwam, in its walled compound with square gatehouse and pepper-pot towers with upper rooms for monks' residences, has now been rebuilt. The old church was burned with the rest of the palace by the Mahdiyya troops in 1888. In 1938 the *Guida* described the ruins – a triple-stepped round podium supported a half circle of ruined arches, inside which the ruins of a square sanctuary could be seen. Contemporary Italian engravings (see Lindhal 1970: 85 for one by Laurenzio Laurenzi) show this ruined circular arcade, on which presumably the restored church now to be seen there was based.

With the church already threatened by the insecurity of the times when Bruce left Ethiopia in 1771, one supposes that after the death of *Itege*

Mentewab a little later its splendour faded rapidly. The glorious figure of Mary, painted, but with her costume of real brocade and silk, overlaid with silver, her necklace, hairpins and bracelets encrusted with gold, the crowns, the silks, costly carpets, ivory and precious metals listed in the annals, can hardly have survived long, given the conditions of the time.

Today, in a small crypt, three skeletons, enclosed together in one coffin, are shown. They are said to be the remains of Empress Mentewab herself, of her son Iyasu II and of her unfortunate murdered grandson, Iyoas. This, however, may be no more than romantic fiction. According to Iyasu II's own chronicle, he was interred beside his father Bakaffa at Tekla Haymanot church. In the chronicle translated by Blundell we are also told that one of the queens of the *zamana mesafint*, *Itege* Esther, was 'buried at Quesquam in the royal tomb of Mentwab' (Blundell 1922: 447–8).

The chronicle of Iyasu II and Berhan Mogasa (Mentewab) describes the church in great detail, though with different measurements in different manuscripts. The *maqdas* was twelve cubits wide, the *qeddest* ten, the *qene mahlet* eight. Takla Haymanot, Heryaqos, Mammo and Nabute, all bearing the title *azaj*, with *Bajerond* Isayyas, chief of the carpenters, built it from brick and mortar, with wooden elements (pillars and roof). It had eight doors in arched double doorways, and eight windows, and was hung inside with silks. Outside the roof was covered with flame-red silks, so that those seeing it from afar cried out 'What is happening? Has Debra Sahay caught fire?' Above this were fixed three hundred and eighty mirrors, whose reflected gleam, it was believed, caused several people in Gondar to fall ill.

The queen had the inside of the church painted. The chronicle describes the paintings, and the *manbara tabot* in the *maqdas* that shone like the sun, and glittered like a precious stone, being covered over with pure gold, its central part encrusted with sapphire. It was constructed of ivory, with four crosses of gold at the corners. Inside it was placed the *tabot* of Mary, Mother of God. The windows of the *maqdas*, thrown open at certain stages of the services, were lavishly decorated with gold, porcelain and rich stuffs. Near the eastern door, Mentewab built two tombs, for herself and her son, under depictions of the *kwerata reesu*, Mary, and the archangels Michael and Gabriel. The roof was topped with a bronze ornament with twenty-four crosses, with a larger one on top, all covered with gold. Among the gifts to the church were velvets, silks, brocades, vestments embroidered in gold and silver, parasols, an ivory manbar (altar), gold and silver crosses, censers, crowns, chalices, other vases and patens, candlesticks, standards, drums and processional crosses, all in vast quantity and all meticulously listed one by one by Iyasu and Mentewab's chronicler. A following list enumerates the substantial library of books in possession of the abbey.

Coffin described the church in 1814:

> The church is well thatched, and the blue silk with which it is lined, and the large mirrors with which it was adorned, by the Queen [Mentewab] are still in a perfect state ... The church, of an oblong square form, has a flat top, and within it is very well plastered with the best clay; it has a kind of portico. The outside is covered with thatch, to preserve the building from being washed down by the rains ... Quosqwom being the most esteemed church in Gondar at the present day, I have been induced to give a fuller account of it.

Thus the first church on the site seems to have been rather different from the later round one, unless – unlikely – Coffin refers to the central square part of the building, within the stone arcade and circular outer wall, as the church proper.

To the south of the church, close to the gateway that leads through a wall dividing the compound into two parts, is a small sacristy roofed with a large dome, built in its own little adjoining compound accessible from the main church compound. Northeast of the church, another small domed structure stands close to the compound wall, serving as the *beta lahm*.

The Residence and Reception Hall

A gate from the church compound, directly beside the small two-storey abbot's house with a dome, balcony and external staircase to the upper floor, leads directly east into the palace area. This is another even larger compound, also walled and with a number of round towers, as well as a gatehouse directly below and adjacent to the reception hall, in other words facing north and not directly towards Gondar, as James Bruce seems to imply. The gate nevertheless opens onto the track leading to Gondar.

Bruce in the 1770s saw this part of the palace in full function, when he went to visit the empress. There were evidently then numerous houses connected with the *itege*'s service in and around the compound, in one of which Bruce himself lived. Today the walled and towered eastern compound adjoining the church compound contains the ruins of the empress's small but attractively ornamented private palace, with her round oratory, decorated inside with blind arcading, to the south. There is no inner court wall any more, although there still remain traces of a structure between the large three-storey reception hall, presumably Bruce's 'square tower', and Mentewab's palace, that might have partly divided the latter off from the area to the east where the reception hall stood.

The palace is an interesting building. Two storeys high, it has arched openings for doors and windows, and some decorative carved crosses. There are seven rooms on the ground floor, with a surviving staircase up one side, some arched recesses and 'cupboards' in the walls, and red and grey stone door jambs. Some small rooms may have served for bathing. To the south, an open wall with round stone pillar bases, two in the side wall and two in the centre, must once have formed a verandah, allowing the empress to sit enjoying the delightful view in complete privacy.

The impressive reception hall, now an empty shell, was a very substantial structure. It has two towers, a round one with a cupola on the northeast corner, and a square one to the southeast. This, now ruined, had a saddle roof that was intact when Rohlfs sketched the place in 1880/1, and there is a kind of undercroft, still accessible, sometimes described as a 'cold house' for keeping food fresh. Inside, at the west end where some fragments of the roof still remain, are a number of wooden elements, looking very fresh although there seems to be no record of this building ever being restored.

There are several interesting carved decorative stones built into the south wall – crosses, lions, one with a rider, one attacking an ox, an elephant – beside and above the three high triple-step arched doorways (which we also find at Barye Gemb, see below). There is a small subordinate door at the west end. Three arched frames surmounted by triangular pediments with elaborate crosses on top flank the doorways, similar to those on Empress Mentewab's palace at Gondar, and there are traces of a long balcony that once ran along the façade at the top.

The compound was evidently defensible. In 1771 Bruce records that, fearing a threat that the king might give the place over to his soldiers for plunder as a punishment for the *itege*'s countenancing seditious meetings there, it was provisioned and prepared for siege: 'The wall was strong and high, the gates lately put into good repair, the tower, or castle, within, in perfect good order.' A sharp contrast, if so, with the state into which the royal palaces of Gondar itself were so soon to decline.

The Muslim Suburb: Islambet

The Muslim area of the town was the main trading settlement of Gondar. It may even have preceded the foundation of the city, if the traditions about Muslim settlements there are true (Solomon Addis Getahun 1997: 3). It is said that Muslims dwelt in this area, then called Godiguadit, in Emperor Yeshaq's time, and that they also lived in the area of the suburb called Gra Bet, whence they were sent to Islamge when the palaces were built. Islamge was situated near the Qaha stream opposite Abwara Giyorgis church, for as James Bruce commented, 'this situation, near running water, is always chosen by the Mohametans on account of their frequent ablutions' – his plan correctly shows it over the stream to the west. Doresse situates the Muslim suburb to the south between the Angarab and Qaha, not far west of Fit Abbo church, as does the 1938 *Guida*, which describes the exclusively Muslim suburb of Addis Alem, referring to it as the former Islam Bet and noting that the old mosque is situated there. Today the suburb is still there, below Fit Abbo church and a new mosque with dome and minaret built on the heights to the north.

A lower mosque, supposedly built some three hundred years ago by Shaykh Muhammad Said, is a very modest square building with an apse projecting at the *mihrab* end. Further up the hill, a round building or *tukul*, now used as a house but with the crescent still present of the roof, is shown as a former mosque. This must be the structure referred to by the *Guida* as 'la vecchia Moschea (tucul)', formerly called Islam Bet.

During the revolt against Iyasu II, in the year 7225 (AD 1732–33), *Dejaz-mach* Warañña's men, as a first foray against the besiegers of Gondar castle, burned part of the 'Eslamochbet', as the chronicle of the emperor calls it (Guidi 1912: 76). Remedius Prutky, who stayed there secretly in return for medical work towards the end of Iyasu's reign in January 1753, described it as 'a small town, below Mt. Abbo, that was inhabited by Mohametans ... three leagues from royal Gondar on the banks of the Kaha, on that side of the city of Gondar that is towards the stream Angareb'. He also seems to mention its name Zelancke (Islamge) when describing their last sight of Gondar:

> below the high mountain where royal Gondar stands, beside the stream An-gareb. Here on either side of the mountain top we saw the site of the town called Zelancke, and between the two mountains a pair of rivers which here flowed together, the Kaha and the Angareb, from the first of which the imperial residence of Kaha takes its name. (Arrowsmith-Brown 1991: 321–2)

The editor, however, in a note situates Zelancke '35 miles northeast of Gondar'.

In the early 1770s Bruce reported that the 'Moorish town at Gondar may consist of about 3000 houses, some of them spacious and good'. In another place he writes 'a thousand houses', which Pankhurst, in *The Economic History of Ethiopia*, and in 'Muslim Commercial Towns ...' took to refer to a second Muslim area or 'an extension of the Muslim quarter' (see Pankhurst 1982: 171, where this idea seems to have been abandoned). Rather later, under Solomon III (1796–97), Muslims from Walqa and Addis Alem were allowed to move elsewhere, being granted land in the Ergeb Ber area (Solomon Addis Getahun 1997: 3).

In the chronicle of Iyoas, it is stated that when news of the defeat of a rebel came to Gondar, joy reigned from Daragenda to Eslambet, perhaps the two extremities of the town at that time. Rüppell (1840, Vol. II: 79ff) estimated that the 'Islambed' quarter in his time embraced some 300 houses out of 1,000 for the whole town (200 in 'Etscheghbed' and 60 in 'Felashabed', the fourth quarter being the 'Residenzschloss der Kaiser'). As for Arnauld d'Abbadie, he stated that 'Islamge', though one of the most populous suburbs of the town, was because of its low position near the Angarab and Qaha the least healthy, and that slave caravans often brought epidemics.

The officer in charge of merchants, the *nagadras*, 'chief of trade', was a Muslim from this suburb in Bruce's time at Gondar. The *nagadras* was an important official, ranking twenty-first in the list of officials in Iyasu I's chronicle, but entitled to a seat and cushion at court. There was apparently no mosque in the Muslim quarter, building one being forbidden. (It has been stated that the Great Mogul sent money to build a mosque in response to an embassy from Iyasu I which had taken gifts of precious African products to India. This seems, in fact, to allude to the gift by Aurangzeb of 2,000 rupees to the merchant Murad for restoring a mosque in Fasiladas' time, as reported by Bernier. The mosque is not stated to have been in Gondar, *pace* Budge, *History* ..., 2: 403, but was apparently one demolished by the Portuguese). Shrines of revered shaykhs, too, are noted in Islambet in later times (Solomon Addis Getahun 1997: 5ff).

In Iyasu II's chronicle, there is a note that when Metropolitan Yohannes came to Gondar in 1745, he entered by the Kayla Meda route. This Kayla Meda is also mentioned on other occasions. Since Kayla is another name for the Falasha, it presumably indicates an open space near the Jewish suburb, twin of the Muslim suburb.

6

SITES NEAR LAKE TANA

Just before the foundation of Gondar, the favourite rainy-season residences of many of the Ethiopian kings had already begun to cluster in certain favoured spots around the great Lake of Dambya or Dembea, now called Lake Tana. The beautiful richly decorated churches and royal dwellings of Amhara had in many cases been destroyed in the incursions of the 1520s and 1530s, and other areas were lost to the newer wave of Oromo invasion. Emperors such as Sarsa Dengel (1563–97), removing himself as far away as possible from the Oromo, and his successors Yaqob, and Susneyos, built or caused to be built a number of castles, palaces and churches in this area, backed by the splendid scenery of the lake and the surrounding hills. Some buildings still survive – improbable ruins in spectacular settings, witnesses of an imperial fantasy that was later to crystallise at Gondar.

Ganeta Iyasu, Azazo

Azazo Tekla Haymanot church is about 12 km. south-southwest of Gondar, near the present airport serving the town, on the (unpaved) route to the lake. Nearby to the northwest a ruined conical tower and other ruins marks the site of Ganeta Iysus, the 'garden of Jesus'. Manoel de Almeida mentions that Emperor Susneyos built a palace 'at Ganeta Jesus, which is one of his pleasances'. Jerónimo Lobo, who lived in Ethiopia for nine years from 1625, refers to it as Ganete Ilhos. In the version translated by Lockhart, Lobo refers to it as the place 'where the Emperor was in some fine palaces and a garden built for him by workmen from India and where he had had us build a fine church and house'. The detail about the Indian workmen is missing in Le Grand's version of Lobo's text.

Ganeta Iyasus was one of the Jesuit residencies, and another church and a two-storey residence were erected to accommodate them. The place offered easy access to the royal camp at Danqaz about twelve miles away. Manoel de Almeida arrived there in 1624, and Patriarch Afonso Mendez came the next year. Later, after the departure of the Jesuits from Ethiopia, the fief of Azazo was granted to the *echege*, who retained it as a residence from c. 1634 to c. 1902 (Campbell 1999).

The attractive sub-circular stone-built enclosure of the church of Azazo Tekla Haymanot, on the hill amid its weeping junipers, is pure Gondar architecture in appearance. It overlooks the site of Ganeta Iyasus. Campbell considers that the 'fortress-residence' of Susneyos was built by Pais on the spot where the church, built of cut stone blocks, now is. He also believes that the wall and gatehouse surrounding it were Portuguese constructions, and that 'the first of the picturesque "castellated" Gondar buildings were probably copied by Portuguese settlers from buildings constructed at Azazo-Ganetta Iyesus by the Jesuits, notably the palace of Susinius, of which some of the buildings and fortified walls remain'. The ensemble would have given rise to similar fortified church enclosures, such as Debra Berhan Sellassie.

A little two-storey battlemented Gondar-style pavilion with a square tower and small cupola lies north of the church, forming part of the enclosure. There is also a square two-storey gatehouse, and round bastion to the rear with a view over the airport and the plain of Dambya. Inside is the round tin-roofed church of Enda Tekla Haymanot Azazo – conspicuous from the main road running southwards from Gondar to the airport. The paths leading to it are fenced formidably by prickly pear hedges with eucalyptus trees inside forming a second shade hedge.

The church, according to legend, was built by Emperor Susneyos. His son Fasiladas is supposed to have lived at Azazo for a time before founding Gondar. Major work seems to have been done by Emperor Yohannes I, the second emperor to build at Gondar, since his chronicler recorded that, in his seventh year (1673–74), he 'introduced the tabot of Our Lady Mary; for the construction of the church of Debra Libanos, of Azazo, had been finished'. The chronicle of Iyasu I not only mentions the church, and the king's attendance at a service conducted by the *echege* in 1689, but refers to 'the apartment that King Seltan Sagad (Susneyos) had built', where the emperor offered a banquet to the dignitaries and the clergy of Debra Libanos. Iyasu II seems to have restored or even rebuilt Azazo, both church and palace, later, as James Bruce tells us. In the reign of Iyoas, in 1760, it was set on fire by lightning, but must have been quickly repaired since Bruce seems to have seen it intact a decade later. The dervishes later burned it again in Yohannes IV's reign, with Gondar.

After describing his first sight of Gondar in its dark wood of *wanza* trees,

Bruce goes on to add: 'Behind it is Azazo, likewise covered in trees. On a hill is the large church of Tecla Haimanout [at Azazo], and the river below it makes it distinguishable.' He describes the building work of Iyasu II there. The emperor 'had begun a very large and expensive villa at Azazo, with extensive groves, or gardens, planted thick with orange and lemon trees, upon the banks of a beautiful and clear river, which divides the palace from the church of Tecla Haimanout, a large edifice, which some time before, he had also built and endowed' [later, Bruce noted that 'the house itself is going fast to ruin, as the kings of this country have a fixed aversion to houses built by their predecessors']. Some ruins and a cistern or pool to the west towards Loza are thought to be the remains of this structure or the earlier palace and garden built for Susneyos.

Guzara

Guzara, near Lake Tana about 60 km. from Gondar, survives as a smallish (18 by 12 m.) but impressive ruin on a hill not far from Emfraz. The new 168 km. dirt road from Azazo to Bahar Dar passes by it, offering an excellent sight of the castle in its dominant position overlooking the lake some distance away to the west. To reach the castle (the road does not go to it), one crosses a sixteenth-century arched stone bridge – perhaps the oldest in Ethiopia – and climbs up the hill.

The chronicle of Emperor Sarsa Dengel states that he came to reside at Dobit in 1571/2 (Annequin 1963; Pankhurst 1982, I: 94-5). Dobit seems to be Guzara, also called Guba'e. The chronicle mentions that 'le roi se dirigea vers Guba'e, s'arrêtant à chaque petit étape a cause des malades et des faibles. Arrivé à Guba'e, il entra dans son château, de belle construction et d'un extérieur admirable.' Emperor Yaqob, too, stayed at Guzara, and Susneyos passed by in 1617. Fasiladas also came occasionally. After that, it seems to have been forgotten.

The main building as it survives is, obviously, of uncertain date, and could have been reconstructed well after Sarsa Dengel's time. It closely resembles the castles of the Gondar compound, and the Ras Gemb. Guzara is a two-storey rectangular structure with two round towers surmounted by round cupolas at the northeast end. A further square tower rose two more storeys at the south corner, but it has now fallen; the roof and floors have also gone. Battlements and wooden balconies ornamented the exterior, and arched windows and doors, with white stones for the arches, and red capitals, added extra elegance. There were five rooms downstairs, the largest about 11 by 5 m. Three of these opened to the exterior. The external staircase common at the castles of Gondar and also familiar in two-storey stone houses at Aksum and Lalibela, for example, was used here, on the northwest side. Niches in the walls supplied storage space or perhaps emplacements for lamps. From the upper parts of the castle splendid views could be obtained over the lake and the plain of Dambya.

There was an enclosure wall, probably equipped with gates, and numerous now completely ruined dependent structures. Annequin noted the ruins of a church some 5–600 m. away. According to Mathew, perhaps following Monti della Corte, the building was constructed by Portuguese from Fremona, the Jesuit establishment in the north near Adwa, perhaps around 1570, but this is uncertain, and may not be relevant to the existing ruin. Anfray suggests that Guzara as we see it today was constructed by Susneyos of Fasiladas (Anfray 1988: 17). Whatever the case, there is little doubt that the style is shared by the Gondar castles more than half a century later than 1570. It could be significant that the chronicle of Yohannes I, when it mentions that the king passed the night at Emfraz in 1677, adds: 'where there is a tower [and] an enclosure surrounding it', perhaps a reference to a still-functioning Gondarine castle, Guzara, there. An improbable legend (Lejean 1872: 6) claims that two Frenchmen, M. Garneau and M. Arnaud, built the palace. Pankhurst derives these names from the nearby rivers Arno and Garno.

Bahri Gemb, or Church of St Mikael

Bahri Gemb Qeddus Mikael is an unusual church supposedly built in the reign of Sarsa Dengel (1563–95), or possibly even earlier, some 32 km. southeast of Gondar on the way to Emfraz. Driving south, it is situated on a hill to the left of the new Azazo–Bahar Dar road about 2 km. north of the small market town of Maksenyit. The *Guida* suggests that it was built early in the sixteenth century, and was later destroyed by Grañ – who did pass close by in 1534, as the *Futuh al-Habasha* relates. Local tradition dates it to the time of Emperor Lebna Dengel, claiming that it was founded by a certain *Dejazmach* Barye. In the chronicle of Emperor Iyoas (1755–69), he is said to have stopped at Menzero 'which is called Bahrey Gemb' in 1768. This is the first – and last – actual mention of the place in the chronicles.

LaVerle Berry (1994: 90) discounts the oral traditions, and suggests that Barye Gemb (Bahri Gemb) is more likely to have been an experimental successor of Gondar-style architecture than a predecessor. He dates it tentatively to the mid-eighteenth century – thus making it the last rather than the first manifestation of the style. It seems to have been a relatively obscure place. Bruce does not mention it in 1770–71. Neither does Rüppell in the 1830s, although Antoine d'Abbadie includes it in his geographical survey a little later.

The 14 m. square building is constructed of basalt, with decorative courses of red tufa, and possesses a large and unusually high dome (c. 11 m. from ground level to the top) supported on a drum. The plan appears to have been a square pierced by four round arches on each side, with an inner sub-circular colonnade of twelve square columns. (This was a common arrangement; the pillars were regarded as representing the apostles, just as every other part of a church possessed some symbolical association. The *Ser'ata Beta Kristyan*, or 'Rules of the Church', linked every facet of the church structure with heavenly protectors or some aspect of the faith.) The layout is not very well planned, four of the pillars touching the corners of the square *maqdas* or sanctuary. The columns and their linking arches support a double vaulted roof, resting on the inside on a further square structure, the *maqdas*. This has the usual three doors at the western end in the west, north and south walls, with arched doorways and red stone corbels. The walls of the *maqdas* support, by means of angle beams, the round drum from which the dome springs. On the exterior a string-course separates drum and dome.

The east wall of the *maqdas* is pierced by a triple window, now blocked. There are double and triple-step arches. (The latter are on the sanctuary doorways. Similar arches can be seen on the Qwesqwam reception hall, and on the doors of the church of Martula Maryam, rebuilt on the ruins of another older church by Father Bruno Bruni and left unfinished on Fasiladas' accession, when Bruni, among others, was hanged.) The façade was originally plastered, and new concrete finishing has now replaced this during recent restoration. Nearby, behind the church, a *beta lahm*, or building for making the bread for the eucharist, has been built, also with a dome in imitation of the main building. There is a low enclosure wall around the buildings with some fine *qolqwal* and other trees inside.

Gorgora

At Gorgora (or Gorgorra in the Portuguese records, Guargara in the chronicle of Susneyos, Pais' Gorgora-Deqana) was a Jesuit residence, later moved to Ganeta Iyasus or Azazo near Gondar. Péro Pais, when he died in 1622, was buried at Gorgora, which he himself had helped to beautify with a royal residence, built in 1614, another palace of white stone, and a church of white stone built between 1618 and 1620.

There were in fact two Gorgoras, the old and the new, the latter founded in 1626, where João Martinez built another church, the surviving one, in 1627. To get to Gorgora, it is wise to take a guide from Debra Sina and the modern hotel there, at today's Gorgora. From here, one continues back towards Gondar for a little before turning off to the left towards the lake, via dirt roads in extremely bad condition paved in many places with rough stone to render them passable, more or less, in the rainy season. The site is about half an hour's journey from Debra Sina.

Built for Emperor Susneyos by Pais on a promontory overlooking the lake above the plain of Dambya, the palace or hunting lodge was said, erroneously, to be the first two-storey house in Ethiopia. Tellez provides an account of its building. First he notes how the royal camp was situated,

> being in a Peninsula almost enclos'd by the Waters of a great Lake, which they call the Sea of Dambea [Lake Tana]. There F. Pays resolv'd to build him a Palace after the European manner, to oblige him, and show the Ethiopians that what they reported of the Palaces, and Monasteries of Europe, was not impossible, as they believ'd. He was encouraged to it by finding in that Place a Quarry of very good white stone, and therefore presently gave Directions for making Hammers, Mallets, Chizzels and all other necessary Tools, handling them himself, and teaching the new Workmen, to dig, hew, and square the Stones for the Fabrick; and the same he did as to all the Joyners, and Carpenters Part. Still he wanted Lime, and found no Stone proper to make it, and therefore made use of a binding Sort of Clay. He rais'd large, and strong Walls, fac'd both within and without with square Stones, well wrought, and joyn'd, so that the building being finish'd, might have serv'd any Prince in Europe for a Country House. Among the Rest, there was one fair Room about 50 Foot long, and 15 in breadth, and on the same Floor, a square Bedchamber, with a spacious Stair Case in the Middle, from the lower to the upper Floor, and from that another which ascended to the flat roof of the house, about which was a handsome parapet. At the Top of the Stairs was a little Room, like a Closet, which the Emperor was much pleas'd with, because from it he had the distant view of all that great Lake, and the adjacent Country, and saw at hand all that came in, and out, without being himself discover'd by any Body. The Father put a Sort of Spring Lock upon the Door, of the Stairs that went out upon the Top of the House, which the Emperor said, would be better alter'd, that he might not always stand in need of the Key to open it, but Father Pays answer'd, Your Majesty may have occasion for it as it is, and how true this prov'd we shall see hereafter. This building amaz'd all the Abyssines, who came from the remotest Parts to behold it, and what most surpriz'd them was to see an upper floor, and having no Name to express it by, they call'd it Babet laybet, that is, a House upon a House.

The lock proved useful shortly after, when, warned of a conspiracy to murder him, Susneyos received the murderers affably, rising and going to the staircase door. Then he shut the door, leaving them unable to reach him.

Lime mortar, incidentally, was shortly to be available, if one can credit Manoel de Almeida. In 1628 he wrote that 'seven years ago an intelligent person from India discovered a kind of fine, light and as it were worm-eaten stone; in … [Gujerat] he had seen it made into lime … Since then with the help of the Emperor Seltan Cegued [Susneyos] and his brother Ras Cella Christos [Sela Krestos] many beautiful churches have been built of stone and lime.' Alvares had noted a century earlier (as recorded only in the Ramusio version of his work) that lime was used to prepare a wash. The tombs at Yimrehana Krestos church near Lalibela (see below) were 'all whitewashed with white lime.'

It is said (Mathew) that in the palace wainscoting was introduced, and there was provision for state apartments, private apartments, queen's apartments and accommodation for nobles, as well as guards' and servants' quarters.

Pais wrote about the church building that he undertook at Gorgora:

> I noticed how the emperor would like to see a specimen of our churches and how they are built. So I tried to build one as well as I could. It is all built of ashlar stone. It was small, 72 palms long and 28 palms broad, but that is only the main body of the church. There is also a chapel outside the church 32 palms long and 24 palms wide. This chapel and the sacristy are built of very good red stone. The church is of white stone, very well carved. The façade and the side doors are decorated with 8 columns, and their capitals and bases and the frieze are so well carved that everyone who sees them says it is not done on earth, but in heaven. There is a choir, a good piece of wood carving.

Despite the identification of the church ruins of today with Pais' church, it seems that the existing ruin heap and sad few fragments of walls still standing belong to the 1627 church, not to Pais' own work.

When approaching the hill on which the ruined buildings at Gorgora stand, beautifully situated, surrounded on three sides by the lake overlooking the isle of Galila, the structures still look quite imposing; the church is (or rather was), entirely Portuguese, 'a piece of Europe beautifully almost absurdly placed in the green forest over the blue lake' (Mathew 1947: 43). However, Gorgora palace – if that is what the ruins are – now exists only as a few traces of a long-ruined wing, not unimpressive, constructed of dark stone, with white lintel stones. Traces of a two-storey structure still survive in one corner; here an upper window can be seen, with part of the floor below it visible in the wall – one can imagine perhaps the 'house upon a house' itself? Both the palace and the church of Maryam Gemb nearby seem to have fallen into disuse with Susneyos' death and the expulsion of the Jesuits.

One long wall of Maryam Gemb still stood until recently. It has now fallen, but a fragmentary part of the walls and vault still standing at the east end still permits one to gain an impression of the decoration. Like the richly decorated church of Martula Maryam, another transplanted European survivor much further south in Gojjam, it is a powerful witness to the quality of some aspects of the Jesuit endeavour in Ethiopia. The church now consists mainly of a massive heap of tumbled stone. The lavish interior decoration of the Gorgora church is to be attributed to its Portuguese origin. Many carved floral motifs, similar no doubt to those described in Pais' building, decorated the pilasters and the coffered ceiling inside, and there were circular windows with scroll borders on the upper level, and arched alcoves in the lower walls with shell-like tops. The roof was a long barrel vault, with lavishly decorated coffering. Despite the state of the ruins – though they have excellent archaeological prospects, everything still being preserved inside the immense heap of stone – Maryam Gemb still offers a remarkable witness to the personal endeavour and exceptional capabilities of the Portuguese in Ethiopia.

Debra Sina

Considerably further east round the lake than Old Gorgora is today's Gorgora. Here a former military camp has been made into an hotel on the lake with a charming garden full of flowering trees, through which one can walk to the round church of Debra Sina, or Mount Sinai, itself in a very attractive compound. Nearby, drawn up on the shore, one can usually see some of the *tankwa*, or reed boats, used on the lake.

A church on this site may originally date back to the time of Emperor Amda Seyon (1314–44). The decoration is said (Staude) to have been painted in the reign of Emperor Tekla Haymanot I (1706–08) at the command of his mother, Malakotawit, the wife (and murderess) of Iyasu I – the queen who was hanged for her crimes on the tree by the palace gate in Gondar (see above). Alternatively, the Malakotawit in question may be the eldest daughter of Emperor Susneyos, and sister of Fasiladas (Jäger and Pearce 1974).

At any rate, the ensemble is regarded as representative of the first Gondarine painting style. This church is not only in a delightful setting, but is an extremely good example of the painted round churches of Ethiopia. The first impression on entering the church is dazzling, a riot of colour and rich imagery. The church has a colonnaded outer circuit whose pillars support the outer part of the roof. The inner circular wall contains the *qeddest*, with twelve wooden pillars, representing the Apostles, supporting carved roof beams. Inside the *qeddest* is the square *maqdas* or sanctuary, with attractive lattice-work wooden windows.

The round drum on top of the *maqdas*, and the four exterior walls of the sanctuary, are all painted. The paintings are similar to, but more numerous than, those formerly in St Antonios' church at Gondar, which are still preserved in Paris. Some, particularly those on the south, are damaged by water, often a problem in these thatched churches. Not all the paintings are in the same positions as the ones in St Antonios, although by far the majority are (see Staude 1959 for more details). The Flight into Egypt and the Sacrifice of Abraham, however, are differently placed. On the drum, apart from God the Father, the twenty-four elders and the Covenant of Mercy (west), there are also the Transfiguration (north), eighteen (local?) saints who are in the position taken in other churches by the Ascension (east), and the Apparition of the Virgin (south).

The church of Debra Sina today has a staff of twelve priests and six deacons, as well as a number of lay canons or cantors, *dabtara*. There are two *debalat*, one dedicated to St Mikael, the other to St Mary.

Danqaz

Manoel de Almeida mentions that Emperor Susneyos had selected one particular spot, Danqaz (Dancaz) – now called Gomnagé or Gomenghe (Pankhurst 1999; Anfray 1998: 14) – as his camping place for ten consecutive years. Susneyos fixed his residence here in 1619; earlier, he passed the rains at Dekhaner, Ayba, Qoga, Gorgora and other places. De Almeida saw the Danqaz camp in 1624. It was situated on a hill, and consisted of 'as many as eight or nine thousand hearths, but as the houses are all of wood, or stone and mud, and thatched, and as they are nearly all round, it seemed more like a mountain of ricks than a city'.

But as well as this village for the accommodation of the royal train, the same sort of thing we must suppose existed around the castle at Guzara, or any of the other royal residences, there was a fine stone palace at Danqaz.

> It is now four or five years since the Emperor, when some stone masons came from India, brought by the Patriarch, built a palace of stone and lime, a structure that was a wonder in that country and something that had never been seen nor yet imagined, and it was such as would have value and be reckoned a handsome building anywhere. It stands inside two very wide and long enclosures in a situation dominating all the rest and is therefore visible a long way off. It has halls and rooms on the ground floor and upper floor, very well proportioned, and terraces from which can be seen not only the camp and the whole of Dancaz, but even very distant places in all directions.

If this is correct, the Danqaz palace must have been built a little later than the Gorgora palace; the chronicle of Susneyos does indeed confirm that 'the Franks built two palaces for him, one at Danqaz and the other at Guagara'. The confusion between Indians and Franks might derive from the fact that Indians from Portuguese India, Goa, were employed as masons, or even, perhaps, Portuguese from India.

Pankhurst (1999) cites Susneyos' chronicle for details about the construction of a palace at Danqaz. The architect is there said to have been an
Ethiopian, Gabra Krestos. The head of the masons and mortar-makers was
the Banyan (Indian) Abd al-Kerim, assisted by an Egyptian foreman, Sadaqa
Nesrani, with other workers from Egypt and 'Rome' (Europeans). Abd al-
Kerim is said by Almeida to have come from India with the patriarch. Barradas
mentions that King Seltan Seguêd (Susneyos) ordered some stone that produced a powder suitable for whitewash for his houses in Danqaz, and that he
sent him five loads.

Combes and Tamisier (1838, Vol. 2: 29ff) visited Danqaz in the 1830s,
describing an edifice 'preceded by an immense court', formerly surrounded
by a wall with a gate, then ruined. In the palace building itself, they remarked,

> at the height of a man, large cut stones where, in a rather rough way, elephants
> and horses with horsemen armed with a lance at the end of which floated a
> standard had been represented. We also observed traces of inscriptions in
> Ethiopian language washed out by the rain; all the apartments seem to have
> been carefully painted … Below the ground floor, an immense cistern had been
> dug, supported by twelve arches, and, despite the humidity of this underground
> spot, the cement was still perfectly preserved; a staircase cluttered with debris
> led to this underground room.

Combes and Tamisier noted also, near the door, a very large trough, supposedly for watering the royal horses. The palace building, they wrote, 'had
a first floor dominated by a terrace; the four angles were surmounted by
conical turrets (flèches coniques)'.

Danqaz is today very difficult of access, but fortunately a few intrepid
scholars (Anfray, Pankhurst and Berry, for example) have managed it, braving
the rapacity of a local (self-constituted?) guardian, and we can cite their
observations. The palace survives in ruins, still impressive but without the
corner turrets and carved elephants, as far as can be seen among the under-
growth, or rather overgrowth, that has begun to invade the masonry itself. A
plan illustrated by Anfray (1988: 34–5) shows an oblong nine-roomed structure; there were arched windows, and one room contains a chimney. The
ruins still exhibit some interesting features, including painting – rosettes in
brown, orange and blue – on the plaster remaining on some of the walls
(Anfray 1988; LaVerle Berry, personal communication, November 2000). The
large cistern, vaulted, that Susneyos had dug there was, according to Barradas,
made in imitation of the one the Portuguese had installed at Fremona. As in
Combes and Tamisier's time, it is still in almost perfect condition, accessible
by an internal staircase. Perhaps this was the example that was later followed
when the large vaulted cistern was installed at Fasiladas' palace at Gondar.

Combes and Tamisier also described the church: 'A large chapel, the ruins of which are still visible ... built beside the castle.' It had 'a vault made of well cut and sculpted stones'. The cruciform church at Danqaz survives, too, in a ruined, or rather unfinished and then ruined, state, its arches still intact at the crossing; the same purely Portuguese church that 'Patriarch Dom Affonso Mendes built at such expense and labour', according to Barradas (1634: 25, 100, 153). Like Maryam Gemb at Gorgora, it was an alien structure, a memory of Portugal planted in a distant land.

Zage

The Zage peninsula can be reached from Bahar Dar by land, about 60 km., or rather more easily by boat.

To travel to Zage by boat is a very pleasant trip of about an hour, past the islands of Entons (St Antonios) and Kebran, with the church of Kebran Gabriel. One can often see local lakeside or island dwellers in their *tankwa*, or reed boats, reminding one of the ancient papyrus skiffs of the Nile, or of the boats used on Lake Titicaca. On Entons are the ruins of a church dedicated to Iyasus. Kebran has a large and conspicuous church dedicated to St Gabriel, which was founded by Amda Seyon and restored by Dawit II and Iyasu II. The building is constructed using Gondar-style masonry in the round style with twelve pillars of red Danqaz stone linked by arches surrounding the cube of the *maqdas*. It contains paintings of fresco type on plaster, and also some others on cloth. The church is famous for its manuscripts, some of which are very old. The island's secure situation led to its being chosen as a safe haven for the manuscripts from other churches endangered by the army of Ahmad Grañ, and several remained here afterwards.

Zage peninsula is characterised by coffee production, but also, like many of the islands of the lake, preserves a rich natural vegetation. There are seven churches on the peninsula. Climbing to the churches from the quay one passes the small coffee plants in their beds, and then through the wooded slopes to the ruined remains of the church of Mahel Zage Giyorgis, St George, founded by Batra Maryam (a new church has been built not far away). Some of the original woodwork of the church lies dismantled at the original site. The priests there show a collection of interesting items, particularly the crowns offered by various emperors as memorials of their visits here. The attributions, not to be credited, are splendidly evocative – Amda Seyon, Fasiladas, Bakaffa and Iyasu I. Bosc-Tiessé (2000: 255) was told that they were presented by Amda Seyon, Zara Yaqob, Yohannes I and Bakaffa! Some old robes with silver appliqué ornament, and a parchment book with paintings executed in the Second Gondarine style, are also shown.

Further up the hill, there is another church dedicated to Batra Maryam, the 'Stick of St Mary'. He was a monk to whom, appropriately enough for Zage, is attributed the discovery of the coffee plant (*buna*), and also of *gesho*, a plant used like hops elsewhere in making the local *tella* beer and mead (*tej*). The church is also called Gedem Zage. It has a fairly typical design. The surrounding outer wooden gallery has attractive carved doors and windows in the inner wall, which is made of stone and mud mortar. Inside are painted ceiling beams, and coloured rush work ceilings surrounding a square *maqdas* or sanctuary, which, with its drum above, is completely painted with modern paintings.

Some fifteen minutes by boat to the south is another large round church, Uhra Kidane Mehret, consecrated to the Covenant of Mercy. The church stands in a walled compound, with some attractive outbuildings and a gatehouse. In the church, a square-pillared outer colonnade acts as a *qene mahlet*, with decorative carved beams. Two bells are suspended in the colonnade. The *qene mahlet* is divided into sections by doors placed across it transversely, an unusual feature. The inner wall exhibits carved wooden windows with painted shutters. Eight doorways lead to the *qeddest*, alternating between single and double arched openings; the inclined plinths of the doorways are carved with different designs. The *qeddest* ceiling has painted beams. Within, the square *maqdas* is covered with dazzling paintings on the outer walls and on the drum above. The paintings date from the eighteenth to the twentieth centuries, some of them being painted in Menelik's time by a certain *Alaqa* Engeda (Bosc-Tiessé 2000: 250). The crowned and enthroned figure of King Tekla Haymanot of Gojjam and his court, with soldiers armed with rifles, is particularly attractive. This church also has a treasury nearby (currently in the process of restoration). Here are exhibited richly embroidered robes said to have belonged to Lakech Makonnen, wife of King Tekla Haymanot of Gojjam, and to Adyam Sagad, Iyasu, as well as elaborate tiara-like crowns attributed – in this case perhaps with reasonable likelihood – to Emperor Yohannes IV, Emperor Tewodros, King Tekla Haymanot of Gojjam, and 'King of Kings' Tekla Giyorgis.

7

HARAR

General History

The Muslim faith is very old in this region, just across the Red Sea from the
cradle of Islam itself. Even if one often thinks of 'typical' Ethiopian history
as a Christian history, Harar represents the other face, the quintessence of
medieval Muslim Ethiopia, whose permanent centre it became. The city of
Harar, long an independent city-state, is the most important Muslim city in
the interior of what is now Ethiopia. The moment when Harar most strongly
impinged upon the Christian state was at a time when there was no walled
city or great castle in a recognised Ethiopian capital city. Emperor Lebna
Dengel (1508–40) and his successors Galawdewos, Minas and Sarsa Dengel
moved about their land, dwelling in tented camps, or passed the rains in one
or other selected spot. Against them, from inside the walls built by *Amir* Nur
in the 1550s, Harar launched its armies.

Muslim shaykhs appear to have been known here before and during the
time of Amda Seyon (1314–44), but the existence of this town is first actually
attested in the chronicle of Amda Seyon's victories over the Muslim kingdom
of Adal in the east. The *Qadi* Saleh, 'whom the kings and governors feared
and honoured like a god', assembled a huge force under sixteen kings, and an
immense number of *makwennen* or governors, to attack the Christian emperor.
The chronicle provides the incredible total of 2,722 kings and governors,
meticulously listing them. Included among them were '3 *makwennen* of Harar.'
Amda Seyon broke their power. When the Arab chronicler al-Umari was
writing later in Amda Seyon's reign there were seven kingdoms of Muslims
in the region, but all were weak and under the authority of the *negus*, the king
of Ethiopia. Harar was in the area called Dawaro. It was later included in
Adal, also called the kingdom of Zayla (Zeila).

177

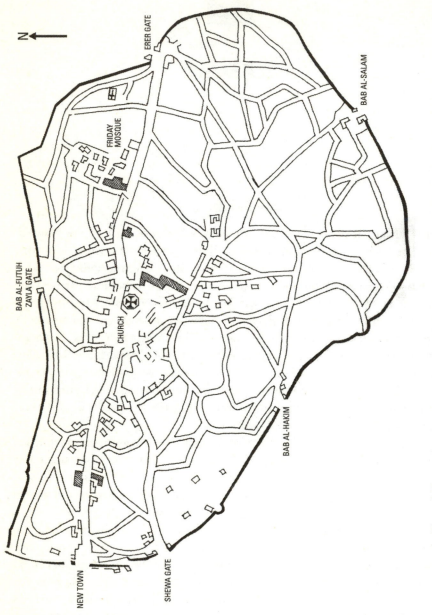

N

ERER GATE

BAB AL-SALAM

FRIDAY
MOSQUE

BAB AL-FUTUH
ZAYLA GATE

CHURCH

BAB AL-HAKIM

NEW TOWN

SHEWA GATE

6. Plan of Harar, showing the main gates in the jugal or outer wall. From the *Guida*, 1938: 447.

Harar became an important Muslim base after Amda Seyon's suppression of Ifat and the other kingdoms. It lay far enough away from the Christian kingdom's borders to be difficult to attack, and could easily avail itself of Afar and Somali assistance if necessary. After the end of the Makhzumi dynasty's dominance in eastern Shewa, the kingdom of Ifat or Adal succeeded as the chief Muslim state in the Ethiopian region. It too was situated further away from the Christian centre, with the Red Sea port of Zayla as one of its most important towns. Adal indulged in constant wars with most of the Solomonid Ethiopian emperors until the reign of Zara Yaqob, and conflict continued up to Emperor Naod's time. The ruling sultans of the Walasma dynasty of Adal grew weaker. *Amir*s or *imam*s, fired with a desire to free Muslim Adal from the Christian emperors' dominance, assumed control in the Harar region. First was Mahfuz, then, even more formidable, his son-in-law Ahmad ibn Ibrahim.

The reigning sultan, Muhammad ibn Azhar al-Din (1488–1518), would probably have preferred to coexist peacefully with his Ethiopian neighbour, Emperor Naod (1494–1508), but the raids against the Christians by Mahfuz, *amir* of Harar, precluded this. Naod, however, defeated the *amir*, and afterwards the sultan and *negus* maintained an uneasy truce. The young Lebna Dengel (1508–40) succeeded to the Ethiopian throne, with his step-grandmother the empress Eleni or Helena as regent. Peace with the Muslim kingdom was preserved, but Eleni nevertheless sent to Portugal for help. Following the advice of Pero da Covilhã, the Portuguese emissary who had come to Ethiopia and was never permitted to leave, an ambassador, an Armenian called Matthew, was despatched to Manoel I of Portugal. After endless problems and delays, this diplomatic tentative finally resulted in the arrival in Ethiopia in 1520 of a Portuguese embassy under Dom Rodrigo de Lima.

Mahfuz had meanwhile assumed the office of governor of Zayla, and attacks on Christian provinces resumed. Emperor Lebna Dengel, young as he was, took the field against Sultan Muhammad and Mahfuz when an attempt was made to infiltrate the territory of Fatagar. Mahfuz was slain, and one of the sultan's castles was destroyed. At the same time Lope Suarez surprised Zayla from the sea and sacked it.

After these successes, Emperor Lebna Dengel could feel reasonably confident. He permitted the Portuguese mission to leave in 1526 with letters proposing an alliance, and some suggestions as to how it might be implemented, but no concrete measures had yet been formally agreed between the two states. The alliance was eventually to be confirmed, and was to be a success for Ethiopia, but by the time this occurred in 1541 it was already too late for Lebna Dengel. Adal had sunk into internecine chaos for a while, several sultans succeeding rapidly on the throne, and this situation assisted the rise of a far more formidable figure even than Mahfuz: *Imam* Ahmad b. Ibrahim al-Ghazi (1506–43). In Ethiopian texts he is often called Grañ, or the 'left-handed'. Based in the Harar region, he had consolidated his power by his marriage to Bati Del Wambara, daughter of the late *Amir* Mahfuz, and by killing Sultan Abu Bakr, under whom the sultanate itself had been moved to Harar in 1520. A puppet sultan was installed as his successor. In the customary way, defiance was expressed by withholding tribute due to Ethiopia. In 1527 Degalhan, governor of Bali, appeared to chastise the Muslim 'rebels'.

Degalhan's defeat after some initial raids was the beginning of the *jihad* or holy war that from 1529 onwards until 1541 nearly destroyed Christian Ethiopia. First Dawaro and Shewa were invaded, in 1531, then two years later Amhara and Lasta. The raids spread into Bali, Hadya, Sidama and Gurage. Tigray was next, in 1535. The old capital of Aksum was sacked, although not before Lebna Dengel had arranged for the treasures of the church to be removed and hidden. The 'Ark of the Covenant' itself was taken under heavy guard to the *amba* of Tabr. The Muslim chronicle of Shihab ad-Din, called the *Futuh al-Habashat*, or 'Conquest of Abyssinia', and the royal chronicles relating to Lebna Dengel's own reign describe the destruction meted out to Christian Ethiopia. They comment, too, on the Islamisation of the population, often through fear.

To demonstrate that the Ethiopian records do not excessively exaggerate when they report vast losses both material and cultural, we can read a description of the sacking of one of many churches in Amhara in the *Futuh al-Habasha*, the often lively and detailed record of *Imam* Ahmad's conquests from the Muslim side. The church in question is Makana Sellassie:

He himself [Grañ] arrived at Makana Sellassie, and penetrated into it with admiration. He entered it with his companions, and in contemplating it they almost lost the power of sight. The interior was ornamented with sheets of gold and silver, on which had been placed incrustations of pearls. The leaf of a wooden doorway was ten cubits long and four wide; it was covered with sheets of gold and silver, and over the gold had been placed incrustations in various colours. The church was 100 cubits long; its width as much as its height over 150 cubits; the ceiling and the interior courts were covered with sheets of gold and ornamented with golden statues. The Moslems were amazed at this work ... they crowded in and he said to them: 'What any man takes shall be for himself, except for the sheets.' They set to work with a thousand axes, tearing down the gold and also the incrustations which were inside the church, from mid-afternoon till night. Each man took as much gold as he wished for, and was rich for ever. More than a third of the gold was then burned with the church.

Alvares confirms the richness of these churches, but in more modest fashion. At Atronsa Maryam, for example, where Grañ's men looted among other things 'a calf with four legs which is called in their language tabot, made of gold', Alvares described the main door as being 'all plated with plates, which at first sight look like gold, and so they told us it was: yet we saw that on the contrary it was all gold and silver leaf'. As for Makana Sellassie, Alvares mentions 'the principal door lined with plates of metal like [Atronsa Maryam] ...; and in the midst of this plating are stones and false pearls well set'.

Emperor Lebna Dengel was helpless in the face of the Muslim onslaught, reduced to fleeing from place to place in the kingdom to escape the *imam*'s pursuit. In 1535 he sent to Portugal to seek assistance, employing João Bermudes, a member of the 1520 mission who had remained behind, as his envoy. Lebna Dengel died in 1540 at Debra Damo, exhausted after the struggles of this disastrous latter part of his reign. His son Galawdewos (1540–59) succeeded him.

Christian Ethiopia had been almost lost to the Amhara emperors when in 1541 four hundred Portuguese musketeers arrived at Massawa under the captaincy of Cristovão da Gama, son of the great Eastern explorer Vasco da Gama. The Portuguese were compelled to traverse a large part of Ethiopia to meet up with the new emperor's forces in Shewa, but in the face of numerous difficulties and dangers they eventually succeeded in doing so. Not all the rulers of the regions they crossed were inimical. The Portuguese received assistance from the *bahrnagash*, Yeshaq, and from other nobles who had managed to retain command of their districts. In addition, they were accompanied, as a clear sign of their alliance with the Christian monarchy, by the queen mother, Lebna Dengel's widow Sabla Wangel. As they moved southwards into the heart of Ethiopia, there were various skirmishes, with encouraging results. Galawdewos, too, had occasional successes. It was certainly a boost for Ethiopian morale to observe that the Muslims were far from invincible. In 1542 Ahmad was wounded at a battle at Ainaba near Lake Ashangi. After another defeat he retired to Zobel on the eastern escarpment, whence he sent for nine hundred musketeers from the *pasha* of Zabid in Yemen.

At the battle of Afla (Wofla) near Lake Ashangi, the Portuguese suffered a major setback when Cristovão da Gama was captured in August 1542. He was soon afterwards executed, the *amir* himself wielding the sword that beheaded him. The loss of their leader, however, did not mean that the Portuguese were reduced to impotence. Those who were left continued on to meet the emperor. Ahmad, meanwhile, suffered a reduction in the number of his Turkish allies, and accordingly in his fire power. In late 1542, Emperor

Galawdewos and the Portuguese finally effected their junction in Semien. Even if both sides of the alliance were horrified at the smallness of each other's force, it was to prove sufficient. At Wayna Dega east of Lake Tana there was another – and memorable – battle. According to one source at least (Bermudes), the Portuguese soldier Pedro Leon shot and wounded *Imam* Ahmad himself. He died shortly afterwards. This was the end of Christian Ethiopia's worst disaster since the seizure of power of the 'queen of the Bani al-Hamwiyya' many centuries before.

But it was not the end of conflict. The people of Harar, stirred up by Ahmad's widow *Bati* Del Wambara, launched another campaign. It ended in defeat, although some captured leaders were exchanged for the emperor's brother Minas, held captive in Zabid. (He had narrowly escaped the castration meted out to other captives, apparently because there was an idea to convert him to Islam and marry him to a member of Grañ's family.) Still Harar was not subdued. Another attempt at resistance resulted in the sack of the city in 1550. Then a further campaign was undertaken under Ahmad's nephew Nur, *amir* of Harar, in 1551. It was this Nur, regarded even today as the town's local patron saint and hero, and nicknamed 'the second conqueror' (his uncle being the 'first conqueror'), who built the walls that eventually were to save Harar from destruction. Del Wambara made the *amir* swear to avenge Ahmad, agreeing that she would then marry him.

A complex situation had arisen, with the Ottoman Turks reaching the borders of the Christian kingdom in Massawa and Arqiqo in 1557. The Christians' attention was now divided between two inimical Muslim groups on the frontiers. *Amir* Nur was proclaimed 'Commander of the Faithful', and invaded Fatagar in 1559. In reciprocation, the emperor sent Hamalmal, his cousin, to attack Harar. The sultan, Barakat b. Umar Din, abandoned Harar and was defeated in battle. However, disaster struck the Ethiopians too. Emperor Galawdewos was killed in battle with *Amir* Nur. His brother Minas succeeded him. The Christian kingdom was once again in a perilous state.

Weakened by the long conflict, both the Christian and the Muslim states were in no condition to meet a new and powerful invader. By 1567 the Oromo or Galla people, in the full flood of their migrations, had swept over the whole Harar sultanate. Only the walled city itself held out. An Arab chronicle of Harar relates how the Oromo devastated the region. *Amir* Nur tried to resist, but died of pestilence following a famine in 1567–68. Harar, although safe within its walls, saw at once its territory and its life-giving trade stripped away from it, while inside the city, factions struggled for political control.

Sultan Muhammad b. Nasir of Harar allowed himself to be tempted into supporting a rebellion in the north of Ethiopia, led by *Bahrnagash* Yeshaq, who also had the support of the Turks. In 1577, the sultan went to war with the *negus*. The result was a major defeat for the Harari forces by Emperor Sarsa Dengel, and the loss of the city state's military power. The sultan himself was captured, and later executed.

Meanwhile the Oromo had seized the remaining Harari territory, even besieging the city itself. The situation was not completely hopeless, however, for in time the Oromo began to convert to Islam in substantial numbers. Harar's markets and long-distance trade were able to revive. Although the sultanate was moved to Aussa in 1577, Harar was to become an independent city-state until the late nineteenth-century conquests by the Egyptians and by Emperor Menelik II. It even issued its own coinage in the eighteenth and nineteenth centuries.

Extant Harari chronicles – though offering very different sets of dates – provide information about the rulers and the main events of Harari history, and the Ethiopian chronicles too offer some brief notes. European sources say almost nothing about Harar until Sir Richard Burton's visit there. It remained remote and unattainable. Remedius Prutky mentioned Harar in passing: 'Adel, the kingdom of the Saracens whose capital is Ara' (Arrowsmith-Brown 1991: 123). James Bruce comments briefly on it: 'Harar is four days journey from Shoa, and seven from Aussa. It is further inland, and a plain country. The chief has the title Emir; and is frequently at war with Amha Yasous in Shoa [King Amha Iyasus of Shewa], who is independent. The people are all Mohametans, called Turks by the Abyssinians.'

Richard Burton visited Harar – the first European to actually enter the city, although Harris and others heard news of it before – in 1855. He paints a picture of the town's degenerate condition under Sultan Ahmad b. Abu Bakr, who ruled until 1866. Burton nevertheless described the town in not unimpressive terms:

> The ancient metropolis of a once mighty race, the only permanent settlement in Eastern Africa, the reported seat of Muslim learning – a walled city of stone houses, possessing its independent chief, its peculiar population, and its own coinage – the emporium of the coffee trade, the headquarters of slavery, the birthplace of the Kat plant, and the great manufactory of cotton cloths.

Burton, in disguise, was received in audience by the ruler of Harar and also met some of the local officials.

When Muhammad b. Ali usurped the throne of Harar, the people appealed to Khedive Ismail of Egypt for help. Ra'uf Pasha, who had already taken Zayla and Berbera in 1870, occupied Harar in 1874, remaining there as the khedive's governor. Vigorous campaigns were mounted against the Oromo, who were defeated and Islamised much more strongly than before.

As a brief social comment, it was remarked by an Egyptian officer of the occupation that the Hararis treated women much better than did most other Muslims at this time. The women of Harar in fact controlled their husbands. All but the *amir* limited themselves to one wife.

It was during the Egyptian occupation, in 1880, that the French poet Arthur Rimbaud set up a branch of an Aden commercial company in Harar. In 1882–83 he explored the Ogaden region, and in 1887 he was involved in some arms dealing with Menelik, king of Shewa. From 1888 to 1891 Rimbaud directed a factory selling coffee, musk and skins in Harar. A letter that he wrote to Alfred Ilg, Emperor Menelik's Swiss man-of-all-work combined with foreign minister, indicates that Rimbaud was perfectly willing to enter the slave trade too, if he could. A house supposedly once occupied by Rimbaud is still shown in the city. It preserves a certain aura of very battered splendour, with an elegant upper room surrounded by an oval gallery, a painted canvas ceiling badly in need of conservation, and a long balcony with coloured glass windows overlooking the town. However, there seems to be no real proof that this building (which is now reported to be undergoing restoration) was really Rimbaud's house.

Between 1883 and 1890 Menelik, king of Shewa until 1899, and after that emperor of Ethiopia, conquered the province of Harar. In 1884–85 the Egyptians left, and Abdallah b. Muhammad was set on the throne of Harar city by the *pasha* and the British Consul. In 1886, after the new sultan's soldiers had massacred an Italian expedition, Menelik defeated Abdallah's forces, annexing the city in early 1887 to his kingdom of Shewa. He appointed his own cousin *Ras* Makonnen as governor of Harar. Aussa too was annexed in 1896.

When *Ras* Makonnen died 1906, his son *Ras* Tafari, later to be emperor under the title Haile Sellassie, succeeded to the governorate. His palace, a large building in a semi-ruinous state, still dominates the town not far from 'Rimbaud's house'. In 1913 Lij Iyasu became emperor. He often stayed in Harar, and was reputed to be considering conversion to Islam. For this, and for other trespasses against certain Ethiopian and European interests during the sensitive years of the First World War, he was deposed in 1917. Zawditu, Menelik's daughter, became empress of Ethiopia and *Ras* Tafari Makonnen was installed as regent.

The Town of Harar

Harar is about 526 km. from Addis Ababa, lying some 1,850 m. above sea level. It is now once again, under the blanket control of the Ethiopian federal government, a self-governing regional polity.

The outer wall, called the *jagol*, the same name given to the defensive hedges or enclosures of a royal camp, is not particularly impressive, but is still more or less intact around its entire circuit. It has recently been restored. Burton commented that it was 'lately repaired, but ignorant of cannon ... pierced by five gates and supported by oval towers of artless construction'.

The gates have different names according to different sources, Ethiopian, Arab, or Somali: on the west side, the Shewa gate (Bab al-Nasri, Burton's Asmadim Bari or Hamaraisa) the south gate or Bab al-Hakim (Buda Ber, Burton's Badro Bari or Bab Bida); the southeastern gate, Bab al-Salam (Sanca, Sofi, or Burton's Sukutal Bari or Bisidimo Gate); the east or Erer Gate (Bab al-Rahima, Burton's Argob Bari); and the north or Zayla Gate (Fellano/Faldano Ber, Bab al-Futuh; Burton calls it Asum Bari or Aksum Gate).

Burton noted that 'at all times these gates are carefully guarded; in the evening the keys are taken to the Amir, after which no one can leave the city till dawn'.

Reading Burton's description of the city as it was in 1855, one finds that much is still the same:

> The material of the houses and defences are rough stones, the granites and sandstones of the hills, cemented, like the ancient Galla cities, with clay. The only large building is the Jami or Cathedral [Mosque], a long barn of poverty stricken appearance, with broken-down gates, and two whitewashed minarets of truncated conoid shape. They were built by Turkish architects from Mocha and Hodaydah: one of them lately fell, and has been replaced by an inferior effort of Harari art. There are a few trees in the city, but it contains none of those gardens which give to Eastern settlements that pleasant view of town and country combined. The streets are narrow lanes, up hill and down dale, strewed with gigantic rubbish heaps, upon which repose packs of mangy or one-eyed dogs, and even the best are encumbered with rocks and stones. The habitations are mostly long, flat-roofed sheds, double storied, with doors composed of a single plank, and holes for windows pierced high above the ground, and decorated with miserable wood-work: the principal houses have separate apartments for the women, and stand at the bottom of large courtyards closed by gates of Holcus stalks. The poorest classes inhabit 'Gambisa,' the thatched cottages of the hill-cultivators. The city abounds in mosques, plain buildings without minarets, and in graveyards stuffed with tombs – oblong troughs formed by long slabs planted edgeways in the ground.

The mosque (here dealt much the same verbal treatment as James Bruce had meted out to Aksum cathedral – see below) is now of much improved external appearance, but the rest of the city is decidedly scruffy. Burton's opinion of the moral qualities of the Hararis was not high either. He added that the Somalis referred to the city as 'a Paradise inhabited by asses', and described the population in fairly depressing terms. He cited also the proverb 'Hard as the heart of Harar'. He describes the administration: 'The government of Harar is the Amir' ... His rule is severe if not just.' The army, commerce, houses, and local diet are also touched on in this first extensive report about the town to reach the outside world.

West of the walled city today is the very considerable new town, laid out by the Italians with a governor's palace and other administrative buildings.

Harar was (and is still) known for a number of saints' tombs – it was an important place of pilgrimage – and for schools of Muslim learning. Itinerant Muslim missionaries from Harar penetrated as far as the Gibé states to the south. The tomb of *Amir* Nur, a little *qubba* or domed structure near Fellano Gate (Bab al-Futuh), not far from the main mosque, was much revered. Another place of pilgrimage is the domed tomb of Shaykh Umar Abadir al-Bakri in the southwestern part of the city. He came apparently from Jidda as an early propagator of Islam in the region. Shaykh Ibrahim Abu Zaharbui, who became a missionary in Harar around 1430, is also revered. Shaykh Ibrahim's tomb is near the Bisidimo Gate (Bab al-Salam). He became addicted to *qat* (or *chat*, *cathus edulis*, the green leaves chewed as a stimulant in this region and in Yemen). Legend claims that Shaykh Ibrahim introduced *qat* into the Yemen; but al-Umari, writing around 1345, already mentions its use there. *Qat* was evidently much loved in the Muslim part of eastern Ethiopia – al-Maqrizi, writing in the mid-fifteenth century, also mentions its use in Ifat to keep drowsy scholars awake over learned tomes, while in the chronicle of Amda Seyon, the Muslim ruler Sabr al-Din boasts: 'I will take Maradi [the Christian's capital at Tagwelat], I will plant *qat* there as Muslims love this plant.'

Harar was also famous for its slave market. Places of interest to visit nowadays are *Amir* Abdallah's house, the Museum, which has an interesting collection of local manufactures, and also a number of houses of typical Harai type, furnished in traditional style. In general, apart from these few tourist spots, the town has a supremely run down and dilapidated air, although the markets seem to flourish. The entire district is marred by a remarkable carpeting of fragmenting plastic bags of different colours that line the roads into Harar and spread over every available space.

Harar preserves a most unusual feature – its language. It is one of the several Semitic tongues of Ethiopia, but possesses its own unique elements. Perhaps it was originally brought by colonists from the north in medieval times – traditions hint at Tigrayan settlers. Possibly, too, some inhabitants later moved on from Harar to the Gurage region, perhaps during Grañ's wars, and there also left the Semitic Gurage language. Harari is today confined to the city of Harar.

8

LALIBELA

General Survey and History

There is no question that Gondar, with its sombre battlemented castles, is imbued with a certain mausoleum-like majesty. The ancient capital of Aksum with its imposing stelae, its ruined palaces and its labyrinth of tombs, is truly awe-inspiring, at least in the vision of what it once was. But Lalibela, younger than Aksum, and many centuries older than Gondar, has not infrequently been ranked, *tout court*, as a 'wonder of the world'. Whatever the arguments about Gondar might be – was it the work of Portuguese, half-Portuguese, or Indian architects and masons, and how much, if any, of the inspiration can be credited to Ethiopians? – ultimately it derives from outside Ethiopia. Aksum and Lalibela, far older, far more accomplished, are indisputably part of Ethiopia's own tradition, even if the Ethiopians themselves give the credit for the mightiest works of their ancestors to Greeks or Egyptians. Aksum and Lalibela have in common that they illustrate the Ethiopians' extraordinary aptitude for stone-working. In the one case this was expressed in the quarrying, dressing and transporting of vast blocks of rock, for use as stele or in building work. In the other, the technique was reversed. At Lalibela, the masons excavated into the mountain itself to form entire buildings from one block of stone, isolated by deep cuttings but still joined to the living rock at one side, at the base, or even at the top.

In about 1137 a new dynasty, known to historians as the Zagwé, took over the government of Ethiopia, or at least of a restricted area in the northern part of the country so-called today. They originated from Bugna in the Lasta region. The name Zagwé is an Ethiopian term of uncertain meaning, perhaps linked to the Agaw ethnic origins of the dynasty. All the surviving Ethiopian sources – those preserved by the rulers who ousted the Zagwé – regard these kings as usurpers from the rightful 'Solomonic' or 'Israelite' dynasty, although

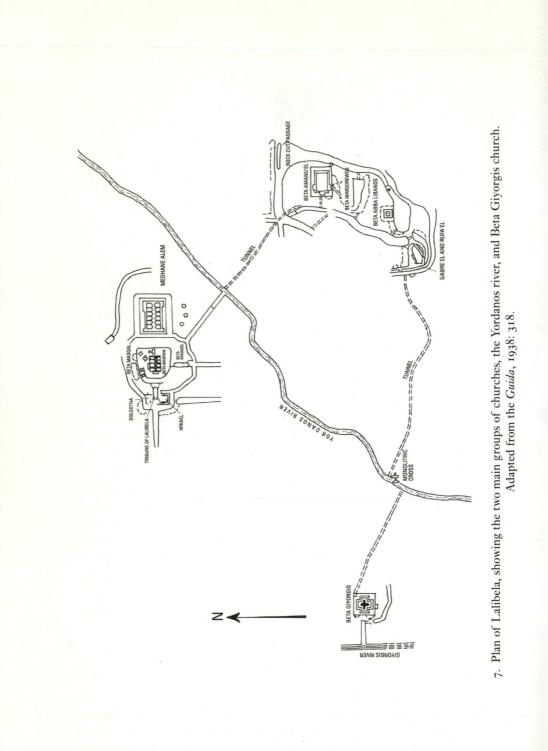

7. Plan of Lalibela, showing the two main groups of churches, the Yordanos river, and Beta Giyorgis church. Adapted from the *Guida*, 1938: 318.

several legends recount the marriage of the first Zagwé ruler to the daughter of the last 'legitimate' king. Nevertheless, some of the Zagwé kings, despite this stain on the dynasty's origins, are accorded reverence for their saintly lives in their *gadlat* or life stories. It is an interesting phenomenon. No less than three kings of a dynasty vilified by the official records of succeeding times are regarded as saints, while none of the 'Solomonic' kings who ousted them – putative relatives of Christ himself by their claim to descend from the Davidic house – have ever been canonised by the Ethiopian church.

The best-known Zagwé monarch, King Lalibela, ruled in the late twelfth and early thirteenth centuries. It is he who is supposed to have been the creator of Ethiopia's greatest architectural wonder, the rock-cut churches of Roha, in the district of Warawar in Lasta, now called Lalibela after him. The name Roha is claimed – speculatively, by modern writers – to originate from the Syriac name of the city of Edessa, Orhay, in Arabic al-Ruha, whose King Abgar was famed in Christian tradition as having received a letter from Jesus himself. Edessa was briefly the capital of a Crusader state, the County of Edessa, until its fall to the Muslims in 1144. It is supposed that the Zagwé, shocked by the disaster, adopted the name Roha for their own city as a memorial.

Lalibela (situated at about 2,630 m. above sea level) might today seem a strange place to select for the capital of a realm, perched on the slopes of Mount Abuna Yosef, in a remote and mountainous region not easy to traverse. It lies one and a quarter hours' flight (in a twin-engined Fokker) from Addis Ababa. From the air, ridge after ridge is visible stretching to the horizon, with roads or trackways following the ridges or the valleys. There is, however, a surprising amount of agricultural land available in the area, in the valleys and on the slopes, despite its daunting appearance at first sight. Groups of round *tukul*s can be seen, or a round church in its grove of trees; sometimes the villages are situated on ledges of the mountains, sometimes on several shelves of a slope, or on a spine or spur at the end of a ridge. Bright yellow ricks are visible amid protective enclaves of euphorbia plants, and numerous threshing floors, surrounded by a patchwork of irregularly shaped fields of teff, sorghum and maize – fields with scarcely a straight line to any of their boundaries. Sometimes the fields lie atop a large *amba*, or sheer-sided flat-topped mountain. The present Lalibela airport (now being enlarged) is in a valley watered by one of the tributaries which swell the Takaze, some 9 km. from the modern town. Francisco Alvares in the 1520s mentioned very numerous and prosperous towns some forty miles away to the east. Achille Raffray in 1882 estimated the population of Lalibela at about 3,000, including pilgrims and those who had come to be cured. Now it is said to be about 7,000, plus some 800 ecclesiastics.

At Lalibela, there are eleven churches, cut in most cases completely out of the solid rock, designed according to legend after a vision by the Zagwé emperor of the Heavenly Jerusalem. They create, to quote Roderick Grierson's apposite terminology, 'a mystical topography' (Grierson 1993: 12). Along the valley of a river – itself canalised in places into a rock-cut channel – called Yordanos after the Jordan, site of the baptism of Christ, the workmen excavated vast pits or trenches. They isolated immense blocks of the living rock, which the masons then in turn transformed into colonnaded, arched and domed churches, faithfully following in stone the special features of the old Aksumite architectural style. Indeed, it has been suggested that the monuments may have been intended to represent a 'New Aksum' as well as a 'New Jerusalem', to replace or duplicate the former imperial capital's pre-eminent holiness in Ethiopia. North of the Yordanos is Debra Zeit (the Mount of Olives) and Bethany; south is Debra Tabor (Mount Tabor, the Mount of Transfiguration). The first group of churches represents Jerusalem; the second Bethlehem. In this way, a new landscape of the Holy Land was constructed in the mountains of Lasta; 'partie intégrante de la montagne' to cite Raffray's apt description.

Whether Lalibela was intended to replace as a pilgrimage centre the real Jerusalem, lost to the Christian world in 1187 when it fell to Saladin, is a moot point. The Ethiopians seem to have had no difficulties with Saladin (see Munro-Hay 1997). We have no evidence, either, that the attributions resulting in that 'mystical topography' were contemporary with Lalibela himself. They might have been a rather later phenomenon, resulting from the popularity of the site as a pilgrimage centre for the 'holy king' Lalibela. The *Life of Lalibela* (*Zena Lalibela*) was written only in the fifteenth century, and we have no means of knowing what basis, if any, its author had for claiming that the emperor had visited Jerusalem, or that the city was carved out in response to a dream of Jerusalem. Nevertheless, it is not inconceivable that the cutting of these churches could have been a deliberate response to provide an alternative for pilgrims for the city that had such a profound grip on the Ethiopian imagination, but was so difficult for them physically to reach. One only need recall, centuries later, *Itege* Mentewab's yearning remark as recorded by James Bruce during a conversation at Qwesqwam:

> You are come from Jerusalem, through vile Turkish governments, and hot, unwholesome climates to see a river and a bog [her unromantic view of Bruce's famous 'journey to discover the source of the Nile']. I, on the other hand, the mother of kings who have sat upon the throne of this country for more than thirty years, have for my only wish, night and day, that, after giving up every-thing in the world, I could be conveyed to the church of the Holy Sepulchre in Jerusalem, and beg alms for my subsistence all my life after, if only I could

be buried in the street within sight of the gate of that temple where our blessed Saviour once lay.

It has been asserted that the Zagwé kings 'imposed multiple layers of meaning on their ceremonial centre. It was a New Roha or Edessa, a replica of Jerusalem and the Holy Land, and it simultaneously presented quotations of two churches at Aksum' (Heldman 1995). By this interpretation Medhane Alem church at Lalibela is supposed to represent Maryam Seyon cathedral at Aksum (although it is dedicated to the 'Saviour of the World' rather than to his mother). The Beta Danagel or church of the Virgins mentioned in the *Book of Aksum* would be the precursor of the dedication of Beta Danagel at Lalibela. But a new Roha, a new Jerusalem and a new Aksum may be rather overstating the case. We do not know for certain that Lalibela's capital was supposed in Zagwé times to be a New Jerusalem – no mention of such identification is found in any contemporary document, or even in any document for several centuries afterwards. In the case of imitation of Aksum, this too is difficult to prove.

Dedications of churches may not always have been the same as they are today in either Aksum or Lalibela. There is, in fact, no clear proof for the designation 'Mary of Zion' at Aksum until well after the fall of the Zagwé dynasty. Indeed, the same caution might apply to Lalibela dedications. The wooden altars that have been found there, with inscriptions apparently dating them to the time of Lalibela and his queen, Masqal Kebra, do not, by and large, share the present dedications of the churches. They might have been *debalat*; alternatively, the dedications might have changed with time.

Lalibela is a still-functioning testimony to the piety of the old Ethiopian kings, perhaps even to King Lalibela himself. There remains, however, room for the suspicion that the origin of some of these churches might be even earlier, in the late or post-Aksumite period when we know that the cutting of rock was a familiar technique. In such a case, King Lalibela may have been responsible for only certain final operations at the site. The *tabotat* or altars just mentioned, and other fragments of wood with inscriptions, which have been found in the sanctuaries of the Gabriel, Medhane Alem, Mikael–Golgotha and Giyorgis churches recently, certainly name Lalibela and his queen, Masqal Kebra (see Gigar Tesfaye 1987). They may be attributable to Lalibela, or they may be pious forgeries dating from a subsequent phase. Yet even if we accept the altars as Lalibela's work, they do no more than indicate that King Lalibela took an interest in the churches – they are far from proof that he had all, or any of them, constructed. Nevertheless, that is the claim of later Ethiopian legend, except in the case of Beta Marqorewos church, sometimes said to have been built by Queen Masqal Kebra after the king's death.

It has often been suggested that the cutting of the Lalibela churches from the rock is in part due to the influence of foreign workmen who came to Ethiopia to escape persecutions in Egypt. Francisco Alvares himself wrote: 'They [the Ethiopians themselves] told me that all the work on these churches was done in twenty-four years, and that this is written, and that they were made by Gibetas [Qibt, Copts or Egyptians], that is, white men, for they well know that they do not know how to do any well-executed work.' This may well have been true in the 1520s. But taking into account the long Aksumite tradition of stone-working, and its continuance with the rock-cutting tradition that has given Tigray and other places a very large number of rock churches, Lalibela is remarkable more for its grandiose conception and finer detail than for any sudden influx of evidently foreign techniques. More, the structural details cut into the rock derive in good part from Aksumite architecture itself. Even elements as yet unknown from ancient Aksum are not necessarily excluded, when it is considered how little we yet know of Aksumite architecture. For example, only during our excavations at Aksum in 1974 was it realised that the Aksumites knew the arch and the vault, and since then there have been few further archaeological excavations to expand our knowledge. The idea of actually isolating the immense rock blocks to be carved is certainly one aspect not seen in the usual rock-cut churches of Ethiopia, but on the other hand Lalibela is on a royal scale, far from the usual relatively small church cut behind a simple façade into a cliff. If there were foreigners in the workforce, they might have been responsible for certain ornamental details, and perhaps for some technological improvements, but otherwise Lalibela – even if its date remains questionable – fits comfortably, indeed inescapably, within the bounds of Ethiopia's own artistic and architectural development.

The *Vie de Lalibela* published by Perruchon from a (nineteenth-century) Ge'ez manuscript of the *Zena Lalibela* now in the British Library tells the Ethiopian version of the construction of the churches. The work may belong originally to the mid-fifteenth century, by which time the king had become a saint in Ethiopia, and Roha an important place of pilgrimage. When God eventually instructed Lalibela to begin the work after the model of the churches he had seen in heaven, the king prepared tools, summoned workmen to whom he gave whatever wages they themselves set, and purchased the land. This latter gesture was to the writer of the story a sign of great bounty: 'for if he had wished to take it, who could have stopped him, being king?' It was a telling remark, for the British Museum copy of this manuscript was prepared for Queen Walatta Iyasus in the early nineteenth century, during the *zemana mesafint*, when royal or princely justice was indeed arbitrary, and the ancient king's act must have seemed a prodigy of saintliness.

According to the *Vie de Lalibela*, angels assisted the excavation of the churches, each night doing much more work than the human labour force could achieve during the day. The king had Beta Maryam cut first from the rock, with Debra Sina and Golgotha in front of it, Beta Masqal to the right, and Beta Danagel to the left. Behind it he had hewn out 'a great church which he had decorated, not with gold and silver but with sculptures cut in the stone; there are seventy-two pillars in this church, like the disciples of the Saviour'. This must refer to Beta Medhane Alem, although there are only twenty-eight interior columns and thirty-four exterior, totalling sixty-two. The number seventy-two may refer to a later attempt to associate the church with the seventy-two disciples of Christ (Heldman 1995). Near these churches King Lalibela caused Beta Gabre'el and Beta Abba Mata'a to be carved out of the rock, two churches made together, separated by an interior wall. This version attributes the name of Abba Mata'a, an alternative name of Abba Libanos, to the church of Rufa'el – the church today called Abba Libanos is not mentioned with the rest. Is this a hint that in the fifteenth century the attributions were different from those found today, at least in certain cases? Beta Marqorewos and Beta Amanu'el came next, then finally Beta Giyorgis. In Golgotha particularly, the author adds, the king had some beautiful pictures painted.

Foreign Descriptions of Lalibela

An intriguing report about Ethiopia comes from Abu Salih the Armenian, author of *The Churches and Monasteries of Egypt*, and incidental collector of a certain amount of current (late twelfth to early thirteenth-century) gossip about Ethiopia and Nubia. Abu Salih was a contemporary of Yimrehana Krestos and/or Harbay and Lalibela. He refers to events between the 1160s and 1208 as happening in his own lifetime. Much of what Abu Salih records may be hearsay, although possibly some of it derived from Abyssinians who came to Egypt. As it happens, just at this period, there was an immense interest in Egypt in matters to do with Ethiopia. A mission arrived in 1200 from the king of Ethiopia to ask the patriarch of Alexandria to seek a new metropolitan bishop for his country, and there was unusual activity later concerning this bishop's deposition and the despatch of a new one in 1210. Abu Salih may have spoken with any one of the different messengers, Abyssinian or Egyptian, or indeed with the deposed Metropolitan Michael, ex-bishop of Fuwa, himself, and thus gained information about the distant Ethiopian kingdom.

The story of these events is quite exceptional in the image we gain of Ethiopia at this time. We learn that the new metropolitan, Isaac, was consecrated for "Arafah, the royal city ... and over all Ethiopia (al-Habashat)'. This indicates that the centre for both church and state was now at the

Zagwé capital in Lasta, named in the *Gadla Yimrehana Krestos* as Adefa. The text confirms that the residence of the metropolitan was in the city of 'Arafah. It then goes on to provide some notes about the king himself, the sole appearance of a Zagwé king by name in any foreign historical source. The king was called Lalibalah ibn Shanuda, meaning 'the Lion', of the tribe of Al-Nakbah. His queen was named Masghal Kabra, 'Great is the Cross'. The dynasty came from a province called al-Bakna (Bugna), and the king's eldest son was called Yabarak (Yitbarak).

After all this very specific information about Ethiopia, its capital, king and dynastic and ecclesiastic situation, we return to Abu Salih. Among other things, he describes the coronation of the Ethiopian kings. They were, he writes,

> crowned with the royal crown in the church of the angel Michael, or the church of St George, beneath their pictures. After that the king does not wear the crown, but the metropolitan blesses him, and lays his hand upon his head, and fastens a band over his head and beneath his chin, and clothes him in a robe of brocade.

What were these two churches, and where? As we have seen, by now Arafah or Adefa is named as 'the royal city' by the *History of the Patriarchs*; it was called Roha also for a time, and is now Lalibela. Some of the edifices there, such as the churches of Mercurius and of the Archangels, might have been parts of the royal residence, only subsequently made into churches. Some of the dedications might have changed. But nevertheless, it is interesting to observe that there is at Lalibela a church with a *tabot* of St Michael, and another dedicated to St George. Could Roha/Adefa, the Zagwé royal city, have been the coronation place described by Abu Salih's informant?

If this was the case, why were there two coronation churches? Lalibela, supposed builder of the churches, was the fifth king of his dynasty. Does this mean that his predecessors were also crowned in these churches? If so, might the rock-cut churches have already been in existence by Lalibela's time? It is an intriguing possibility – but no more than that in the present state of our knowledge. Earlier Zagwé kings might have been crowned in Adefa, in conventionally built churches dedicated to Mikael and Giyorgis.

One might speculate about other details of the information about Ethiopia in Lalibela's time gleaned from Abu Salih and the *History of the Patriarchs*. In the latter, a story is told about the magnificent dwelling Metropolitan Michael constructed for himself; it had corridors so long that 'he who enters them becomes weary before he reaches their lowest part and their highest part'. There are traces of large monuments built on the surface at Lalibela, perhaps the remains of other royal or ecclesiastical installations, and one should probably think of a substantial town of lesser houses of more perishable materials, wood, mud and thatch, or rough stone, like the houses of the present day. The palace and the House of the Metropolitan may perhaps be among the apparently originally secular constructions such as Beta Marqorewos or Beta Gabre'el Rufa'el, perhaps combined with some of the remains on the surface. Certainly the tale about the corridors will ring a bell with anyone who has wandered around Lalibela's vast underground maze.

If, as Abu Salih records, the Ark of the Covenant itself was kept among the treasures of the royal church at the Zagwé capital (see Grierson and Munro-Hay 1999), which church might have been meant? Gerster suggests that the church of Amanu'el 'may have served the king as the palace chapel', doubtless because of its particularly careful cutting and decoration. Perhaps, following the report of the *History of the Patriarchs*, we may imagine King Lalibela here amid the perfumed smoke of the aloe-wood and incense as Metropolitan Michael, robed in his golden jewelled cape, entered the sanctuary every Sunday.

When Europeans first started to learn something about Lalibela is uncertain. An early example seems to have been Alessandro Zorzi. On 7 April 1523, in Venice, he collected notes about an itinerary in Ethiopia from Brother Thomas, an Ethiopian 'Franciscan' from Ganget. Brother Thomas said that from the castle of Asquaga one went on to Urvuar (Warawar, yet another name for the Lalibela region); 'and there is a king in the said great city, where are 12 churches of canons and a bishop, and the tomb of a holy king that works miracles, and has the name of Lalivela; whither go very many pilgrims from all the lands'. From there one journeyed to Bugna, the district that lies just north of Lalibela. A certain Brother Antonio, who actually came from Urvuar, was also among those who supplied an Ethiopian itinerary to Zorzi.

Francisco Alvares, once again, is of key importance in the history of the revelation of the churches of Lalibela to a wider world. Some time after 1520 he travelled in Lasta, viewing the splendid church of Yimrehana Krestos in a cave near Lalibela, and then visiting Lalibela itself. He returned again later with the ambassador Saga Za-Ab, appointed by Lebna Dengel to go to Portugal. Alvares was amazed by what he saw: 'At a day's journey from this church of Imbra Christo are buildings, the like of which and so many, cannot, as it appears to me, be found in the world, and they are churches entirely excavated in the [living, soft] rock [or tufa], very well hewn.' Alvares described the churches – in a way very difficult to follow, although one can just about recognise the churches in question. He then added his famous disclaimer:

I weary of writing more about these buildings, because it seems to me that I shall not be believed if I write more, and because regarding what I have already written they may blame me for untruth, therefore I swear by God, in whose power I am, that all that I have written is the truth (to which nothing has been added), and there is much more than what I have written, and I have left it that they may not tax me with its being falsehood (so great was my desire to make known this splendour to the world) and because no other Portuguese went to these buildings except myself, and I went twice to see (and describe) them because of what I had heard about them.

So he defended himself against the same accusations of immoderate exaggeration as would later be levelled at James Bruce concerning such incredible matters as cutting meat from a living cow. In Ramusio's 1550 Italian version of Alvares' work, plans of eight of the churches, of uncertain authorship, and sometimes difficult enough to reconcile with the originals, were included.

In a plain two days distant from Lalibela, Alvares was told there are 'other buildings such as those of Aquaxumo, like stone chairs and all other buildings, and that the residences of the kings were there'. This is reminiscent of Monti della Corte's description of a stone 'throne of Imraha' close to Bilbola, west of Arbaat Ensesa near Lalibela (1940: 165, and Tav. XXXVIII):

> Prima di allora, il santo e potente monarca aveva la sua sede vicino a Bilbolà … il 'trono' attribuitogli dalle leggende indigene, un sedile formato di tre pietre squadrate profondamente infisse nel suolo e circondate da un muricciolo a secco, certo assai posteriore, benchè anche in esso appaiano, commisti a sassi informi, vari blocchi tagliati che son da ritenere provenienti dai ruderi di un più antico edificio. Queste 'trono' si trova su una piccola altura, coronata di piante, su cui, semiterrati, si notato traccie della arenaria rossastra, che presentano traccie della mano dell'uomo. L'altura stessa e forse in parte artificiale e nasconde un ammasso di rovine antichissime. E' a un'ora e mezza circa da Bilbolà Gheorghis, in direzione Nord-Est.

Miguel de Castanhoso was the chronicler of the adventurous expedition under Cristovão da Gama, and, after his death, with the remaining Portuguese to offer military assistance to the Emperor Galawdewos. He relates that in 1543 they came to a region 'on the skirts of the sea called Jartafaa'. He continues:

> We marched in this way for eight days, straight from the lake to the sea … we continued on until we came to a hill on whose top were twelve monasteries of friars, or churches in which religious men lived, a few men to each, and each one dedicated. Each church was formed from one stone, excavated on the inside with a pick; like ours are, with two lofty naves and pillars, and vaulted, all from a single rock, with no other piece of any kind, with a high altar and other altars, all of the same stone; as I say, in the whole edifice of the church there was

nothing brought from the outside, but all cut from the same living rock ... I measured the smallest to see how many paces it was, and I found it fifty paces; the others were very much larger.

He then repeats that the Abyssinians say they were

made by white men, and the first Christian king of this country was a stranger. Whence he came is unknown; he brought many men with him to work at this rock with pickaxes, and they cut out a cubit a day, and found three finished in the morning; and the King died a saint after he had completed these edifices. They showed us the place of his burial ... I heard them say that the King of Zeila came to see these edifices, and that two Moors tried to ride in, but when they came up to the door their horses foundered ... The Moor [Ahmad Grañ] ordered his men to leave the place, as Mafamede [Muhammad] did not wish him to destroy such noble edifices.

This record renders unlikely the stories that Grañ in 1533 filled the excavations in since he could not set them on fire, or that the Ethiopians did the same to protect them. Grañ's soldiers probably thoroughly plundered the site, but had neither time nor the energy to spare to wreak much greater havoc. In fact, the *Futuh al-Habasha* confirms this, recording that:

Ahmad ... learnt that the idolators had assembled near the church called Lalibela; he marched against them across the mountains, and by a very difficult road ... They reached the church, where the monks were collected to die in its defence. The Imam examined the church and found that he had never seen the like. It was cut from the rock, as were the columns supporting it. There was not a piece of wood in all the construction save their idols and their shrines. There was also a cistern hewn out of the rock ... Then he burnt their shrines, broke their stone idols and appropriated all the gold plates and silk textures he found. (From Whiteway 1902 and Basset 1897–1909)

The future *abun* or metropolitan bishop of Ethiopia, and patriarch of Alexandria – if his splendid but contested titles are admitted – João Bermudes, was also part of the Portuguese expedition. He claimed in his 1565 book that 'the Moors ... wished to destroy these churches but could not either with crowbars, or with the gunpowder which they exploded in them, doing no damage at all'. His description was very general:

There are here certain churches cut out of the living rock, which are attributed to angels. Indeed the work appears superhuman, because, though they are of the size of the large ones in this country [Portugal], they are each excavated with its pillars, its altar, and its vaults, out of a single rock, with no mixture of any outside stone.

After this, no other foreigner records seeing the churches – although they appear in unreal splendour on a map in Livio Sanuto's *Geografia* of 1558 – until Rohlfs (see below). Nevertheless, Lalibela and its churches continued to be known and described. Pais quoted Alvares' descriptions and Ludolf wrote of the 'magnificent structures' hewn from 'whole solid Rocks'. Bruce merely remarked that:

> having before him as specimens the ancient works of the Troglodytes, he [Lalibela] directed a number of churches to be hewn out of the solid rock in his native country of Lasta, where they remain untouched to this day, and where they will probably continue till the latest posterity. Large columns within are formed out of the solid rock, and every species of ornament preserved, that would have been executed in buildings of separate and detached stones, above ground.

Rohlfs, who accompanied the 1868 Maqdala expedition to Ethiopia, was the next to report on the churches. (Ullendorff writes that Antoine d'Abbadie, who was in Ethiopia between 1838 and 1848, visited Lalibela. This would make him the first of the modern explorers to see the site, but I have not been able to trace any record of this visit, nor is it noted by Perruchon in the introduction to his *Vie de Lalibela* of 1892.) Rohlfs considered it wrong to attribute all the churches to Lalibela. He thought that he could detect an older and less fine style, in contrast to a more modern and delicate one. He considered Beta Abba Libanos to be the oldest, then Beta Marqorewos. Rohlfs mistook the word *selassie*, trinity, for a saint's name, mentioning that as well as the tomb of Lalibela, in Golgotha church there was also the tomb of 'another celebrated saint of Abyssinia, Selassé'; this is in fact the Chapel of the Trinity. It seems that Rohlfs had no problems at all in gaining access everywhere, including the sanctuaries of the churches. The priests even allowed his Muslim interpreter to accompany him.

Only some of the exterior columns of Medhane Alem church then remained intact. Rohlfs also noted the stone cross on the road leading to Beta Giyorgis. He estimated that some 1,200 to 1,500 people lived at Lalibela, but he added that the remains of old churches, roads cut in the rock, and the ruins of stone houses of better construction than those occupied in his own time were evidence for Lalibela's greater importance in the past.

The French vice-consul, Achille Raffray, to whom we are indebted for some excellent drawings, visited Lalibela in 1882. He, like the writer of the *Zena Lalibela*, emphasised the wide variety in the architecture of the churches; he recorded ten churches, describing them and providing measurements. His companion, M. Herbin, prepared plans. Raffray concluded that the churches were built in the twelfth century. However, following his estimation that

Lalibela was the fifth Christian king of Ethiopia after Abreha and Asbeha and Kaleb (at Aksum), and two other kings at Lalibela, he calculated that Lalibela might be supposed to have ruled in the fifth century.

Gabriel Simon followed in 1885, publishing plans and descriptions of eleven churches, with drawings of interesting architectural or artistic details. After this, visitors became more frequent. Perhaps the most significant record of the churches is offered by the series of etchings prepared by L. Bianchi Barriviera for the 1940 publication by Alessandro Monti della Corte. In more modern times, for sheer splendour of presentation, as well as for a good outline text, Georg Gerster's 1970 book *Churches in Rock* can hardly be equalled.

The Churches

There are two groups of churches at Lalibela, one north of the Yordanos, one south of it and a little east. In addition there is a single further church situated separately to the west. Although Lalibela itself is in a splendidly scenic situation, surrounded by mountains in this wild region of Lasta, nothing of the churches is visible at first sight, because of the very style of their setting, opening out on to the base of huge pits carved from the rock. Only if one goes up one of the mountain paths, like that leading to the rock-cut church of Asheten Maryam in the cliffs high above Lalibela, do the great scars in the rock in which the churches are concealed become visible. Not only are the churches excavated from the rock, but the surrounding pits containing them are linked with a complex of trenches, tunnels or channels, some of which have now become disused and blocked. Once these formed a complex of 'processional roads and circuits through which the churches could be reached by going up them and not down' (Lindahl 1970). Clearly, apart from this ceremonial aspect, in a land where torrential rains can be sometimes expected, there had to be an efficient system of drainage for all the deep trenches and access tunnels – there were cisterns, too, that filled during the rains. To the casual visitor today, usually whisked around the main church complexes during a two-day tour, the sheer complexity of the tunnel system is hard to appreciate, and, in addition, many of the tunnels are now blocked or disused. It seems never to have been ascertained where the workers put the immense amount of excavated rock from these cuttings, trenches and tunnels, not to mention the chippings from the work of carving out the churches themselves.

Descriptions of these wonderful churches cut into the coarse-grained reddish sandstone or tufa of Lalibela range from the lyrical to the technical; in both styles there is a great deal to say. My descriptions will be relatively

8. Examples of the decoration in the Lalibela churches, including the Star of David, from Raffray's book.

brief, summarising the main features of the architecture of the churches in the following order:

Group I, the Northern Churches:

Medhane Alem, the Saviour of the World
Beta Maryam, the Church of Mary
Beta Masqal, the Church of the Cross
Beta Danagel, the Church of the Virgins
Beta Qedus Mikael, the Church of St Michael
Golgota, Golgotha

Group II, the Eastern Churches:

Beta Amanu'el, the Church of Emmanuel
Beta Marqorewos, the Church of Mercurius
Beta Abba Libanos, the Church of Abba Libanos
Beta Qedus Gabre'el Rufa'el, the Church of St Gabriel, which is combined with that of Raphael

and finally, to the west:

Beta Giyorgis, the Church of St George.

Group I, the Northern Churches

Medhane Alem, the Saviour of the World This is the greatest and in some ways the most impressive of the Lalibela churches. It stands on a plinth in the middle of a huge 40 by 38 m. excavation in the rock, with entry passages in the northwest and southwest corners. There are some tombs and storage caves cut into the walls of this pit. The church is rectangular, 33.5 m. long, 23.5 m. wide, and 11 m. high.

All round the outside are rectangular or square pillars cut to form an exterior colonnade, and aligned with the interior columns; Raffray's drawings of the church show that most of these, and part of the overhanging roof they supported, had collapsed. They have now been reconstructed, as can clearly be seen by the outline of the blocks on them. Nevertheless, this restored outer colonnade, shading the vast body of the church, makes a most impressive sight as one surveys the church from the surrounding courts. On the roof, which is pitched, are carved eight large arches on each of the two slopes, reflecting the eight inner bays of the church, and on the overhangs above the external colonnade rows of blind arches are carved. The corner columns are joined at the top to the flanking columns by panels carved with crosses.

Inside the church are a vaulted east–west nave and four flanking flat-

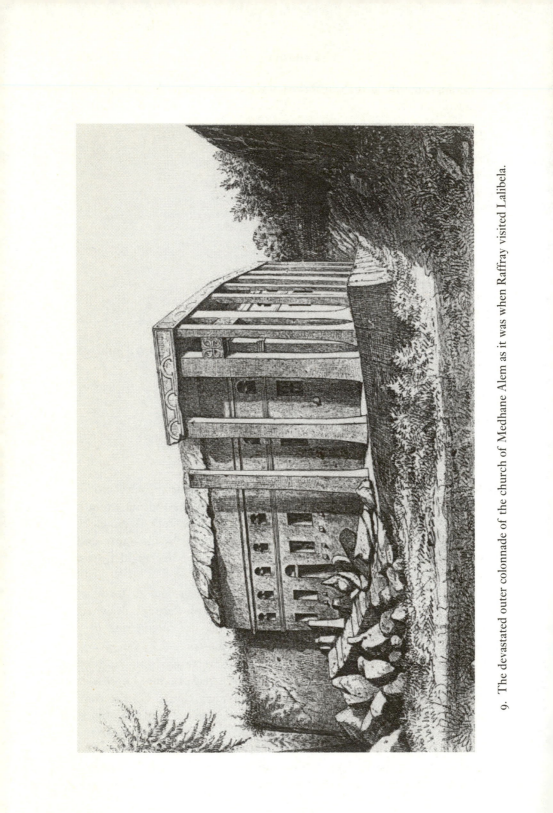

9. The devastated outer colonnade of the church of Medhane Alem as it was when Raffray visited Lalibela.

roofed aisles, two on each side – forming a so-called 'five-aisled' church. The aisles are delineated by four rows of seven massive square columns joined in both directions – except across the nave, which has higher arches springing from corbels, following the curve of the vault – by arches with corbels, with equal rows of pilasters on all four inside walls. There are thus eight north–south cross-bays, of which one at the west end constitutes a sort of narthex, and two at the east end constitute the sanctuary, whose floor is at a higher level than the rest.

The effect is very powerful, as the columns are completely undecorated, while the arches and spandrels are decorated only by the simplest of linear borders – a forest of columns united to the stone floor and ceiling without any interference beyond the corbels. In the northeast part of the church near the entrance to the sanctuary three tombs cut into the floor are shown; they are attributed to Abraham, Isaac and Jacob. There are windows in most bays in which there is no door. These are rectangular in shape on the lower level, round-topped with corbels on the upper level. Externally, on the south side there are four square monkey-heads to each window, one at each corner of a rectangular frame. On the north side, unusually, there are only two rudimentary representations of the square monkey-heads at the base only, and no frame is indicated. The decorative infill of the lower windows is quite varied, and very attractive. There are three doors, in the usual positions, all in the western half of the church, in the north, south and west sides. They have arched and corbelled openings. Opposite the west door is a narrow passage in the rock leading on into the court surrounding Beta Maryam church.

The sanctuary is entered through curtains, beyond which other curtains conceal the last bay where the *tabot* and the 'about eight' *debalat* are kept. This is lit by pierced decorative windows. The two outer side aisles have doorways of Aksumite style leading into the two easternmost bays, while the entrances to the bays in the inner aisles flanking the sanctuary arch are blocked by walls. At the narthex end of the church (west), the bays are also blocked. The northwest bay has an Aksumite-style doorway. The doorway from the narthex into the main body of the church (from the *qene mahlet* to the *qeddest*) is also of Aksumite style, partly narrowed by stone blocking added later.

One is usually shown a cavity in one of the nave pillars where the 'Lalibela-style' processional cross that the priests exhibit to visitors is said to have been found. This very attractive and individual style of cross (whose specific attribution to the Lalibela region is common but unfounded) shows a sinuous central bar to which are attached twelve protuberances. These are generally claimed to represent the twelve disciples. The (brass?) cross – which has a name that can be interpreted as meaning 'the invincible, doer of miracles' – is described as being of solid gold, and is supposed to have been the

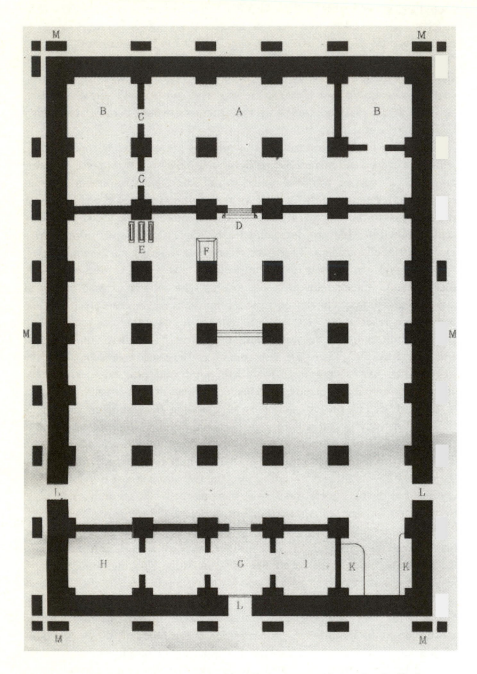

10. Plan of the great church of Medhane Alem, Lalibela, after Raffray.

11. Beta Maryam church, Lalibela, after Raffray.

processional cross of King Lalibela himself. It was stolen in March 1996 by a priest, but by good fortune was retrieved in Belgium in May 1998, and returned.

Is this extraordinary church of the Saviour of the World 'a copy of the coronation cathedral in Aksum' (Gerster 1970), a rock-cut version of the old five-aisled church of Maryam Seyon at Aksum? If so, it is surprising that it is not more apparently 'Aksumite' on the exterior, as is, for example, Beta Amanu'el. Where are the 3,815 monkey-heads and 91 gargoyles of the old metropolitan cathedral (see Chapter 11)? Was there anyway, in Zagwé times, a coronation cathedral in Aksum? The old city had long been abandoned by the monarchy, the Arab historians reporting that a place called Kubar had become the capital by the ninth century at the latest. Could Lalibela, so Aksumite in its architecture, be Kubar? No coronation is known to have occurred at Aksum until Zara Yaqob's 'revival' of the ceremony in 1436, although it is designated as a church for the coronation of vassal kings in an itinerary of 1400.

Not far from Lalibela is another, three-aisled, church, more modest in scale but of very similar design to Medhane Alem, with an external colonnade. It is called Gannata Maryam, the Garden of Mary. It is attributed to the reign of the man who deposed the last Zagwé king, Yekuno Amlak.

Beta Maryam, the Church of Mary Standing isolated in the middle of an excavated courtyard, the church of Mary is a splendid structure with three arched and pillared porches, the southern one rebuilt of stone blocks. These porches are closed except at the arched top on the sides, and open at the front, each with a central column with corbels and a carved capital at the front, and another column in the middle of the portico. The porches – which when Raffray sketched them in 1882 were covered with straw roofs supported on wooden pillars – lead into the western half of the church in the usual way, on the north, south and west sides. Cut into the courtyard to the east by the entrance tunnel from Medhane Alem court are a baptistery with wide external steps, and two small interior staircases, and another tank or cistern, and there is a little cross-shaped baptistery sunk into the rock at the northeast corner of the church.

Beta Maryam lies between the façade of Beta Masqal on the north, and the little church of Beta Danagel on the south. The church is 15 m. long by 11 m. wide, and 10 m. high, with a pitched roof. There are three aisles divided by four slightly irregular columns making five cross-bays, the sanctuary being at the east end. In sharp contrast to the stark simplicity of Medhane Alem, much of the church of Mary is beautifully decorated with painting and carving on the pillars, capitals and corbels, and the soffits of the

12. The Amda Berhan in the church of Beta Maryam is always kept veiled from sight. It is said that on it the secrets of the past and future are inscribed.

arches. The ceilings between the arches are also painted. The vaulted ceiling too was once painted – only fragments survive now. The painting on the columns, executed on plaster, have mostly disappeared as well. Designs include rosettes, haloed saints, Mary and Elizabeth, the Annunciation, the sun, the man who 'took up his bed and walked', the woman of Samaria, Christ with the loaves and fishes, and some animal and bird frescoes. The general feeling inside the church is of richness and colour. The paintings, supposedly contemporary with the assumed period of cutting out the church by Lalibela, are thus dated to the early thirteenth century. If this is correct – and I am assured by Stanislaw Chojnacki, the expert in this field, that they resemble the late Coptic style of Fatimid times in Egypt, which tallies well – they are the earliest surviving church paintings so far known in Ethiopia. This, of course, does not necessarily mean that they were done at the same time as the church was originally excavated. On some of the pillars are attractive carved motifs, crosses with floral embellishments, bands of decorative work and the like.

There is a narthex with a central pillar at the west end of the church, inside the west portico. The centre aisle, or nave, is much higher than the outer aisles, and there is a gallery above running the length of the church, with the 'Aksumite frieze' decoration of alternate square openings and filled-in panels each flanked on all four corners by square monkey-heads. At the east end of the nave in front of the *maqdas* there is a very tall column with a corbelled capital rising right to the centre of the transverse arch, a most unusual architectural addition. Legend says that King Lalibela, in a vision, watched Christ touching this pillar, and the past and the future of the world are now inscribed upon it – but it is always now veiled from human sight by draperies. Alternatively, it is claimed that a letter from Christ to King Lalibela is inscribed on it (perhaps a reference inspired by King Abgar of Edessa's letter to Christ). The column is referred to as *amda berhan*, the Pillar of Light; it is said that once it was unveiled, and flooded the area with light.

A more prosaic account claims that there is a Coptic inscription on this pillar, a dedication of some sort. Some new information can now be added to this. By chance, through the kindness of a friend, I have recently been able to see a photocopy of a photograph of a part of this pillar, two faces presumably somewhere about middle height on the column.

Some elements are clear. The pillar is quite elaborately decorated. In the higher section visible on the photograph, the painted plaster shows a bird (an eagle?), wings and claws spread; the head is off the picture. At the same level on another face is a six-pointed Star of David, with, in the interstices of the arms, some decoration including illegible Arabic writing. This appears to be carved, like much of the other decoration in the church, rather than painted. Below the eagle, written on the plaster, is the Arabic text (*a* or *I)rahima ya rabb* (?), 'have mercy, O Lord' (?) with *habr* (?), 'bishop' (?) next to the Coptic abbreviation for Christ below it, and next to and below that more Arabic text,

13. An engraving from Achille Raffray's book, a line drawing of the interior
of Beta Maryam church.

al-r-i 'amila (... made) *al-k-m-l-sa* (?) perhaps not an Arabic word? This text appears to be incomplete and perhaps there are missing parts on the other sides of the pillar. Another suggestion postulates the translation MXC for the Greek/Coptic letters, providing the date AH 1090 (?), or AD 679, and a reading *al-kanisa*, 'the church', for the last part of the lower line (Rachel Ward, Venetia Porter, personal communication). The style of the writing implies a date not earlier than the twelfth century. Just below this inscription the plaster is broken, and only the stone of the pillar is visible. At the level of the inscription, on the other face, below the Star of David, is a painting of a haloed and bearded figure, perhaps a saint, with two circular medallions (?) on his costume at shoulder level.

The lower windows of the church are square with Aksumite-style square monkey-heads at the corners. There are waterspouts on the porches and on the roof. At the sanctuary end, four windows, set one above the other, show various different infill decorations. In the north wall a swastika window filling surmounts another with a cross. Three plain rectangular windows form a third level on the sides of the church, while on the west front above the porch are two arched windows with corbels below a quatrefoil window. Under these and above the west porch is a rough carving of two men on horseback, one apparently St George killing the dragon, over the west porch on the exterior façade. Some have supposed that this is later than the rest of the church, and it has even been attributed to a sixteenth-century Portuguese sculptor. Two bells hang in the arches of the west porch.

Facing the west porch is the double-arched entry of a passage, with a cell above it at the eastern end – the so-called tribune or 'royal box' of Lalibela. The passage is open to the sky, but has holes cut in the walls all along it on both sides, very probably for inserting beams to provide some sort of temporary roofing material – straw or cloth? The twin arched entrances with bracket capitals are preceded by two steps flanked by short square pillar plinths with square capitals. The Sellassie chapel approached from inside the church of Golgotha (see below) lies beneath this passage. Access to the upper cell is from a door in the southwest corner of the court, via a small entrance door which leads to a staircase cut in the rock. The staircase descends to an arched opening through which one can see the east façade of the Mikael-Golgotha churches, while a side door provides access to another staircase leading up to the cell. From the cell one can look over the court to the west end of Beta Maryam through twin openings, in one of which a bell is suspended, and, from the other side, down to the open passage and beyond to the stone round or oblong houses of Lalibela village. The west end of the passageway opens via an Aksumite-style window to a view over the monolithic block called the Tomb of Adam.

Beta Masqal, the Church of the Cross This church, 10 m. long by 3 m. wide, has an elegant southern façade decorated with blind arcading extremely similar to that over the external colonnade of Medhane Alem church. There are three doors, the two on the south side facing Beta Maryam supplied with Aksumite-style square monkey-heads at the four corners, and with separate entrance steps. They are flanked by two square pillar-like plinths. Further east on the wall are two windows, one with a double-cross design and the other with a Greek-cross and flower tracery design reminiscent of some of the crosses inlaid into the western portico of Maryam Seyon church at Aksum. The western door in the south façade leads to an ante-chamber (about 2 m.) and some rock-cut tombs, the eastern door leads into the church itself. The doorway in the northern side of the church leads to a narrow trench cut along this side and communicating with the entrance trench to Medhane Alem court and with a western entrance near the Tomb of Adam.

Beta Masqal's architecture is strange for a church, since it has only a central row of four columns, three square and one cross-shaped in section, reflected by pilasters on the south wall only. It may originally have been a treasury or similar building. To the east is an open cave with some burial cells off it.

Beta Danagel, the Church of the Virgins Beta Danagel is a small church on the south side of Beta Maryam, partly in a cave cut in the rock, partly outside it. It measures about 5 by 5 m. The church is accessible either from the west through a cell with a single-pillared double-arched entrance opposite the south porch of Beta Maryam, which leads through an ante-chamber opposite the altar, or by a small side entrance further east in the court. It is very irregular in shape, and has four square columns inside. Another entrance in the south wall leads through a cave into a rock-cut passage running southwards to steps from which access can be gained to the right to the Mikael and Golgotha churches, or straight on through a cut at the end of which one turns east towards the eastern group of churches, or west to reach Beta Giyorgis. This passage may also be entered by passing directly through the cell opposite Beta Maryam's south porch. Inside the sanctuary of Beta Danagel, which opens eastwards from the pillared *qeddest*, there is a half-dome cut in the rock over the altar.

The Virgins of the dedication are said to be the fifty virgin martyrs of a convent in Edessa, purportedly killed by Emperor Julian the Apostate. Heldman suggests that originally the church was given the dedication following a parallel with the Beta Danagel of Dabtara mentioned in the *Book of Aksum*, and only later came to be associated with the virgin martyrs of Edessa. This would also be the reason why Alvares referred to the church as the church of the Martyrs. However, as with many other structures in this court, one wonders whether originally this too was not intended to be a church, but formed one of the subsidiary installations connected with the main church of Beta Maryam.

Beta Qedus Mikael, the Church of St Michael, and Golgota, Golgotha These churches really belong together, being two parts of a whole. St Mikael's church is sometimes called the church of Debra Sina, Mount Sinai. They are not completely isolated from the rock, Golgotha church being joined on two sides (east and north), with a chapel called Sellassie opening from it into the rock on the eastern side. The church of St Mikael is surrounded on the exterior by a trench in the rock, above which the church stands on a triple plinth 3 m. high. There are beautiful exterior window carvings on two levels on the walls, and three doorways as usual in the western half, the northern one leading into Golgotha church. There is another doorway leading from the chancel into Golgotha near the entrance to the Sellassie chapel.

Access from the south side of Beta Maryam court is from a corridor which passes Beta Danagel, leading to a descent of a few steps, at the base of which there is a trench to the right which curves round to enter another trench-like court at the southeast corner of Beta Qedus Mikael, 6 m. below the level of the Beta Maryam court. Steps cut into the lower of the three stages of the 3 m. high triple plinth on which the church stands give access to the south door. Opposite are numerous caves cut in the rock and a passageway accessible from a bridge over the trench.

St Mikael's church (9.5 by 8.5 m.) has three divisions (nave and two aisles) divided by two rows of four columns each, cross-shaped in section, and repeated by pilasters on the walls. The two rows of pillars are linked by arches. There are thus five cross-bays. The altar is in the raised chancel section in the east central part of the church.

Golgotha church (10.5 by 6 m.) is entered through the church of St Mikael. It has three columns, cruciform in section, running east–west in the centre, and a fourth pilaster in the west wall, forming two aisles; flattened arches join these, with corbels at the base of the arches. The west wall exhibits arches, the tops open as windows, with crosses pierced below. Viewing the façade from the outside one can see a rectangular window above these, looking out from the west end of the passage constituting the 'tribune' or box where Lalibela is said to have installed himself to watch the church ceremonies. This window shows Aksumite-style square monkey-heads on the exterior wall.

King Lalibela is supposed to be buried in a vault under the floor in the north aisle of this church, and a tomb is shown above. If it is true that Grañ's soldiers sacked the churches, one would expect the grave of the 'holy king' to have been desecrated as well. At the east end of the north aisle is the altar. In a grilled recess in the northeast corner there is a relief carving of a recumbent figure and an angel; this represents the Tomb of Christ. Most unusually, there are carvings of full-sized human figures in arched and painted niches around the church; four are labelled, Yohannes, Giyorgis, Qirqos and Estifanos, but this writing is thought to be a later addition. Altogether, there are traces of seven surviving figures. Alvares merely noted 'two great images carved in the wall ... of St Peter and St John'. The figures are massive and solid in appearance, stiffly robed, with haloes or turbans, holding a book in one hand and a cross on a staff in the other. There may have been two others if the chancel doorway to St Mikael's church and the door to the Iyasus (or Kidane Mehret) chapel at the east end were later pierced through other statue niches. It has been suggested that they perhaps represent some of the Nine Saints, but this seems an unlikely theme here; another suggestion is that if there were nine here, they, with three others in the Sellassie chapel, would represent the twelve apostles. The Iyasus chapel has a beautiful ogival window visible from outside beside the east side of St Mikael's church.

East of Golgotha church, accessible from its south aisle, is the mysterious Sellassie or Trinity chapel (trapezoidal, c. 4.5 by 7 m.), which it is not possible to visit. However, a photograph in Gerster's superb book *Churches in Rock* shows a view of the quite exceptional presence of three *manbara tabot*, altars cut from the rock with the three steps in which they are rooted. The central one has on it carved images of the four evangelists, with the head of a man, eagle, ox and lion respectively, and a cross above, while the side ones have only the cross. On the left altar is written Krestos, Christ; on the right altar, Paraqlitos, the Paraclete. Shallow niches behind contain damaged carvings, perhaps depicting the three persons of the Trinity, or perhaps three apostles, as noted above. Before the altars stands a single central column direct to the barrel vaulted roof, draped in cloths – this can be glimpsed through the entrance doorway from the church of Golgotha. The vault is horseshoe-shaped in the rear section – another reminiscence of Aksum, where horseshoe arches and barrel vaults were found in the Tomb of the Brick Arches and the so-called Brick Vaulted Structure in 1974; the sanctuary arch at Debra Damo is also slightly horseshoe-shaped. Possibly this chapel once served as the sanctuary for the church of Golgotha. Directly above the chapel is the cell at the west end of an open passageway, the so-called tribune of Lalibela.

To the northeast of the church of Golgotha is an abandoned rock-cut chamber, consisting of a cave with two square pillars supporting the roof, opening to a further rock-cut passageway. West of Golgotha church, accessible from the steps of the triple plinth surrounding the church of Mikael, is a small cell, the upper part of the Tomb of Adam. Below, the Tomb of Adam forms the entrance to the group of churches from the west. Adam is said to have been buried on Golgotha, and many Ethiopian paintings show the crucifix on Golgotha with a skull at the base, with Christ's blood running down to it as a symbol of salvation. Sergew Hable Sellassie (1972) mentions this place, and indicates it on his map; 'northwest of Golgotha is a cross hewn from solid rock called Qeranio. The place beneath it is called the Tomb of Adam.' Approaching from the west through an avenue cut deep into the rock, the Tomb of Adam is seen as an oblong block, with a doorway reached by steps, and above, cut into the façade, a cross. Behind, the view is closed by the western wall of Golgotha with its arched windows, with, above them, the Aksumite-style west window of the open passage leading from Beta Maryam court.

Group II, the Eastern Churches

Amanu'el, Emmanuel A most beautiful church, spoiled at the moment like almost all the Lalibela churches – though for the wisest of reasons – by a roof erected over it to protect it from the elements. Lalibela, a monument of supreme importance, and recognised as such by UNESCO, needs urgent and competent preservation and restoration work, as well as archaeological in-vestigation. At the moment there seems to be little progress towards these aims.

Looking at the church of Emmanuel (and also at the church of Yimrehana Krestos in a cave not far from Lalibela – see below), one can imagine what a section of, perhaps, the palace of Ta'akha Maryam at Aksum might have looked like in its original splendour, although at the Emmanuel church there are no round monkey-heads above the longitudinal ribbing of the façades, the smooth surfaces instead representing a plastered finish over the stone and woodwork. The building is of an even pinkish-red colour.

Beta Amanu'el can be approached directly from the west by a long rock passage with a door and three windows, opening opposite the west door. An alternative route approaches by a series of chambers from Beta Marqorewos, entering the court by some steps descending from a doorway in the southwest corner. A third route enters from the southeast – no more than a hole with some steps on its east side – to the court. This entrance emerges from the immense cut in the rock outside the Emmanuel court to the east. The cut leads in one direction (north) past a cistern to some rock-cut nuns' cells and on towards the northern group of churches. In the other direction (south) it descends by a staircase into a further, deeper, cut, then passes through an exceptionally tall and narrow tunnel (possibly designed so that processional crosses or standards could be carried without lowering them) to further cuts, and steps leading through to another large court facing the south façade of

14. The façade of the church of Dabra Libanos, Lalibela, after Raffray.

Abba Libanos church. This gigantic rock-cut gully isolates this whole group of buildings on all sides save the west. From this gully one does not appreciate that behind the vast curved rock walls to the west is another great pit, excavated to leave only a central block – the splendid church of Beta Amanu'el – and a small treasury (*beta gabaz*) to the south of it.

The rectangular church, 18 m. long, 12 m. wide and 12 m. high, is completely isolated by the surrounding trench 24 m. deep; further, as we have noted, this whole group of buildings is isolated by a gigantic rock-cut gully on all sides save the west. The church stands on a plinth of three steps, which widens at the doors where there are four steps. The structure exhibits externally the pattern of regular salients and re-entrants familiar on Aksumite plans, reflected inside by the arrangement of the columns. There are three Aksumite-style doorways in the western half of the church in the customary positions, one in the centre of the west end, and others in the north and south sides, with external landings. At the northwest corner of the church is a sunken circular baptistery, with two steps leading down into it.

Inside the church, the nave and flanking aisles running east–west are separated by two rows of four columns each, the central four square in section, the eastern and western ones cruciform; all are reflected by pilasters attached to the side walls. Arches join the columns above corbels. There are thus five cross bays, that at the east end being divided off to form a domed sanctuary with two flanking rooms. At the west end, in the northwest bay, is a staircase ascending to a low gallery and some small cells. The centre bay forms a porch or narthex inside the west door. In each bay there are windows on three levels, the lower Aksumite-style with square monkey-heads and cross-shaped internal divisions, the middle set with corbels and arches, the topmost square and empty but framed in Aksumite style with square monkey-heads. The nave, unlike the flat-roofed side aisles, is vaulted above two rows of 'Aksumite frieze' decoration, the lower blank, the upper pierced in some cases to admit light from the side aisle galleries or lofts.

It is not difficult to imagine, as has been suggested, that this was a royal church, a perfect Aksumite palace cut into the rock of Lasta.

Beta Marqorewos, the Church of Mercurius   Access to Beta Marqorewos is gained through a number of entrances. One leads in from the west, entering Beta Marqorewos beside its raised open court. A second route is by a tunnel, long and curving slightly, leading from the so-called Faras Bet, emerging from below into the northern part of the complex. A third way leads from the southwest corner of the Amanu'el court, where one can mount some steps, passing through a doorway into a room overlooking the court by a window. This room has a square hole cut into its floor, the base of some vanished object. From this room, one passes through some other chambers to Beta Marqorewos.

An unusual building, 31 m. long by 25 m. wide, and 6–8 m. high, Beta Marqorewos may not originally have been a church. It is most remarkable for its massive columns; eighteen of an original twenty pillars, somewhat unevenly spaced, still survive. Sixteen of these pillars were arranged in two rows of five, flanking two rows of three; the extra two at each side flanked a small raised open court, which has holes in the floor along the edge and in the centre, perhaps for erecting poles for a tent or awning. Three arched openings carried on two more central pillars opened from the main columnar hall northeastwards into three small rooms – the sanctuaries – beyond which through the rock and across its surrounding trench is the southern façade of Beta Amanu'el, visible through a tribune or windowed box reached from the central room. Finally, a northwestern addition is supported by two more columns; it is from here that, through a number of doors and halls, access to Beta Amanu'el is possible. Beta Marqorewos has suffered collapse in places. The immense columns are plain, narrowing only a little towards the top. But one still shows a number of crowned and robed figures painted on it. It seems probable that this was originally some important secular 'building' of the town, perhaps a royal or ecclesiastical dwelling.

Beta Abba Libanos, the Church of Abba Libanos A very attractive church, located inside a large court accessible through tunnels and cuts from the huge gully that passes by the east side of the Amanu'el church. Beta Libanos is freed of the rock on all sides by means of a cut going right round, but joined at the roof. The church is 9.5 m. long, 7 m. wide and 7 m. high. It is rectangular in shape. The façade shows six pilasters on the wall and five indentations between them, four with windows of the lower level with Aksumite-style square monkey-heads and cross-shaped openings, and one with a similar Aksumite-style doorway reached by a number of steps. The middle-level windows, of which there are only three, are ogival. The top level shows, above a horizontal cornice, simple rectangular blank windows for (non-existent) aisle galleries. Raffray illustrated a drawing of this church with a straw-roofed structure attached to it on one side.

The internal plan is extremely similar to that of Beta Amanu'el, but without the second level of 'Aksumite frieze', and with the staircase-well left solid. However, there are flat beams instead of arches except for the sanctuary at the east end, and the narthex at the west. Outside, the church lacks the salients and re-entrants of Beta Amanu'el, unless these are represented in a symbolic way by the pilasters. The church is supposed to have been constructed as a memorial to Lalibela by his wife Queen Masqal Kebra. It is said

15. Sketch by A. Raffray of the church of Amanu'el at Lalibela, engraved for his 1876 book.

to be served at present by about one hundred and fifty ecclesiastics (priests, deacons, *dabtara*).

Beta Qedus Gabre'el Rufa'el, the Church of Sts Gabriel and Raphael

To reach this church, also called Gabre'el Rufa'el, or the church of the Archangels Gabriel and Raphael, it is necessary, approaching from the north, to mount a declivity until the arches of the façade of Beta Gabre'el appear. Turning towards them to the right, one passes some large stones, the remains of a now-vanished structure. Crossing over a rock-cut trench by a bridge, the way leads through a rock-cut corridor with an open pillared gallery facing south towards the imposing northwest façade of the twin 'churches' of Gabriel and Raphael. One then crosses another wooden bridge over a 15 m. deep trench cut on the north side of the churches to the entrance stairs, which rise from a deep plinth excavated on three sides right down to the base of the trench. Several cisterns are visible below. There is another trench on the south side of the church.

The massive monumental façade, dignified and imposing, is decorated with tall attached columns from top to bottom separating the arches of a deep blind ogee arcade with corbels, forming seven niches, with doors in the third and sixth, and ogival windows in the others. The main door to the east is of Aksumite style. The west door, which opens on to a high stone terrace, has the same corbels and ogee arch as the arcade.

Inside there are two chapels (unoriented) in the 19.50 m. long by 17.50 m. wide church. The room entered by the steps fronting the wooden bridge is more or less rectangular with two central columns repeated in pilasters in the walls, with a second room to the east opening in turn southeast to another which overlooks the trench behind (or southeast of) the church. From the main room, a door with steps leads down giving access to this trench. This may have been the original entrance, being considerably more convenient. The western chamber is entered from the main room, and is irregularly shaped with two central columns.

This church seems to be the one called Belem or Bethlehem by Alvares. However, there is every likelihood that this monument, with no conventional signs indicating its function as a religious building, was not intended to be a church, but formed part of the royal palace. Above are some large hewn stone blocks, which might suggest that the upper level above the rock-cut buildings we see today was once fortified. In 1993, excavations near here in pits revealed metal crosses. One, in a plaited, approximately fourteenth-century style, might indicate occupation in post-Zagwé times under the subsequent 'Solomonic' dynasty, and the discovery of fetters might hint at the existence of a prison under the palace, if that was what it was (S. Chojnacki, personal

16. The splendid façade of Beta Rufa'el-Gabre'el at Lalibela, perhaps once a palace. After Raffray.

communication). There is a large cistern in the trench below the façade, and wells in the floor. From nearby a tunnel once led west to the Yordanos, where another passage continued on to Beta Giyorgis. At the point where these tunnels join the Yordanos valley, there is a large cross left standing from the rock when it was hewn away.

If one passes straight through the entrance gallery opposite the churches, a tunnel leads on to a rock chamber with a window overlooking the east end of Beta Gabre'el. This room has a massive and magnificent iron-studded wooden door, presumably part of the original installations here. Further passages beyond this door lead to the ground level overlooking the Faras Bet, from which area one can approach the other churches either over a bridge, or by a rock-cut descending staircase leading to the tunnel-like cut that continues on to the Faras Bet itself.

The Faras Bet is a round room cut in the rock, with openings in the upper part. The name (Horse House) comes from the legend that it was Lalibela's stable. It may have been a *beta lahm*, for preparation of the eucharistic bread, the windows of the upper part being designed for letting the smoke escape.

The Western Church

Beta Giyorgis, the Church of St George This unusual and beautiful church – also sometimes referred to as Hamara Noh (Noah's Ark) – consists of a great block of red-coloured rock cut into the shape of a cross. It stands in the midst of a trench 12 m. deep. Situated apart from the other Lalibela monuments, it is reached from the northern group of churches by passing southwards from Beta Maryam court through the passage beside Beta Danagel, descending the steps, and continuing straight on towards the Yordanos valley through a cut in the rock, then turning right (west). One passes a tree with a phonolith (stone 'bell') suspended on it, and then descends to a flat sloping rock platform with splendid views, in the midst of which is the great pit containing the church.

A rock-cut passage lower down the slope descends gradually down to the courtyard around the church; the terrifying alternative is an eighteen-step ladder made from eucalyptus, which leans against the rock wall in one corner of the courtyard, where there is a rock-cut stepped plinth. In the walls of this court are several openings leading to hermit's dwellings, ossuaries, or chambers where drums and other church paraphernalia are kept.

The church measures 12 by 12 m. At the top it is distinguished by two crosses, one inside the other, cut on the flat roof following the shape of the church itself. There are very attractive upper windows, ogival in shape, but broken by ribbed capitals, surmounted by sinuous flowing curlicues which

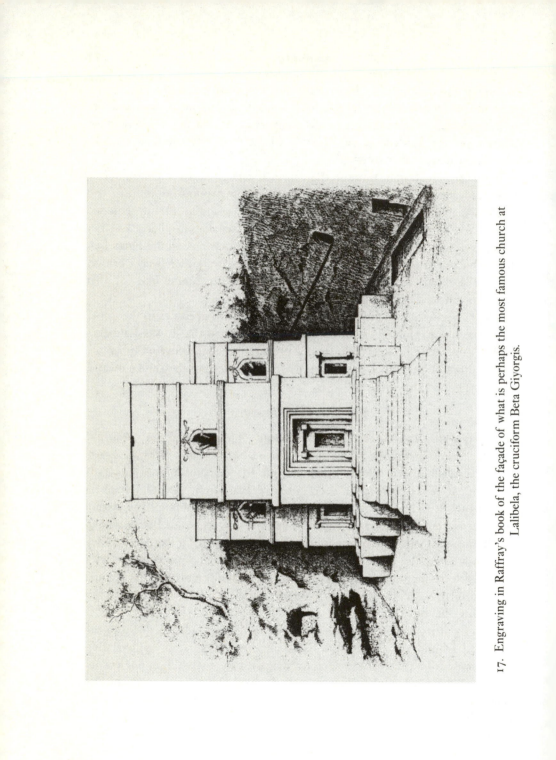

17. Engraving in Raffray's book of the façade of what is perhaps the most famous church at Lalibela, the cruciform Beta Giyorgis.

18. Some decorative features from Lalibela churches published among
the engravings in Raffray's book.

descend to frame the windows themselves. There is one such window on each
of the twelve sides of the building. The church appears tall for its width,
standing on a triple-stepped plinth, but this is counteracted to some extent by
the 'string courses', cut in the rock above the level of the doorways, below and
above the upper windows, and finally between the latter and the roof itself.
There are three doorways, very plain with Aksumite-style square monkey-
heads at the corners, in the three sections of the west façade, the central one
alone having an access staircase, the others merely opening on to a broader
part of the main plinth.

The interior is spacious and quite well lit by the three ogival windows set
high above a dado in each of the four arms of the cross, of which only the
eastern, or sanctuary, arm is domed, the others having flat roofs. The sanctuary
dome (a feature similar to those in some of the rock-cut churches in Tigray)
bears a cross pattée carved on it, the other flat roofs exhibit plain crosses. The
crossing is defined by four arches with bracket capitals at the level of the
dado, and has a higher, flat, roof. At the lower level each section of the wall
in which there is no door shows instead an Aksumite-style window with
square monkey-heads; but these are blind, not appearing on the interior.
Everything about this church is simple and elegant. It is sometimes suggested
that this was the last church excavated here. Local legend, however, attributes
Beta Libanos to Queen Masqal Kebra, after Lalibela's death, while the king
is supposed to have caused all the others to be cut during his lifetime.

19. Window designs at Lalibela, from the book by Achille Raffray.

9

THE CHURCH OF YIMREHANA KRESTOS

History

Labouring up the slopes of Mt Abuna Yosef, mounting ever higher in the bitter cold, Francisco Alvares approached the church of Yimrehana Krestos. Even the indefatigable Portuguese royal chaplain had almost had enough. Despite being hauled along at the end of a rope pulled by a strong slave, he 'was near dying ... from the great ascent'.

Tradition dates this church to the reign of the twelfth-century Zagwé king Yimrehana Krestos, who preceded Harbay and then Lalibela himself on the throne. Yimrehana Krestos is another of the Zagwé royal saints, said to have been priest as well as king, celebrating the mass himself. He reigned, the traditions record, for forty years – suspiciously, so did King Solomon of Israel, and, according to the same traditions, almost all the other Zagwé kings as well. Yimrehana Krestos, apart from these brief allusions to him in the hagiographies, is otherwise completely unknown to history, although perhaps Abu Salih's description of the kings of Abyssinia as priests might have been based on information about this ruler that had reached Egypt.

Alvares visited the church of Yimrehana Krestos in the 1520s. He remained there two days, seeing among other things a copy of 'a chronicle or life of this King' – the *Gadla Yemrehana Krestos*. In Alvares' account of his travels, he first recorded the monastery of 'Our Lady, named Iconoamaleca' (i.e. attributed to King Yekuno-Amlak, 1270–85). This monastery, now called Jammadu Maryam (a place also distinguished by a medieval church in a cave), owned, two days' journey away to the west, 'a large and rich church in another cave; according to my judgement three large ships with their masts would find room in this cave. The entrance to it is not larger than to allow two carts with their side rails to enter.' This was the church of Yimrehana Krestos.

Alvares continued:

> This church which is in this cave is very large, like a cathedral, with its large aisles, very well worked, and well vaulted: it has three very pretty chapels, with well-adorned altars. The entrance to this cave is to the east, and the backs of the chapels are that way, and if one goes at the hour of tierce there is no seeing in the church, all the offices are done with lamps. There are in this church (as they say) 200 canons or Debeteras, according to their language: I saw an infinite number, and they have not got monks; they have a Liçaquanate [*liqa kahenat*, chief priest], a very noble prior: he is over all of them, as has been said before. They say that it has much revenue. These canons are like well-to-do and honourable men. This church is named Imbra Christus, which means path of Christ [Yimrehana Krestos means 'May Christ guide us']. Entering this cave a man faces the chapels, and on the right hand when one enters are two painted chambers, which belonged to a King who lived in this cave, and who ordered this church to be built. On the Epistle side [the south] are three honoured sepulchres, and as yet we had not seen others such in Ethiopia. This is specially high, and has five steps all around it [all whitewashed with white lime]. The tombs were like this. This tomb is covered with a large cloth of brocade, and velvet of Mequa, one cloth of one stuff, and another of the other, which on both sides reach the ground. It was covered over, because it was the day of its great festival. They say that this tomb belongs to the King who lived here, whose name was Abraham. And the other two sepulchres are of the same fashion, except that one of them has four steps, and the other three: and all are in the middle of the cave. They say that the larger of these two belongs to a Patriarch of Alexandria, who came to see this King, having heard of his sanctity, and he died here. The smallest and lowest belongs, they say, to a daughter of this King.

Alvares also mentions that in the book he saw was a picture illustrating the miracle by which angels supplied Yimrehana Krestos daily with the bread and wine requisite for the mass. He added: 'so it is painted in the chancel' – a painting that is not there today. Indefatigable, Alvares went on upwards to find the quarry from which the building stone came, and examined it and the stone of the church itself, thus ascertaining to his own satisfaction that the monks made a false claim when they said it had come 'from Jerusalem'.

The Church Today

This very impressive and sumptuously decorated church is built in a large cave in a ravine not far from Lalibela (though six hours' journey away since there is no road for vehicles). The journey from Lalibela is arduous, and is accomplished partly by mule – an animal whose surefootedness even on these tiny tracks is legendary – and partly by walking and climbing in the very thin mountain air, which quickly exhausts those not used to it. Leaving Lalibela one descends to a relatively well-watered agricultural valley in which there is a church dedicated to Gabra Manfas Qeddus. Then come patches of scrub, and eucalyptus forests with tiny tracks bordered with aloes and other spiky plants with scarlet flowers. Some rich valleys, and some poor ones, alternate with green meadows grazed by animals, with rocky, desolate patches, or with different areas of vegetation. Views become more and more spectacular, and the paths more and more precipitous. Fold upon fold the mountains of Lasta stretch away, etched by the shadows cast by the sun into jagged rows, retreating one after the other into the distance. A juniper forest has to be traversed, on a steep slope, silent but for the cicadas and the call of the occasional exotic bird. The roots of the trees form a sort of staircase as the path winds down. Just before this, extraordinary in such a place, and a sign of the efforts now being made for soil conservation, much of the hill has been recently terraced. Finally, a village on a knoll is reached, small *tukul*s set in their enclosures of protective poisonous euphorbia. Then comes a stone staircase leading past a round two-storey house, and, at last, the cave mouth, buried among juniper trees. One tree, fallen, supplies a convenient terrace wall in front of the church.

Yimrehana Krestos cave is nowadays blocked by an ugly stone wall supplied with two gates, one with rudimentarily carved animal figures on it. Inside the cave, another short wall, built with the same wood-and-stone technique as the church, and with two high wooden arched openings, in one of which bells are suspended, links the northeast corner of the church with the main wall. The cave is large, deep and relatively low, with a craggy roof that seems to have been trimmed to some extent by man. From outside the wall, one can only glimpse the tops of the twin 'towers' of the north facade of the church.

The church – to contradict Alvares, perhaps impressed by the glorious interior to enlarge it in his memory – is a relatively small one, about 12 by 9.5 m. in size. But it is extremely unusual and attractive. In basic exterior ground plan it is like Debra Damo (see below), with re-entrants and salients in the walls, which rise from a plinth of red dressed stone; there are two recesses in the long sides, one in the shorter sides. The parts of the building that protrude at the corners are built a little higher (to a height of c. 6 m.) than the central section. One presumes, considering a remark by Kosmas Indikopleustes about the 'four-towered' royal palace of Aksum, that this was also the case with the Aksumite palaces, whose plans show similar protruding corners. Greater height, if it had been desired, was impossible here without a considerable amount of extra work, as the cave roof limits it.

The outer walls resemble those of Beta Amanu'el at Lalibela, having a striped effect because of the alternate black horizontal beams and light-coloured plaster courses. The long horizontal beams are set back a little, and the stone layers heavily plastered. What is conspicuously missing from the 'classical' Aksumite design in these churches in Lasta is the monkey-head element; there are none of the round cross-members as seen on the Aksum stelae or at the church of Debra Salam, Asbi, for example.

Inside, the decoration makes Yimrehana Krestos the most elaborate of all known ancient Ethiopian churches, although on the lower level there is only a plain paved floor and the striped walls. After the comments above about the lavish adornment – which are nevertheless true – it comes as a disappointment to observe that the rich decoration is by no means immediately obvious. As in so many Ethiopian churches, the prevailing gloom, and the curtains festooned unattractively here and there on poles stretched at hazard across the nave and aisles from the capitals of the columns, scarcely enhance its appearance. In addition, the soot from lamps, tapers and rushlights, and the jumbles of miscellaneous goods lying in the corners, detract yet further from the splendour that should be visible. The paintings and ceilings are much obscured.

The plan of the church is very simple – an Aksumite palace in miniature. The church has the usual basilical plan with the customary three (Aksumite-style) doorways. A main west doorway gives access into a part of the church acting as a narthex or vestibule, and two others in the western part of the north and south sides lead to the aisles. Alvares watched the faithful receiving communion at all three doorways when he was there, on the feast-day of the founder, when he estimated that some 20,000 people came to participate. There are four columns, two on each side separating nave and aisles, reflected by pilasters in the side walls. These, except for the pair opposite the west door, are all linked by arches, unlike Debra Damo, but like many – but not all – of the Lalibela churches. The stone columns, rather low, are built of alternate light and dark stone (the former also darkened by smoke). They support carved and painted wooden bracket capitals. Like the pilasters, the dark layer on the columns projects, the opposite of the pattern on the walls. The soffits of the arches are painted with cross designs or interlacing motifs bordered by a design of interlacing circles. There is an arch leading to the sanctuary, which is flanked by two other rooms. The sanctuary is domed; the dome can be seen from the outside as well. A sort of low stone platform opposite the north door is used for exhibiting books, carved *manbara tabot*, and so forth.

The first bay of the nave has a flat ceiling, as do the aisles. Some of these ceilings are very elaborately decorated, with inlay in the form of double crosses and squares, or by squares set to form repeated hexagons, which are themselves painted with numerous animal, cruciform, star and other designs (Gerster illustrates many of them). The colours being obscured by soot, the effect is rich but sadly muted. The second two bays of the nave are higher, the arches here being surmounted by a row of wooden 'Aksumite frieze' decoration, infilled with painted designs except for two on each side which are windows opening on to the roof. A few wall-paintings are visible, close up by the ceiling.

Above this, there is a splendid high trussed roof, not dissimilar in shape to the now-destroyed one at Debra Damo but with a flat central section, doubtless caused by lack of space near the cave roof. A trussed roof of the same type is found also in the mediaeval stone church at Bethlehem in Gayn. The roof at Yimrehana Krestos church forms a long gable-like spine above the roof on the exterior; it does not, after all, need to be waterproof. The central truss is carved and painted, and rafters and purlins give the ceiling a coffered appearance, each of the dozens of panels thus created being painted with geometrical designs. There are undoubted associations with Islamic design and technique in these inlaid ceilings. In the dim light of the place they are hard to see unless one is armed with a good torch, but in the swift illumination of a flashbulb some of their splendour becomes visible for a moment. The priests, unfortunately, use smoky tapers to light them for tourists, adding, day by day, slowly but inevitably, to the grime that is obscuring them. Mythical beasts on painted panels fixed to the lintel of the north door may derive from some Eastern coffer or similar object.

The wooden tracery filling of the windows – which are on two levels, giving the impression from outside of a two-storey building, although there are no upper rooms – includes a number of swastika and cross forms, which also occur at Lalibela. There are also stone window infills, with variations of the 'keyhole' design – based on arches and capitals – cut from single blocks. Some of these infills have double rows of arches, others arches over a cross, others lacy patterns based on interlocking circles and cross shapes. Sometimes a running guilloche pattern ornaments the arches or the frame of the designs. These infills are painted white, and make a fine contrast with the dark wood window frames with their square monkey-heads at the corners.

By the northeast corner of the church is a covered hole filled with water. It is said that the water runs under the church, and that, by a miracle, when Yimrehana Krestos wanted to build a church here, the cave was formed by instantaneous separation of roof and floor.

Beside the church (or facing it to the north) is another building constructed with similar techniques, presumably the royal dwelling noted by Alvares. It is, unlike the church, not oriented, standing at an angle to the church. This structure is larger than the church (c. 17.5 by 7.5 m), and is now used as its treasury. It had (Gerster 1970) two rooms, one large and one smaller, and two doors, with a number of plain Aksumite-style windows, oblong in shape with a simple horizontal bar. Now it consists simply of one room, a three-pillared hall. The building is a plain rectangle in plan with no indentations, although the striped exterior is the same as that of the church. A raised bench runs along the facade, broken where steps lead up to the doors. Tradition makes this building the royal dwelling of the priest-king Yimrehana Krestos. If so, it is the only known secular construction attributed to Zagwé times, if we discount some of the 'churches' at Lalibela, which possibly originally had secular use. If Alvares is right, and it had 'two painted chambers', this is the first record of internal painting in a royal dwelling in Ethiopia. Nothing of the sort is now visible.

South of the church there is now only one major tomb, a substantial cloth-covered structure attributed to the king, beside another small one said to belong to Ebna Yimrehana Krestos, the king's slave. It is also said that in the depths of the cave behind the church are many skeletons of monks and others, who have been buried in this holy spot, some dating from Yimrehana Krestos' time.

AKSUM

The Aksumite Kingdom: Historical Outline

Modern dictionaries or atlases of ancient times barely mention Aksum, and exhibitions in the great museums of the world can show virtually nothing to represent the life of ancient Ethiopians. The British Museum exhibits, as the sole representatives of one of Africa's greatest civilisations of antiquity, two coins and a few pots and beads. Until the publication in 1998 of David Phillipson's book *Ancient Ethiopia*, even in the Museum book shop there was no further information available.

The region lying west of the Red Sea and north of the Horn of Africa has been not infrequently in the news since the 1970s because of its tragic political, social and economic condition, and was back there recently thanks to the savage border war with Eritrea, just ended. But the area remains almost completely unknown outside specialist publications for its splendid past, when the province of Tigray in northern Ethiopia and the southern part of the now-independent country of Eritrea as far as the coast were ruled by the kings of Aksum.

We still know extremely little about early Aksum – hence the great import-ance of Dr Neville Chittick's excavations in 1972–74 and their sequel (see below). Even more revealing in some respects have been the recent excavations under the direction of Dr Rodolfo Fattovich on the hill called *Amba* Beta Giyorgis overlooking the modern town, confirming the earlier origin of the town, on the hill at least, in pre-Aksumite times, from perhaps the seventh to the fourth centuries BC (Fattovich and Bard, 1994; Fattovich et al. 2000). For the Aksumite kingdom itself, ancient literary references supply some useful information. A Greek document of the late first century AD called the *Periplus of the Erythraean Sea* (Huntingford 1980) mentions *Basileus* (king)

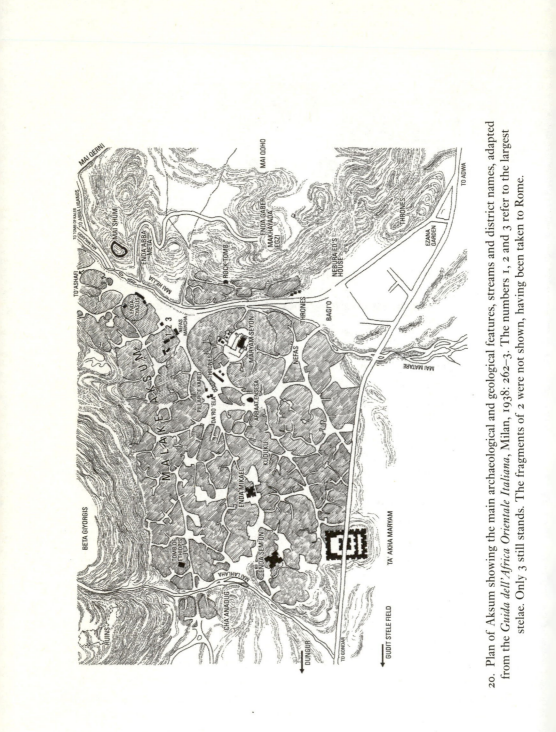

20. Plan of Aksum showing the main archaeological and geological features, streams and district names, adapted from the *Guida dell'Africa Orientale Italiana*, Milan, 1938: 262–3. The numbers 1, 2 and 3 refer to the largest stelae. Only 3 still stands. The fragments of 2 were not shown, having been taken to Rome.

Zoskales, ruler of a large slice of upland and coastal Ethiopia from the *metropolis* of the Aksumites. The document is exceptionally sparing in its use of the terms *basileus* for king, or *metropolis* for a city, but it employs both in the section describing the region ruled from Aksum. This seems to indicate that even then the Aksumite kingdom and its capital city were becoming something notable. The *Periplus* – before returning to its real theme, commerce in the Red Sea and Indian Ocean – adds a personal touch, noting that King Zoskales was a man greedy for gain, but well-versed in Greek literature.

In the regional commercial network, Adulis, Ethiopia's ancient port (near modern Massawa) played an important part. Like the Roman historian and geographer Pliny, writing at about the same time, the *Periplus* mentions Adulis, the Aksumite port.

> After Ptolemais of the Huntings, at a distance of about 3000 stades, there is the customary mart of Adouli, lying in a deep bay that runs southwards; in front of it is an island called Oreine ... opposite Oreine on the mainland, 20 stades from the sea, is Adouli, a village of moderate size, from which to Koloe, an inland city and the first ivory market, it is a journey of three days; and from this, another five days to the metropolis called the Axomite ... Zoskales rules these parts, from the Moskhophagi to the other Barbaria [these are other coastal regions that the author describes elsewhere], mean [in his way of life] and with an eye on the main chance, but otherwise high-minded, and skilled in Greek letters.

Zoskales' kingdom, like those of the Arabian kings, was deeply involved in the local Red Sea commerce as well as in trade towards the Roman Empire in the north, or India and Ceylon to the east. The *Periplus* gives a list of Aksumite imports and exports, the latter consisting of ivory, tortoiseshell and rhinoceros horn. Pliny, too, had noted these same trade goods, with the additions of hippopotamus hide, monkeys and slaves.

During the first centuries AD Aksum came rapidly to dominate the whole region; the vague description from the *Periplus* already indicates a substantial sphere of influence for the nascent state. Britannia was only the most distant province of the far-flung Roman Empire in the third century AD, when Aksum, with its capital over a mile above sea level on the 'roof of Africa', was listed by the Persian prophet Mani as the third kingdom of the world. During the first centuries AD cities and towns were founded – or succeeded their Di'amat precursors – in many places in what is today Eritrea and Tigray province in Ethiopia. Immense stone-built palaces were erected, constructed in a distinctive architectural style, dominating lesser streets of houses built haphazardly in an organic fashion. One of these structures, the relatively modest-sized palace of Dungur, excavated by the French archaeologist Francis Anfray in 1966–68, is conserved in its cleared state just to the west of modern Aksum. The ruins of this substantial villa or palace convey a good idea of the setting in which some grandee of ancient Aksum lived. If the finds discovered there are ever published, we will have an even better idea of the lifestyle of the prosperous citizens of the ancient capital at one stage in the city's history.

Ranking after the capital, Aksum, granite-built and splendid beyond the possibilities of provincial towns, came a number of lesser but still substantial towns. Only one, now called Matara, in Eritrea, has been excavated. A team working under Francis Anfray found several major buildings of limestone, with innumerable other finds revealing aspects of the daily life of the inhabitants. On the Red Sea coast, Adulis, with its palaces and churches of local basalt (one of which was excavated by the British Army during the Maqdala expedition of 1868), became the kingdom's chief port. From here, the treasures of Africa – gold, emeralds (i.e. beryls), obsidian, ivory, costly animal skins, aromatic gums and incense, and slaves – were shipped away to Egypt, Rome, India and Sri Lanka. In return came costly metalwork and weaponry, wine and olive oil, fabrics of various kinds, and other valuable imports.

Building on their trading wealth and the agricultural and pastoral resources of their country, the rulers of Aksum were to become ever more powerful. Their titles as we know them from inscriptions (written in Greek, the trade language of the Red Sea, in south Arabian script, and in their own Ge'ez or Ethiopic language), grew more and more elaborate. The titulary, and the content of the inscriptions, finally claim conquest overseas into modern Saudi Arabia (Leuke Kome, Najran) and the Yemeni kingdoms of Saba, Himyar and Hadhramawt. King Ezana – famous as the first Christian king of Aksum, which was, after Armenia and Georgia, one of the earliest independent countries in the world to adopt Christianity as its state religion, c. 340 AD – calls himself the King of Kings, King of Aksum, Saba, Salhen, Himyar, Raydan, Habashat, Tiamo, Kasu, and the Beja tribes. The four names appearing after Aksum represent two of the Yemeni kingdoms and the palaces in their respective capitals. The rest of the names refer to places in Africa; Habashat is 'Abyssinia', Tiamo perhaps a memory of old Di'amat; Kasu is Meroë, the biblical Kush, in modern Sudan, in the Red Sea coastal region of which country the Beja people, too, still live.

The African empire of Ezana and his dynasty is very little known, but the text of an inscription survives that seems to belong about this period. It was copied by a visitor from the Roman world called Kosmas Indikopleustes, who published it in his book, called *The Christian Topography*. Kosmas recorded this inscription at Adulis, and it is therefore commonly called the *Monumentum Adulitanum*. It provides a kind of gazetteer of the Aksumite king's conquests.

Kosmas copied it at the request of the *archon* or governor of Adulis, who wanted to send the copy to King Kaleb of Aksum, then preparing for his invasion of Yemen. The unknown king says:

> I entered valiantly into battle and subdued the following peoples; I fought the Gaze, then the Agame and the Siguene, and having conquered, I reserved for myself half of their lands and peoples. The Aua and Singabene and Aggabe and Tiama and Agathous and Kalaa and the Samene people who live beyond the Nile in inaccessible mountains covered with snow where tempests and cold are continuous and the snow so deep a man sinks up to the knees, I reduced to submission after having crossed the river; then the Lasine, and Zaa and Gabala, who inhabit the very steep mountains where hot springs rise and flow; and the Atalmo and the Beja and all the people who erect their tents with them. Having defeated the Taggaiton who dwell up to the frontiers of Egypt I had a road constructed going from the lands of my empire to Egypt. Then I fought the Annine and the Metine who live on precipitous mountains as well as the people of Sesea. They took refuge on an inaccessible peak, but I besieged them on all sides and captured them ... I defeated also the barbarian people of Rauso who live by the aromatics trade, in immense plains without water, and the Solate, whom I also defeated, imposing on them the task of guarding the sea-lanes.

He later sums up: 'I have submitted to my power all the peoples neighbouring my empire: in the east to the land of Aromatics, to the west to the land of Ethiopia [here probably referring to Meroë in modern Sudan] and the Sasou.' Not content with this African dominion, this unknown ruler also invaded Yemen:

> I sent an expedition by sea and land against the peoples living on the other side of the Erythraean Sea, that is the Arabitas and Kinaidokolpitas, and after subjugating their kings I commanded them to pay me tribute and charged them with guaranteeing the security of communications on land and sea. I conducted war from Leuke Kome to the land of the Sabaeans.

This last section doubtless furnished the justification King Kaleb sought for reasserting Aksumite control over the Arabian kingdoms in the sixth century.

The validity of these claims can be inferred from some of the objects and inscriptions found in Yemen itself. The Arab royal inscriptions of the third century AD tell us – first-hand evidence, though written by the Arabian rulers of Saba and Himyar, the 'enemy' of the time – how the Aksumite kings sent their sons with fleets and armies to ally with rival Arabian tribes, an exercise of the principle of 'divide and rule' which allowed the Aksumites slowly to carve themselves out an Afro-Asiatic empire spanning the Red Sea.

We know something of Aksumite progress through a number of these south Arabian inscriptions found in the Yemèn. The kings called GDRT and 'ADBH are mentioned in inscriptions at the great temple called Mahram Bilqis, Marib. These reveal that the king of Saba, 'Alhan Nahfan, and his two sons Sha'ir Awtar and Yarim Ayman, made a treaty with GDRT (perhaps pronounced Gadarat from an Ethiopian name Gedur, Gadara), 'king of Habashat' in the early third century AD: 'They agreed together that their war and their peace should be in unison, against anyone who might rise up against them, and that in safety and in security there should be allied together Salhen and Zararan, and 'Alhan and GDRT.' Later, in the 240s, the Sabaean kings Ilsharah Yahdub and Yazzil Bayyin found that Himyar and Abyssinia (Habashat) were in breach of a treaty during a war in which the Ethiopian ruler 'ADBH (Adhebah?), 'king of Aksum', supported a certain Shamir Dhu-Raydan, almost certainly to be identified as Shamir Yuhahmid, king of Himyar. An inscription tells us that 'Shamir of Dhu-Raydan and Himyar had called in the help of the clans of Habashat for war against the kings of Saba; but Ilmuqah granted ... the submission of Shamir of Dhu-Raydan and the clans of Habashat'. More wars followed under King Karib'il Ayfa' of Himyar, who fought both Saba and Habashat. Two Aksumite kings, DTWNS and ZQRNS (Datawnas and Zaqarnas?), were also in the Yemen in the 260s fighting with King Yasir Yuhan'im of Himyar. Even the last king of Saba, Nashakarib Yuha'min Yuharhib, before his state was finally absorbed by Himyar, was still engaged in conflicts with Ethiopia.

It was at the end of the third century that the prophet Mani, outlining his schema of the four world powers of his day, put his own Persia and the Roman Empire first, then Aksum as the African ingredient, and finally 'Sileos', perhaps an Indian kingdom or even China: 'There are four great kingdoms in this world. The first is the kingdom of Babylon and Persia, the second is the kingdom of the Romans, the third is the kingdom of the Aksumites, the fourth is the kingdom of Sileos (?).' Even if this arrangement were largely symbolic or mystical, adopted from a customary quadripartite listing of 'the four quarters' or the 'four kingdoms of the world' – east, west, south, north – the inclusion of Aksum as typifying the south in such a listing shows how well known the African empire had become in international terms.

The native inscriptions and coins clearly indicate that Aksum became Christian in the mid-fourth century under King Ezana. The story of Frumentius as preserved by Rufinus has been told above, and archaeology corroborates it. First-hand evidence for the conversion comes from a Greek inscription of Ezana, in which he proclaims his conversion by ceasing to call himself the 'son' of the war god Mahrem, but puts himself instead under the protection of the Christian Trinity. His coins too abandon the ancient symbol of the disc and crescent and adopt the cross.

At first, it seems likely that there was little missionary endeavour, although the fact that Christianity had become the royal religion doubtless encouraged its adoption at least in court and city circles. But by the fifth and sixth centuries, hagiographies preserve the accounts of the lives of a number of 'Roman' saints who came to the country to establish their faith in more remote regions. Even if the saints are themselves largely the stuff of legend, this might be regarded as the memory of a second more popular phase of conversion, contrasting with the more specifically royal conversion of the earlier period. From this time, or perhaps even earlier, biblical translations were prepared, Christian religious art was produced, and the Christian faith of northern upland Ethiopia proceeded apace to become one of the country's most distinguishing features.

Some two centuries after Ezana, Kaleb, king and saint, added to the imperial expansion of Aksum a third of the kingdoms of Yemen, the Hadhramawt (southeastern Yemen) and 'all the Arabs on the coastal plain and the highlands'. This occurred around AD 519 after his defeat of the Jewish king, Yusuf Asar Yathar, 'king of Himyar, king of all the Tribes' as the south Arabian inscriptions call him. The exact position of the Aksumite kings in Arabia is still uncertain. We have seen that there were extensive campaigns in the third century, and that Ezana still claimed at least suzerainty over Saba and Himyar in the mid-fourth century, although by then powerful Arabian rulers evidently controlled their own destiny. One Syriac document, describing the events in Kaleb's reign, claims that the Aksumites appointed the Arabian kings; if so, it must have been little more than a formality. Kaleb's expedition changed things for a brief time. His empire – perhaps best regarded in terms of vassal states more or less under Aksumite suzerainty – then embraced, in modern terms, all northern Ethiopia, part of the Sudan at least to the Nile, and the whole of Yemen.

The Yemeni war of Kaleb, conducted ostensibly as a champion of Christianity against the persecutions of the Jewish ruler Yusuf, may have also involved practical commercial interests. One text states that the Yemeni king was interfering with the Roman merchants who came to trade there. Interestingly, some of the actions of the war are known from Yusuf's or his officers own inscriptions. For example, one of his chiefs or *qayl*s tells of 'a campaign by wadi beds and a river valley for their lord the king Yusuf Asar against the Habash in Zafar [the capital city of Himyar]. They overthrew the church'; exactly as the Christian Syriac writers also confirm. This was dated in year 633 of Himyar, AD 518 or 523 (the Era of Himyar may have begun in 115 BC, but 110 is also possible). The Aksumite invasion, perhaps a pincer movement of forces sent via the west coast of Arabia, and south via Qana in the kingdom of the Hadhramawt, was not long in subduing the country.

Kaleb installed an Arab viceroy, Sumuyafa Ashwa, as king. He survived for about five years, before being overthrown in a military coup by Abreha, an Aksumite, who seized the crown. Kaleb could not oust the usurper, but in due course Abreha is reported (by the contemporary Byzantine historian Procopius) to have vowed allegiance and tribute to Kaleb's successor. Abreha's successors ruled Yemen until the Persian conquest around AD 570.

The theoretical submission of Abreha to Kaleb's son may be confirmed by the fact that the sole known inscription of King W'ZB (Wa'zeba?), who calls himself 'son of Ella Asbeha' (Kaleb), continues to use the conventional title of king of Saba and Himyar, but abandons the expanded reference to Hadhramawt and the Arabs of the coastland and the plateau.

In 1987 the Department of Antiquities in Aden invited me, as a member of the Mission française en Yémen du Sud, to study and catalogue a remarkable discovery, a hoard of 1,194 gold coins, 336 late Roman gold pieces with 858 gold coins struck for the kings of Aksum. The treasure had been found in a pot by farmers. This single find enlarged by three times the entire number of Aksumite gold coins known to date. It had perhaps been buried at the time of Kaleb's expedition, since his coins are the latest to be included in it. The earliest pieces in the hoard are from an issue struck by Ezana after his conversion to Christianity c. AD 340.

During the period of Aksumite expansion and prosperity, in the capital city itself substantial stone-built mansions were constructed. The largest of these, which were presumably royal residences, were discovered by the Deutsche Aksum-Expedition led by Enno Littmann in 1906. The expedition published, in 1913, a magnificent four-volume work in which archaeological and inscriptional material was included with excellent photographs and plans. Some of the palace buildings were cleared and planned in 1906. Fuller excavation had to wait until the work of Francis Anfray at the smaller villa at Dungur, 1966–68, and the 1972–74 expedition led by Neville Chittick. Even then, only relatively small areas were properly explored.

The great buildings were constructed of granite blocks or rubble, mud mortared. They apparently consisted – only the lower courses now survive, as at the Dungur palace – of towered square pavilions mounted on high podia. Perhaps this design originated as an anti-flood measure, as well as emphasising the prominence of the central person dwelling there. The main building was approached by monumental granite staircases. Kosmas Indikopleustes, a sixth-century Greek visitor to Aksum, wrote of the 'four-towered palace of the King of Ethiopia', and the plans of excavated structures in Aksum, Matara and Adulis (as well as stone-carved successors at Lalibela) seems to indicate that this was a common design. Staircase wells confirm that there was an upper storey, or at least a roof terrace. These massive and solid structures, which form the centre of similar complexes found in all Aksumite towns so far excavated, were surrounded by courts, themselves completely enclosed by ranges of domestic buildings. This gave the inner structure both defence – if it were needed in the unwalled Aksumite towns in a land that was itself a mountain fortress – and privacy.

Within the great structures, elaborately shaped granite pedestals and capitals adorned the columns, which may themselves have been of granite, or in some cases perhaps of wood. There were brick ovens, underfloor drainage systems, marble flooring and panelling, and almost certainly carved wooden decorative work. The architecture was distinctive. The ground plans show indentations and salients along the walls, the corners are reinforced by cut granite blocks – with sometimes a horizontal row of blocks for extra strength – and the elevation displays a regular shelving of the wall, each stage being topped with flat slate-like stones. All this was doubtless designed to strengthen walls constructed without the use of a binding lime mortar, in a land where the rains could be heavy and persistent at times. In addition, not so far discovered surviving at Aksum, but visible on the stelae and on some of the rock-cut or stone-built churches of Tigray (Debra Damo, Debra Salam at Asbi, and the Geralta churches), there was a further system of binding the walls by a wooden matrix. This consisted of longitudinal beams, cut square, inserted in the wall, over which lay transverse round beams passing either right through the wall, or at least well inserted into the stonework, clamped over the longitudinal beam by a cut in the underside, firmly linking the whole together. The exposed round ends of the transverse beams form the familiar 'monkey-heads' imitated in stone on the Aksumite stelae, and seen as actual functional elements at Debra Damo and other built churches. Window and door structures were made on the same principle, but with square 'monkey-heads'. This can be seen imitated in stone at Aksum on the stelae, the 'Mausoleum' door, and the door-slab of the Tomb of the False Door, as well as at Lalibela, while wooden examples occur at Debra Damo, Yimrehana Krestos near Lalibela, and many other old churches in Ethiopia.

The Aksumite kings also dedicated granite-carved thrones to celebrate their victories, inscribing them with detailed accounts of their military campaigns. Rows or clusters of these thrones – or rather their pedestals – still stand, broken and desolate, around the city. They were dedicated to the gods of the Ethiopian pantheon – Astar (the planet Venus, a male deity in Ethiopia); Beher, the Sea; Meder, the Earth; and Mahrem, who is identified with the Greek war god Ares in the Greek version of the inscriptions. Statues of gold, silver and bronze were erected to Mahrem, the dynastic god; he was the theoretical 'father' of the reigning king. The statues have now disappeared, but the inscriptions proclaiming their setting-up can still be read. One statue-base, recorded and photographed by the members of the Deutsche Aksum-Expedition (DAE) in 1906, still bore the fixing-holes for the feet of a statue; each foot was 92 cm. long. Many of the throne pedestals are provided with two slots at the base in front of the seat, which seems to confirm that figures were once seated upon them. Slots at the sides and back were apparently for fitting large stone slabs, on which inscriptions were carved.

But nowadays the most impressive remains at Aksum are the royal tombs and their fabulous markers, the stelae or obelisks. In the very centre of the modern small town, on a stone terrace reconstructed in the position of one of Aksumite date, still rise many dozens of granite needles or obelisks, customarily called *stelae* after the Greek *stele*, or standing stone. Even the plain examples are impressive, cut from the hard local grey-green nepheline syenite, a kind of granite. But truly staggering in scale is a series of six enormous carved ones. These may depict in a stylised fashion the royal palaces of the dead kings, whose tombs were discovered lying beneath them during Neville Chittick's excavations (see below). The stelae perhaps represented a symbolic stairway to heaven for the dead rulers of Aksum. At the base are granite plates furnished with carved wine-cups for offerings – perhaps sacrificial blood, perhaps only wine, mead or beer – to the spirit of the deceased.

Exceptionally for an ancient sub-Saharan African state, Aksum struck its own coinage. This seems to have come as a successor to the South Arabian coinage, which was probably terminated a relatively short time before the Aksumites commenced their own issues. Chronologically, the coin-issuing rulers span from about the late third century AD, when the coinage commenced under King Endubis and King Aphilas, to the seventh century, when Aksum's power began to wane. Few contemporary states issued their own independent coinage in gold. It was a statement of absolute sovereignty only achieved at the time by Rome, Persia and the Kushan kingdom in north India and Afghanistan. On the coins issued by the kings of Aksum, of gold, silver and bronze – the latter two, uniquely, sometimes overlaid with gold on important symbols such as the cross, the crown, the royal head – we can read the names of over twenty of these otherwise totally unknown kings. Despite some recent discoveries and studies, the Aksumite coinage remains one of the rarest and least-known in the world.

The kings can be seen on the obverse of the gold pieces, wearing the elaborate high Aksumite tiara supported on a little colonnade of columns. The rulers wear fringed robes, and are adorned with necklaces, bracelets, armlets and probably finger-rings. They hold a sword, a spear, or later in Christian times a hand-cross. The bust of the king is framed by two wheat-stalks, doubtless representing one of the vital crops on which Aksum's prosperity depended. Most unusually, the king is also represented on the reverse of the gold coins, but this time wearing not the tiara but a sort of close head-cloth or helmet. On silver and bronze coins this latter image is the norm for the obverse, with a variety of reverse designs, although in the later series crowned heads appear on the obverse of these lesser metal pieces too.

Perhaps the most characteristic reverse motif is the cross. Ethiopian art has exploited the cross form to a high degree, and on these coins some of the earliest developments can be seen; Latin and Greek crosses, cross-crosslets, diamond-centred crosses inlaid with gold, and other variants. It may be – indeed it seems almost certain – that the Aksumite kings were the first to place the Christian cross on their coins.

The legends on the coins appear at first in Greek, on all three metals. Later there is a gradual change, Ge'ez coming to predominate on the lesser metals while Greek is retained for the gold – an indication of its status in the international commerce of the time, when Greek was the lingua franca. Doubtless one of the motives behind establishing a national coinage for Aksum was the encouragement of trade. In addition, the kings could send messages to their people by this useful propaganda medium – some of the earliest Christian examples show the cross in the centre surrounded by the words 'May this please the people', doubtless a form of conversion manifesto. Other legends declare 'By the Grace of God', or 'By this [cross] he will conquer'. Later messages read 'Joy and Peace to the People', 'Christ is with us', or 'Mercy and Peace'.

One eyewitness description exists of a king of Aksum. When King Kaleb, about AD 518/19, conquered the Jewish King Yusuf of Himyar in Yemen, the Byzantine Empire sent an embassy to propose that Aksum's merchant fleet try to join in the silk trade, buying from Indian merchants in an attempt to exclude Rome's inveterate enemy, Persia. One of the ambassadors witnessed the king's arrival, and later described it in a note that has luckily been preserved by the sixth-century chronographer John Malalas. The scene was one of great splendour. Kaleb stood high on a chariot-like dais, bound round with golden leaves, and set on a wheeled platform drawn by four elephants. He wore a gold and linen head-dress, with fluttering golden streamers. His collar, armlets, and many bracelets and rings were of gold. The king's kilt was of gold on linen; his chest was covered with straps embroidered with pearls. He held a gilded shield and lances, while all round him musicians played flutes and his nobles formed an armed guard.

The blaze of all this magnificence, fuelled by commercial riches and a successful war, was soon to fade away. Around AD 570, the Persians finally conquered Yemen from Abreha's son Yaksum. Not long afterwards they seized Jerusalem and Alexandria. The Red Sea trade with the Roman Empire and

India slipped from Aksum's control. The coinage that had publicised the glory of the King of Kings of Aksum ceased to be issued.

With the rise of Islam around 640 a new map of the world was drawn, which almost excluded Aksum. The early *hijra* or emigration to Abyssinia recorded in the *hadith*, the accepted body of traditions of Islam, indicates that the Arabs were accustomed to travel across the Red Sea to their nearest African neighbour. Muhammad's followers fled to Ethiopia from the plots of the Quraysh tribal authorities of Mecca. The Ethiopian king, commemorated in the later Arab literature by the title and name of *Najashi* Ashama ibn Abjar, received the prophet's followers, refusing to extradite them at the request of the Quraysh. He thus gave the new religion the respite it needed to consolidate itself. When the time was right he allowed the exiles to return, and they and the prophet himself are recorded in Arabic literature as having praised the justice and order of the *najashi*'s rule. Two of the prophet's wives, Umm Habiba and Umm Salama, both among the exiles in Ethiopia, are said to have described the paintings in an Ethiopian church – perhaps the main church at Aksum, an early version of the present church of Maryam Seyon – to the prophet. The rise of Islam was to destroy the old Red Sea trading system and wipe out one of Aksum's greatest resources, the sale of African products to the Roman world. With Egypt lost to the Muslims after 640, the Roman or Byzantine empire no longer had access to the Red Sea and Indian Ocean. Their ships ceased to come to Adulis. Forced into a narrower mould, Aksum fell into obscurity.

The stories preserved in the Arab records mention revolts and battles at this time in Ethiopia. Modern studies of the geo-archaeological record point to an environmental decline. There is also the tantalising possibility that the great plague that struck Byzantium in the 540s originally emerged from Ethiopia, where it may have left the land as badly stricken demographically as the great northern empire was to be (if we credit the historians' accounts). This may provide another factor for the ultimate failure of Aksum in Arabia, and the oncoming decline of the city and the state. Aksum itself, for over six hundred years a great capital, was left with an exhausted environment. For centuries trees had been felled for charcoal and agricultural expansion, and the topsoil had washed away. Even the weather changed, according to recorded Nile flood-levels in Egypt, which depended on Ethiopian rains. Its hinterland incapable of supporting the swollen population of an imperial city, Aksum was doomed to become a backwater, of no political importance, a forgotten place outside Ethiopia.

The decline of Aksum was not the fall of the Ethiopian Christian kingdom, only a shifting of emphasis. The Muslim *khalifa*, al-Walid (705–715), caused a fresco showing six of the kings with whom early Islam had come into contact to be painted on the walls of his desert castle, Qusayr Amra, in Jordan. The names of four of these rulers still survive, the Ethiopian *najashi*, together with the Roman Caesar, the Persian King of Kings, and Roderick the Visigothic king of Spain. The metropolitan bishops still continued to come from Alexandria, by permission of the Muslim authorities in Egypt. In Ethiopia, new capitals arose, each a little further to the south as the Christian kingdom became landlocked. Arab authors tell us something about Ethiopia after Aksum. They wrote of a vast realm, ruled by a king from the city of Kubar, the site of which is now unknown. The kings remained powerful, as Arab geographers such as Ibn Hawqal and al-Mas'udi continue to report. Kubar is mentioned from the ninth century.

Muslim states came to control the sea-coast, blocking Ethiopia's foreign commerce. In the tenth century a queen conquered the kingdom; in AD 979 she sent a zebra ('striped female donkey') to the king of Yemen, who sent it on to al-Bahliyar, ruler of Iraq. Ancient Aksum faded into insignificance – except as the traditional site for royal coronations (after the Zagwé period), and for its cathedral dedicated to Mary of Zion. This church is still today the holiest shrine in Ethiopia – the reputed resting place of the Ark of the Covenant itself, said to have been brought back to Ethiopia by the first emperor, Menelik, reputed son of Solomon and the Queen of Sheba. A very few of the mediaeval and later kings were crowned here, employing one of the ancient Aksumite stone throne pedestals in the church enclosure as their coronation seat.

The Town in the Past

'Ham begat Kush; Kush begat Ityopis, and after his name Ethiopia is known until today … Ityopis begat Aksumawi; Aksumawi begat Malakya Aksum. And he begat Shum, Nafas, Bagi'o, Kuduki, 'Akhoro, Farheba. These six sons of Aksumawi were the Fathers of Aksum.' According to this local legend collected by Enno Littmann from an old priest, Aksumite and Ethiopian origins date back to the days of Noah's progeny. Like many other peoples, Aksumites recall that there was once a golden age, long ago, a wonderful time of plenty: 'zemana hambasha neru imni', when stones were bread.

Historically, the beginnings are more prosaic. Apart from the *Periplus*, there is a brief note in Ptolemy's *Geography* that the royal palace was at Aksum. Though originally written in the second century this text may contain, in the manuscripts that have come down to us, somewhat later information. Otherwise, it is Ezana, king of Aksum, who himself provides the earliest topographical information about Aksum. In two of the inscriptions of Ezana (recorded by the Deutsche Aksum-Expedition (DAE) as nos. 10 and 11) the king declares 'I have set up a throne here in Shado.' Because one of these inscriptions (no. 10, after Monneret de Villard) is said to have come from a spot close to the original position of the famous trilingual inscription of Ezana (DAE 4, 6 and 7), it is supposed that that place was Shado. The DAE plans and photos do indeed show the stone with the inscription, together with a number of throne pedestals, standing at this spot, and it is possible that the inscriptions were once associated with the pedestals. The *Book of Aksum*, which includes a brief description of the town in Ge'ez that dates in its present form from perhaps the fifteenth century, also mentions a place called Sado, where there was a church, near another spot called Me'raf. This Me'raf is mentioned in medieval accounts of the royal coronation as the place where the king first stopped on entering Aksum. These descriptions confirm that there was a stone standing there, inscribed in an unknown language. This must be the stone that we now know to have been erected by Ezana. It has since been moved to the Ezana Garden (see below).

The first foreign description of a monument at Aksum is by Kosmas Indikopleustes, writing in Greek. (For texts of many of the descriptions of Aksum in their original languages, see Ugo Monneret de Villard's excellent compendium, *Aksum. Ricerche di Topografia Generale*). Kosmas, who was at Aksum in the first quarter of the sixth century, briefly recorded that he had seen bronze statues of unicorns in the four-towered palace of the king of Ethiopia. There may be traces of such a palace in the large buildings excavated by the DAE in Aksum: Enda Sem'on, Enda Mikael and Ta'akha Maryam. Little survives of these structures, and they are at present undateable; they are illustrated in plan and by photographs in the DAE report. Other examples, such as the Dungur mansion, exhibit similar plans, consisting of a central edifice with the four corners forming salients, as if indeed they formed the bases of protruding corner towers.

Charters attributed to medieval – even to Aksumite – kings are preserved in the *Book of Aksum*. We might well be suspicious of those attributed to the legendary kings 'Abreha and Asbeha', Gabra Masqal, or Anbasa Wudem. As far as the medieval ones are concerned, however much they might have been altered to enhance the fame, and the property claims, of the cathedral as later copies were made, we may be on surer ground. King Sayfa Arad (1344–71), Amda Seyon's son, is the earliest whose charter survives, and others emanated from Zara Yaqob, who lived for three years in the town, and underwent his tonsuring ('coronation') ceremony there in 1436. For a brief moment, the ancient glories of the quondam capital might have been revived. But three years of residence of the locust-like medieval Ethiopian court and its horde of attendants must have thoroughly exhausted the town's resources. Zara Yaqob issued a decree ordering that the people need not offer food and tribute to a visiting monarch unless they wished to, and no subsequent emperor ever spent very long there.

Although it is customary to assert that Aksum was the 'coronation city' of the medieval kings, in reality the truth is very different. True, Zara Yaqob's son Baeda Maryam took the trouble to summon Aksumite officials to his own coronation at Jejeno in Amhara, and at one time ordered preparations to be made for his coronation there, but almost a century and a half elapsed before the next Aksumite coronation, that of Sarsa Dengel in 1580. In the interim, Lebna Dengel had visited the town, organising the flight of the revered stone object called the 'Ark of the Covenant' and giving the other treasures of the church into the hands of guardians. Aksum and its cathedral had been burned by Ahmad Grañ in 1535, and rebuilt on a much smaller scale. Emperor Susneyos was crowned at Aksum in 1608. Further reconstruction of the church followed, and the building may have taken something like its present form under Fasiladas, whose daughter Yodit was present at its dedication in 1655. Iyasu I was crowned there in 1693. After that, Aksumite coronation was revived only by Yohannes IV in the late nineteenth century. Coronation at Aksum was, in truth, an event of exceptional rarity.

The Venetian Alessandro Zorzi collected notes in 1519–24 about the routes within Ethiopia and on to Jerusalem. He was able to meet certain Ethiopian monks in Venice, and talk to them about their journeys. Only a few of these itineraries mention anything about Aksum. Brother Raphael, for example, was a Franciscan of Jerusalem 'who came from the land of Presta Jani [Prester John, the usual term for the emperor of Ethiopia at that time] from a city called Axon, where all are Christians baptized with water like us and not with fire'. The last note alluded to a current belief that Ethiopians bore facial scars because they were 'baptized with fire'. Zorzi met Brother Raphael in Venice on 1 March 1522, and conversed with him in Latin. 'And first he described to me the itinerary he made when he went from Axon, his native place, to the chief city of Presta Jani called Barara.' Aksum (Axon), he describes as 'a great city', three or four days distant from the Nile. It was very hot. Crops were gathered 'twice a year as in all the lands of Presta Jani', there was honey and sugar, and among the fauna the rhinoceros and great serpents are noted. Raphael added comments about local clothing, weaponry and metal deposits. There were paintings in the churches, but sculpture was not permitted. His note about great vaulted lead-roofed temples reminds one of Francisco Alvares' description of the cathedral made at more or less the same time. There were also palaces, forts, monasteries, and manuscript books written in the old script. The monastery of Lelia (Halleluya) was two days from the city; here were three great churches and five thousand monks, not far from 'a very great river called Marab'.

The 'Franciscan' brother Thomas of Ganget came via Jerusalem. In his conversation with Zorzi on 7 April 1523, he praised Aksum to the skies. Aksum was 'one of the greatest cities in these provinces, and another and greater Rome for grandeur and splendid buildings, ancient and wondrous; and that there are columns as great as the campanile of San Marco in Venice, with great arches also and worked stones with great Chaldean letters that few can read'. This description at least allows one to recognise the stelae and, perhaps, the exposed inscription of Ezana at Me'raf.

Apart from these modest notes, the first major description of the town, by the Portuguese chaplain Francisco Alvares – who was in Ethiopia between 1520 and 1526 and who spent eight months in 'Aquaxumo' by order of Emperor Lebna Dengel – comes almost exactly a thousand years after Kosmas. Alvares and his successors over the next century, Manoel de Almeida, Péro Pais (and Balthasar Tellez following them), present the ancient remains of Aksum very much as they are today. As a rule they describe the stelae more fully than anything else. Alvares, writing before the destruction caused by the war with Imam Ahmad Grañ, noted a few things that have now disappeared or at least are not certainly identifiable. The most important is of course the former much larger church of Maryam Seyon, destroyed in 1535 or thereabouts. Another structure, the Ambaçabet, is noted below in the section concerning the votive thrones.

In Alvares' book Aksum is named as the residence of several queens – the queen of Sheba, Makeda, Candace, and Gudit – whose names crop up occasionally in Ethiopian history. It was 'the city, court and residence (as they say) of the queen Saba [whose own name was Maqueda] who took the camels laden with gold to Solomon, when he was building the temple of Jerusalem'. It was also 'the principal residence of Queen Candace [whose own name was Giudich] who was the beginning of the country's being Christian. She was born (as they say) half a league from here, in a very small village, which now is entirely of blacksmiths.' This Candace, he adds, is supposed to have built the 'very noble church, the first there was in Ethiopia; it is named St Mary of Syon'. The curious identification of the Candace of the Bible with the destructive Queen Gudit in the tenth century is an addition in the Ramusio edition.

Manoel de Almeida confirms the extent of the ruin that befell Aksum in the sixteenth century, commenting that 'today it is a place of about a hundred inhabitants. Everywhere there are ruins to be seen, not of walls, towers and splendid palaces, but of many houses of stone and mud which show that the town was formerly very large.' Pais around 1620 saw in 'Agçum' only about '150–200 mud houses, very small and miserable, covered with straw' as well as a few of stone, in narrow unordered streets. Barradas merely commented

36. No one knows what happened to the vast quantities of rock that must have been hewn out to form the intricate network of rock-cut passageways and tunnels leading to Lalibela's churches.

37. Left isolated when a new channel was cut from the river Yordanos (Jordan), a cross hewn from the rock stands proudly amid the vegetation of the river valley.

38. Subtle touches of decoration, the pierced-stone windows relieve the mass of the great stone block of the church of Medhane Alem at Lalibela.

39. Varied, elegant, though carved from stone, the windows of the church of the Saviour of the World admit a dim light into the greatest of Lalibela's churches.

0. Legend says that from this gallery the royal saint, Lalibela, would watch the religious ceremonies enacted in the courtyard below.

41. The rock cut labyrinth of Lalibela sometimes offers tantalising glimpses of hidden splendours. Here, from a staircase leading also to the so-called Tribune of Lalibela, an opening reveals the church of Golgotha.

42. Sometimes all that can be seen of the wonderful structures within are windows cut from the solid rock of the courts at Lalibela

43. Like a vision from the past, the west façade of Beta Amanu'el church evokes, carved from the living rock, one of the great palaces that once adorned the ancient capital of Aksum.

44. An imitation rendered in solid stone of one of the windows of the typical old Aksumite style in the church of Amanu'el at Lalibela.

45. The massive stately columns and the raised court of the church today called Beta Marqorewos may originally have belonged to a royal palace at Lalibela.

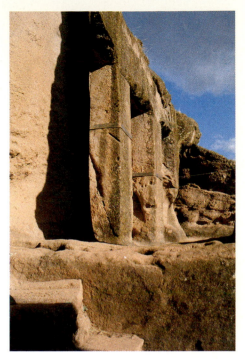

46. Beside the exit from one of the underground passages leading to Beta Marqorewos church, a discarded and broken wooden door lies where it fell long ago.

47. A crowned figure, perhaps a king or saint - one of the faded paintings still visible in the church of Beta Marqorewos.

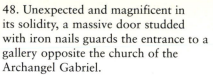

48. Unexpected and magnificent in its solidity, a massive door studded with iron nails guards the entrance to a gallery opposite the church of the Archangel Gabriel.

49. The delicate form of one of the windows within the ogive arches of the façade of Beta Gabriel church might once have lit not a church, but a royal or episcopal palace.

50. The faithful in Ethiopia were called to prayer not by the clang of a bell of cast metal, but by lithophones, bells made from stones that, suspended from trees by ropes, emitted a musical note when struck.

51. Elegant and refined, a finely decorated window in the magnificent cruciform church of St. George, Beta Giyorgis, at Lalibela.

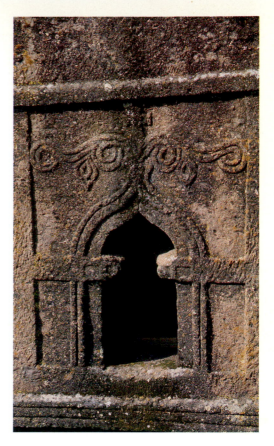

THE CHURCH OF YIMREHANA KRESTOS

2. A jewel in its casket of rock, the west nd of the north façade of the church of imrehana Krestos, situated in the emote mountains of Lasta.

53. One of the most elaborate ancient churches surviving in Ethiopia, the church of Yimrehana Krestos exhibits elegant capitals and archways dating from mediaeval times.

54. Dingy, blackened with the smoke of tapers, one can see little in the church of Yimrehana Krestos until the flash bulb illuminates the hidden splendour. Two of the elaborate painted and inlaid wooden ceilings of the church.

55. Modern artistry captures the traditions of the past: paintings
and silverwork in the shop of Haile Mariam Zerue at Aksum.

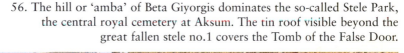

THE ANCIENT SITES

56. The hill or 'amba' of Beta Giyorgis dominates the so-called Stele Park,
the central royal cemetery at Aksum. The tin roof visible beyond the
great fallen stele no.1 covers the Tomb of the False Door.

57. A decorated granite column base from one of the vanished palaces of Aksum, in the 'archaeological cemetery' created by the Italians, the Ezana Garden at Aksum.

58. Demonstrative of the restrained and elegant taste of the ancient Aksumites, a stepped and chamfered column base of granite from one of the palaces lies today in the Ezana Garden.

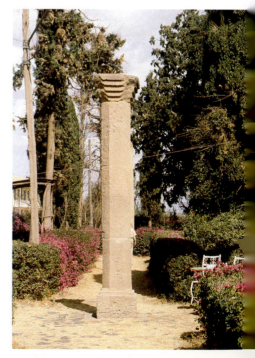

59. Sometimes wooden columns might have held up the roof of the muti-columned halls of the palaces of ancient Aksum, but this one, today re-erected in the Ezana Garden in Aksum, is of solid granite.

60. Perhaps the greatest single stone monument ever erected by man, the now-fallen stele no.1 at Aksum smashed onto the roof of another massive structure, the tomb called the Nefas Mawcha, resulting in the ruin of both.

61. Beside some of the typical 'monkey head' beam ends carved into the granite of the great fallen stele at Aksum, a window cut into the house

62. The great stele at Aksum represented a building of thirteen storeys. Here, the windows of one storey can be seen.

63. The Aksumites were absolute masters of stonework. The walls and staircase descending to one of the tombs at Enda Kaleb, where the royal saint King Kaleb and his son Gabra Masqal are said to have been buried over fourteen hundred years ago.

64. Empty sarcophagi, carefully carved from stone and later desecrated and broken, lie in one of the underground burial chambers in the so-called 'Tomb of Kaleb and Gabra Masqal'.

65. The gatehouse leading to the holiest spot in all Ethiopia, the inner enclosure of the church Mary of Zion at Aksum. The west façade of the church of Maryam Seyon is visible beyond.

66. Between the modern and the ancient churches of Maryam Seyon - the attractive building called the Treasury of Yohannes.

7. Lying where it was found during the excavations of 1959, a large stone slab of unknown purpose discovered near the church of Maryam Seyon, Aksum.

68. The simple elegance of the west façade of the 17th-18th century church of Mary of Zion at Aksum, with its terrace, bell tower and magnificent flight of stone steps deriving probably from older structures on the site.

69. Perched high on a conical hill just outside Aksum town, the church of Abba Pantelewon, one of the famous 'Nine Saints' of Ethiopia.

DEBRA DAMO

70. From afar, the imposing 'amba' of Debra Damo presents its steep-sided profile. Access to the church on this mountain, gained only after being hauled up on the end of a leather plaited rope, is forbidden to women and to all female creatures, even hens.

ROCK CHURCHES IN THE WUQRO REGION

71. Cut into the rock, the façade of the church of Medhane Alem – the Saviour of the World – at Addi Qesho.

72. In the church of Mikael Milahayzengi, the architects were not deterred by the intransigence of the solid rock to make this fine carved ceiling design.

73. Seen from the west, the massive walls of the temple at Yeha, oldest and most splendid of all the surviving buildings in Ethiopia.

74. A stele of unknown purpose stands in front of the *qwolqwol* or *euphorbia candelabra* tree in the enclosure of the church and temple at Yeha.

75. Embedded in the wall the rebuilt church, a frieze stylised ibex, symbols of ancient god dating from t time of the temple at Yeha.

that 'I call Acçum more of a village than a town because that in fact is what it is, no other name could be given it today, despite what it may have been in the past', even though 'this one is the principal one of this kingdom' (Barradas 1996: 119–20).

Dr Charles Jacques Poncet visited Aksum (which he confusingly called Heleni) in 1700 during a journey to Gondar to cure Emperor Iyasu I or his son of a skin disease. The Frenchman, whose account appeared in 1704, provides a few brief notes concerning the remains to be found at 'Heleni'. Poncet wrote that

> in the middle of the large space which is in front of the church, one sees three pyramidal and triangular needles of granite, covered with hieroglyphs. Among the designs on these needles, I noticed on each face a lock, which is very strange, as the Ethiopians do not use locks, and do not even know how to use them.

'Pyramidal and triangular' does not really describe the stelae very well, and by 'hieroglyphs' Poncet seems merely to mean elaborate carving rather than writing. He describes the church as 'magnificent ... the most beautiful and the largest that I saw in Ethiopia', but goes wrong again when he adds 'it is dedicated to St. Helena, and it is apparently from this church that the town took its name Heleni'.

The Armenian Yohannes T'ovmacean (see Nersessian and Pankhurst 1982) was another of the visitors to Aksum who did not, apparently, learn its real name. He notes that three days out of Adwa

> they rested at a village called Saba which was in ruins. This city was named after a woman of ancient times called Saba whose numerous, very tall, and beautifully carved stelae were erected in more than 10 places. Some of these stelae are still standing, while others have fallen and lie buried. The woman Saba also built a palace for herself. It was made of stone like that in a nearby mountain. This stone, after being cut and fashioned, was used to erect a three-storey structure with several halls and rooms, beautiful staircases, doors and windows, as well as a dining room, attics, basements, granaries, and a yard with stables. The roof and floors were cut from a single rock, and the palace was altogether a remarkable edifice. However, because it was not used, and perhaps on account of wars, one side of this palace, as well as various other parts of it, had fallen to ruin. Half the building was nevertheless still standing, and T'ovmacean personally inspected it completely.

What T'ovmacean saw was probably the 'Tombs of Kaleb and Gabra Masqal' and their ruined superstructure.

The Scottish traveller James Bruce of Kinnaird followed in 1770. He too described the town, in general correctly, but with his customary energy and positivism, which led to some inaccuracies or flights of the imagination. These Henry Salt pointed out with some relish some thirty-five years later. Bruce of course mentioned the stelae area: 'In one square, which I apprehend to have been the centre of the town, there are forty obelisks, none of which have any hieroglyphs on them.' This last remark was evidently directed at Poncet – although Bruce took care elsewhere to defend Poncet's geographical information, and his claim to have been to Ethiopia. This claim was questioned by eminent contemporary French scholars such as the abbés Renaudot and Le Grand – although they themselves never visited Ethiopia. Nevertheless, such details as the route taken to reach Ethiopia, and the description of the lock carved on the stele door, proved Poncet's trustworthiness as far as Bruce was concerned.

Bruce, too, was often very wide of the mark in his interpretations. In particular, he ascribed almost every monument in the town of any distinction to Ptolemy III Euergetes, king of Egypt (246–221 BC) and even found – made up, suggested Salt later – the name on a block of stone lying near the row of thrones in the cathedral court. He further wrote: 'I apprehend [the standing decorated stele], and the two larger that are fallen, to be the work of Ptolemy Euergetes.' In the middle of his description of the contents of the annals of Iyasu I, when Bruce diverged into his defence of Poncet, he demonstrates how reluctant he was to give the Ethiopians the honour of being responsible for Aksum. 'I believe it to be the magnificent metropolis of the trading people, or Troglodyte Ethiopians, called, properly, Cushites … as the Abyssinians never built any city, nor do the ruins of any exist at this day in the whole country.' He believed 'Axum … to have been much adorned, if not founded, by the Ptolemies'; and again states that:

> Ptolemy Evergetes, the third Grecian king of Egypt, conquered this city and the neighbouring kingdom; resided some time there; and being absolutely ignorant of hieroglyphics, then long disused, he left the obelisk he had erected for ascertaining his latitudes, ornamented with figures of his own choosing, and the inventions of his subjects, the Egyptians, and particularly the door for the convenience of private life, to be imitated by his new-acquired subjects, the Ethiopians, to whom it had hitherto been unknown.

All this, apart from constituting a very bizarre explanation for the stelae, is simply imagination. The choice of this particular Egyptian king was based on the fact that Kosmas Indikopleustes, in publishing his copy of the *Monumentum Adulitanum*, presented a stele of Ptolemy, also at Adulis, as part of the same inscription as that of the anonymous Aksumite king quoted above.

Bruce also had an idea that 'Axum, being the capital of Siris, or Siré' (the province of Shiré directly west of Aksum) therefore had a connection with the dog-star, Sirius. From this he deduced that the one hundred and thirty-three pedestals hewn at equal distances into the five-foot high parapet wall of red marble which he saw on the left of the road after the Bazen obelisk (on the right of the present main road), had once borne statues. They were statues, he surmised on unknown grounds, of 'Syrius the Latrator Anubis, or Dog Star …'. Bruce continues: 'only two figures of the dog remained while I was there, much mutilated, but of a taste easily distinguished to be Egyptian. These are composed of granite, but some of them appear to have been of metal.' He mentions these figures several times. Once he declares that 'the prodigious fragments of colossal statues of the Dog-Star, still to be seen at Axum, sufficiently shew what a material object of their attention they [the 'Cushites'] considered him to be'. Again, he states that

> there is not in Axum (once a large city), any other hieroglyphic but of the dog-star, as far as I can judge from the huge fragments of figures of this animal; remains of which, in different postures, are still distinctly to be seen upon the pedestals every where among the ruins.

In addition to this extraordinary account of what seem to be the Aksumite throne pedestals, Bruce mentions other pedestals 'whereon the figures of the Sphinx had been placed'. As Monneret de Villard commented, only Bruce or perhaps only his fantasy ever saw any of these. It is certainly strange that although Bruce surely must have seen something to give him these ideas, no other visitor to Aksum, before or after him (except Kosmas Indikopleustes, who saw 'unicorn' statues) has ever recorded anything of this sort. Did he perhaps see the remains of some sort of statue on one at least of the pedestals? Rather than accuse Bruce, as so many have, of deliberate deception in some of his stories – Horace Walpole suggested that his drawing of the Abyssinian lyre should rather be 'the Abyssinian liar' – it might be recalled that he left Ethiopia in the early 1770s, and his work only appeared in 1790. Even if certain details might have become blurred, and his own strongly held theories might have distorted other elements, his work nevertheless remains one of the great monuments of Ethiopian studies.

Bruce considered that the town of Aksum 'may have about six hundred houses', which, if true, indicates a substantial increase; although Sapeto later (1838) counted only about three hundred and fifty houses, with some 1500 inhabitants, and Ferret and Galinier 'trois ou quatre cents masures' in 1841. Von Heuglin and his companions estimated a population of some 2,000 to 3,000 in 1861, while Achille Raffray considered that about 2,000 people lived there in 1874.

The first published plan of Aksum seems to be that drawn by Henry Salt in 1805 (published in Lord Valentia's *Voyages* …, 1809, III), which indicates the main outlines; most of this he confirmed during his 1810 visit. In the centre is the church compound with the cathedral, steps, throne pedestals and gatehouse, and 'a small running stream' (Mai Hejja) leading from a tank or reservoir (Mai Shum) between a North Hill and an East Hill (Beta Giyorgis and Mai Qoho). The central and southeastern groups of stelae are shown, and the Ezana inscription with three thrones, another five being indicated beside the 'rocks resembling a wall' (at Mehsab Dejazmach Wolde Gabriel). Further east Abba Lucanes (Abba Liqanos) and Abba Pantalewon are indicated. The latter is situated on a hill called 'Mantilles' after Bruce, which other travellers variously render as Mentelen, Mendelen, Mentiellen or Mentale, apparently all in fact deriving from Pantalewon through a Tigrinya dislike of the sound 'p'. A path is shown leading to the 'catacomb of Calam Negus', the tombs of Kaleb and Gabra Masqal. It is possible that some of the 'remarkable stones seen by Mr. Salt' shown in one corner of his plan, and said to be three furlongs southwest of the standing decorated stele, were part of the great tomb called Nefas Mawcha (then partially built over by houses); although the distance quoted seems too great. It is more probable, perhaps, that they were the visible remains of one of the palaces such as Enda Sem'on and Enda Mikael or Ta'akha Maryam, which the DAE later planned. Lefebvre in 1841 mentioned in the west of Aksum the foundations of a structure with six columns of 1.60 m. length, on an emplacement of 50 by 60 m., which might also be part of one of these palaces. As for the local housing of the time, for Salt the village seems to have been clustered west of the stele (Malake Aksum area), with some further houses on Beta Giyorgis. The area later known by the names Bagi'o and Nefas is marked as 'marshy ground'.

After this, several other visitors began to fill out the plan of the town in their publications, some meagrely, some richly. Among them were Rüppell 1833, Combes and Tamisier 1838, Sapeto 1838, Lefebvre 1841, Steudner 1862, von Heuglin 1862, Schimper 1864–65 (BM add. 28506, a beautiful hand-painted map 'Gegend von Axum und Adoa'), Rohlfs 1868, 1880–81, Lejean 1872, and Bent 1893. The culmination was the extraordinary work of the Deutsche Aksum-Expedition (DAE) in 1906, published in four volumes in 1913.

The Town Today

The present small town of Aksum is generally reached by air, although the main (unpaved) road from Gondar to Asmara, the 'strada imperiale' of the Italian occupation, passes through it – and directly over the now almost invisible remains of the palace of Ta'akha Maryam, cleared and planned by the DAE in 1906. The town, situated at about 2,100 m. – about 1.37 miles

– above sea level, lies at the base of two prominent hills, Mai Qoho to the east (c. 100 m. high), and *Amba* Beta Giyorgis to the north (c. 150 m.). These hills were called Laheah and Gobo Dirah by W. Steudner; Edda Girges and Edda Egsiéna by Schimper. Gobo Dera or Gobedra is actually another hill to the west of Beta Giyorgis.

Mai Qoho is a more or less barren rock, though scattered with grasses after the rains and with some seepage of water in places. This is, in fact, the significance of its name – a rocky mountain with water. On top of it are the remains of a stone stockade occupied at one time by Yohannes IV, the last emperor to be crowned at Aksum. Beta Giyorgis, somewhat higher, dominates the town from the north. It has now been carefully terraced with stones to aid water and soil conservation, and planted with eucalyptus trees, which with some small local shrubs and grasses have softened the much harsher silhouette seen in older photographs. On top of this mountain are some Aksumite ruins, and the remains of an Italian fort built above them. Further away, among the pleasant fields and smallholdings on a plain high above Aksum, is another stele and tomb field. Both hills offer superb views over the town and the surrounding plains and mountains.

From the valley between these two hills to the north-northeast of Aksum descends a seasonal stream, known by several different names along different parts of its course. In its upper levels it is called Mai Malahso (with a tributary, Mai Qerni, descending from Mai Qoho hill); in the centre of the town it is known as Mai Hejja; and as it enters the plain, Mai Matare. Another seasonal stream bed, Mai Lahlaha, descends in the boulder-strewn western part of the town, skirting the area called 'Addi Cha'anadug.

A huge reservoir called Mai Shum, 'Chieftain's Water', collects the waters from Mai Qoho hill. Perhaps in ancient times an earth dam across the Mai Malahso helped augment this supply. Interestingly, the name Aksum is suggested to derive from two words, *ak* and *shum*, also meaning Chieftain's Water, and certainly water would have been a prerequisite for the city's long life as a capital. A smaller temporary reservoir directly to the east of the larger one is called 'daughter of Mai Shum'. Many wells, and the juniper, sycamore fig, jacaranda, 'wanza' (*Cordia abyssinica*) and other trees that shade the town, testify to the presence of water at no great depth, despite the generally barren appearance of the town's surroundings especially before the rains.

The old airport of modern Aksum – a new one has just been opened to the east beyond Abba Pantalewon's monastery – is in the plain opposite the town to the south, in the area called Farhaba according to the Italians. This plain, west of the plain of Hasabo, is occupied by several villages and other features, but the name Farhaba seems to be unknown today. In the easternmost part is Semorat with Gebgeb behind (to the south of) it. Further west, up to the low hills to the south is Mai Ako, with the hill of Addi Qerni, the Horn, and Addi Berah behind it. Next comes the part of the plain and the village on a hill called Sefoho, with Enda Arbaat Ensesa hill and Da'erika further south. In this area is the rock-cut church of Abba Mata'a, visible only as a white façade with a red double door and a window halfway up the wall of a gorge. Medogwe, with its green-roofed church of Medhane Alem, lies further to the west. Returning from a visit to Abba Mata'a, one can see the whole prospect of Aksum and its surrounding hills and mountains. To the east is the sharp pointed shape of Damo Galila, then, moving westwards, its equally precipitous sisters the mountains of Adwa, and the high peak crowned with the monastery of Abba Pantalewon. Flanking the town are the crests of Mai Qoho surmounted with a radio antenna, and the more evenly contoured eucalyptus-covered block of Beta Giyorgis with Gobo Dera to the west. Further west still than Sefoho, there is another hill called Addi Hankera, with Seglamen behind it.

When the Italians first constructed the airfield in Aksum, they demolished all the houses south of the main road, but now there are substantial suburbs on this side. There were three main districts in the town in former times, according to the DAE. Malake Aksum lay west and north of the modern Stele Park and curved west under the shelter of Beta Giyorgis. Kuduku was situated between that and the main road (divided by Lejean into Safaha in the west, with 'Addi Kilte east of it, although the name 'Addi Kilte is now given to the region west and south of 'Addi Cha'anadug). According to the DAE report, Dabtara was the ecclesiastical district surrounding the church of Maryam Seyon, including the enclosure of the Church of the Four Animals (of the visions of Ezekiel and St John), *Arbaat Ensesa*, on its west side. The market place was in the area called Nefas, and on the other side of the Mai Matare south of Dabtara was Bagi'o.

These names are sometimes still remembered, but generally new ones have replaced them in common usage – if they were not erroneous in the first place. Thus Hawelti (the word for 'stele') is the name of the suburb west of the Stele Park. Dabtara is a name completely unrecognised today by Aksumite *dabtara*, the *nebura'ed* and the local people, who call the ecclesiastical quarter simply Geza Falesti, monks' houses, or Awda Mehret, the ward of mercy, or Asada Beta Kristyan, a name applied to every church courtyard or compound. Outside the cathedral enclosure gate to the west is the large fig tree, surrounded by steps, called Da'ro 'Ela, the 'place where a pond (or well) is found'. Cha'anadug ('donkey loading', alluding also to the Palm Sunday celebrations of Christ entering Jerusalem on a donkey) is on the way to Egzi Hasara, '(the place which) the Lord Protects' further west. Mik'a Kabaro ('beating the drum') lies south of Arbaat Ensesa church, and Addi Kilte is further west towards Dungur, where 'the queen of Sheba's palace' stands. South of Geza Falesti is Geza Amus, apparently referring to a former prostitutes' district, with Godif (with a reference to waste or garbage) next to it towards the east. Directly next to Geza Falesti, near Aksum Museum, is the round Tigray house formerly belonging to the family of the *ras* of Tigray, in the area called Enda Rasi.

Proceeding from the Stele Park up the valley of the Mai Hejja/Mai Malahso on the Beta Giyorgis side one passes the church of Enda Iyasus (the place of Jesus) and then the area formerly called Enda Negus – another name that no one seems to know nowadays. Beyond this is the Northern Stele Field, now more or less a eucalyptus wood. On the eastern flanks of Beta Giyorgis is the district called Geza 'Agmai. Paths from here lead on in different directions. One leads to 'Ashafi or Addi Sehafi, where there is an ancient rock-cut wine- or olive-press (NB on the DAE map the road is shown correctly to the northeast, but in the text (p. 76) it is described as 'nord-westwärts von Aksum', also correct because of the curved route taken by the road). Another goes to Addi Guatiya, where there are some rock-cut tombs, and Enda Kaleb, with the so-called 'Tombs of Kaleb and Gabra Masqal'; and along the valley of Megfa Hansi to the church of Abba Liqanos (Schimper indicates a valley called *melhad* or *malhad* between Edda Girgis and 'Abuna Licanos'). This church is built on Aksumite ruins. The Italians constructed a fort here. In recent fighting before the fall of Mengistu the church was badly damaged, although it has since been reconstructed.

On the opposite side of the Mai Hejja stream bed, facing Enda Iyasus church, is a hill, part of Mai Qoho, crowned nowadays by the Yeha Hotel. The hotel is an unobtrusive building, modestly placed, but with a superb view from the terrace over the greater part of the central stele area at the base of Beta Giyorgis hill, and over the ecclesiastical district to the south. In 1975, when construction work commenced, an Aksumite building was found below it (excavated by Wilding and Godet, and never published). Just below the hotel, in the place called Enda Abba Meta (or Mata'a, after one of the Nine Saints, also called Libanos) directly above the Mai Shum reservoir, a new church dedicated to Abba Aregawi has been built over the *sebel*, or source of curative holy water, known by Abba Mata'a's name. Here the religious ceremonies of *Timqat*, centred on the celebration of the baptism of Christ, take place. The ritual, for the blessing of the waters and asperging of the people, requires to be conducted near water.

The main road passing through Aksum from east to west first skirts the southern side of Mai Qoho hill. Some distance before Aksum stands the steep hill of Enda Pantalewon, crowned by the church of this particularly Aksumite member of the group of the Nine Saints. At the entrance to the town, just after the Aksum Touring Hotel, and before the triangular space popularly called the Ezana Garden, the stele above the tomb of Bazen rises prominently on the lower slopes of Mai Qoho, marking an area of tombs and the southeastern Stele Field. The tomb is accessible by a road that runs directly behind the Aksum Hotel, below the prominence of Mai Qoho marked by a radio antenna. Another stelae has been re-erected in the garden of the Aksum Hotel nearby.

At the Ezana Garden, the road into Aksum veers right to follow the Mai Hejja stream bed and the contours of Mai Qoho hill towards the Stele Park. The main road carries on west through new suburbs, and out of the town towards Shiré and Gondar. After leaving the Ezana Garden and the new white marble-clad Telecommunications building on the left, the right fork of the road, past the tomb of Bazen, enters the town. This road was constructed by the Italians in 1935, when a bridge was built over the Mai Hejja, and the stream bed itself, which formerly filled this space, was consolidated. The road is now called 'Denver Street' in honour of Aksum's new sister city, Denver, Colorado, whose Ethiopian population effected the introduction between the two cities, and whose citizens have helped to finance the paving of the road. The road passes the remains of a number of stone Aksumite throne pedestals on the right. There are now four of these, the second inscribed with three Ge'ez texts describing the campaigns of a ruler of Aksum called *Haseni* Daniel, with a little further on the battered remains of a column base or capital and another granite fragment of Aksumite date. Between the thrones and the two capitals, today sealed off by barbed-wire fences, a track to the right gives access to Mai Qoho hill. Part of the track is 'paved' with discarded tank tracks, and on top of the hill are the remains of many lorries and even a complete tank, brought up to dominate Aksum during the recent civil war.

The main road leads past the Tigray National Regional Central Zone Administration building and the marketplace, opposite which, on the Mai Qoho side, is the imposing rather Dutch-style house that formerly belonged to the *nebura'ed*, the civil governor and chief ecclesiastic of Aksum. It was built by Dejazmach Gabra Sellassie of Adwa, restorer of the façade of Maryam Seyon church at the beginning of this century; he was named *nebura'ed* of Aksum by Emperor Menelik. The house has just been restored with the financial assistance of Dr Sehaye Teferra. Inside are a number of vaulted rooms, a galleried upper hall, and the infamous 'torture-room' where the officials of Mengistu's government punished their Aksumite suspects; it is now a bathroom.

In the garden are two Aksumite stone thrones lying at the foot of a bank of reddish rock. One consists of the base-plate, with an integral throne base rising from the centre. The throne base is pierced with a single (fixing?) hole for a statue (?). A second base-plate is more complex, with a channel cut in the base-plate, into part of which a square area has been cut with five holes (for fixing a statue?), and two small cuts at the front for the feet (?). We are necessarily vague about these details, as no actual figure survives, although Ezana's inscriptions indicate that real statues of metal were made and dedicated to the gods. Excavation in any of the throne areas may reveal traces, but this has so far not been undertaken.

A modern monument of some sort is at the moment under construction at the crossroads outside the former *nebura'ed*'s house, employing the red stone which comes from Degwe, some fifteen kilometres away. (Local legend claims that Christ came here, asking for water. He was grudgingly given a cup, which he angrily threw down, and which is there to this day.) Beyond the *nebura'ed*'s house, which is apparently destined to become a cultural centre/ museum, is the office of the Culture, Tourism and Information Department, Central Zone (Tigray). Between these two buildings a narrow entrance passes through the rock 'wall' to the right, allowing one to see clearly that it is indeed a sort of wall, though apparently natural.

A little further on is the Post Office on the right, after which three more granite throne bases can be seen, set on a natural rock wall behind which is a basin-like area called Mehsab Dejazmach Wolde Gabriel. Beyond this on the right is a suburb called Gazash Moshan. Here are some steps cut into the rock of Mai Qoho, and a rock–cut tomb. Salt (Valentia 1809, Vol. III) describes this tomb – which is just visible from the present main road behind some houses – as 'the appearance of a double door-way excavated in the rock on the western side of this hill'. The description is correct. The rock has been cut back to form a flat surface, in which a shallow depression has been cut out like a doorway, with a deeper depression inside. It could perhaps be a single grave, intended to be covered with a sealing stone, or perhaps it is merely unfinished, and was intended to be much deeper.

Monneret de Villard, noting that this is the sole cave-like excavation in the rock in Aksum, suggested that it could be identified with the 'Grotto of the Slave' (Ba'ata Barya), mentioned in the fifteenth-century (?) description of the town called the *Mashafa Aksum*, or *Book of Aksum*. This asserts that the shadow of the cross of Abba Salama or Frumentius, the first bishop of Aksum, could be seen there; 'when he rested and sat by that stone, the glorious shadow of his Cross became delineated thereon'. The text may, however, refer to some other spot. It certainly gives the impression that the stone in question must have had some sort of cross carved on it, and there are plenty of such stones in Aksum, though no longer associated with a cave. From Gazash Moshan a track leading off the main road to the right mounts to the hill of Mai Qoho behind the Yeha Hotel.

Directly above this part of the town, on Mai Qoho hill, is a place called Makhayada Egzi' (Schimper's Edda Egsiéna, a name still in use; Enda Egzina, the place of Our Lord). Here the Italians constructed a fort in 1935 using stones from a ruin nearby called Enda Gaber, possibly named after the renowned Ethiopian saint, Gabra Manfas Qiddus. Monneret de Villard speculated about the possible identification of the ruins with the church of St Michael mentioned by Alvares. The name Makhayada Egzi' refers to 'the imprint of the Lord's feet', and there was formerly a foot-shaped depression there that people used to fill with water they carried there, before using it to anoint eyes or other diseased parts of the body. The rock, now marked only by a dead juniper tree, very conspicuous from afar, is directly above the east end of the cathedral of Maryam Seyon. The mystic stone itself was cut away recently by soldiers of the Derg, and either removed elsewhere or smashed.

Opposite Gazash Moshan the small Aksum Museum stands on the left at the back of a large garden. Here one must buy tickets to visit the Stele Park. The road continues to a wide more-or-less triangular open space with a central fountain basin, opposite the largest of the still-standing stelae and its smaller satellites. To the right are the tracks leading to the Mai Shum, to the Yeha Hotel – this one is now paved – and to Enda Iyasus; to the left are the great fallen stele and the tomb called Nefas Mawcha.

The road to the left continues westwards past the so-called Pillar of Yared, now standing together with another fragment of an ancient column in a protected position inside an enclosure with a doorway. The pillar, according to legend, was erected at the place called *miwrade qal*, where the Holy Spirit descended on St Yared to inspire him to compose the sacred songs. This event is commemorated by an inscription on the concrete threshold of the enclosure. Next to this is Da'ro 'Ela, the open space named after a giant sycamore tree in the centre of it. Several roads meet here. The road continuing west divides Malake Aksum from Kuduku, and goes on to Cha'anadug, Addi Kilte, Beles Bahari and Dungur. The road to the south skirts the church compound, passing the church of Arbaat Ensesa on the way to the market place, and another road leads northwards; on Lejean's map of Aksum this divides Malake Aksum into two districts, Takha Haimanot (= Tekla Haymanot, conceivably the dedication of the round church that formerly stood in Enda Iyasus compound?) to the east, and Tahtai Gheza to the west. The church of Arbaat Ensesa is sometimes called Tekla Haymanot's church today, as there is a *dabal* of that saint, but this does not seem to be in the right position.

On the map of the west part of Aksum drawn by Ruth Plant with the help of local informants, the suburb of Kuduku is divided into several smaller districts; Miginta and Geza 'Adam next to Da'ro 'Ela (Da'ro 'Illa), Geza

'Amus south of Arbaat Ensesa church, Goduf Abba Qifle Yohannes south of
that, with Beles Bahri, Miwqa Keboro, Miwqa 'Akhoro, Miwqa 'Ofay and
Inda Sim'on forming the central part of the suburb from north to south. To
the south are Goduf and Addi Kilte. The Mai Lahlaha watercourse is shown
passing east of the tomb of Ityopis and west of Ce'andug (Cha'anadug),
through Mezbir (Mazeber), then south past Da'ro Addi Kilte towards the
main road. Some of these names are recognisable in the list of ruined churches
in the *Book of Aksum*: 'Among them is Mika'el 'Ofay in the quarter of Malake
Aksum; the great guardian Ta'eka in the quarter of Walda Kuedekui; Sem'on
in Maya Sama'et (in the quarter) of Walda Akuaro.' These names were later
bestowed by the DAE on the palace ruins they found, Enda Mika'el, Ta'akha
Maryam and Enda Sem'on, although it seems improbable that these ruins
were really related to the *Book of Aksum*'s churches.

Opposite the Pillar of Yared is the outer gatehouse leading into the Mannagasha or coronation court of the cathedral, where a row of stone Aksumite
thrones, and two separate ones called the King's and the Bishop's Seats, can
be seen. There is also a small mound called Gudif Maryam. From here
another gate leads into the inner court of the cathedral – today containing
two cannon mounted on gun carriages, dated in Arabic to AH 1280 and 1281
(AD 1863–85). Women cannot pass here. A stone flagged path leads on to the
massive flight of steps rising towards the west façade of the cathedral.

The western suburbs of the town, Cha'anadug, Negusta Saba, Addi Kilte,
and on to Dungur constitute the district of the 'palaces' or great mansions.
Nowadays the paved road running through the town on the Adwa to Shiré
route veers left at the entrance to these suburbs, while an unpaved road
continues straight on into the mass of stone houses. There are many mounds
in this area, some of which undoubtedly represent Aksumite 'palaces' of
considerable size underlying the present houses. The evidence for this lies
not only in the excavations undertaken here by the German team in 1906,
and the British in 1973–74, but in the many vestiges that are still visible,
though sometimes hidden in private compounds. This was the area of the
mansions the DAE called Enda Sem'on and Enda Mika'el. If one continues
directly along the paved road towards Shiré, following its left turn instead of
going straight on into the suburbs, the fragmentary remains of the palace
called Ta'akha Maryam are visible beside the road.

Continuing along the main paved road westward, some way beyond the
town on the right is the excavated palace of Dungur, and opposite it the
Gudit Stele Field. Further away near the area called Se'qudur is the ruin
that the DAE called the Tomb of Menelik, in Mazeber (Monneret de Villard
later suggested that Mazeber was actually east of the town near Enda Kaleb
– the word means 'ruin', so possibly several places were so called). From

here a path continues west towards the mountain of Zala (a name apparently not used nowadays, when it is generally called Gobo Dera; it was named *Amba* Gollo by Schimper) and to the quarries. On the southern flank of this mountain is the rock of Gobedra (Gobo Dera – '*gobo*' signifying mountain) where one part of the rock face is carved with the image of a lioness. The quarries are in Gobo Dera, opposite the hill called Addi Hankera on the south side of the Shiré road. On a hill west of the Tomb of Menelik, at the edge of the plain, are the ruins called Wuchate Golo, where in 1958 a curious Aksumite monument, perhaps a baptistery, was excavated (de Contenson 1961).

The Ancient Sites

The archaeological work at Aksum, as it was left in 1974 with the Ethiopian revolution, was eventually published after Neville Chittick's death in *Excavations at Aksum* (Munro-Hay 1989), as part of the Memoir series of the British Institute in Eastern Africa. This offers detailed accounts of the excavation of many of the sites in Aksum, and the finds from them, as well as a bibliography for Aksumite sites not described. From 1993, a five-year programme under the direction of David Phillipson resulted in the clearing of the most important tombs found in 1974, and a certain amount of additional work at other sites in the town (Phillipson 2000).

Mai Shum reservoir   There is no real evidence for the dating of the Mai Shum reservoir, without archaeological investigation. Salt (Valentia 1809, Vol. III: 97–8) heard that it had been constructed in the reign of Yeshaq (Isaac) king of Abyssinia, by the Abuna Samuel, 'who died at Aksum three hundred and ninety-two years ago [i.e. 1413] and was buried under the Da'ro tree still remaining near the church'. Yeshaq became king in 1413 and reigned until 1430; Abuna Samuel cannot be the contemporary metropolitan bishop, at that time Bartolomewos, but might instead refer to Samuel of Waldibba, or of Debra Abbay, a famous ascetic of the period who came from an Aksumite family. There is no evidence as to whether in the time of Yeshaq there was already a cistern there, which the ecclesiastic might have restored, just as it was restored and enlarged during the governorship of Ras Mengesha Seyoum much more recently. The *Book of Aksum* mentions the name Mai Shum only when describing the 'house' under the stelae. Bruce, however, noted a Mai Shum on the road going west to Shiré, before reaching Selaklaka. He and his companions departed from Aksum at 7 o'clock, partly by 'the remains of an old large causeway, part of the magnificent works about Axum', and, after a pause to watch steaks being cut from a living cow, pitched their tents at 11 o'clock 'in a small plain, by the banks of a quick clear running stream; the spot is called Mai Shum'. This, however, is in the opposite direction from the reservoir, and evidently was situated a certain distance away from the town.

Water for the cistern derives largely from run-off from the Mai Qoho hill, where also steps cut into the stone facilitated access to the basin. Most of the water seems to come from the east side of Mai Qoho. There was formerly a pond called Gual Mai Shum, 'daughter of Mai Shum', on this side of the main reservoir, where children used to swim when the rains had filled it, but now it drains into Mai Shum by a channel cut in the rock. There may have been a small spring feeding the cistern as well. At Enda Kidane Mehret further up the stream there is a *sebel* or permanent source for holy water, as also at Enda Abba Mata'a, but these are apparently mere seepages of water from Mai Qoho. The Mai Kerwah of the *Book of Aksum*, or Mai Kirah, situated northeast of Aksum (north of the cathedral near the house of Gabra Masqal according to the *Gadla Yared*), may have provided a permanent flow, but this runs in the opposite direction. Here Yared – the famous sixth century ecclesiastic to whom is attributed the splendid traditional Ethiopian church music – met with Cyriacos, bishop of Behnesa and Abba Labhawi the Syrian. The Virgin Mary having commanded them to instruct Yared in the office and liturgy, they mounted a gleaming cloud and came to 'Mai Kerwah in the land of Aksum'. Meeting Yared, they gave him their books and instructed him, before returning three days later.

Francisco Alvares also noted that 'at the back of this great church [Maryam Seyon cathedral] is a very handsome tank or lake of spring water of masonry, at the foot of a hillock where is now a market, and upon this masonry are as many other chairs of stone as those in the enclosure of the church'. Unless some confusion has crept in between two places, and this refers to Mai Shum – probably merely an excavated cistern, without masonry retaining walls or throne pedestals, though perhaps lined with stone as the DAE photos of 1906 show – Alvares' tank must refer to the Mehsab Dejazmach Wolde Gabriel (see below). Nevertheless, it seems strange that so acute an observer as Alvares could have missed a major feature of such importance as Mai Shum during his many months of residence. Even today, the constant coming and going of women with large black water-pots on their backs, or donkeys carrying two such pots on panniers, is a very notable aspect of life in the town. Even if he did not remark this, Alvares can scarcely have missed passing the reservoir when he went up to see the tombs of Kaleb and Gabra Masqal (see below).

Emmanuel Barradas, who was in Ethiopia between 1624 and 1633, saw a 'small lake or large tank' fed by a small spring, from which both people and livestock were supplied, although 'the greatest public attraction in all the village are the wells which after only minimal digging give good water good not only for sanitary purposes but also for drinking' (Barradas 1996: 119). The 'small lake' can hardly be anything but the Mai Shum.

Bruce wrote that 'Axum is watered by a small stream, which flows all the year from a fountain in the narrow valley, where stand the rows of obelisks. The spring is received into a magnificent bason of 150 feet square, and thence it is carried, at pleasure, to water the neighbouring gardens.' Ferret and Galinier describe more or less the same thing after their 1841 visit, and von Heuglin too, in 1861, noted a streamlet feeding the basin. A small plan of Aksum provided by Schimper (BM add. 28506) indicates the position of the church, obelisks, and May Shum, marked 'perenn.' However, the DAE in 1906 specified that then this situation no longer prevailed, and Monneret de Villard, observing the stream in 1937, and consulting elderly local residents as well, pointed out that unless the hydrography of Aksum had changed, there was no perennial stream in the Mai Hejja. It is easy enough to imagine that certain visitors, in Aksum only briefly at a period when the stream was flowing, assumed it to be permanent. The *Guida* (1938: 264) notes that the Mai Shum was known, erroneously, as the Queen of Sheba's Bath.

Mehsab Dejazmach Wolde Gabriel   The name of this place presumably commemorates the Wolde Gabriel, who was *dejazmach* of Tigray in the 1780s. It consists of a rock barrier or embankment, which, despite the opinion of Alvares and Bruce, seems to be retained by a natural rock wall (as Salt too ascertained). It is presumably in this area that Bruce remembered a five foot high wall of red marble with pedestals cut into it. Such a rock 'wall', dark red in colour, even with a façade in places sufficiently vertical to give the impression of having been cut, does still exist behind the *nebura'ed*'s house, forming the back wall of the compound. Two throne bases lie below it here, which could easily have once surmounted it. Possibly these throne bases are the ones referred to by Barradas when he wrote:

Apart from this standard [the Ezana inscription], nearby in the direction of the church, leaning against the foot of the hill on the right-hand side, are some stones which are perfectly square and must measure some four or five span, the thickness at the ends may be a span but towards the middle the thickness increases, as in the pedestals of our own columns. They are placed on top of other rough ones with the largest portion being on top. Ancient traditions asserts that these were the seats of the Umbares when they judged. Umbares are similar to our desembargadores, and these Umbares are held to be descendants of those who came of old from Jerusalem, sent by Solomon with his son by Queen Sabbâ, named Milelec, to bring justice. (Barradas 1996: 120–1)

The 'wall' continues in a rather less imposing way towards the Stele Park. The rock here, even in its present fragmented state, retains its reddish tinge, and on top of it, now crooked and partly undermined, stand three throne bases. Four were recorded by Rüppell, five by the DAE (nos. 16–20). These are reminiscent of the position of the 'chairs of stone' mentioned by Alvares near his masonry tank. Rüppell considered that the embankment had been hewn out of the nearby cliff, but partially destroyed through time, and Lefebvre (1841) noted that 'the Silico-ferruginous rocks of the base seem to have been made by the hand of man'. Von Heuglin, after his 1861 journey with Dr Steudner and H. Schubert, described it as 'a path hewn in the cliff, or a water conduit'. Possibly at one time the wall retained water in the basin-shaped area behind it; the word *mehsab* means 'washing-place', which would seem to confirm this possibility. The market place was situated nearby in 1861, as it is today. Alvares noted that his tank was 'at the foot of a hillock, where is now a market'. The market may have moved, or there may have been more than one. However, the present position near the entry road to the city would seem far more probable a place to situate a market than up the valley by Mai Shum.

Wells and water sources Several writers on Aksum from Alvares onwards comment on the many wells that provided water for the inhabitants, apart from the Mai Shum reservoir. The *Book of Aksum* states that there were seventy-two sources of water. Alvares merely noted 'very good wells of water, of very beautiful worked masonry,' and that 'in the town of Aquaxumo, where the Queens Saba and Candacia were, there are many wells and tanks made with good masonry'.

Nathaniel Pearce, around 1814, recorded that 'the pool of standing water at Axum became so very muddy, that it caused many horses and mules to die daily'. This might have been Mai Shum, or perhaps another pool like the marsh shown on Salt's town plan. Pearce also noted

> there is no river within two miles of Axum, but the inhabitants have good well-water; there are many wells hidden, and even in the plain have been found, but the people are too lazy to clear them from rubbish. It appears probable that, in ancient times, almost every house had its well, as I have been at the clearing of four, situated not more than ten yards from each other. The stone of which they are constructed is the same kind of granite of which the obelisks are formed.

One such well was found during the excavations conducted by Chittick in the Stele Park.

The Southeastern Stele Field and the tomb of Bazen The 6.5 m. high dressed stele marking the tomb attributed to Bazen is the most prominent monument in the southeastern Stele Field of Aksum, which lies on the flank of Mai Qoho below a height called Medfa Walatu (where another Italian fort was built in 1935). In 1805 Salt noted the stele, and wrote that there were fourteen others visible. He indicated them on his plan, lying to the right of the upright one. Rüppell in 1833 saw only four, although Sapeto – perhaps simply taking Salt's figure – also records fourteen fallen and one erect. The DAE photograph of this area in 1906 shows the standing stele (as no. 1) alone in a completely barren landscape, with the fallen no. 2 (also a dressed stele, 5.20 m. long) below it some 25 m. away, and two other rough stelae (nos. 3– 4) nearby. The text notes that there are a few others – there seem to be eight indicated on the plan (fig. 29). Monneret de Villard, whose report barely suppresses his irritation at the way the Italian military engineers had dealt with Aksumite monuments, thought that some of the stelae had even been used in construction of the road. In 1961, the manager of the Touring Hotel (now the Aksum Touring Hotel) discovered a dressed stele in his garden; it is considerably smaller than nos. 1–2 at 3.50 m. It has been re-erected at the open-air restaurant in the hotel garden.

During excavations conducted by M. Jean Doresse in 1954, it was found that there were in the immediate neighbourhood of the standing stele a number of rock-cut tombs. That of Bazen is directly below the stele. A near neighbour is slightly to the left and behind it, a row of arched grave loculi cut from a large oblong pit. These are the most impressive tombs, although there are a few other shafts and pits nearby.

Bazen is the name given to several kings of Ethiopia in the different lists, the most notable being the Bazen supposedly reigning at the time of the birth of Christ. The king lists say that Christ was born in the eighth year of his reign, but the king is unknown save from these very late Ge'ez lists. The name occurs also on a stone built into the north wall of the staircase leading to the terrace in front of the western façade of the old cathedral of Maryam Seyon. The existence of this stone was first mentioned by Salt, who saw it in 1810. It reads 'This is the sepulchral stone of Bazen', or 'the stone of the Hall of Bazen'. The fact that it is in vocalised Ge'ez, and that it begins and ends with a cross, implies that it is at least later than the fourth century in date. Recent reading suggests that the name is 'Lazen' rather than 'Bazen'; Lazen is the 'Bisi'-name of King Kaleb.

Bazen's supposed tomb consists of a staircase cut into the rock, with some small burial loculi cut to the sides, and a shaft descending just above the entrance. Inside is a hall with low small chambers opening off it for burials. It was obviously a multiple grave. The most notable of the other tombs in the area is the one mentioned above, consisting of an oblong pit with arched openings along one side, for the insertion of burials. It is difficult to date these tombs. However, given the appearance of the two (now three) dressed stelae known in the immediate neighbourhood, and comparing them to others in the main and northern stele field, they might belong somewhere in the third or fourth centuries AD.

The Ezana Garden This small triangular garden, which an indignant Monneret de Villard referred to as 'a species of archaeological cemetery', contains a number of ancient objects, exhibited in the pleasant setting of a hedged garden, in which there is also a cafe and benches for video shows. De Villard's complaint arose because the military, when building the new road into the town in 1936, had moved a number of monuments without recording their previous position, even levelling a 'funerary tumulus' near the stele of Ezana. He thought it very probably the tomb of Ezana – the existence of major tombs under the stelae was then unknown – and published some intact pots that came from it, which the military had preserved.

The Ezana Inscription (DAE nos. 4, 6 and 7) The most prominent monument in the Ezana Garden, and the reason for its name, is the famous stele of Ezana recounting his war against the Beja. The stele is now covered by a circular hut for protection. It is carved with an inscription in Greek on one side, well preserved, and in Epigraphic South Arabian (ESA) and Ge'ez, very badly worn, on the other. Another almost but not exactly similar text was discovered carved on a second stele, now protected by a small stone hut on the track from Mai Shum reservoir to the Tombs of Kaleb and Gabra Masqal.

If the plans in the 1906 DAE report and the 1938 *Guida dell'Africa Orientale Italiana* are correct, the original stele bearing the inscription must have been moved slightly southwards when the new road was built in 1936. This is confirmed by Monneret de Villard, who supplies a list of the ancient objects moved at the time. The road followed the line of a former track, enlarging it by cutting away part of a small hill. It seems that when Bruce, Salt and others came to Aksum, the road from Adwa into the town passed between Mai Qoho and a small oval-shaped hill. On the southern end of this hill were the ruins of the church of Maryam 'Ammaq, and on the northern end another ruined church called Arbaat Ensesa. Only a track led past the stele on the other side of Arbaat Ensesa. The DAE plan shows both tracks, while the Italian plan of 1938 in the *Guida* shows only the road south of Arbaat Ensesa, forking from the main road at the newly laid out Ezana Garden.

There were some Aksumite throne pedestals between the two ruins. Four throne pedestals were seen by Rüppell, the nearest to the stele bearing Ethiopic inscriptions (of *Haseni* Daniel) on the base-plate. Sapeto vaguely recorded 'some'; while five were noted by Lefebvre and in the DAE report (nos. 21–25). Today there are four throne bases lying to the right of the road, the second with the inscriptions belonging to *Haseni* Daniel, plus a base or capital from a column and another unidentified Aksumite stone object. Some fragments were removed to the Ezana Garden, while the larger throne bases remained where they were.

The inscribed stele has long been known. While Alvares only mentioned in passing that among the ruins in the plain before Aksum were 'many of these chairs [thrones] and high pillars with inscriptions; [it is not known in what language, but they are very well carved]', Emmanuel Barradas in the next century was more specific. He noted that the inscription was on the road from Fremona (the Jesuit station) just before entering 'the village', Aksum. It was

> a square dark stone ... placed in the ground. It is five or six span in height and more or less one span in width. It leans a bit to the east and bears writing here and there. The letters on the western side from top to bottom seem to be Amharic, but antique and old so they cannot be read, not only because they are quite worn but because differences can be found in them from those letters now used.

This is a perfectly fair description of the Ge'ez/Epigraphic South Arabian side of the stele. 'As to the letters on that part that leans to the east, some of them seem to be Greek, others Latin, but from none of these languages can perfect sense be made, despite the efforts of visiting priests who knew both' (Barradas 1996: 120). The stele was also mentioned by Manoel de Almeida, who like Barradas arrived in Ethiopia in 1624, remaining until 1633. He wrote that 'a bombard shot away' from the great stelae – many of these ecclesiastics supply measurements according to the convention of the time, using the current military terminology –

> is a broad stone not much higher than a man on which a long inscription can be seen. Many Greek and some Latin letters are recognisable, but when joined together they do not make words in Greek, Latin, Hebrew or any other known language, and so the meaning of the writing is not discoverable.

Balthasar Tellez repeated much the same description as Manoel de Almeida in his abridgement and revision of de Almeida's book published in 1660.

Patriarch Afonso Mendez in a letter of 1626 opined that the Greek and Latin letters on this stele indicated that all these works [the stele and inscription] were by European workmen of the time of Justinian or other Eastern Emperors, who had close relations (as Procopius attests) with the King of Ethiopia. The mixture of languages came from the lodging together in tents of soldiers speaking both languages.

He also noted – the only one among all these learned Jesuits apparently to be able to read one word of this really rather well-preserved and clear inscription – that the word Basileus ('king' in Greek) was visible. Later in a 1728 French translation of the *Itinerário* of Jerónimo Lobo (in Ethiopia from 1625 to 1634, died 1678, the last survivor of the Ethiopian mission), Mendez' remarks are cited, but the word is written 'Basilius'. This is the reading attributed by Bruce to Poncet (see below).

Manoel de Almeida added, when writing of the coronation of the medieval Ethiopian kings at Aksum, that the royal cavalcade approached the town from the east until they reached 'the stone which I said above has an inscription which no has been able to read for many years'. At this spot, the young women designated 'daughters of Zion' awaited the king, holding a cord with which they ceremonially blocked the entrance to the Holy City, Aksum. The chronicle of Emperor Sarsa Dengel recounts that:

> The Daughters of Sion ... [stood] ... in the middle of the road where there is a small obelisk. This obelisk is covered from top to bottom with inscriptions cut by the ancients in Greek letters. The name of this place is Mebtaka Fatl, that is, the cutting of the cord.

At this spot, which others call Me'raf, the king dismounted and underwent a ritual questioning as to his identity. He then cut the cord as women cried out 'Truly you are King of Zion,' accepting him into Aksum, and thereby into the kingship of the New Jerusalem.

Henry Salt, during his visit to Ethiopia as part of Lord Valentia's expedition in 1805, saw the Greek inscription, and copied it with his servant and companion Nathaniel Pearce's help. It was published with an illustration in Vol. III of Valentia's account of the voyage. Salt even dug about a foot and a half of the inscription out of the ground – the first step in Aksumite archaeology! – so that he could complete it. He went to inspect the inscription again in 1810, and re-published it with a new illustration and a modified translation. At the same time, he got his companion, Mr Stuart, to copy what he could distinguish of the lettering on the other face of the stone, which has versions of the same text in two scripts, Epigraphic South Arabian and Ge'ez, although both are composed in the Ge'ez language. Bent in 1893 was able to take an impression of this face of the inscription, which Müller attempted to translate in his appendix to Bent's book. The text had to wait for the DAE report before it was realised that two scripts were involved (DAE nos. 6 and 7; the Greek text was numbered DAE 4). Lefebvre's expedition in 1841 again cleared the base of the Greek inscription and copied it; it is illustrated in the *Atlas* volume, Pl. 14.

Finally, Müller noted in his appendix to Bent's book that 'in the year 1808 Salt discovered, in the rubbish heaps of Aksum in proximity to the celebrated Greek inscription, three large limestone tablets ... on which old Ethiopian inscriptions were engraved'. There is no record of this discovery in Salt – who, on the contrary, expressed his disappointment that despite many enquiries he could trace no other inscribed stones – nor was he in Abyssinia in 1808. It seems that Rüppell in 1833 was in fact the first person to see and copy these inscriptions. He states that they had been found three years before, in 1830. They were all the same size and all had Ge'ez inscriptions on them. Littmann was told that part of the one he labelled DAE no. 8 came from near the Ezana inscription, but this is very uncertain. Monneret de Villard relates the long history of two of them (seemingly DAE nos. 8 and 9). They were first seen in the garden of the *Qese Gabaz* Qalamsis not long before 1839, when Sapeto recorded them as found in 'a field near the town'. At the time they served as the border for a well. Further rumours of them (by this time supposedly four inscriptions) were reported by Lefebvre in 1841:

> there were four others near the reservoir which is opposite the obelisk: but Akalemsis, the guardian of the library, a self declared descendant of Solomon, had them moved to his house, to make a profit out of them, and the exorbitant demands which he made of us in order to show them, prevented us from seeing them. M. J. Sapeto has one of them, which is in Ge'ez; two of the others are in unknown characters and hieroglyphics.

Ferret and Galinier, also in 1841, made the same (?) 'discovery':

> if we wished to pique ourselves on discoveries, we might add that we found, in the garden of a priest called Johannes, two inscriptions: one in Ge'ez language, the other in Himyarite language. The first has little interest, the second at least is of very great antiquity. This is engraved on a stone covered with dust, and divided along its length in two more or less equal pieces.

This is certainly DAE no. 8, broken in half along its length. Steudner and von Heuglin in 1861, and Lejean in 1863 reported further sightings of these inscriptions. Von Heuglin commented that one of the four he saw in 1861 'contains many horizontal and vertical lines, in which stand single signs, I conjecture that it represents a calendar or astronomical table'. Lejean, twenty-two years after Lefebvre had failed, found a different abba Kalemsis [father Apocalypse] ... the old priest was charmingly obliging to me, and allowed me, without asking a centime from me, to copy what I pleased of his beautiful inscriptions. The one in Ge'ez is known, and naturally I chose the other, the mysterious one. Lefebvre, who admits that he did not see it, was wrong to say it was hieroglyphic; it is in very beautiful Himyarite writing, and easily readable. Unfortunately the workmen who found it broke the left hand edge of the stone, which does not help make it easy to interpret. MM Ferret and Galinier, who in 1841 had the same privilege as I, said that the stone had been broken lengthwise into two more or less equal fragments; they did not say if they had seen the second fragment, which I have never heard spoken of, with their own eyes.

Finally in 1893 Bent was able to copy nos. 8 (the right half only – the left was eventually located in 1906 in the courtyard of Arbaat Ensesa church) 10, and 11 for Müller, and in 1906 Littmann could copy, study and translate them with more success. Several of the ancient inscriptions copied by Rüppell, Bent and Littmann were taken into the treasury of Maryam Seyon. Some inscriptions are now stored in an office next to the *nebura'ed*'s office near the new church of Maryam Seyon, while others are in Aksum Museum. The 'astronomical table' has never been traced.

An inscribed object was dug up in Aksum and acquired by King Tekla Haymanot II around 1770. Bruce was told at the empress's palace at Qwesqwam that 'the king had got a stone for me, with writing on it, of old times, which he was bringing to me; that it had been dug up at Axum and was standing at the foot of his bed'. This was the small magico-medical stele or cippus of Horus, dating perhaps to the 30th Egyptian dynasty, that Bruce illustrated in his book. It is odd that, given his mania for Egyptianising everything he saw in Aksum, he should have been given one of the very few genuinely Egyptian objects found in Ethiopia. The cippus has, extraordinarily enough, been rediscovered in Edinburgh recently.

Other Ancient Objects

The Ezana Garden also contains a number of other Aksumite relics. At the entrance is a well, flanked by two granite throne- (?) bases each supporting a round granite column drum. To the right beside the café is another throne-base, with on top of it a square column-base and part of the shaft. The right hand section of the garden contains the battered fragment of a throne (?), a granite drainage conduit, and two pillar-bases probably from the peristyle in the centre of the south wing of the palace called Ta'akha Maryam. In the left-hand part of the garden is another stepped column-base, four-tiered with three square steps and a round upper part. In the centre of the garden is a granite column with a stepped capital, and two bases of votive thrones that once stood on the edge of the Arbaat Ensesa mound behind the inscription of Ezana. One of these supports a round-topped stele, the other a round column drum.

At the east end of the garden is the top of stele no. 4, one of the decorated stelae, brought there just before Monneret de Villard's visit in 1937. It is one of only two (see also no. 6, lying broken near Enda Negus) that have a second circular emplacement at the summit for the insertion of a decorative plaque (?). The missing part between the stele and this top section is the so-called 'Stele of the Lances', which is now mounted on the north wall of the west staircase of the cathedral, above the 'Stone of Bazen'. Salt saw it embedded in the pavement 'on a paved way leading to the flight of steps before the church' and in his 1814 book included an engraving of it together with two others depicting re-used lion-headed water-spouts from the cathedral compound. Sapeto also recorded it. Rüppell, Lefebvre, Raffray and Bent saw the fragment of the stele in the same place between 1833 and 1893. The DAE failed to find it, but by 1937 Monneret de Villard remarked the fragment in its present position on the church terrace. He was the first to realise that it belonged to stele 4.

The Central and Northern Stele Fields Here are the great monuments of Aksum, the stelae erected by the ancient kings and the royal tombs beneath them. The *Book of Aksum* states that there were fifty-eight obelisks at Aksum, some fallen, some still erect. Alvares merely noted that there were more than thirty, and de Almeida 'counted some twenty that were standing and seven or eight that have been thrown to the ground and broken in many fragments'. Patriarch Afonso Mendez, in a letter of 1626, recorded '16 or 17 pyramids' which seemed to him to be 'mausoleums of the ancient kings'. Bruce mentions forty stelae. Salt in 1805 was told there were fifty-five originally, four of the size of the standing one; Sapeto follows Salt. Von Heuglin in 1861 reported 'more than 60', Bent in 1893 'somewhere about fifty'. The DAE report noted seventy-eight in the Central and Northern Stele Fields. In the latest study (Munro–Hay 1989, based on Ruth Plant's 1973 schedule of stelae with 1974 additions) one hundred and forty-one were recorded in the central and northern area; there are certainly many more buried complete or in fragments in the cemeteries.

So far, in the main Stele Field formed by the Stele Park and the Northern Stele Field, the monuments have been noted in an area extending from beside the east wall of the Tomb of the False Door, along the whole area of the Stele Park (Central Stele Field), and in and south of Enda Iyasus churchyard, past Enda Negus opposite Mai Shum, and on into the eucalyptus woods by the Mai Malahso and below Geza 'Agmai (Northern Stele Field). Something of a chronology of the stelae was attempted in *Excavations at Aksum*, when all the information from the numerous trenches dug to explore the setting of the stelae was examined. Some stelae were found, still standing with their base-plates intact, but buried by later building work. The different levels indicated different stages in the process of their erection. Occasionally there was the chance for radiocarbon dating. The general result indicated that the stelae advanced, in an overlapping sequence, from smaller rougher examples, through a development to dressed stelae, and finally to the large decorated ones. This progression was accompanied by the construction of platforms and terraces, over a period of some centuries from about the time of Christ until perhaps the end of the fourth or beginning of the fifth century. After that, it seems, 'house' tombs such as those of the False Door, and Kaleb and Gabra Masqal, were built. The stelae were abandoned, perhaps partly for religious reasons with the coming of Christianity, and partly for practical reasons after the fall of the great stele, no. 1.

Who raised them, when and why has not much preoccupied the Ethiopians of the past. The *Gadla Marqorewos* attributed to them a diabolical origin. Lefebvre, too, commented that 'les Abyssins, dont la paresse et l'inertie sont sans example, ne pouvant comprendre que des mains humains fussent capables d'édifier de semblables monuments, en attribuaient l'origine au démon'. Bruce, of course, had his usual answer: 'I apprehend this obelisk [the standing stele DAE no. 3] and the two larger ones that are fallen, to be the work of Ptolemy Euergetes' (and see below for some even odder suggestions). Henry Salt in 1805 was told that they were set up by the eponymous ancestor of the Ethiopians, Ethiopis (Ityopis) 1,544 years before.

Salt, however, in his own book of 1814 offers a new and surprising detail. He writes

> the tradition of the country ascribes them to the reign of the Emperor Acizana, which took place upwards of three hundred years after Christ, but I should rather be inclined to believe that the workmen of that age were scarcely equal to complete so chaste and highly finished an undertaking.

In modern times the results of excavations in the Stele Park confirm this 'traditional' dating. But it is a puzzle to find 'Acizana' (= Aeizana, Ezana), whose name was totally absent from the Ge'ez lists and traditions, cited as coming from a local source at this time. Much more probably, this attribution was the result of Salt's own ideas resulting from the interpretation of the Ezana inscription.

Theodore Bent associated the stelae not with tombs, but with sun worship: 'Aksum in its best days must have perfectly bristled with these stone monuments of a primitive form of piety ... here at Aksum we seem to have before us a highly perfected form of stone worship, associated with sacrifices to the sun.' Modern Aksumite interpretation – even the tourist guides relate this as fact – attributes the standing decorated stele to King Romha, Romah or Romhay. This king seems to be an invention derived from the incorrect reading of the name Armah on the coins of this king. The word Negus, or 'king', is written to the left of the royal bust on the coins together with the A of Armah's name, while the other side reads RMH. The letters are unvowelled, and are read as a group ignoring the A on the other side; hence Romah, Romha. Some of the Ge'ez lists include the other version, Ramhay. He is also said to have been the first to mint coins, although modern numismatic studies place Armah nearly at the end of the coinage sequence.

The cause of the collapse of some of the stelae has also given rise to many conjectures. The fact of their fall is not at all extraordinary when it is known, as it is after the excavations of recent times, that even the largest are generally rooted in the ground by only a relatively small percentage of their whole length (one-twelfth in some cases). Their emplacements were only meagrely – if at all – consolidated with stone supports. Bent imagined that the washing away of the soil 'by the stream, the Mai Shum' had undermined them.

Henry Salt thought that 'Aboona David' had overthrown the stelae and the 'temple', citing reasons derived from his interpretation of a Ge'ez inscription on a throne pedestal in the cathedral enclosure (see below). The priests, however, told him that in 1070 Gadit (Gudit) had come from Amhara and thrown them down, a common tale told in local schools until today. Manoel de Almeida and Afonso Mendez reported, certainly wrongly, that they were overthrown by the Turks during the revolt by Bahrnagash Yeshaq in 1578, during the reign of King Malak Sagad (Sarsa Dengel): 'the old men of this country say that a few years ago, in the time of King Malaac Cegued, and the Viceroy Isaac, who rebelled and brought in the Turks to help him against the Emperor, they overthrew the six or seven that lie on the ground in fragments'. Barradas description of Aksum written in 1633–34 (Barradas 1996: 119) enters into more detail about the stelae and their supposed fate:

> The real fame of this place, Açcum, is that it was the seat of the Queen of Sabbâ, and of the kings who succeeded her over a long period of time and about whom there are still some memories, as we shall see. The truth is that it was once a place of great and notable majesty, to which still testify today the tall and handsome columns or pyramids which remain standing, two of which, the most notable (according to those who have seen these and others), can compete with the largest and best of Rome. They are made of blocks of dark stone, very well worked, with each of the four sides with carvings of rooms.

What shows above the ground must measure some fifty or sixty cubits in height, a width of 10 to 12 palms and a depth of five or six. Like these two, another is lying on the ground in pieces, knocked down by artillery fire directed at it by the approaching Turks. Apart from these there are several others that are erect, some large others smaller, some well-carved others rough, some upright others leaning in such a manner that they may have served the important people as monuments or as grave markers. All of which suggests a grandeur and majesty more of Egyptians accustomed to their pyramids than to Romans or other nationalities.

Monneret de Villard rightly rejected the story about the Turks. Not only had Alvares seen the stelae already lying fallen years before, but the chronicle of Sarsa Dengel, in its detailed account of the war, mentions no such extra-ordinary event as a bombardment of Aksum by Turkish artillery. It is true that Yeshaq and the Turkish pasha were at Aksum in the reign of Minas, but again no bombardment is mentioned by his chronicle. De Villard, investigating the second largest stele during the process of raising its five fragments for transport to Italy in 1937, was absolutely certain that the fractures did not come from artillery. He also found underneath the stele fragments of pottery, which he dated to the tenth to eleventh centuries, from their similarity to others he had found in cemeteries along the Atbara and between that river and the Mareb; a possible indication of the approximate date of the stele's fall. It is difficult to accord any accuracy to such a comparison, given the very meagre knowledge of Aksumite and later pottery in 1937, and even today.

In 1906, the DAE found the Stele Park area built up with houses and compound walls from just west of stele 3, and just behind stelae 19–20. From stelae 3 and 19 eastwards there were no buildings in front of the level of Enda Iyasus churchyard wall. Beta Giyorgis hill, incidentally, was completely bare at this time, except at the base where a considerable suburb of round straw-roofed houses with some scattered trees extended some way up the lower slopes, with a few even higher up around Geza 'Agmai. The major change in appearance of this area in the last ninety years or so has been the abandonment of the round type of house, the replacement of straw roofs with metal, and the importation of eucalyptus trees.

The terrace The stelae facing the cathedral of Maryam Seyon, in the centre of the town, now stand on a stone-faced terrace of Aksumite style. This, completely invisible earlier – although its presence was divined by von Heuglin in 1861, who noted that the main stelae stood on 'a low, perhaps artificial terrace' – was discovered by French archaeologists working in the 1950s (Leclant, de Contenson). It has now been reconstructed more or less on its former line.

The great fallen stele (no. 1)   The largest of all the stelae is certainly among the biggest stones ever hewn out by man from the quarries of the ancient world, weighing an estimated 500 tonnes or more. It is a testament to the magnificent self-esteem of the unknown ruler who caused it to be extracted and dragged several kilometres to its final site – a testimony also to the skill, artistry and *main d'oeuvre* of the designers, quarry-men and stone-masons who decorated and raised it. Probably over 33 m. tall originally – the shattered top does not permit a complete restoration, but just over 31 m. survives – this single massive stone is carved in the hard grey-green granite of the region to represent a tower. It is carved on all four sides. Front and back are shown with a door and ring handle, 'entresol' windows, eleven further storeys represented by windows, eight with plain divisions and three with elaborate window-tracery. The sides depict the round monkey-heads and windows corresponding to those on the front. This monstrous stone soon fell – if indeed it ever actually stood for more than a few seconds after being levered upright, with only about 3 m. of undecorated base to support it. It smashed down on to the roof-block of a great tomb lying nearby, the Nefas Mawcha (described below). No base-plates have ever been found – another possible hint that it collapsed immediately, before these could be installed – and only one fragment of the top with a small section of the curve of a shaped apex seems to have survived the impact with the Nefas Mawcha top-stone, or later removal of the fragments.

Study of the stratigraphy of the area leads to the conclusion that the great stele fell in the late fourth century, since a coin of the early Christian King Ouazebas of Aksum was found overlying some of the fragments (see Munro-Hay 1989).

Other stelae   Northeast of the Nefas Mawcha still stands the great stele's largest surviving neighbour, stele no. 3, 21 m. high, with an estimated weight of some 150 tonnes. Salt's 1805 drawing shows it very well. Utterly different is the engraving James Bruce supplied in his book; this 'geometrical engraving, servilely copied, without shading or perspective, that all kind of readers may understand it' is in fact extremely inaccurate, showing windows in only one storey. The romantic view of this stele in the Lefebvre expedition *Atlas* volume shows it with seven storeys, with to the left a partly broken and fallen stele no. 2(?) – Pl. 2 also supplies several drawings of stelae. Incidentally, just as Salt criticised Bruce, so Ferret and Galinier criticised Salt in their 1844 article 'Obélisque d'Axoum', at the same time introducing many more errors than had Salt.

At the time of Salt's drawing the base plate was free of the ground at the front, and a huge *da'ro* or sycamore tree stood to the right. The folio acquatint engraving, based – with much romanticisation – on a sketch he drew from the viewpoint of the roof of Maryam Seyon church, shows a different angle, and has flattened the ground somewhat, as well as showing the base-plate flush with the ground. The flanking stelae and *da'ro* tree are adjusted in Salt's different drawings so as not to interfere with the main view. The considerable gap below the base-plate, which was visible in 1906 (DAE) as in 1805, was filled in by the 1950s. Later the slope was paved over and strengthened by the cement steps that today lead from the esplanade up to the stele. It is to be hoped that this will prevent the materialisation of Gerhard Rohlfs' prediction, written after noticing in 1868 that the earth in front of the stele had sunk: 'perhaps only a few more rainy seasons, and the centre point of the vertical will become unaligned with the base, and then the last witness of the wonder-buildings of Aksum will also lie like its brothers in pieces on the ground'.

Stele 3 is about 21 m. high, but the depth of its underground part is unknown. On its south face there is a door with a square lock and bolt. Above are the 'entresol' windows, eight storeys, and a shaped summit with fixing-holes. The back has a round shield at the top, with five circular pellets in the centre. This is reminiscent of the design on a shield on a newly discovered gold Aksumite coin of King MHDYS (published in the 1995 *Numismatic Chronicle* – the royal name is not vocalised, and the exact pronunciation is unknown). The sides show round monkey-heads and 'entresol' and other windows corresponding to the front design all the way up. The shelved rear base-plate is plain. The front one, however, not only includes four holes for offerings, but a running design of vine leaves and bunches of grapes is provided as a border, very similar to the decorated pillar with this design in Maryam Seyon church vestibule (DAE II, Abb. 144). This would seem to be the base-plate described by von Heuglin, when he writes that 'one such base-plate bears a peculiar decoration, representing a row of human hands (?)'. The five-pointed vine leaves do look a little like spread-out hands.

Von Heuglin seems to have been the first to speculate on what might have been inserted at the top of the stelae. He suggested a metal cross. Bent, on the contrary, decided that 'there is still to be seen a representation of the solar disc', and later adds that study of the stele fallen into the stream (no. 5) allowed him to 'satisfactorily establish that it was not a cross which had been placed here, as ardent Jesuit travellers have stated'. This presumably meant Alvares – not in fact a Jesuit – who according to the Ramusio Italian translation of his book, stated that 'the top ... is like a half moon in which are five nails, on the side looking south, nailed to the stone in the shape of a cross. When it rains the rust from these nails running down the stone from the nails is like congealed blood.' Another version suggests that the holes resembled *quinas*, the five dots on dice, which on the Portuguese royal arms represented the five wounds of Christ. Symbolism and ardent Jesuitry aside, the holes are exactly as Alvares reported. Littmann illustrated a reconstruction of the top of stele no. 1 with a disc and crescent. Bruce, when describing the large still-standing decorated stele, mentioned that 'they are all of one piece of granite; and on top of that which is standing there is a patera, exceedingly well carved in the Greek taste'. Does this mean that he thought that the carving on the top, on the shaped upper part of the stele, represented a shallow wide cup (patera); or is there a mistake here, and he refers instead to the base-plate? Probably the latter, since later Bruce notes that 'upon the large block of granite, into which the bottom of [the stele] is fixed, and which stands before it like a table, is the figure of a Greek patera'. In fact the standing stele no. 3 does not show a 'patera' or kylix carved on the base-plate, like stelae nos. 4, 5 and 6. Instead, there are four holes.

The second largest stele, 24 m. tall, of which 3 m. form the base, is decorated on all four sides. The front and back show a door with a ring handle, 'entresol' windows, nine storeys, and a shaped top, but with the depression and fixing-holes for an ornamental plaque on the front only. The sides exhibit round monkey-heads and the same sequence of windows as the front and back. The plain front base-plate only has been found. A fragment supposedly from this stele – but really from stele 4? – lies in the inner enclosure of the cathedral, directly in front of the Chapel of the Tablet of Moses.

Stele no. 2 was taken to Italy during the Italian occupation of Ethiopia in the late 1930s and still stands in Rome, restored, but far from its original home. There are moves afoot to have it returned to its original home, moves which hopefully will shortly be successful. According to the mayor of Aksum, Ato Wondimu Yohannes, in 1997 Italy formally agreed to return the stele. All expenses of its repatriation were to be borne by Italy. At a conference in Italy, studies relating to the complex questions of its transport and re-erection were commenced. Bringing it back from Italy will be a monumental task. But if it could be done in 1937/8 it can be done again, and presumably the technical possibilities are much improved. The difficulties involved set back the originally envisaged deadline. Late 1997 became early 1998. In Pankhurst's book *The Ethiopians*, published in 1998, it is twice stated that it had already been returned. However, the war with Eritrea seems to have put paid for the moment (late 2000) to any chance of its return. It has not yet even been taken down and dismantled.

There will also be important archaeological work to be done at the spot where it is to be replaced, or re-erected. There is almost certainly a tomb connected with the stele that should be investigated before re-erection. There may be other underground complications as well – neighbouring tombs, robber tunnels and the like. I recall walking around in 1974 below the Stele Park in the very large chambers of the tomb we called Catacomb C, the southern extension of which (Chambers 7 and 8) approaches extremely close to the site of stele 2. If such substantial underground chambers, never filled with debris beyond a mud wash, stand below, it is imperative that the emplacement be thoroughly investigated before trying to re-import and even re-erect stele 2. In addition, it will need to be decided how it is to be replaced. Will the more authentic arrangement of restoring the broken pieces to the site as they were observed by earlier travellers, and photographed and planned in detail by the DAE, be enough? Or are we to see a major change in the skyline of Aksum, if – who knows how many centuries after its collapse and shattering – it is raised again to dominate its slightly smaller neighbour? Whatever happens, care must be the watchword – stele 3, nearby, must be more than susceptible to any tremors occurring in the neighbourhood.

Some work has been done on the emplacement of stele 2, as reported recently by Bertrand Poissonier (Poissonier 2000). He found that there was a solid mass of cemented rock under the stele, a foundation reaching down to bedrock, and covered with a large stone. He conjectured that, instead of being inserted into a hole, the stele actually stood on this stone, above ground, consolidated by a surrounding podium 2.8 m. high (the height of the undressed bole of the stele). The podium would have been topped by the base-plates and reached by steps. His work, however, stopped at bedrock, and did not establish whether any open rock-cut chambers lie directly below the proposed emplacement of the stele. A robber trench, which might have been the cause of the collapse of the stele, was found. An associated coin of Gersem might hint at the approximate time of the collapse.

Three other carved stelae lie smashed in or above the bed of the stream to the east, near or just beyond the church of Enda Iyasus. Stele 6 is the furthest north, about 13 m. high with a 2 m. rough base, carved on the front (south side) with a blank doorway, 'entresol' windows, and two storeys above, and terminating in a double top with two circular depressions with many fixing-holes. The two sides have simple monkey-head decoration only, and the rear (north) base-plate, the only one known to the DAE, shows traces of a border of circles. The DAE illustrated a proposed restoration based on the front plate of no. 4. But fortunately, during Chittick's work at Aksum, the missing base-plate was recovered. It is in fact quite different from that of stele 6, having only one level, and one central kylix. It is perfectly preserved. The edging of holes surrounded by a narrow border gives an impression of a running guilloche pattern, as seen on some of the gold coins of King Aphilas of Aksum in the later third or early fourth century. This stelae might perhaps be more or less contemporary with Aphilas' reign.

Stele 5 now lies right in the bed of the Mai Hejja stream. It measures about 15.5 m. in height. Its decoration is curious, probably because it was altered at some point. Perhaps the stone broke early on during the preparation of the decoration. The front shows an undecorated area of about 2.5 m. with part of a window frame already cut out. This was abandoned, and new decoration started above. A blank door, with 'entresol' windows, is surmounted by two further storeys. Then, on a much thinner upper part, two further storeys are depicted, with the windows only in the centre part, a frieze of little columns and capitals (?) and a single shaped depression at the summit with fixing-holes. The back of the thinner top part is blank, but the lower part shows the beginning of work in the form of four and a half rows of square monkey-heads, probably for windows on which work was abandoned when the original stele broke. The sides show circular monkey-heads, in rows of three on the lower part, two only on the thinner upper part. The base-plates are both stepped, the rear one undecorated, the front one almost exactly the same as the stele 4 plate, with a central kylix on a raised step, and three others lower, but without any border of holes.

Stele 4 is about 18 m. tall. The 'Stele of the Lances' and the top part now in the Ezana Garden add 2 m. to the surviving 16 m. still lying in front of Enda Iyasus churchyard. The approximately 2.2 m. undressed base is interesting in that it still retains some of the quarrying marks. The stele is decorated on the front (south) side with a blank door, 'entresol' windows, four storeys above, the two spears or lances, and a double top with two circular depressions with fixing-holes. On the north or back face, there is a round shield – or so one imagines it to be, both from its appearance and the association with the lances – and, visible today only on the 'Stele of the Lances' section, the same architectural decoration as on the front. The base-plate (long since illustrated by Salt in Valentia 1809, III), has a raised centre section with a kylix, and a lower step with three others surrounded by a border of small holes. As Bent observed, runnels in the corners are a sure indication that some sort of liquid offerings were made here. Bent (who calls these plates 'altars') considered that the kylix was cut 'to receive the blood of a slaughtered victim. Channels cut at two corners enabled the blood to flow on the lower platform, where again we have three more recipient vessels cut, and a complete series of holes all round, and two more channels at the corners to enable the blood to flow on the ground.' This may be true; but also the kylix shape appears in a wine(?)-press found at 'Ashafi near Aksum, so the base-plate cups may not have been designed for anything other than wine, beer or mead offerings. The kylix, and the lion-heads on the 'Ashafi press, as well as the general workmanship, make it likely that the press dates to more or less the same period.

In addition to the six decorated ones, there are a number of other decorated stelae. These are not cut into a regular shape, and are of much simpler design. Probably they are of earlier date – precursors of the great decorated monuments. One, no. 7, now fallen, is carved with an Ionic-style column supporting a pitch-roofed shrine (?), with another smaller depiction of the shrine alone on the other side. The stele lies just opposite Mai Shum, a little way up the valley from Enda Iyasus churchyard, on top of another fallen stele (no. 36). Salt (Valentia 1809, III) illustrates this stele, described as a 'small obelisk', standing, but buried to a point some way below the base of the smaller shrine. One wonders if this is really how he saw it. If the proportions are right he must surely have been able to see the other, more interesting, side with the column as well. Perhaps he 'restored' what he actually saw fallen and partly buried – unless the level of the earth covered the top of the column, and he simply assumed there was only another depiction of the shrine on that side. The stele was also illustrated in the Lefebvre expedition *Atlas* volume, Pl. 1.

A second decorated stele nearby, no. 34, directly outside Enda Iyasus churchyard, presents a simple version of the beam and monkey-head style of architecture. If the larger stelae, with their accurate and complex design, had not existed, it would have been more difficult to explain this very rudimentary design as imitation architecture – something that becomes obvious when the more elaborate examples are at hand.

Another stele lying inside the Enda Iyasus churchyard itself, is decorated simply on the side that now lies uppermost, with a chevron carved above a circular object (shield?). Further up the valley, a stele exhibits a small *ankh*, the sign of life in ancient Egyptian, carved near to the base.

The more elegantly shaped plain dressed stelae of the Stele Park are generally broad but relatively thin, and with carefully rounded tops. They may have belonged to other members of the royal family or to important officials of the court, buried at the same time as the kings who employed the great carved stelae.

In the northern part of the stele field there are a number of stelae on which the quarrying marks are clearly visible, just the same as those to be seen in the quarries themselves in Mount Zala, Gobo Dera.

Tombs in the main stele field Underneath the Stele Park, as the land-scaped part of the larger stele field has been called by archaeologists, is an extraordinary series of tombs. This is the underground maze that the team led by the late director of the British Institute in Eastern Africa, Neville Chittick, began in 1973–74 to explore and clear. It seems that some at least of these tombs had been entered and disturbed frequently, up to relatively recent times. Knowledge of them seems to be recorded in the *Book of Aksum*.

Tomb of the False Door   The distinguishing feature of the westernmost of the tombs so far discovered was a false doorway like those on the larger decorated stelae. The Tomb of the False Door was excavated and cleared. It has now been covered with a corrugated iron roof, and can be visited. It requires, however, consolidation and restoration to give a clear idea of its original appearance.

The tomb was found in 1973 in a road that then passed from the northern suburbs of the town on the lower flanks of Beta Giyorgis hill towards the cathedral. Excavation revealed that the tomb had been constructed in a large pit. First, a huge stone had been placed to act as a base, on which a burial chamber surrounded on three sides by a corridor-like ambulatory had been constructed using finely cut granite blocks. Two staircases provide access to a vestibule leading to the tomb chamber, and to the outer ambulatory respectively. On top of the central structure, another huge stone was placed, acting as a roof for the chamber. Above the staircases the false door slab was raised, forming part of the façade of a square superstructure constructed above the tomb. In front, a large paved court was laid out. Finally, one supposes, the two large stones that covered the staircases would have been placed in position. The one that would have covered the tomb chamber staircase has completely disappeared, but the other is intact and still in place. Close below it, one of the iron clamps that held the courtyard stones together is also still in position.

The tomb seems to date to the late fourth or early fifth century. The false door, with its ring handle and ribbed lintel – found on a separate block that had fallen into the front courtyard – is exactly the same as that on stele 2, and very similar to that on stele 1 (where, however, there is no ribbing on the lintel). The 'cyclopean' masonry has something in common with that in the tombs attributed to Kaleb and Gabra Masqal.

Directly beside this tomb to the east was another structure, built with brick vaults, and with horseshoe-shaped brick arches. It was never completely excavated, and its purpose and plan remain obscure. Conceivably, it was connected with the largest of all the tombs found by Chittick's team, the vast structure named the 'Mausoleum', which lies somewhat to the southeast at the base of the great fallen stele.

The 'Mausoleum'   This tomb, named from a first impression of its great size, lies directly beside the great fallen stele, to the west. I can recall the first exploration of the tomb, not long after the discovery of one of its three entrance shafts amid the enormous quantity of sterile granite fill that had been laid over the area, presumably to level it up after the construction was finished. Wedged into a gap between giant granite roof-beams and the earth fill of the corridor, I scribbled down some quick notes as Neville Chittick crawled along under the tremendous roofing stones, calling out what he saw: 'Another chamber ... ten in all ... enormous ... seems to be plaster on the wall ... another shaft coming down here ... roots between the stones ... ouch! ... at the end, the top of a brick arch ... it's blocked ...'.

Later excavation by the great stele revealed that a courtyard had been prepared, with a granite doorway in its west wall, a perfect copy in stone of the typical Aksumite-style doorway. It led into the central corridor of the tomb, which had three shafts giving access from above. From this passage, 16 m. long by 2 m. wide, ten chambers led off, five on each side, each measuring about 6.6 by 1.75 m. The tomb thus covered an area of some 240 square metres. There were traces of lime plaster on the walls of one chamber, Chittick reported during his preliminary venture inside, and a brick arch at the far end of the corridor. The excavation of the tomb was continued by David Phillipson in recent years, but little of its contents apparently remained within. It was found that the entrance and the side chambers all had brick arches on stone lintels, and that the arch at the end of the corridor led to a similar door as that by the stele. The corridor itself was paved with stone slabs.

The Nefas Mawcha The name of this prodigious structure (supposedly Tigrinya, according to the DAE, but in fact Amharic, and a well-known place-name) means 'the place of going forth of the winds'. The modern name may derive from a legend recounted in the *Book of Aksum*:

> it is said that there is a large house at the base of the great broken stele; at its four corners there are four other large houses [or corridors]. The first which has its exit towards the east, extends as far as Mai Shum; the one with its exit towards the west extends as far as Edda Taray [i.e. Addi Seray, where the Tomb of the False Door was found]; that with its exit to the north goes to Nahso [apparently, therefore, the name of the area behind the Stele Park, immediately below Beta Giyorgis], and that which has its exit to the south goes as far as the church. When one enters there with lights, a wind puts them out, and everything remains in shadow.

Local people say that they do not know the name 'Nefas Mawcha', only having learned of it from my book *Excavations at Aksum*. They appear to have no special name for the giant roofing stone, although one informant, a *dabtara* of Aksum, called it *emni admas*. This was interpreted to mean the 'skyline' stone; a stone that came from some infinitely distant spot. The term refers locally to the magic 'machine' that many people at Aksum believe was used by the ancients to mould, shape or hew out the stelae and other stones. It is thought to be buried beneath the Nefas Mawcha. In the Geralta region it is called *ibna mahaw*, and is supposed to have been used for cutting out the rock churches.

The description in the *Book of Aksum* is intriguing, because Neville Chittick's excavations have now proved that as well as the Nefas Mawcha, there certainly are 'corridors' at the base of the great stele. To the west lies the so-called Mausoleum, and to the right a still unopened tomb that we called the East Tomb, as its doorway faced the Mausoleum on that side – it may prove to be related to stele no. 2, now in Rome. Local memories, even occasional discoveries when digging for building stone, may have kept in the minds of the Aksumites the existence of some of these monumental underground edifices. The *Book of Aksum* reinforces the description after making a note of the tombs of Kaleb and Gabra Masqal: 'And there is a house like it at the foot of the obelisk, with a great many doors on the right and the left, on the west and the east.' This is certainly a reasonable description for the Mausoleum, and perhaps of the unexplored East Tomb as well.

When the great stele fell, the Nefas Mawcha capstone, itself measuring about 17 by 7 by 1.5 m., was not broken, but the stele separated into three major fragments, its top section being completely smashed by the impact. However, the Nefas Mawcha capstone was forced downwards by the blow. The ingenious arrangement of balances that maintained the Nefas Mawcha proved unable to resist the impact; the interior of the tomb underneath it was partly crushed. The inside edges of the roofing blocks of an inner passageway – or more probably a rubble-filled supporting wall – were forced downwards by the weight. These blocks had been cut at one end to fit under the great roof block, and at the other end were trimmed to slot under a second series of stones that roofed an outer passageway all round the structure. With the shock of the stele falling, the outside edges of the blocks shed the metal cramps that held them in place, and rose upwards. Some of the outer roofing blocks simply slipped off the inner ones, others were completely somersaulted over. When Dr Chittick's team dug underneath the monument, we found that there was no evidence for the suggestion in the DAE report that there had been a ceiling of blocks under the great roofing slab, supported by cross-walls dividing the structure into several compartments. The blocks were, instead, part of a paved floor. For an account of the excavations and the finds, see Munro-Hay 1989.

The Nefas Mawcha was not recorded by early visitors to Aksum unless, as noted above, some of the 'remarkable stones seen by Mr. Salt' actually belonged to this building. Possibly the *Book of Aksum*'s description of a building 'at the foot of the obelisk' actually refers to the Nefas Mawcha rather than to the tombs. When the DAE arrived in Aksum, only part of the Nefas Mawcha lay outside a compound wall which included stelae nos. 1–2 as well. The German team was able to plan and explore only a part of the monument.

Platforms and shaft tombs In the central area of the Stele Park a number of platforms were found, faced with shelved walls of Aksumite date, and covered with layers of white and red earth. Some had been extended later. These platforms seem from their position in the cemetery to have had some ritual significance, and to be related to the tombs found in the same area. Some parts of the platform complex seem to date from the very beginning of our era, confirming the idea drawn from the *Periplus* that Aksum was already in existence around the beginning of the first millennium AD.

In the same area of the Stele Field, several shafts were found, varying from a very large one (leading to Shaft Tomb A) retained with stone walls of typical Aksumite style, to mere holes leading into tunnels or down under fallen stele and displaced base-plates. The shafts – associated with some of the platforms mentioned above – gave access to rough rock-cut chambers below, some completely filled with loose earth, others almost clear so that it was possible to walk into them and plan them without excavation. In Shaft Tomb A, large flat stones were installed in two of the chambers, possibly mortuary slabs on which the bodies of the deceased had once been placed. On all sides tunnels were found opening out – some doubtless dug by grave robbers – containing fallen stelae, skulls and bones, pottery, metal, and piles of other grave-goods.

Entering these tombs for the first time has left some lasting memories. John Manley, one of Neville Chittick's team in 1974, discovered a narrow hole in one of the trenches, leading down under a fallen buried stele to a narrow shaft disappearing deeper into the earth. It was the entrance to Shaft Tomb C, once marked by the now fallen stele no. 136, which stood directly behind the standing decorated stele no. 3 and a little north of stele 19. I visited the tomb shortly after it was opened. A rough wooden ladder was inserted, and I descended into the hole. At the bottom, darkness, and the heavy, moist air of an ancient tomb. A ball of string to guide my return, a candle – we were primitively supplied – and I set out into the gloom. The candle barely illuminated a large rock-cut chamber. On through a rough doorway, through room after room. I concentrated on what the flame dimly revealed – a floor covered with shiny dry mud; the walls and roof were imperfectly seen in such feeble light. Here a skull, gleaming white suddenly in the light, lying close beside the entrance to another chamber; there the greenish tint of some ancient bronze fragment fitfully illuminated; pots lay still intact where the servants of the dead – or later robbers – left them. Suddenly I realised the candle was dimming. There was no oxygen – I found myself gasping for breath, and had to beat a quick retreat.

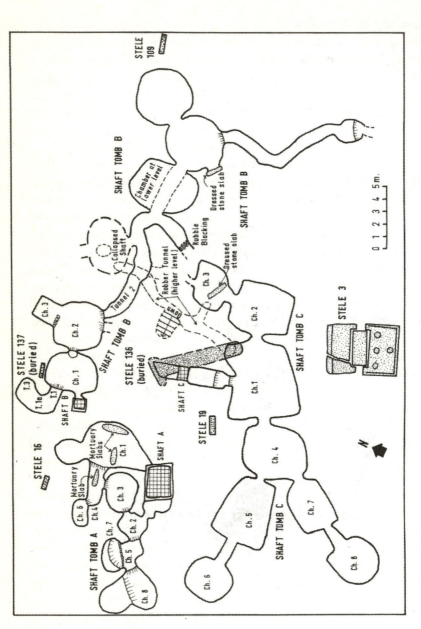

21. Plan (from S. Munro-Hay, *Excavations at Aksum*, 1989) showing the complex of tombs and tunnels around the still standing stele 3. Stele 2 once stood only a few metres to the left of Ch. 8 in Shaft Tomb C – and the plans we have may not entirely accurately represent the relationship between underground and above ground features. Evidently, re-erection of this stele, if it is ever undertaken, could risk problems perhaps even involving stele 3.

When Shaft Tomb C was planned it became clear that its central room, 5 by 6 m., lay only some 5 m. north of the still erect stele 3; and there is almost certainly another tomb, possibly of not unimpressive dimensions, beneath stele 3 itself. In another tomb, Shaft Tomb B, a honeycomb of tunnels and chambers a little to the north, a huge dressed stone blocked further exploration. All this emphasises the need for thorough exploration before stele no. 2 comes back from Italy and any attempt is made to replace it in its original position.

Tomb of the Brick Arches   Only in the Tomb of the Brick Arches was there time to carry out proper clearing in the 1974 season at Aksum. This was an important tomb, dating perhaps from the fourth century AD. It was distinguished by a long staircase leading down to a horseshoe-shaped brick entrance arch, something totally unknown in Ethiopia before.

The tomb lies immediately to the east of the Stele Park area, beside the east wall. Once a broad flight of steps led down from the eastern part of the stele terrace to a superstructure distinguished by standing stones set upright all along the base of its walls. The staircase itself was roofed over by large rough granite blocks. All this is now badly ruined. The superstructure and the upper part of the staircase were first uncovered by Jean Doresse in the 1950s. Strangely, his investigations went no further then a few steps below the first landing. Some twenty years later, working with Dr Chittick's team in 1974, with the aid of Doresse's plans and notes, I was able to relocate the staircase and reveal the entrance arch. It was fascinating to watch the slow unfolding of the work. First, the staircase was cleared – with some difficulty, as the western retaining wall had completely collapsed. A landing appeared, then more steps; there were seventeen steps and three landings. Eventually, a granite lintel appeared in the north wall. Then, below it, totally unexpected at that time, a brick. The diggers cleared the top of an arch – the received dictum of the time stated 'the arch was unknown in Aksum'. More clearing followed. The arch was horseshoe-shaped; a new paragraph to be written in the history of architecture. Then came the stone blocking. Unfortunately, it was broken, and we knew others had been there before.

Neville Chittick had the west wall of the staircase, of which some lower parts were found to be still intact, rebuilt by a local workman. The work looked exactly the same as the old Aksumite work, but during the night after its completion the whole wall collapsed again.

Inside the tomb it was found that the blocking of all the interior arches too had been broken. It was evident that robbers had penetrated into all the chambers. Work was difficult. I had to wear a straw hat continuously, despite the unpleasantly hot and stuffy atmosphere, as the heat from my lamp – we had no electricity – dried out the rough rock-cut roof, and jagged stones would occasionally fall on me. The discomfort was well worth the result. In the tomb many grave-goods still remained, presumably valueless to the robbers but a treasure trove for the archaeologist. I found fragments of gold and silver jewellery, a silver amulet case wedged in the blocking of one of the rear loculi of the first chamber, and many hundreds of beads. Beads from one necklace, of glass balls overlaid with gold leaf sealed over by a further layer of glass, were found in the first chamber and in one of the side chambers, as though the necklace, in being torn from its place by robbers, had broken and scattered its beads over the tomb. There were bronze objects, including plaques backed with iron, with traces of wood, presumably formerly fixed on a wooden box or chest. The bronze plaques were inlaid with glass in floral or geometric patterns. A most attractive object was a bronze belt buckle inlaid with silver crosses and blue enamelling – none of which was visible at the time, the whole object being green from its long burial. There were also iron weapons and a hammer with both shaft and head in solid iron, exquisite glassware goblets and flasks (all, alas, broken into fragments), beautifully decorated pots of many different shapes, even fragments of wood and leather preserved by the damp. Only part of the large pile of material in the first chamber was cleared at the time, as the season came to a close long before the work could be completed. Further in were small loculi, perhaps the burial places where the dead were laid to rest. These too had once been sealed with blocking walls, now broken. Though planned, they were never touched. They were left to await the resumption of work.

All this material was installed with the occupants of the tomb – perhaps a ruler and his family – when they died, doubtless to ensure that they had everything required for a luxurious life in the afterworld. We know from the Aksumite inscriptions of the period prior to the conversion of King Ezana to Christianity, that Ezana at least, and by inference perhaps other kings as well, bore the title 'Son of Mahrem', and that Mahrem was identified in Greek versions of the inscriptions with Ares, God of War. Whatever the actual rank of the person buried in this particular tomb, there can be little doubt that the rich furnishings and splendid granite tombs and stelae in the Stele Park area are a confirmation of the semi-divine status the Aksumite royal myth bestowed on their kings.

Neville Chittick, fired by the surprising quality and quantity of the finds of the 1974 season, wrote of Aksum as 'the last of the civilisations of antiquity to be revealed to modern knowledge'. He was premature about the revelation. Events in Ethiopia in 1974–75 moved rapidly past the possibility of resumption of the excavations. Only just recently have the great tombs and other structures we discovered been reopened and the work resumed. In

1993 Dr David Phillipson, who had accompanied Neville Chittick during the earlier excavations, recommenced work for the BIEA. Like the 'Mausoleum', the Tomb of the Brick Arches was reopened. Work on clearing of the heap of grave goods started again after nearly twenty years. More of the bronze plaques and some other metal debris, including a disk, c. 34cm. in diameter, decorated with a cast brass face surrounded by an Ethiopic inscription came to light in a cache under the floor in the outer vestibule. It is conjectured that such a disk might have decorated one of the decorated stelae.

In the first chamber the clearing was to continue to a considerable depth. New discoveries amid the mass of material heaped in the room were ivory tablets, square with a pattern of concentric circles and a bronze central stud, and two splendid carved ivory tusk-ends. They were decorated with running vine ornamentation similar to that seen on the stele 3 base-plate, and animal carvings (Phillipson 1995), and might perhaps have formed part of an ivory throne. The account of the excavation of the small loculi to the rear of the tomb – the innermost chamber only was completely cleared – has been published by Dr Phillipson. Readings from the tomb show dates from the late third century to the end of the fourth century AD. It is suggested that the second half of the fourth century is the most probable date for the tomb's use. An elderly woman, a middle-aged man, and probably one other person were buried there.

The Beta Giyorgis Stele and Tomb Field   On top of Beta Giyorgis mountain is another stelae field, which seems to have generally escaped notice until the work of Lanfranco Ricci and Rodolfo Fattovich brought it to attention relatively recently. Access to Beta Giyorgis can be achieved by several routes. A good way up is to take the road directly west of the main Stele Park, past the Nefas Mawcha on the right. This leads to a crossroads where there are the remains of (two?) stelae, of the round-topped dressed variety, lying broken in the middle of the road. They lie directly behind the Stele Park, and hint that the royal necropolis continues in this direction.

The track mounts the side of the hill, which is scattered with large rocks providing an easy ascent. One is soon higher than Mai Qoho, with an aerial view of the Yeha Hotel. Monkeys are common here, and the eucalyptus trees supply a pleasant shade. Reaching the summit of the hill, a plain is visible, scattered with houses and fields of teff and millet. Behind the house of Berhane Wolde Khael, with its underground grain store, there is a square rock-cut pit, probably a tomb. A little further away groups of two and three rough stelae are found, the first fallen, the others still erect. Nearby is another tomb, now covered by a tin roof. It consists of a shaft cut in the rock, revetted with stone around the top, and a single small sub–rectangular chamber opening out about two metres below ground level.

About 100 m. distant is another group of stelae, more impressive. All are fallen and broken. The first stele one sees on arriving at the spot bears the quarry marks that show the method of extraction. A row of holes were excavated to the length of the stelae desired, and wooden plugs inserted into them. These would be watered, and would swell accordingly, eventually breaking the stone off from the mother rock. After that the stele could be transported to the spot where it was to be erected, and cut into the desired shape and style on site. There are, besides this stele, c. 5–6 m. long by c. 1.5 m. wide, another six fragments, most reasonably well–cut and perhaps forming an intermediate stage towards the more finely dressed plain stelae in the Stele Park below. Close by is a tomb, now covered over for protection, and several other rough stelae. There was evidently a fairly sizeable cemetery here.

The star object in this cemetery lies yet a little further away, close to another dressed stele lying fallen (some 8 m. long as far as can be seen before its summit disappears into the ground, including a rough base about 1.5 m. long). Near this, Fattovich found a unique monument, a double stele, of dressed stone. From a single rough base rise two stelae, separated for their whole height, but joined by two cross-bars of granite left intact during the cutting. The longest (c. 8 m.) of this pair, on the left, has a rounded top. The other is broken. No other double stele of this type has previously been recorded.

It is possible, depending on the season, to return to Aksum by a track which descends via the watercourse Mai Lahlaha, filled with huge rocks fallen from the hill, to the suburb of Beles Bahari (cactus of the sea?). Dungur (a name referring to a stony area, in the region now generally named for 'the queen of Sheba's palace') is visible below. In the upper course of this seasonal streamlet, two large stone-lined cisterns are found sunk into the water course itself close to the summit of the hill. These seem to be relatively modern. Just above them (in a field where no trace is now visible) Ricci and Fattovich excavated two basilical Aksumite churches. Their positioning on this western part of the hill seems, together with the 'palace' suburb below, to hint that the main part of the ancient town was situated towards the west. Incidentally, two structures that once bordered Mai Lahlaha in its lower part, the so-called Tomb of Ityopis and the mansion excavated by Puglisi, appear to have completely vanished.

West Aksum

The Addi Kilte mansions The remains of several substantial mansions still survive in the Addi Kilte district of Aksum. Many are in private compounds, and cannot be seen from the outside, but the general contours of the suburb clearly reveal where the main ancient structures are.

Following the dirt road leading into the suburb from the paved main road, which it prolongs in a straight line westwards, at the second crossroads on the right numerous ancient fragments are visible, the granite cornerstones of a palatial structure. This was the site called ES (Enda Sem'on) by the 1973–74 expedition under Neville Chittick, although it was not in fact the same site as the DAE's original Enda Sem'on (see Munro-Hay 1989: 11, no. 10 on the plan Fig. 2.2). A cornerstone of granite, two other large Aksumite stones embedded in a wall, five others in the road to the right, and a cluster of four cornerstones opposite with another further along the side road in a wall indicate that an important Aksumite building once stood here. A house on the corner exhibits eight dressed stone steps, which were dug from below the present ground level. Behind the house, still partly buried, is another very large step-like stone of the same type, and another lies in the area to the side of the house directly beside the main road. Occasional coins have also been found here, but they have long since been sold, and were never identified. A little further up the main road a stepped stone lies partly buried in the road itself.

At the next crossroads, if one turns left and then right, a granite stone can be seen in the road, which mounts here to a reddish area – the site of excavations in 1974 in the area called IW (no. 5 on the plan noted above). This stood for 'Iron-works', as it was assumed from the burning that traces of that activity would be revealed there. Instead, several rooms from a burned Aksumite mansion were discovered, the walls still partly standing, but the wooden elements calcined by a violent conflagration.

Returning to the main road of the suburb, a large open grassy space is next reached from which five roads diverge. That to the left leads to the IW area. A trench was laid out in 1974 in the centre of the open space itself, with little result, perhaps because it lay in a former courtyard. But the second road to the right off this space leads to an Aksumite stone in the wall, and the mound beyond this open space conceals major remains. First, in a small alleyway to the right, is a very large cornerstone resting on another almost buried. Then, in a gateway are two granite stones now employed as steps. Inside the compound here are several substantial Aksumite granite stone blocks or slabs, and there is one more embedded in the road a little further west. Nearby compounds contain granite pillar shafts later used as mortars, large flat stones, one pierced with a round hole, and other fragments of Aksumite work. Local tales tell of passages underground from point to point, not completely improbable if some rooms of these vanished structures remained more or less intact underground.

After a further crossroads, the summit of the hill is reached, and a final crossroads brings one to the end of modern Aksum in this direction. The remains here belong to the DAE's Enda Sem'on (no. 6 on the plan in Munro-Hay 1989) and to smaller nearby structures (nos. 26-7 on the plan). A gully curves round and down to join the main road east of the queen of Sheba's palace (Dungur), between a road bridge and the generator station. The generator house is the first modern building in Aksum when one approaches from the west.

Somewhat further to the northeast from the large open space mentioned above, moving towards the bell-tower of the cathedral and Da'ro 'Ela, are two more very large and impressive corner blocks of granite with another just visible below them. These stones are visible in an alcove built into the wall of the house of the late *Kere Geta* Wolde Yohannes. There are two further sets of blocks inside the compound as well, one consisting of three levels of blocks, and another single stone is visible in a side road outside the house. Around the base of the house are blocks and other fragments collected in the compound. This site bears witness to another substantial mansion rather to the north of the three (?) noted above. It is the DAE's Enda Mika'el palace (no. 9 on Fig. 2.2 in Munro-Hay 1989).

Further south, straddling the main tarmac road, are the remains of another mansion, the very substantial Aksumite palace building that the DAE called Ta'akha Maryam (no. 3 on the plan). The remains today are very meagre. A stepped pillar-base survives, turned on its side as part of the wall of a compound to the left of the main tarmac road approaching from the east. A massive stone pierced with a drainage canal stands by another such base on the same side of the road further west, outside the *woreda* (district) court. Inside the court compound is another square stepped base. Opposite on the other side of the road two large paving slabs still remain. The compound behind these exhibits an Aksumite stone used as a gateway step, and an entire staircase of many steps made from ancient stones found on the site, while another compound to the right contains Aksumite stones, and a pillar shaft hollowed out to serve as a mortar. A compound rather further north also contains Aksumite remains (no. 4 on the plan cited above).

By far the most interesting surviving section of Ta'akha Maryam is part of the peristyle in one of the palace courts, which still stands south of the main road in the compound directly next to (east of) the *woreda* court. Here can be seen the massive stones forming the base, sitting on a foundation of smaller stones, with at either end two large L-shaped stones with stepped ends forming a second level. These finely cut stones, still almost intact, offer a sad impression of the architectural splendours now lost under this drab quarter of the town. Somewhere here, according to local informants, on the north side of the main road, buried to a depth of about one metre in a compound, the great statue pedestal with the enormous footprints that was published by the DAE still survives. Further ruins, of a mansion excavated by Puglisi (no. 28 on the plan in Munro-Hay 1989), and of the structure called the Tomb of Ityopis (no. 7 on the plan), belonged to this western quarter of the town, but they have vanished from sight, dismantled or buried.

Dungur: The 'Queen of Sheba's Palace' The ruins of the 'Queen of Sheba's Palace' as local people began to call this structure soon after its discovery, lie to the west of Aksum opposite the Gudit Stele Field at a place called Dungur or Dungur 'Addi Kilte. In fact, the building is a substantial Aksumite mansion – really part of the same district of the ancient town described above. The mansion was excavated by Francis Anfray in 1966–68 and has been left uncovered as one of the interesting archaeological sites of the town. Although nothing remains of the mansion and its surrounding structures but the lowest levels and the podium, it still gives a good idea of the sort of dwelling that a prosperous Aksumite, perhaps a noble or high official of the fourth to sixth centuries AD, might have constructed for himself.

Regrettably, apart from a plan and a few notes on the finds (Anfray 1972), this excavation – like all the others undertaken by the French in Ethiopia in Haile Selassie's time – has never been fully published. One would particularly like to have details about some of the small finds, as they might offer a hint as to the activities undertaken in the outer range of buildings, and suggest a date for the complex as a whole. Karl Butzer, studying the geo-archaeology of Aksum and its environs, dated the structure to the seventh century, but it could very easily be much earlier.

The mansion and its dependencies covers an area of some 3,250 square metres. The plan of the central block resembles that of the large palace of Ta'akha Maryam recorded by the DAE in 1906, the 'four-towered' plan with each corner marked by salients that could represent the base of corner towers. The outer buildings surrounding this structure and its courtyards are rather irregular in layout, but basically form a large square with many indentations and salients in typical Aksumite fashion. At the northern angles stood two rough stone stelae.

Originally, a double staircase led into the complex through a portico, which in turn led into one of the courts surrounding the central edifice. All that now remains is the lower level, or podium, of the buildings, following in profile the shape of the mound to which the whole structure had been reduced as it fell into ruin. The highest surviving part is the central 'pavilion', which was approached by three sets of stairs to the top of the podium – one from the east, the most important, and two sets of double steps from the south and west. The pavilion may have had an open portico, supported by columns; the bases and the paving are still there.

The typical Aksumite masonry style is well exemplified by this building: façades with re-entrants and salients, graduated or stepped construction with shelving as the walls rise, corner blocks of dressed masonry for strengthening the structure, and small granite stones bound by mud mortar. The most unusual feature here is the single row of cut blocks along one level at the top of the stepped part of the podium. Similar work has been noted so far only in the Aksumite work at the base of the Maryam Seyon cathedral podium, and at the 'Tombs of Kaleb and Gabra Masqal'.

In the dependent buildings surrounding the courts, a number of fitments can be observed. Among these are stone piers presumably for supporting wooden columns or floors, a brick installation that the excavator suggested might be a 'hypocaust', and a brick oven. The precise nature of the surviving part of these dependencies is sometimes obscure. The 'rooms' with stone piers have no doorways, and the piers presumably supported floors, but occasional divisions on the same level do have doorways, implying that not all the lower level was merely a podium for a higher floor level. Possibly some rooms were entered from within by ladders (personal communication, Professor Steffen Wenig).

Gudit Stele Field   West of Aksum is another substantial group of stelae, amid the rocky desolation of fields where local farmers endeavour to scratch a living with their wooden ploughs drawn by paired oxen. Lefebvre in 1841 noted fifty-two stones or remains of obelisks, three being of dressed stone. When Bent visited in 1893 he commented that the stele were all undecorated and unhewn. He evidently missed the dressed ones (nos. 1–4, 6). The DAE counted forty-four, and the BIEA used the same numbers, finding no more stelae. In 1974 several areas were excavated, and a certain amount of grave-goods was found. Some of the stelae, Monneret de Villard noted, had been raised again haphazardly, without real information as to their original position.

The most interesting finds came from one modest, probably non-royal tomb in this cemetery, where a considerable deposit of grave-goods was revealed. It was excavated by Warwick Ball, as part of Dr Chittick's team. Among the finds were a set of almost intact clear glass stem goblets with trail decoration, and a set of small beakers, six of each, with a large collection of iron tools and weapons and about seventy exquisitely finished earthenware pots. Much of this material is exhibited today in the Aksum Museum – where the visitor is told by an imaginative official that the goblets came from the 'Queen of Sheba's Palace', and belonged to the queen herself! The tomb appeared to be little more than a small roundish roughly cut chamber, marked with an undressed stele, yet the possessions of the owner seem to represent a fairly prosperous way of life.

J. T. Bent, after his brief note about this field of monoliths, added: 'then there is a large circular artificial mound which probably contains a tomb, and which we longed, but owing to the stress of circumstances, were unable, to open'. Monneret de Villard assumed that this mound was the so-called Tomb of Menelik, which Ferret and Galinier mentioned as a 'petite monticule' some 2 km. from the town – but they indicate that this mound was situated 'to the southeast', not to the west. Bent's mound could just as easily have been the mound then covering Dungur mansion, the contours of which can still be clearly seen around the now-excavated building. Since Ferret and Galinier mention that 'bricks and cut stone' were to be seen near the mound, and bricks, generally rather rare at Aksum, were found in several installations at Dungur, the published direction may just be a mistake. For the DAE in 1906, the 'Tomb of Menelik' was the mound already opened by Gabra Sellase, governor of Tigray, in 1904–05 to the west of Aksum by Se'qudur. The bones found in it were taken to the church of Maryam Seyon. The DAE planned the simple small four-roomed building (fig. 289) – or rather podium for a building – and some other later structures built on to the east.

Tomb of Ityopis (Ethiopis) The *Book of Aksum*, in a corrupt passage, mentions this tomb of the father of the 'Ityopyawiyan', or Ethiopians:

> Again, there is the tomb of Ityopis the father of the Ethiopians, son of the son of Kam [Ham], whose name Ityopya was given to the throne (manbar) of the district of Malake Aksum [or, in Conti Rossini's version, *Liber Axumae*: 'again, there is at Mazeber, land of the commander of Aksum, the tomb of Ityopis, father of the Ethiopians, son of the son of Kam, who call themselves Ityopya']. And there was an obelisk standing as high as the stature of a man; but today it has become ruined. Now they wish to set up a stone as before. And if they spread dung there in the evening, they find that it has become ashes by the morning, so that if they throw rags down they are burnt.

The DAE identified this ruin cautiously with a building they found on the left bank of Mai Lahlaha, which they called Gebäuderest D. The published photo illustrates a very substantial wall with six surviving 'shelves'. The German team thought that this wall might belong to the podium of a large building. Ruth Plant's map shows 'Ityopis tomb' on the other side of the stream bed.

Gobo Dera (Gobedra) and 'Mount Zala'. The Lioness and the Quarries
At the outcrop of Gobo Dera (Gobedra) about four miles west of Aksum at

the foot of the mountain of Zala, Lefebvre in 1841 recorded the figure of a lioness, carved on a large rock some way up the hill (see the *Atlas*, Pl. 5). He also noted 'enormous detached blocks, as if they had undergone the beginning of squaring, which made us think that this place was one of the quarries where the stones which served for all these buildings had been extracted'. J. Theodore Bent too thought this, noting the 'massive granite projection' above 'Gobederah' 'from which I imagine the ancients obtained their large blocks of granite'. The DAE also described the place, supplying a good illustration (II, Tafel XV). D'Abbadie in 1868 marked it on his map as Kabanat; 'lion sculpté sur le rocher'.

On a smoothed area of a large projecting rock, the lioness is naturalistically modelled ('quoique très peu correct', adds Lefebvre) bounding along, mouth open and tongue lolling through powerful-looking teeth, as if in pursuit of a ball-like object floating off to the right. The carving is in shallow relief, without much detail except in the head and claws. The 'ball' seems in fact to be the typical Aksumite flared-arm Greek cross seen so often on fifth-century coins and on stones set up in various places in churches and other structures.

The quarries for the stelae are found a short distance away from this spot. It can clearly be seen how the stelae were extracted, by the rows of cuts in the rock in which wooden wedges would be inserted, which, when swollen with water, would split the rock along the selected line. There is one large stele (c. 9 m. long and 2 m. wide) lying there apparently ready for transport to the city. But its rounded top is broken on one side, perhaps when it escaped the ropes being used to manipulate it. It seems to have fallen against another stele in the process of being cut out. This stele is about 12.5 by 2 m., with a flat end not yet shaped; it shows the sectional method of cutting along one of the sides. Not far away is another stone, clearly marked with the holes cut for the insertion of the wedges used to divide the stone.

Closer to the road, below a stone marked in white with the number 7700, there is a very large partly dressed stone resembling in shape the Nefas Mawcha topstone. It measures perhaps 9.5 by 4–4.5 m., and is neatly cut on one long edge, less so on the other. Work seems to have been abandoned on this stone, and it was destined never to reach Aksum.

From the top of the mountain of Gobo Dera there are wonderful views in all directions. A strange building survives at the highest point, built solely of huge quantities of piled-up stones. There is an outer wall of considerable size, and within it various other structures, all of the same unusual construction. This peculiar fortress seems to be the building mentioned in local legends that recount the tale of Queen Gudit's campaign against the city. In order to count her army she commanded every soldier to add a stone to a pile

– and this building, the 'stones of Gudit' is the result. To cite Sergew Hable Sellassie's translation from a modern chronicle assembled by the *qese gabaz* of Aksum, Tekle Haimanot:

> One day because she [Gudit] wanted to show the number of her army, she ordered each one to go to a high mountain called Gobedra carrying in his hand a stone and to leave it there. The heap became like a mountain. The heap of stones is found there to the present day.

The structure is now filled with rusty tins, from its recent occupation by soldiers watching the main Gondar road below during Mengistu's time. I have been able to find no further explanation for this bizarre structure.

Gobedra is also the site of prehistoric remains, excavated in 1974 at a rock-shelter there (Phillipson 1977).

East Aksum

Tombs of Kaleb and Gabra Masqal: history A substantial Aksumite structure housing two large granite-built tombs some way outside the main town of Aksum has long been known. The fifteenth-century (?) *Book of Aksum* describes it:

> And there is the house of Kaleb and his son Gabra Masqal, built in the heart of the ground, with stone pillars [or obelisks]; it may be seen from the outside to this day. But inside, they say, it is filled with gold and jewels. There are those who say, 'We have seen with our own eyes when jewels came out through holes when they pushed in grass wet with saliva. One of its gates is Aksum, and one of its gates is Matara.'

The last phrase is perhaps an allusion to the legend that King Kaleb of Aksum passed with his army to Matara by means of a tunnel, to chastise some pagans of Bur near Matara. Local legend claims that he took with him the *tabot* of Abba Pantalewon to aid him in his war. Alvares, of course, came here and described the structure:

> Above this town, on a hill which overlooks much distant country on every side, and which is about a mile, that is a third of a league, from the town, there are two houses under the ground, into which men do not enter without a lamp. These houses are not vaulted, but of very good straight masonry, both the walls and the roof … the blocks are set in the wall so close one to the other, that it all looks like one stone, for the joints are not seen. One of these houses is much divided into chambers and granaries; in the doorways are holes for the bars and sockets of the doors. In one of these chambers are two very large

chests ... and in the upper part on the inner side they are hollowed at the edge, as though they had lids of stone, as the chests also are of stone. (They say that these were the treasure chests of the Queen Saba.) The other house, which is broader, has only got a portico and one room.

Presumably, the partial fill of earth, or some later forgetfulness on Alvares' part, accounts for the slightly erroneous descriptions. There are in fact three sarcophagi in the central chamber of Gabra Masqal's tomb, and three chambers off the hall in Kaleb's. For some reason, when Beckingham and Huntingford, editing Alvares' book *The Prester John of the Indies*, suggest in a note that Alvares refers in this passage to the tombs of Kaleb and his son, they add 'which were connected by a narrow underground passage about forty yards long'. There is no record of such a passage, and it certainly has not (yet) been found by any recent researchers, although the existence of a tunnel to Matara, Jerusalem, or (Sapeto after *Dabtara* Tesfu, 1838) Enda Pantalewon, was a common tale.

Subsequently other Portuguese visited the tomb. Péro Pais (1620) even provided a sketch plan of the tomb of Kaleb, and Mendez and Barradas also came to see it. Mendez was quoted by Balthasar Tellez in his 1660 book, translated into English in 1710. He writes, after discussing Kaleb's association with Abba Pantalewon:

> in the mid way, between Auxum and Beth Pantaleon, there are three Caves, within one another and hew'd out by Hand in the Rock, one of which is the Entrance, and has the Door to the West, being 15 Cubits long and 4 in Breadth; and at the end of it are two other little Rooms, in the nature of a Cross, to the Entrance, each of which is 10 Cubits long, and that on the Right Hand, or to the Southward is 4 Cubits wide, and that opposite to it 6. All the ground lying under these caves has a square Wall about it.

This presumably means that the patriarch saw only, or at least described, only one of the tombs.

Barradas refers to the buildings as 'two houses made of black stone, squared and well cut. Both are placed under the ground.' A candle was needed at mid-day to see them. Barradas heard that in one of them

> dwelt in penitence the holy King Caleb and there ended his days ... the other, which is quite nearby, and can be entered at one jump, as it has a hole for a door instead of a courtyard, belonged to one of his sons, who retired from the world with him, who lived there and died in saintliness like his father. Both are buried in the church of Saint Pantalião.

Barradas learned, in addition, that 'not long ago, in our time' bodies had been discovered at Pantelewon's church, and one of them 'as it must be there written' had been discovered to be that of Kaleb. He also related the tale of the passageway from the king's 'house or pit' to Matara in Bur (Barradas 1996: 124–5).

Henry Salt and Nathaniel Pearce, too, came in 1805 (Valentia 1809, Vol. III). They arrived from Adwa, turning off to the north before reaching Aksum by a track which their guide told them led to an interesting spot called 'Calam Negus'. Turning west they travelled across 'a plain fully six miles in extent', and so by this back way came eventually to the tombs. All they were able to see were the underground tombs themselves – including, their guides told them, 'the road by which Calam Negus went to Jerusalem, and "if any person should take a candle into it at night, he would distinctly see the whole way to that holy city"'. Thus local legend had expanded Kaleb's expedition to Matara. Salt noted the Aksumite style of the door in Gabra Masqal's tomb. The tomb was nearly closed with earth, so that he and Pearce had to creep in on hands and knees; but he would not be 'deterred by any trifling difficulties'. He described the three stone sarcophagi, which are still there. Above, he saw only some 'large loose stones, ready squared for building'.

Among Pearce's papers in the British Library (BM add. 19347, fol. 152) is a record of an odd Greek inscription that he transcribed here (?). After a letter dated 'Auxume Sept 26th 1815' he added the following:

ΩΔΗΨΜΜΟΥΙΟΙΣ ΥΙΣΙΣΚΟΡΕΣΙΛΦΔ

§15°

this is the only sign of the original inscription I can (propably = properly?) trace out with a candle in a very dark place indeed the stone is allmost worn bare of every letter some of them may not be perfect as there is not more than three that remains perfect. N. Pearce.

Not much sense can be made of this.

Others followed to explore these tombs. Lefebvre illustrated an engraving of King Kaleb's tomb (Caleb-Negousse) with a most inaccurate plan (*Atlas*, Pl. 5, also illustrated in Beckingham and Huntingford's edition of Alvares, pl. IV). The DAE cleared large parts of the upper structure, and as usual prepared meticulous plans. The BIEA excavations in 1973–74 also investigated the surroundings of this building. It was found that on the south and east there were other structures, generally inferior in construction. They were earlier in date on the east, later on the south.

Tombs of Kaleb and Gabra Masqal today The superb setting, with views in all directions, makes Enda Kaleb a pleasure to visit. Today the building has been cleared and the tombs left open, though partially roofed over with tin. The area has been walled, with the north side of the building itself forming part of the enclosure near the entrance gate. The massive cut granite Aksumite cornerstones can be seen on arrival at the entrance gate from the road that leads here from Aksum, passing the Mai Shum reservoir and the new church built over the *sebel* or holy well of Kidane Mehret.

The front wall (west) supports a terrace reached by a stone staircase, from which a central higher terrace can be reached by a much wider staircase, with two flanking side flights of steps leading to the buildings housing the two tombs. The upper terrace opens to two equal-sized entrance porticoes, each with a single column-base on one side. The column-base on the Kaleb side is square and stepped, the Gabra Masqal side-base octagonal. The octagonal pillar belonging to it was found by the DAE; it seems to be the one now re-erected in the Ezana Garden. These areas appear to have been open paved porticoes, which in turn lead to two larger paved columnar halls, of which the one to the south – Gabra Masqal's, according to legend – is larger than the northern one. Both open to further groups of rooms to the west, above the tomb entrances themselves. Staircase wells indicate that this part had an upper storey or at least a roof terrace. The tomb staircases were probably sealed, after the (multiple) burials inside were installed, by heavy stones, a few of which survive over the staircase on Gabra Masqal's side.

It seems quite probable that the superstructures over the tombs constituted either churches or memorial chapels. In the Gabra Masqal hall there are traces at the eastern end of some sort of installation where an altar or similar object might be expected. Three out of four corner emplacements remained for the DAE to plan, but now only one remains. A limestone central plate showed two fixing-holes, and other traces resembling the shape of feet. Quite possibly, a statue (of the king ?) stood here under a baldaquin supported by pillars set into the emplacements. Behind were other rooms, which have never been entirely cleared or planned. The general design of these buildings, with their staircases and porticoes, seems to have been rather elegant, and it is a pity that the complete design is still unknown.

The tombs beneath the chapels – if that is what they are – are fascinating. (NB a good torch is needed to visit them.) Kaleb's (so-called) tomb is reached by a staircase opening directly into a transverse hall of some 7 m. width. From this in turn three rooms open to the east. The masonry is curious, and very labour-intensive. It is of the irregular type called 'cyclopean', composed of large stones skilfully cut like a jigsaw to fit each other at all sorts of different angles. The stones are therefore of many different shapes and sizes. Two large modern stone piers, installed to support the roof, now obscure the left-hand room.

In the tomb of Gabra Masqal, a staircase and a short passage open into a transverse hall about the same size as that in Kaleb's tomb, and again three rooms open off it towards the east. However, in this tomb the door facing the stairs has a splendid Aksumite-style frame with squared monkey-heads. The holes for the wooden door hinges at the top and bottom are visible, and another hole for the bolt. The room is rather larger than the equivalent room in Kaleb's tomb. It contains three sarcophagi of stone, one with a cross cut on the end. The two side rooms are narrower and longer than those in Kaleb's tomb – in the room to the right there is a cross cut on the wall. These crosses could, of course, have been cut at some later date when the tombs were opened, but there seems in fact to be no reason to believe that they do not date from the time the tomb was built. This seems to have been in relatively early Christian times in Ethiopia, perhaps indeed from the period of Kaleb and his son (see Munro-Hay 1989). There are two further rooms opening to the west off the hall in Gabra Masqal's tomb, the southern one also being equipped with an Aksumite-style doorframe; the northern one is damaged. The masonry in this tomb is laid in horizontal lines, but the masons still employed occasional odd cuts to accommodate the corners of certain stones. In general, the work rather resembles the masonry of the Tomb of the False Door in 'Addi Seray by the Stele Park.

Addi Sehafi Addi Sehafi (Ashafi) is an Aksumite site reached after some two hours walk, leaving by the road northeast of the town, beyond Geza 'Agmai and the end of Beta Giyorgis hill called Gobo Nebrid. To reach Addi Sehafi one follows the road past the very extensive Muslim cemetery.

Muslims cannot be buried in Aksum, and their recent attempt to build a mosque there aroused local Christian fury. Government attempts to arbitrate apparently received a reply intimating that only when the Muslim authorities of the holy city of Mecca permitted the construction of a Christian church there could the holy city of Aksum consider a mosque. This not unreasonable attitude is not new; Dervla Murphy quoted exactly the same argument offered in 1968. The Muslim cemetery outside Aksum consists of innumerable graves marked by stones with small 'stelae' headstones in Muslim fashion. The graveyard stretches for a long way along the sides of the road.

One passes the famous water source called Mai Kirah, where Yared met foreign saints sent by St Mary to teach him the liturgical chants. Today, there is a stone-walled well surrounded by a few trees. Not far from here is the village of Ma'kono, reputed to be the dwelling of many goldsmiths and silversmiths, people still regarded with a certain reserve, not to mention fear, by many Aksumites. It is said, among certain of the less educated elements in this intensely conservative society – to the victims' anger – that they employ certain magic arts. Particularly they are accused of being *buda*, or werewolves, persons who can transform themselves into hyenas or other beasts, or cast spells resulting in illness. This accusation is – or was – also levelled against the Falasha. Conventional Aksumites still shun those who work with metal, and will not intermarry with them. The reason is the usual one of fear of persons who have skills that are hard to comprehend for those who lack them. Aksumite gold- and silversmiths, incidentally, are spread far and wide through Ethiopia and Eritrea, the skill of working these metals being part of the Aksumite heritage.

Further on, before one reaches the *sebel* of Enda Abbate (where water employed for curing skin diseases emerges from the rock), the Akeltegna area with the church of Maryam Sehay, Mary the Sun, can be seen to the right. The path to Addi Sehafi curves northwards here, crossing the Mai Goda stream to the left – named, legend says, after a monk who died after washing himself in its waters. The stream bed is filled with large water-worn rocks, and the water flows north to join the Mareb. From here, the mountains of Eritrea are visible. Crossing the river, one mounts towards the church of Arbaat Ensesa at Addi Sehafi – the village of the Secretary or Recorder – passing another well walled with stone called Mai Hirus (water of the ploughed land), and several hills and fields scattered with huge boulders. At Addi Sehafi one enters stone-walled lanes surrounded by euphorbia, olive, wanza and other trees.

In this village of dispersed houses and fields, below the church under a *da'ro* tree, are three large Aksumite stones (an estimated 1 m. by 80 cm. by 30 cm.) arranged as seats. One block has four shallow cuts out of the long sides at both ends. The other two appear to be plain. These alone would make one suspect that there must be other Aksumite features nearby, and a short distance away lies the proof. A very large rock can be seen with a cut out of the top of it. Climbing it – it now has a stone-walled passage leading up to it – the 'wine' press can be seen. The installation consists of two rectangular depressions cut into the rock. One is deeper and larger, and one shallower and smaller. Both lead via channels pierced through the rock and decorated with carved lion heads at the ends, into a much deeper basin. At the base of this is carved a rock-cut kylix with two handles, similar to those on the stelae base-plates at Aksum. Various holes and ledges seem to be associated with entry into the basin, or perhaps with supporting shelves for working at a lower level. Given the presence even today of olive trees in the region, possibly this was an Aksumite olive press?

Nathaniel Pearce was shown this olive (?) press, which he considered to have been 'made by the ancients to prepare some kind of cement in for building' – a most unlikely suggestion. His Ethiopian friend invoked the tale

still known in the countryside: it had been designed as a container for serpent's food.

Local legend relates many snake/dragon stories about this region. One tale
claims that the snake, attaching its tail around a tree near Enda Abbate, could
reach to the Mareb river with its head. An alternative was that it attached its
tail to the small sugar-loaf mountain nearby, while the craggier hills beside
it are called 'Hard for the Snake to Climb'. In these stories, the destruction
of the serpent is attributed sometimes to St George, sometimes to the Nine
Saints.

Small Antiquities around Aksum

Pillars, capitals, water-spouts and crosses A number of pillars, bases
and capitals lie scattered around Aksum. The DAE recorded three in the
Maryam Seyon church compound. Two were near the King's Seat – a single
broken limestone pillar now lies south of the thrones in the Mannagesha
Court – and another on the mound called Guduf Maryam (Gudif Maryam).
Outside the Da'ro 'Ela gate of the church compound, at *miwrade qal*, the
pillar of Yared with a round stone drum on top of it serves as a resting-place
for the *tabot* during processions. Another pillar formerly stood, partly buried,
nearby. This is probably the second pillar that stands today inside the enclosure
of the pillar of Yared. Some eight paces away was a third pillar with a cross
cut on the capital. This seems to be the pillar found today inside the inner
compound of Maryam Seyon, west of the new cathedral and north of its
campanile. It stands on the right as one enters, beside a section of a round
column. Opposite these two on the left is another large granite stone cut with
a deep cross. The two pillars in the Maryam Seyon courtyard seem to be parts
of Aksumite columns, one a simple shaft, the other with the characteristic
Aksumite chamfered edges, and an integral capital with a *cross pattée* carved
on it. On top of this a round stone drum is now positioned.

Two richly carved pillars – very similar to many of the vine-decorated
door-jambs from ancient Yemen – were formerly kept in the vestibule of the
church. Only one of these is there now, embedded in the wall of the *qene
mahlet* porch of the church to the right of the central door. Other ancient
fragments were built into the structure itself. Several fragments, including a
capital and many stones decorated with carved crosses (frequently found inlaid
in the west walls of churches), were photographed built into the exterior wall
of the porch of Maryam Seyon in 1906. When the porch was rebuilt in
arched form during the 1908 restorations, many of the stones were replaced
in slightly different positions. The palmetto capital illustrated in the DAE
report (fig. 241) was not replaced. One such capital lies now near the Treasury

above the 1958 excavation site. Another similar one is embedded in the west terrace wall above the long staircase, together with two stone crosses, two lion-headed water-spouts, and other fragments. On the western terrace of the old cathedral, near the south bell-tower, what seems to be the remains of a carved decorated granite column shaft lies near the terrace wall. Many other fragments lie scattered in the enclosure of the cathedral, in Arbaat Ensesa church compound, and in the Ezana Garden and the throne-field opposite.

Decorative lion-headed waterspouts are not uncommon in Aksum. Examples are to be seen at Maryam Seyon church, some in the west terrace wall, some in the south terrace, some by the entrance to the Stele Park built into the wall. Others are kept in the Museum. They are often mentioned, and sometimes illustrated, by travellers from Alvares' time onwards.

Bowls and fonts Rüppell in 1833 saw a very large stone bowl, which had recently been found in a rubbish heap in the old city. It was shallow with two projections, one on each side, acting as handles, and an inscription in Ge'ez on one side. The bowl was stored in a private house, where it was used to feed the donkey. Lefebvre's expedition illustrated it in their *Atlas* volume, Pl. 1. The DAE team was unable to find it again, but published the inscription as no. 18. The unvocalised Ge'ez inscription seems to record a certain Ahlali as having made the bowl for a place of pilgrimage.

In 1881 Rohlfs saw another basin or font, this time half filled with earth in the court of 'Tekla Haimanot church'. This seems to be the alternative name of Arbaat Ensesa church, and the bowl may be the same as the stone bowl that Bent mentions:

> there is also another church hard by [the Maryam Seyon enclosure], just the ordinary round Abyssinian church where women may worship [presumably the church of Arbaat Ensesa, also known as the women's church]; and outside this is a font where children are baptised, for no unbaptised people are admitted within the walls of a church, and it has an old Ethiopian inscription around it.

In 1906 the DAE did indeed find a font in the court of the church of Arbaat Ensesa, a broken bowl carved in one piece with a square flat base. The inscription was recorded as DAE no. 17. It notes the consecration of the baptismal basin to 'the King of Peace' in Heaven and on the Earth. A certain HKF apparently cut the inscription, which is written in unvocalised Ge'ez. It may be this basin, or another, that is now in use built into the covered font in the baptistery beside the gateway of Arbaat Ensesa church. However, another old stone font with two side bosses was recorded near the new (square) church of Enda Iyasus by the DAE. As we have noted above, Lejean refers to the eastern part of Malake Aksum as 'Takha Haimanot'; perhaps this was the original name of the old round church in what is now the Enda Iyasus compound? Another large stone bowl survives at Abba Liqanos church, and there are others in Aksum Museum.

Houses and house models Archaeology is not just about royal monuments, but the perishable nature of humbler dwellings at Aksum, as in so many other places, means that little remains to indicate how the ordinary people lived. However, some clay models of houses were found which are described here.

The general impression of Aksum from the 1906 photographs taken by the DAE was of a town primarily consisting of single-roomed round thatched houses, although some of the larger ones boasted several inner divisions. Nevertheless, there was formerly quite a rich architectural variation here, with round houses, sometimes with a circle of interior pillars, other round houses with square interior arrangements – not dissimilar from the typical Ethiopian round church – and different types of square houses, some even possessing three storeys. There were also round two-storey private houses, and some rectangular two-storey gatehouses providing the entrance way into compounds, very attractive and elegant. Stone exterior staircases were common. Some of this survives today, although modern building methods are replacing the traditional styles in many instances. Many older houses were built of the local granite, employing small stones held with a simple mud mortar. Traditionally, thatch was used for roofing, with a central terracotta finial to cover the peak. Attractive carved window- and doorframes may also be seen.

These house styles have a long history in Tigray. From Hawelti near Aksum, came some pottery house models dated to somewhere between the third century BC and the first century AD. They included a round type with conical roof, layered thatch, rectangular doorway and possibly wooden ribbing on the walls – the type of *tukul* or *agdo* of the present day. There was also a rectangular type with doorway and windows, monkey-head beam-ends under the roof, and even a water-spout draining through the parapet on the flat roof. From the excavations at Aksum came other models of rectangular houses with pitched roofs covered with layered thatch, ribbed lintels, and typical Aksumite windows with square monkey-heads.

CHURCHES OF AKSUM

The Cathedral of Maryam Seyon

The church or cathedral of Maryam Seyon or Mary of Zion is among the most important ecclesiastical buildings in Ethiopia. However, visiting it today is not always a pleasure. There is frequent harassment of foreign visitors in the enclosure of Mary of Zion church by 'officials' (indistinguishable as such by any special badge or uniform) checking admission ticketing. This could be prevented by ensuring that a properly uniformed official was in attendance, with notices at the gates explaining the rules. With the disestablishment of the church in Ethiopia, money from tourism is much needed, but at present the church administration earns much adverse criticism because it has made no arrangements to implement the relatively simple mechanisms required to receive visitors properly.

To be fair to the ecclesiastical establishment at Aksum, the greater number of the priests and *dabtara* (lay canons and cantors affected to the service of the church) are completely uninterested in visitors, being immersed in the rituals and the service of the church. In addition, there are other reasons for reserve in the attitude of the church authorities. There have been thefts from both the church (by local priests, who are now in jail) and the neighbouring museum (apparently by a German tourist, who, scandalously enough, was connected with a museum in his own country). There is also concern and unease over the publicity surrounding the claim that the 'Ark of the Covenant' is kept in a chapel above the treasury (see below), publicity much enhanced by Graham Hancock's claims in the book *The Sign and the Seal*, and subsequent Internet and film coverage.

There are two churches at the site nowadays. One is a modern round edifice built in the reign of the last emperor – the most ostentatious building in Aksum today. The other, built or restored by order of Emperor Fasiladas in 1655 (or 1657 according to Salt), is constructed on the remains of several previous churches dating right back to Aksumite times. The new cathedral, inaugurated in 1964 by Emperor Haile Sellassie with Queen Elizabeth II as his guest, has just been equipped with a copper covering over the dome, and has undergone a number of other necessary repairs. There is also a large, very prominent bell-tower, broadly based on the shape of the Aksumite stelae. This new church has the advantage that it is accessible to women, something totally forbidden for the older structure, except briefly in the seventeenth century when Catholicism prevailed. Between these modern buildings, by the always empty blue-tiled water-tank, is an old column shaft with a cross on its capital, surmounted by a round stone, and another pillar; these seem, as noted above, to be the same pillars that formerly stood by the Pillar of Yared.

The older church is a substantial oblong structure of stone. Although it is often referred to rather optimistically as the 'great church' of Aksum, or by similar hyperbole, it is in fact smaller than many ordinary parish churches in other Christian countries, and possesses no ornamental stonework or other architectural features of note. Inside, too, it does not in any way compare to the description in the late fourteenth-century account, *Iter de Venetiis ad Indiam*, where the church of 'Chaxum' is presented as a gold-encrusted coronation church. Nor is it to be compared with the much larger cathedral that Alvares saw and described around 1520. The seventeenth-century rebuilt church that survives today is plain, and although it possesses a certain exterior stateliness with its sombre battlemented walls, splendid stone staircase and flanking domed towers, the interior offers a rather run-down appearance.

The church is surrounded by a low plinth of three or four steps, constructed with large stones possibly recuperated from the older cathedral that stood here until the sixteenth century. Many of these stones are equipped with one, two, or three bosses, perhaps originally designed to assist with their transport. The line of the plinth steps is broken by the doorways. On all sides the building is battlemented, with waterspouts on the long sides to drain away the rain from the roof. There is a pillared and now closed portico at the west end from which three doorways lead into the *qeddest*. Henry Salt was quite right when he commented (Valentia 1809, Vol. III) that 'the first impression on beholding Axum church, is its great resemblance to the Gothic seats of noblemen in England'. It belongs in a general way to the castle-like architectural school of Gondar. Its date of dedication, 1655, is contemporary with the earlier manifestations of this style under Emperor Fasiladas. Part of it could date from an earlier restoration under Sarsa Dengel, in which case it might merit comparison with the pre-Gondarine castle of Guzara; but it seems that the existing castle there is not the original one of Sarsa Dengel.

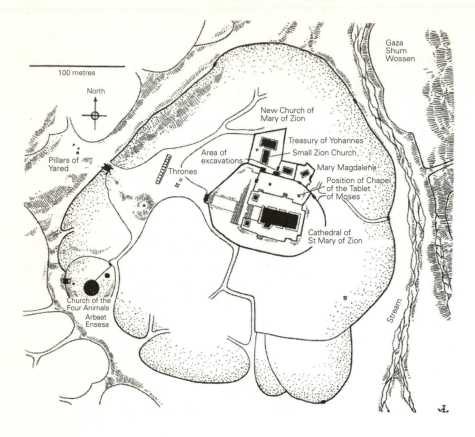

22. The compound of Maryam Seyon church at Aksum, showing the buildings as they were in 1906. The position of the new round church and Chapel of the Tablet of Moses built in the 1960s is noted. All the adjacent buildings except the treasury of Yohannes have now disappeared. Adapted from D. Phillipson, *The Monuments of Aksum*, 1997: Fig. 167.

The portico originally had a flat architrave, and was open to the west – as Salt's illustration in Lord Valentia's book shows. Lefebvre's illustration is similar, with apparently some sort of decorative frieze at the top including three Greek-style crosses (*Album*, Pl. I). Later the gaps between the columns were screened in with wooden strap-work, and finally, in 1908, the present arches were installed. At the southwestern corner of the building is a battle-mented tower containing the staircase to the roof. The roof was flat when the DAE saw the building, and is now pitched.

The high walls, built of small stones rather than cut blocks, are relieved only by a number of arched windows and doorways. Unusually, there are three doorways in each of the long sides, one pair leading into the vestibule at the west end of the structure, one pair into the *qeddest*, where communion is received, and the last into the sanctuary area. Prominent water-spouts jut from the top of the walls, in which there are inserted a few decorative features, usually stray blocks from Aksumite times. Among these may be noted, at the east end, in the centre, two blocks, one with a sinuous cross motif, one with a diamond shape cut out in the centre, and, to the south, an octagonal column-base incorporated flat into the wall. On the south side, in the door pillar east of the staircase tower, a palmetto-style fragment has been incorporated.

On the roof at the west end of the main building stood an ornamental arch flanked by two little towers – after Salt. The Lefebvre illustration shows a more or less classical pediment with a central arch. In the photos included in the DAE report, the arch is filled in with wooden strap-work. This was crowned by a large open-work metal cross with seven ostrich eggs on spikes surrounding it, set on a cone hung with chains and little bells – another similar finial was on the old battlemented Treasury of Yohannes. Today the cathedral roof is pitched and supports a small square tower with arched windows, four corner finials, and a central crown-shaped support for a metal cross.

Within the tree-shaded, tranquil and fascinating setting of the inner and outer enclosures that form the sacred area within Aksum, the cathedral stands on a large high terrace or podium, accessible by flights of steps on the west, north and south. Much of the terrace is composed of ancient materials probably dating back in part to the earlier churches or other structures on the spot. The inner enclosure round the church is forbidden to women, although sometimes the church treasures are set out on exhibition, and can be viewed by women through an iron screen to one side of the new Treasury. This part of the compound is reached by a staircase descending beside the new cathedral, behind the Treasury of Yohannes, to the *nebura'ed*'s offices – in the end room of which are kept three ancient Aksumite inscriptions – passing round the east side of the 1958 excavation area.

Below the terrace of the old cathedral, inside a grille, is a modern two-storey structure crowned with a green dome and a silver cross, the chapel of the Tablet of Moses (*enda sellat*, or sometimes *sellata Muse*) with the treasury (*eqa bet*) below. The chapel – a curious mélange of architectural themes from the stelae and the neighbouring cathedral, covered with green tiles – is constructed against the northeast corner of the cathedral terrace. The new chapel, built by the late Empress Menen, replaces the chapel of the Tablet of Moses, a building that earlier this century stood, oriented north–south, beyond the northwest corner of the terrace, directly next to the Treasury of Yohannes. This structure was described briefly by Doresse, and shown on his plan (Doresse 1956: 47). There are also some illustrations of the paintings on the façade and vestibule. The chapel is the same building as the 'little church of Zion' recorded and planned when the DAE visited Aksum in 1906. The new chapel is supposed to house the Ark of the Covenant on the upper floor. East of the Treasury and chapel is the *beta lahm*, where the bread for the eucharist is baked by women specially appointed for the purpose.

Many of those foreigners who came to see the cathedral in the nineteenth century commented on its status as a place of sanctuary, where, by ringing the bell in the porch and proclaiming one's intention, a criminal could be safe from the pursuit of the law. An area around Aksum cathedral is called 'hasura la Seyon', the 'compound of Zion' in recognition of this. It is also a place of pilgrimage, particularly for the festivals of *Hedar Seyon*, a feast celebrated on 21 Hedar, or 30 November, associated with the coming of the Ark of the Covenant and also honouring Mary, and *Hosanna*, Palm Sunday.

Inside, the church meets the requirement for three separate areas for the religious ceremonies by the use of the porch as an outer room, the *qene mahlet*, where hymns are sung and the *dabtara* stand to chant during services, from which three doors enter a four-pillared *qeddest*, the part of the church where the administration of communion occurs. The flat ceiling shown in the DAE report has been replaced by a vault, the columns now being linked by arches instead of flat beams. The central elevated vault allows the entrance of light from side windows. From the *qeddest*, access to the inner sanctuary area, or *maqdas*, is gained.

The *qene mahlet*, or porch, also vaulted, has two exterior doors north and south, and three doors leading to the *qeddest*. Left of the central door to the *qeddest* is a stone cross of the type seen on fourth- or fifth-century coins, built into the wall. To the right is a column carved with vine leaves and a sinuous stem, surmounted by a typical Aksumite cross in a circle, exactly as seen on coins of the fourth century. There is also a fragment of another type of decorative cross, reminiscent of another cross embedded in the exterior wall of the east end of the church. Above the central door to the *qeddest* is a large and rather elegant painting depicting Emperor Yohannes IV engaged in battle with the dervishes, flanked on the right by an unfinished picture of the Holy Trinity visiting Abraham and Sara, and on the left by another unfinished painting of Mary, Protector of Virgins. There are a number of other paintings, some very new. By the north doorway is a picture of King Gabra Masqal listening to the famous chanter Yared, very appropriate in the area of the church where the *dabtara* sing the songs of Yared himself – who was reputedly a native of nearby Medebai. Embedded in the jamb of the south doorway to the exterior is a curious carved fragment.

Next comes the stone-flagged *qeddest*. Four very massive plastered columns support the vaulted ceiling by arches, and on these columns are some paintings covered by curtains. On the north side of the first column to the right on entering is a painting of the Virgin and Child, and on the west side are pictures illustrating the crucifixion and burial of Jesus. The second column to the right exhibits, on the west side, a picture of Mary above the prone figure of the donor, the *Nebura'ed* Iyasu (nineteenth century). On the first column to the left one can see the journey of Mary to Egypt, the death of Mary, the killing of the infants by King Herod, and the Annunciation, by a painter called Isisnos. One picture shows Mary standing on the crescent moon. The south side of this column also carries a picture, of Mary and the Child Jesus. Finally, the second column on the left illustrates, on its west face, the Trinity (Father, Son, and Holy Spirit as a dove) with Mary, surrounded by angels playing trumpets; this is signed by a well-known painter, Berhane Masqal Fisseha. In the southwest corner a door leads into the staircase tower.

The sanctuary screen wall has a central door into the *maqdas*, and two others into the side chapels. Above the central doorway are three wooden windows, and above the other doorways, double windows. On either side of the triple window are stone crosses set into the wall. A large painting of the Holy Trinity depicted as three old men occupies the central upper register above this. Immediately below are other pictures, one with the names of the donors *Bajerond* Gabra Sadek and his wife Semeñish, a second showing Adam and Eve in Paradise, with a subordinate scene depicting Eve taking the fruit from a tree with the Serpent in it, and a third scene illustrating the expulsion from the Garden of Eden. Below, from left to right, are numerous scenes flanking the three doors; all the paintings are veiled with curtains. First are depictions of the revered monk Abuna Medhanina Egzi', Mary and the Child, and Abuna Samuel riding a lion; then to the left of the central doorway St George and the Dragon, and a scene of Maryam Seyon church itself with worshippers, a king and priests. On the doors themselves two large figures of Mikael and Rafael, the archangels, appear above a scene showing the army of Pharaoh drowning in the Sea of Eritrea (Red Sea), and another illustrating how Rafael saved a church dedicated to him from the attack of a large fish. To the right of the main doorway Mary and the Child are painted, in memory of *Grazmach* Afework and his wife *Wozayro* Turas, above another panel painted with the figures of the Nine Saints. Finally, to the south of the third doorway, are paintings of Mary and the Child Jesus, in memory of 'Ras Mikael, Head of the Princes of Tigray', with three quintessential saints of Ethiopia, Gabra Manfas Qiddus, Tekla Haymanot and Abba Aregawi.

Beyond this, about half of the building is curtained off to form the *maqdas*, or *qeddesta qeddusan*, the Holy of Holies, where the *tabotat* are kept, and to which entry is not permitted to the public in any Ethiopian church. There are two side chapels. The sanctuary and side chapel walls are covered with paintings, repainted in the 1950s by Aleqa Yohannes. As usual, the Trinity is depicted above, high in the vault, while Mary with the Infant Jesus and St George and the Dragon flank the sanctuary entrance, with other scenes below.

History of the Cathedral of Maryam Seyon

Doubtless the special position of the church of Maryam Seyon in Ethiopia descends directly from the earliest days of Christianity in the country, when a church was built in the city of Aksum, then an imperial capital. Historically, King Ezana is known to have been the king who converted to Christianity in about AD 340. In Ge'ez texts, the conversion is attributed to two royal brothers called Abreha and Asbeha, and the name Ezana is unknown. There may, however, be an explanation. Aksumite kings – and their successors in Ethiopia – employed several names and titles. For example, in his sole surviving inscription King Kaleb is also called 'Ella Asbeha' – many foreign references to him call him by the name Ellesbaas or variants – and he also bears another title, 'Be'ese LZN'. Generally these names are viewed as constituting a personal name, a throne name or epithet commencing with Ella- ('he who ...'), and a clan name preceded by the word *be'ese* or *be'esya* ('man of ...'). Ezana's own inscriptions supply his clan name, Be'ese Halen, but never an 'Ella-' name, although they mention his father's 'Ella-' name of Ella Amida. Thus, there remains the possibility that Ezana reigned under the 'throne'-name Ella Abreha. With an event so radical as the change of faith, he might have changed this to Ella Asbeha, 'He who has brought the dawn'; later Ethiopian kings not infrequently changed their throne names in just this fashion.

As for the story of the two royal brothers, it is known from Ezana's inscriptions that he had at least two brothers, called Sazana/Saiazana and Hadefan. Saiazana is linked with Ezana in a very close way as joint addressees of a letter written by the Roman emperor Constantius II c. 356 on the subject of Frumentius, bishop of Aksum. We therefore know that Ezana had a brother for some reason closely involved with ecclesiastical matters little more than a decade and a half after the conversion. A combination of these elements might have given rise in the Ge'ez records to the legend of two royal brothers Abreha and Asbeha reigning at the time of the conversion.

A further Ge'ez legend is recorded about the foundation of the cathedral in the *Book of Aksum*.

A third time it [the city of Aksum] was built by Abreha and Atsbeha [at the place] where is [now] this sanctuary of the cathedral of Aksum. Now the foundation was performed by means of a miracle, for previously there was [there] a great lake; and the holy kings Abreha and Atsbeha climbed a great mountain called Mekyada Egzi'ena and prayed that [God] might reveal to them where they should build a cathedral for the dwelling-place of His name. And Our Lord descended and stood between them, and took earth, and cast it where it is now; and above [the place] there stood a column of light; and there they built the sanctuary; and behold it is there to this day.

A little further on the book mentions: 'Again, there is a miraculous mark where the foot of Our Lord stood; there is outlined in the rock to this day the shape of His sandals'. It is tempting to wonder if this second mention might not be associated with the Aksumite stone statue-base marked with the imprint of huge feet (92 cm. long) found by the DAE in a ruin mound in the western part of the Kuduku suburb, and drawn and photographed for their report (figs 81–2). Underneath it was the socle on which it stood. The DAE report suggests that with feet of this size, the statue could have been some 5 m. tall. The knowledge that this stone existed might have amplified and confirmed the legend of Mekyada Egzi'.

The Ge'ez legend about the foundation of Maryam Seyon cathedral may draw on some ancient memories of a time when the Mai Hejja overflowed. However, archaeological evidence indicates that in Aksumite times there was already a long history of building in the area of the present church. Far below the battlemented terrace on which the seventeenth-century church now stands, at its eastern end in the graveyard below, the terrace rests on a very substantial Aksumite basement or podium. All the characteristics are visible: the squared corner-blocks, the shelving topped with flat stones, the re-entrants and salients, as well as an unusual feature, a complete row of cut stones, paralleled only – to my knowledge – at the Dungur mansion and the Kaleb and Gabra Masqal tomb superstructure. More, the 1958 excavations just north of the present terrace (de Contenson 1963) revealed several levels of building. A substantial structure built on virgin soil, on a different orientation from the church of today, associated with coins of pagan Aksumite kings including Ezana himself, ran approximately along the line of the northern wall of the later oval inner enclosure. Conceivably this was a temple – although the only reason for suggesting this is that a church was later constructed on the site, and religious sites often have a long history. Over this was later built another monument, oriented like the church of today, of which the southern wall disappears under the northern part of the terrace wall. There was also, north of this building, part of a large enclosure on more or less the same orientation as the pagan structure, with rooms and courts similar to the outer wings of most typical Aksumite mansion/palace structures. These later buildings, both associated with Christian period coins, may represent a sacred enclosure and some structure annexed to the original church, which presumably lies – perhaps several levels – below the present one; unless, of course, this oriented central building was the original church of Ezana itself, and the present podium dates only from a rebuilding of, say, King Kaleb's time. Perhaps – in the absence of permission to conduct excavations at Maryam Seyon itself, which seems highly improbable – if ever the account of the excavations of the Dungur mansion are fully published, and a date for the edifice settled, the similarities of architecture, particularly the long row of cut blocks, with the Maryam Seyon church podium may provide a clue as to the date of the latter. The BIEA excavations at the Kaleb and Gabra Masqal tombs certainly suggest that this feature was a sixth-century practice.

As noted above, it is possible that the Ge'ez legend recalls a time when the sacred area was subject to floods. Not only were Aksumite buildings in general constructed on elevated podia, but excavations indicate that attention was paid in the earlier buildings around the present cathedral terrace to the provision of drainage systems under the courts.

If the original church at Aksum was built by King Ezana, he – or some ecclesiastic at his court, perhaps even Frumentius, his bishop – might have had in mind the example of such churches as the 'five-aisled' basilicas of the Holy Sepulchre in Jerusalem or the Nativity church in Bethlehem, both begun in 327. ('Five-aisled' indicates buildings with a nave and flanking double aisles all of the same width.) Marilyn Heldman (1995, and in Grierson 1993), however, asserts that some the Aksum churches were 'quotations' – architecturally or by their dedications – of famous Jerusalem sites, associating Maryam Seyon cathedral with the sixth-century Church of the Apostles on Mount Sion. One day, perhaps, an archaeological investigation on the platform of the church might establish whether the five-aisled church there – which we know of only from c. 1520 – really dated originally from Ezana's time, from Kaleb's reign some two centuries later, or even from some other unrecorded reconstruction. It may be that, if Ezana did indeed create the first five-aisled church on the site, the dedication to Mary of Zion dates only from Kaleb's time. Or it may be that this dedication, which is not mentioned in any Aksumite document – indeed it is not mentioned in its complete form until the time of Zara Yaqob, and then only in a later copy of a text – is a much more recent attribution. (The dedication to Mary of Zion and other aspects are discussed at length in a book now awaiting publication as a sequel to Grierson and Munro-Hay, *The Ark of the Covenant*.)

In the *Gadla Libanos*, the life story of St Libanos, there is a brief statement that in the twenty-fourth year of King Dawit I (1406) the cathedral at Aksum was restored by royal command. The *Iter de Venetiis ad Indiam*, an account of a journey from Venice to India (as so often, meaning Ethiopia) written at the end of the fourteenth century and now in Florence, mentions that in

'Chaxum' the kings subject to Prester John were crowned. The basilica was said to be the most beautiful in the world, very richly ornamented with gold. While it is easy to suppose that everything far away, and in the mysterious East, was for Europeans of the time viewed through a gilded haze of misinformation, we have in the Arabic record called *Futuh al-Habasha* confirmation of the accounts of the sacking of numerous churches in Ethiopia in the 1530s, and confirmation that very rich ornamentation was indeed found in them, not excluding gold plating, or at least covering with gold leaf. It is true that Aksum's church was not specifically included among the descriptions of the spoiling of these splendidly furnished treasure houses, the document unfortunately being deficient at that point. But another document preserved in the *Book of Aksum* details the precious objects from the church that Emperor Lebna Dengel consigned to the chiefs of Temben, Sahart, Salawa, Agame, Abargale, to the *ba'ala gada* Amde, and to Robel, governor of Tigray, presumably for their concealment and protection from Grañ's soldiers. One thousand, seven hundred and five objects of gold are listed.

The *Book of Aksum* describes 'the state of the constitution of Our Mother Seyon the cathedral of Aksum' in technical terms which give little idea of its general appearance. Included are depth of foundations, thickness of walls, height of the vaults, number of columns, shutters, 'wheels' (= round-headed windows?), arches, monkey-heads and gargoyles. Of the latter two there were 3,815 and 91 respectively. This piece of information at least permits us to suppose that the church – or the perhaps considerably altered version of the original church still extant in the fifteenth or early sixteenth century – must have looked rather like the churches of Debra Damo, northeast of Aksum, or Debra Salam near Asbi, Tigray, which is built in a cave. These are two famous and still extant examples of the classic monkey-head style of building seen also on the Aksumite stelae.

Only from Francisco Alvares do we get something of an idea of the great church of Aksum in its sixteenth-century glory – although his description is in some places hard to follow.

> This church is very large; it has five aisles of good width and great length, vaulted above, and all the vaults closed, the ceiling and sides all painted. Below, the body of the church is well worked with handsome cut stone; it has seven chapels, all with their backs to the east, and their altars well ornamented. It has a choir after our fashion, except that it is low, and they reach the vaulted roof with their heads; and the choir is also over the vault, and they do not use it. This church has a very large circuit, paved with flagstones like the lids of tombs. This consists of a very high wall, and it is not covered over like those of the other churches but is left open. This church has a large enclosure and it is also

surrounded by another larger enclosure, like the enclosing wall of a large town or city. Within this enclosure are handsome groups of one storey buildings and all spout out their water by strong figures of lions and dogs of stone. Inside this large enclosure are two mansions, one on the right hand side and the other on the left, which belong to two rectors of the church; and the other houses are of canons and monks.

After this, Alvares describes the 'House of Lions' and the votive thrones in the large enclosure (see below).

The DAE report illustrates a possible restoration of the ground plan of this church, fitting it over the still existing basement walls at the east end. It would have been more than twice as wide as the present church, and much longer as well. However, only excavation can give a genuine idea of the old church. This great building was destroyed in 1535, when Ahmad Grañ – according to the abbreviated chronicles – came 'and burned Aksum, Halelo, Bankol and Lagaso'. Rohlfs, von Heuglin and Huntingford all dated Grañ's attack to 1535, as do the chronicles. Salt, doubtless drawing his information from the priests at Aksum, and Sapeto, preferred 1526, and Monneret de Villard opted for 1541(?).

Emperor Sarsa Dengel (1563–97) rebuilt the church, perhaps just before he came to be crowned at Aksum in 1579. In 1604–05 F. Guerreiro described this new church as having three naves, that is, a nave and two aisles, and a thatched roof. We do not know how much of the internal arrangements of the older church, inner walls, pillars and so on, still standing like the outer walls (see below), might have been incorporated in Sarsa Dengel's smaller church, but it is reasonable to suppose that some did survive the burning. In 1608, on 18 March, Emperor Susneyos was crowned in Aksum, entering the church to hear Mass. The Oromo or Galla invasion of 1611 seems to have resulted in this replacement church being burned – it is recorded in an annual letter reporting on events in the province of Goa for 1612 that in Acçumu the church was set on fire by the Galla and 'voracious flames consumed it'.

Yet the remains of the ancient larger church were still there years later, when Manoel de Almeida was at Aksum at some time between 1624 and 1633. He saw 'a church of stone and mud, thatched ... built among the ruins and walls of another, ancient, one, the walls of which are still visible ... but very wide apart'; the ruins of the former much larger cathedral. The stone and mud mortared church was the one built or reconstructed by Malak Sagad (Sarsa Dengel), as de Almeida himself noted; he added that it 'exceeds in size all the others in Ethiopia ... and in memory of the ancient one is held in such veneration that the same emperor came here to be crowned'. Apparently the church that Manoel de Almeida saw was no more than a restoration of Sarsa

Dengel's church, of which the walls would have been left standing after the Galla raid; a ruin within a ruin. Thomas Barneto in a letter of 1627 recorded that the church in the ruins was built by 'Mala Seguet' (Malak Sagad), and Emmanuel Barradas, who was in Ethiopia at the same time as de Almeida (between 1624 and 1633), also visited this church, noting its square wooden columns and thatched roof. This presumably indicates that in Sarsa Dengel's building he saw none of the massive stone columns used in the construction of the present church. There may be other parts of the old church preserved in the sanctuary area, and thus invisible to modern visitors.

Barradas provided a description of the church as it was when he was in Aksum. He gave special attention to this church of 'Acçum' because it was 'the principal one, not only in this kingdom of Tygrê but in all of Ethiopia, both for its antiquity and for being the one to which the kings are accustomed to go to receive the imperial crown, and where those of old held their royal seat' (Barradas 1996: 118). Barradas adds that 'even though many have written of it and its greatness ... something new can always be found to say that others may have missed or ignored or not deemed worthy of mention'. According to Barradas:

> The supports of the old church, or to be more exact, part of the walls, which today seem to be reasonably high off the ground, well prove it to have been a very large structure when the Moor Gran destroyed it. The part used today was built within the ruins of the first and because the walls are rather distant from the other partly collapsed ones it is sufficiently large and usable. The outside walls are of black stone, the stone work is very fine and well fitted together. The columns are of square blocks of wood, the framework is in like manner, but the church roof is entirely covered with straw. Over the threshold of the main door is a not very large landing cut from black stone from which some steps of the same material lead downstairs. One of the steps has a small round cavity into which is thrown the hair that is cut from the Emperor upon his coronation. It would be large enough to bury him in, although not very decently, if it were covered, however it is always left uncovered and open to view. Walking down the stairs to the ground floor and a short distance beyond to where rises a high, square wall which can be seen surrounds the entire church and acts as its enclosure. (Barradas 1996: 123)

A description of the church – apparently the ruined older one – is provided by Le Grand in his Second Dissertation, 1728, with a marginal note referring to MS Alf. Mendes, Ch. 6, thus presumably dating the description to before 1634. He describes

> Les restes d'un temple magnifique, qui se sont conservés contre le tems. Il

pouvait avoir deux cens-vingt palmes de longueur sur cent de largeur; il y avoit deux aîles de chaque côté & un double vestibule; on y montoit par douze degrés. Le Roy d'Ethiopie s'arrête dans le vestibule intérieur & s'y assied sur un trône de pierre, lorsqu'il est couronné dans cette Eglise.

In 1655 (*Book of Aksum*) or 1657 (Salt), the present church was built, or at least partially reconstructed. Al-Haymi, Yemeni ambassador to the court of Emperor Fasiladas in 1648, admired the castle then being built at Gondar by an Indian (see above), and certainly Aksum Zion cathedral is of the same genre as the battlemented and towered castle of Fasiladas. The emperor is said to have given 'an incalculable quantity of money' to make the church 'marvellous and magnificent'. The automatic attribution by earlier writers to the Portuguese is no longer current, although certainly their influence had some impact on styles and techniques both in Aksum and at Gondar and other places. According to Mathew, Péro Pais 'in his early years in Ethiopia … constructed at Aksum the palace on one floor made of worked stone and cedar wood' (although I have found no other mention of this Aksum palace elsewhere, either in the Portuguese reports, or the chronicles). The Portuguese were represented by a viceroy at Goa in India, and most of those who came to Ethiopia came via India, so mixtures of styles, techniques and nationalities of artisans might be expected. Whoever the masons or architects were, the church of Fasiladas' time may have retained a good part of its walls from the three-aisled church of Sarsa Dengel, which in turn may have preserved, particularly at the eastern or sanctuary end, some elements from the internal walls and fixtures of the more ancient church destroyed by Grañ. We know only that it did not embrace the outer walls of the older church, the quality of whose stonework Barradas so admired. These, after a long time standing ruined, were demolished, one supposes, for building material when Fasiladas' restoration was in progress.

In 1678, during the rebellion of Fares, governor of Salawa, the rebels behaved scandalously, 'breaking the links of Christianity, to burn Aksum, the city of Zion', but perhaps the church escaped with little damage. At any rate, it served for the coronation of Iyasu I in the 1690s. Emperor Iyasu II in 1749–50 ordered more restoration to the church, and presented many gifts, after visits to Aksum in those years, and there seems little doubt that the appearance of the structure as we see it now is largely the result of the joint work of Fasiladas and Iyasu II. There have been a few restorations, alterations to the portico and roof, and other additions of minor importance since then, but by and large the church remains as it was.

The cathedral was both praised and denigrated by later visitors, suffering its worst insult from Bruce's description: 'a small, mean building, very ill kept and full of pigeons' dung'. As we have seen, Poncet, surprisingly for a man whose own king was the builder of Versailles, was most complimentary about it, calling it 'magnificent' and 'the most beautiful and the largest that I saw in Ethiopia'.

Salt on his 1805 visit was a little indignant with Bruce, whom he said had 'most unjustly depreciated it, since … compared with all others in Tigré it has no rival (except Chelicut) with respect to size, richness, nor sanctity'. Combes and Tamisier, however, after their 1835 visit were to describe it as 'la plus remarquable de l'Abyssinie, quoiqu'elle soit même inférieure à … nos greniers ordinaires'. They felt that Salt's description was exaggerated. Bruce's judgement appeared to them more exact. A plan and a view of the façade of the cathedral of Maryam Seyon are provided on Plate 1 of the *Atlas* volume of the Lefebvre expedition, in Aksum in 1841. The plan is incorrect, as it indicates a staircase tower halfway along the south side, and a sanctuary protruding far out from the centre of the east end. The elevation shows the façade as an open porch of three bays with flat architraves, but horseshoe-shaped arches are indicated in the two flanking bays.

Today the church of Maryam Seyon and its compound are rather attractive, generally well kept and shaded with many trees. The church is far from magnificent, and indeed is rather scruffy, but it retains a certain aura, compounded of its sanctity for a large part of the local population, and its prominent position on its terrace. The new cathedral with its huge dome and whitish concrete does rather detract from the old stones of the earlier structures, and there are more new works being undertaken, but the atmosphere of the place has not been completely lost.

In the treasury are kept a number of objects used by the church for processions and other ceremonial occasions. These include drums with silver casings and gilding, parasols elaborately decorated with silver appliqué ornaments and tassels, brocaded and embroidered robes, some splendid hand or processional crosses, and a collection of massive crowns presented by various Ethiopian emperors when they have visited the church. The treasury, or *aqabet*, of the church is also the guardian of its greatest glory; the 'Ark of the Covenant'.

The 'Ark of the Covenant'

One of Christian Ethiopia's most dramatic and mysterious claims relates to possession of the Ark of the Covenant, constructed by Moses at God's command, and later installed in the Temple of Solomon at Jerusalem. Now it is said to be guarded by the monk who is the treasurer of the church in a special chapel beside Aksum Seyon church. Such a tremendous claim, incubated in the remote isolated world of Ethiopian Christianity, has aroused relatively modest interest until recently. Perhaps not surprisingly, none of the earlier scholars of Ethiopian history took the trouble to investigate this odd tale very closely; on the face of it, the documentation on which it is based seems a farrago of nonsense. But now, with the vast widening of boundaries permitted by modern communications, and the attentions of modern journalists, it has become a major theme of discussion in a wider Christian and Jewish world. For a recent study dealing with certain aspects of the story of the Ark, written as a response to some of the more extreme recent theories about Templar and Masonic conspiracies and the like concerning the Ark in Ethiopia, see Grierson and Munro-Hay 1999; a second volume concerning the story of the Ark, the history of the mysterious *tabotat* of Ethiopia, and the history of the church of Maryam Seyon, is awaiting publication.

The Ethiopian legends preserved in the book called *Kebra Nagast*, 'Glory of the Kings', relate the story of the meeting of King Solomon of Israel and the Queen of Sheba (who is an Ethiopian queen called Makeda in this version). Returning to Ethiopia, the queen bore a son, Ebna Hakim, from their union. Ebna Hakim means 'Son of the Wise Man' – i.e. of Solomon; he is also called David or, in other later versions of the legend, Menelik. In due course, as a young man, Ebna Hakim went to visit his father in Jerusalem. Solomon eventually appointed him king of Ethiopia and sent him home. He and his companions, the eldest sons of the high priest and other notables of Israel, took with them the Ark of the Covenant, which they removed by stealth from the temple, fleeing with it by night from Jerusalem.

The Ark eventually reached Aksum. There are various stories about its previous resting places, or places to which it was withdrawn in time of danger, including Tana Cherqos island in Lake Tana, an island in Lake Zway, Digsa in Bur northeast of Adwa, and Yeha. The *Kebra Nagast* records only that King David (i.e. Ebna Hakim), son of Solomon, brought it to his mother Makeda's capital, Debra Makeda, the 'Mountain of Makeda', installing the sacred object under guard in the fortress. Abu Salih the Armenian, in his *Churches and Monasteries of Egypt* written in the early thirteenth century, mentions that the 'Ark of the Covenant' was then in Ethiopia, and that it was carried in procession to the royal palace at the capital, which at the time, in Lalibela's reign, is known to have been Adefa/Roha, the city later called Lalibela after the king himself. It contained 'the two tables of stone, inscribed by the finger of God with the commandments which he ordained for the children of Israel'.

Abu Salih even described the Ark:

The Ark of the Covenant is placed upon the altar, but is not so wide as the altar; it is as high as the knee of a man, and is overlaid with gold; and upon its lid there are crosses of gold; and there are five precious stones upon it, one at each of the four corners, and one in the middle. The liturgy is celebrated upon the Ark four times in the year, within the palace of the king; and a canopy is spread over it when it is taken out from [its own] church to the church which is in the palace of the king.

This is clearly a Christian object, not much reminiscent of the Ark of Moses. The way it is carried to the royal palace sounds exactly like the sort of processions still seen regularly at church festivals in Ethiopia today, when the *tabot* or altar tablet, veiled, is carried out from a church. (The Ark is called *tabot* in Ethiopic, a word which, although it means an ark or box, is used also for the stone or wood *tabotat* or altar tablets. The word for tablet is actually *sellat*, as in *sellata hegg*, 'tablet of the law', given by God to Moses at Mount Sinai.) Does Abu Salih's comment about the Ark's journey to the church in the royal palace indicate that the relic – whatever precisely this was – was lodged at Adefa or Roha during the Zagwé period? It would certainly seem likely that a king who left a reputation as pious as that of Lalibela would wish to have such a relic, if it were in his country, kept close by in his own capital.

Ethiopian tradition asserts that the Ark has long reposed at Aksum. Once it was kept in the Holy of Holies of the church of Mary of Zion, but now it apparently rests in the domed *enda sellat* just to the south above the new treasury. It is uncertain when first the cathedral of Maryam Seyon at Aksum came to be regarded as housing the Ark, but reliable evidence is entirely lacking from early times. No documentation from pre-Aksumite or Aksumite times confirms the story of the *Kebra Nagast*. No document except the ambiguous record of Abu Salih mentions the Ark in Ethiopia, although the tablets of Moses do enter Ethiopian mythology rather earlier. The *Book of Aksum*, the earliest surviving copy of which is seventeenth century, but which apparently describes the pre-Grañ church, does not specifically mention the Ark. However, the cathedral is referred to as 'Our Mother Seyon the Cathedral of Aksum', and land grants of Sayfa Arad and Zara Yaqob also include this dedication (not to mention others purporting to date from the time of the legendary monarchs Abreha and Asbeha, Gabra Masqal and Anbasa Wudem, although these refer simply to *gabaza Aksum*, the cathedral of Aksum, and only the last employs the name Seyon). For the appearance of the Ark itself in Ethiopia, we have to wait until the much later; and that is in a Jesuit report and a Christian Arab document, not in an Ethiopian source. Detailed study of all this documentation, and of its significance, is to be published in the sequel to *The Ark of the Covenant* noted above.

Alvares merely noted of the church that

it is named St Mary of Syon … because its altar stone came from Sion. In this country (as they say) they have the custom always to name the churches by the altar stone, because on it is written the name of the patron saint. This stone which they have in this church, they say that the Apostles sent it from Mount Sion.

There is no mention of the Ark.

Arab-Faqih, author of the contemporary *History of the Conquest of Abyssinia*, noted that Imam Ahmad (Grañ)

returned to march against the town of Aksum, which is said to be an ancient town … [The king of Abyssinia] brought forth the great idol from the church of Aksum; this was a white stone encrusted with gold, so large that it could not go out of the door; a hole had to be pierced in the church because of its size; they took it away and it was carried by four hundred men in the fortress of the country of Shire called Tabr, where it was left.

Whatever this object was – presumably the 'Ark' or *tabot* of the church (the same as that recorded by Alvares a few years earlier?) – it does not seem to have been the wooden box-like object one would expect for the Ark of the Covenant.

In a Jesuit annual letter from Ethiopia for March 1626–27, Manoel de Almeida records a claim that for the first time since Abu Salih mentions the Ark itself. He states that instead of a consecrated stone

they have a casket that they call Tabot of Sion, that is to say Ark of the Covenant brought from Mount Sion; and they are so devoted to this that all the altar stones they call Tabot. And in the principal churches the altars were as all the churches had in ancient times, made in the form of boxes.

He then tells a strange tale, claiming that the emperor (then Susneyos) and others affirmed that inside the *tabot* was enclosed a 'pagoda, or an Idol, which had the figure of a woman with very big breasts'. Manoel de Almeida asserts that the emperor, at the time of his coronation at this church, was insistent that he be allowed to look inside; but the '*dabtaras*' did not permit it. Later, some zealous priests, 'obstinate in their errors', seeing that the Catholic faith was gaining ground, took the *tabot* and other precious things and fled, hiding them until the persecutions passed. The Catholics meanwhile removed the *manbara tabot*, the tabernacle, which they sent to the Jesuit centre at Maigoga (Mai Gwa-gwa) or Fremona (near Adwa) so that it might not be replaced, and installed an altar to their own specifications. During this period alone, women were permitted to worship in the church of Maryam Seyon as in all other Catholic churches. Manoel Barradas recorded that the *tabot* or Ark was taken to Bur to conceal it from the Catholics, and he heard that it had been restored at Fasiladas' orders just as they were leaving in 1633 (Barradas 1634: 122).

Balthazar Tellez enlarged a little on this, writing long after the Catholics had been driven from Ethiopia. He declares that the Abyssinians

> thought they added much Reputation to their Church of Auxum or Aczum, by saying their Chest or Tabot, was the very Ark of the Old Testament that was in Solomon's Temple, and that God brought it so miraculously to Ethiopia ... The Abyssines to gain more respect to this little Chest of theirs, always kept it so close and conceal'd, that they would not show it even to their Emperors. They call it by way of excellency Sion, or Seon, as they pronounce it, and for the same Reason the Church, where they kept this to them so precious a Relick, being dedicated to the Virgin May, had the name S. Mary of Seon. Not many years since, perceiving that the Catholick Faith began to spread abroad, and fearing lest this litle Chest of theirs should be taken away, or disregarded, the most Zealous of their Monks remov'd it thence, and very privately convey'd it to the Territory of Bur, near the Red Sea, where they hid it among close Thickets and vast high Mountains, in order at a convenient Time to restore it to its ancient Place, in the Church of Auxum or Aczum, where in all likelyhood it now is, since their Revolt. (quoted from the 1710 English edition)

The *Book of Aksum* confirms that the Ark went to Bur during this period of persecution.

It seems that one emperor, quite exceptionally, was able to view the Ark or the tablets kept at Aksum. When Iyasu I came to Aksum in 1690/91, according to his chronicle, he rode on horseback up to the principal door, the door of the Ark of Zion. The king entered the sanctuary of the Ark of Zion, kissed it, and seated himself on the throne. Later he received communion in the *qeddesta qeddusan*, the Holy of Holies, and gave a banquet to the clergy. The next day the king entered the *beta maqdas* and ordered the priests to bring the Ark of Zion to show to him. The *tabot* of Seyon was deposited in a coffer with seven locks, each having its own key. The keys were brought, and six of the locks were opened, but they could not open the seventh. Brought, still locked, to the king, it opened of itself. The king then saw the Ark, and addressed it 'face to face like Esdras'. The Ark responded, giving him advice and counsel about his rule. The chronicler's tale is not quite as simple as it seems; it has been interwoven, in flattery to the emperor, with the account in Revelation of the opening of the seventh seal.

Iyasu in 1687 had already been generous to the cathedral, according to a land charter (Huntingford 1965: 63):

> with the help of our Lady Mary of Seyon the Mother of God ... in the seventy-

second year after the previous kings [Susneyos, in 1615] abrogated [the laws], we restored to our Mother Seyon the Cathedral of Aksum all her laws and ordinances, and all her charter lands, and the administration of her possessions by the nebura'ed.

On this occasion too Iyasu, at the principal door of the church, with the drums beating, confirmed all the fiefs. In 1693 Iyasu returned. This time, the chronicle records that he entered the 'chamber of the Ark' with Sinoda the metropolitan bishop, the *Echege* Yohannes and the dignitaries, all on horseback; probably in this account the 'chamber' actually means the enclosure of the church.

James Bruce was very dismissive of the 'fabulous legends' about the Ark, although he did add that 'some ancient copy of the Old Testament, I do believe, was deposited here, probably that from which the first version was made'. He claimed that when he was in Ethiopia King Tekla Haymanot II told him concerning the Ark that 'whatever this might be it was destroyed, with the church itself, by Mahomet Gragn, though pretended falsely to subsist there still'. The king may perhaps have told him some such thing, but it seems unlikely to have been true. Arab-Faqih would surely not have missed recording so enormous a blow at the Christians' morale as the destruction of their most revered 'idol', if it had in fact not escaped the invaders, as he himself recorded.

Combes and Tamisier described a richly decorated chapel dedicated to Sellaté Moussé in the church compound. Lejean in 1863 identified Maryam Seyon church itself by the name Sellata Mousi. As Monneret de Villard noted, this must stand for '*Sellata Muse*', the tablet of Moses, and is a further reference to the sacred object kept in the cathedral enclave. Combes and Tamisier, however, wrote that 'this (female) saint for whom the Abyssinians have great veneration, was of the line of Solomon'! They perhaps saw the little church of Zion, north of the cathedral, in which the DAE heard the 'Ark' was kept. Local people today still refer to the object kept in the new chapel where the Ark is supposed to be as *sellata Muse*.

Only two people actually claim to have seen the Ark, or rather the tablet of the law contained in it; Yohannes T'ovmacean and R. P. Dimotheos. T'ovmacean saw the relic in 1764, when he went to look at the church in 'Saba'.

There was also a large and ancient Abyssinian church where they said a piece of the stone tablet of the Ten Commandments carried by Moses had been preserved, and they took T'ovmacean and Bijo (his companion) into the church, and showed him a closed altar said to contain this tablet of the Ten Commandments, but they refrained from opening it. However, on the insistence of

Bijo, who claimed that he was a relative of the King, they very hesitatingly obliged. They took out a parcel wrapped in cloth, and began ceremoniously to unwrap it. There was a packet wrapped in another parcel of velvet, and it was not until they had removed a hundred such wrappings that they at last took out a piece of stone with a few incomplete letters on it, and, kneeling, they made the sign of the Cross, and kissed the stone, after which the object was again wrapped up, and put back into the altar which was then closed. This was a great relic – if it was indeed a piece of the tablet of the Ten Commandments which God gave to Moses.

As far as Dimotheos was concerned, as one of the party accompanying the legate from the Armenian patriarch to Emperor Tewodros, the priests must have felt that they had to satisfy him. He writes that in 1869 he was taken by the priests to see the Ark:

When we arrived at the church everyone went into the vestibule, and we alone were taken by several of the clergy into the sacristy, built outside the church to the left, at the end of a row of other rooms. Inside this sacristy on the ground floor, was a sort of wooden attic, which one went up to by a movable ladder. One of the priest who accompanied us went up, and having entered, took up two planks of the ceiling to give room for two other priests who followed him there; then a deacon with a censer in his hand approached a coffer, which he censed, and presented us the censer to do the same. The coffer was a casket of Indian work; when it was opened we saw revealed the Tablet of the ten commandments. We removed it to look at it more closely. The stone was a pinkish marble of the type one ordinarily finds in Egypt. It was quadrangular, 24 cm long by 22 wide, and only 3 cm thick. On the edges it was surrounded by engraved flowers about half an inch wide; in the centre was a second quadrangular line in the form of a fine chain of which the interior space was empty, while the space between the two frames contained the ten commandments, five on one side, five on the other, written obliquely in Turkish fashion; at the base of the tablet, between the two frames, were three letters.

He then notes the letters, one a figure non-existent in the Abyssinian alphabet (elsewhere he mentions that the text was in 'Abyssinian' language) indicating 'ten', and the other two representing the sounds '*tsa*' and the unvoiced French 'e'. Although these do not indicate numbers, he thought that nevertheless a date was meant, but no one could explain it. On the other side the tablet was ornamented with more flowers, but of different workmanship. Dimotheos added: 'this stone was near entirely intact, and showed no sign of age; at the most it might go back to the thirteenth or fourteenth century of the common era'. It seems likely that – like T'ovmacean? – he was shown a *tabot*, or altar tablet, of a more than usually elaborate kind; one in the British Museum collection (kept at present in the Orsman Road store, no. 1868-10-1-21) is fairly elaborate and has a similar decorative arrangement, with a considerable amount of writing on it.

In 1881, Gerhard Rohlfs questioned the *nebura'ed* of Aksum about the Ark, and whether it had been left undamaged by the Muslims when the church was burned. He was assured that it was still in the church. It was not an ordinary copy, as one could find in the Holy of Holies, but the original, built into the church wall and accessible only by means of a secret door. The clergy, emperor, *echege*, even the *abun* could not see it; they would not be able to bear the sight of it. Only the guardian and his successors were permitted to see it: 'So it was thousands of years ago,' added the nebura'ed, 'and so will it be until the last days.'

The Inner Enclosure

Around the terrace on which the church stands is an oval-shaped enclosure. On the east and south sides of the church terrace is a graveyard, reached from the southern side of the podium of the church by a staircase of fifteen steps. It is from here that the visible remains of the older Aksumite podium can be seen, on the south and eastern sides of the present podium. It is extremely impressive. On the south are the remains of one rebate in the walls, and a projecting corner, built in the typical Aksumite style with massive corner-blocks of granite holding together shelved walls of smaller stones. An exterior plaster survives here, but how old it is cannot be said; however, it may well be that the exterior walls of Aksumite buildings were plastered in such a way. A characteristic, rare in Aksumite structures, is the continuous row of stone blocks above the third shelf of the wall. This is also visible on the east end of the Aksumite podium, where it includes one very long stone. The east end consists of three projecting parts divided by two rebates in the wall, but these have now been blocked, and newer walling brings them out to the same level as the projecting parts. Fragments of the far (northeast) corner of the last projecting part can be seen on the other side of the wall east of the *enda sellat* and the treasury courtyard. The original Aksumite structure must have been sizeable and impressive, rising from this elegant base.

In the south wall of the later upper part of the podium are set five water-spouts, some with lion-heads, some broken; there are three to the west of the south staircase, two to the east. At the base of the southwest corner of the podium is another large Aksumite stone, probably not *in situ*. Two further sets of monumental steps descend to the west from the terrace to the en-closure. The upper steps are now flanked by two bell-towers, towers that were not there when Salt sketched the church, or at least were not included in his picture – as we have seen, he was perfectly willing to alter nature in the interests of art. However, the towers are not mentioned by any other description either, being first noted by Heuglin in 1861 – which did not prevent Leroy (1965) from citing them as a possible indication of Portuguese influence in the building of the cathedral. On top of the north retaining wall of the upper flight of steps are a number of ancient objects; an octagonal column base like the two in the Ezana Garden and the one fixed into the east exterior wall of the cathedral; a lion-headed water-spout; a stepped pedestal; a curious shaped stone, rather like a head-rest; another water-spout; and the 'Stone of Bazen' with the 'Stele of the Lances' fragment on top of it. At the top of the steps on a plinth in the centre was a large round stone (photographed by the DAE and illustrated in Vol. III, fig. 222). Monneret de Villard believed that this object might be the mysterious *berota eben* described in the *Book of Aksum*:

> Then there is the berota 'eben near the throne, the name of which is Jerusalem. It is completely round like a shield; in the centre it is red and round like a dish. And when a person makes a journey, they ask him 'Where is your country?' And they say to him, 'Do you know the *berota 'eben*?' And if he says, 'I do not know it,' they say to him, 'You are not an Aksumite.'

Since *'eben* means stone, this was apparently some sort of round stone object.

Bruce, of course, noticed the 'two magnificent flights of steps, several hundred feet long [in fact about 50 m. or 165 ft. at their longest], all of granite, exceedingly wellfashioned, and still in their places'. They were, he thought

> the only remains of a magnificent temple. In the angle of this platform where that temple stood, is the present small church of Axum, in the place of a former one destroyed by Mahomet Gragn, in the reign of David III [Lebna Dengel]: and which was probably the remains of a temple built by Ptolemy Euergetes, if not of a time more remote.

At the north end of these steps on the first terrace a particularly large stone, perhaps three metres by one and a half metres in size, is laid flat on the ground – one wonders if it might not bear an inscription on the other face. It lies at the base of some steps mounting eastwards to a small garden area directly in front of the *Sellata Muse* chapel. Mounted in the western terrace wall at this point above the long stairs are two stones bearing crosses, two water-spouts with lion-heads, and at the corner of the battlemented terrace section of the wall is part of a square stone column. There is also a weathered marble column and base or capital fragment. (One tends to forget, amid the omnipresent granite of Aksum, that the durable, massive style of monumental building work must once have been tempered by other softer materials, marble, wood and plaster, with perhaps considerable areas being plastered or painted as well.) On the first terrace are also two stones pierced with pairs of holes, which it is said were for inserting flagpoles at the time of the royal coronation; similarly one is told that another square hole was for the oil of myrrh used on those occasions. Flanking the base of the long lower steps are two stones placed erect, each pierced with a square hole. These appear to be corner pillar-supports from one of the row of stone thrones in Mannagasha Court, but according to local report were for the royal shoes when the king removed them to ascend to the church.

In the small garden in front of the Chapel of the Tablet of Moses there is a sizeable fragment broken from one of the decorated stele (no. 4, in addition to the Stele of the Lances fragment, and the apex in the Ezana Garden). There is also an erect chamfered column with a capital (or rather a rectangular stone on top) standing in the centre, and, lying about in the grass, two column drums with capitals or bases attached, and two doorway fragments of the type found *in situ* by Chittick in a double doorway at Enda Sem'on palace. There is also a lion-headed water-spout emerging from the north terrace wall of the cathedral podium, and by the entrance to the podium nearest to the chapel of the Tablet of Moses, another granite pillar fragment. Stairs from this garden lead down towards the old excavations and the treasury grille, past a palmetto capital in limestone. An exit towards the new cathedral through a gate passing between the excavations and the pool by the bell-tower leads past an inverted chamfered column shaft with a double palmetto capital.

By the south wall of the cathedral podium, next to the inner fenced area around the chapel of the Tablet of Moses, are four large Aksumite granite blocks, while inside the fence beside the façade of the chapel are several marble capital or base fragments, and marble slabs, one carved with a cross. Against the east wall of the podium terrace are many other objects: a chamfered column shaft fragment, then in the bay formed by the eastward extension of the terrace, two granite blocks, a 'throne' formed by two chamfered column shafts and a granite throne-base (?), a round granite drum, a square chamfered fragment, a block with an attractive carved motif similar to the palmetto designs found elsewhere, and two more granite blocks.

From the base of the wide western flight of stairs, a broad paved path or court, flanked by various ancient stones, leads westwards to a staircase mounting towards an inner gateway protected by a gatehouse. Conspicuous among the stones in this staircase is a massive Aksumite granite slab pierced with two square holes. To the left among the trees lies a granite fragment with two oblong protrusions, resembling the stones found in a double doorway in the palace ruins called Enda Sem'on in 1974 (see Munro–Hay 1989). From the gatehouse, leading up to the outer enclosure to the west, are seven steps, the top one consisting of a very large Aksumite granite stone. Inside the two-storey gatehouse are two cannon. A fire is burned here nightly, and its ashes are said to have curative powers; they can be used to mark the sign of the cross on the forehead, or can be mixed with water as medicine. The signs of this fire are very apparent on the blackened ceiling beams and outside the doors, where the walls are marked with smoke. Outside the gatehouse, flanking the entrance, are two granite objects of Aksumite date, one possibly a pillar-support from one of the granite thrones in Mannagasha Court, the other a pillar-base of four steps.

Just inside this gate on the right when leaving the cathedral is a stone sunk into the ground; it is regarded as holy, and those entering the inner court often stop to kneel before it and kiss it. There are various tales about it. According to one, a slight depression visible on it is said to be from St Tekla Haymanot's foot, when he remained for many years praying, standing on one leg. A priest provided me with a different tale: it was the grave of Inberam – the pre-Christian High Priest of Aksum who assisted in the education of Frumentius at Aksum is supposed to have borne this name. Someone else gave it the name Enbarat, evidently a variant. Priests collect gifts for the church here at times of festival.

Beside the treasury (*eqa bet*) with the chapel of the Tablet of Moses (*enda sellat, sellata Muse*) is the still open excavation trench of 1958 with the exposed remains of the ancient structures that preceded the churches built on this spot. These are situated to the north of the present church and its battlemented terrace wall in the inner enclosure. A very large flat washing (?) slab, part of a doorway like those found in the Enda Sem'on palace, many corner-blocks, paving slabs, numerous rooms and other features are still distinguishable among the excavated features.

There were, at the time of the DAE visit in 1906, three small enclosures to the north of the church. These contained, to the east the church of Mary Magdalene, and in the centre the small treasury with the tomb of *echege* Theophilus southwest of it. To the west was a gatehouse, leading to the little church of Zion (built on a north–south axis, not oriented), with beyond it the battlemented treasury of Yohannes. Only the latter now remains. The little church of Zion, where the 'Ark' was kept, was identical with the chapel of the *sellata Muse* mentioned later by Doresse and others, now replaced, in a different position, by the *Itege* Menen's green-domed chapel. The so-called Treasury of Yohannes is locally said to be the burial place of a member of the family of Emperor Yohannes, possibly of *Ras* Mengesha Yohannes his son. Apparently it is currently used as a dwelling for monks, and a place for their induction into the monkhood. The candidate is washed with blessed water, and prayers are said over him by the priests. He is then covered with a new cloth, like one dead, since from this time on he is dead to the world. Finally he is given the hat (*qob*) of a monk.

The Outer Enclosure

Outside all this, another much larger enclosure delimits the whole of the large ecclesiastical compound. In the northern part of this Emperor Haile Sellassie constructed the new round church of Maryam Seyon in 1956, the arrangements unfortunately ignoring the enormous archaeological opportunity that was offered to look further into the history of this very important part of the town. An Aksumite granite column stands in the outer enclosure near the new campanile. It was upright but partly buried when the 1958 excavators cleared it. The French archaeologists discovered that it rested on layers containing relatively recent pottery, proving that it was no longer in its original place, so it was re-erected at modern ground level in the same spot.

The Votive Throne Pedestals

In the outer enclosure of the church compound, in the Mannagasha court opening by a gatehouse towards the public space called Da'ro 'Ela, stands a row of throne pedestals, with two further pedestals directly in front of them, and two others some 20 m. distant. These have been described almost as often as the church itself. The thrones in the court were numbered by the DAE; no. 2 is the 'Bishop's throne' next to no. 1, the so-called 'coronation throne'; the others are nos. 3–15. In other parts of the town are DAE nos. 16–18 at Gazash Moshan, 19–20 at Mehsab Dejazmach Wolde Gabriel, 21–25 by the Ezana inscription, and 26 in a quarry to the right of the road to Enda Kaleb. A small mound near the thrones in the church enclosure is called Gudif Maryam. This mound is associated by the *nebura'ed* with 'a legend of our ancestors'; it originated from the rubbish (*gudif*) transported from the church site after the cathedral was burned by Queen Gudit in the ninth century.

The pillared 'coronation throne' (DAE no. 1) seems always to have been recognised as such, but the others in a row, and similar pedestals elsewhere in the town, have sometimes been regarded as altars, offering stones and the like, destined for sacrifices. Raffray, for example, after seeing the line of thrones in the cathedral enclosure in 1874, wrote of 'autels ayant servi aux holocaustes'. Similarly, Rüppell, von Heuglin, Ferret and Galinier and others employ the terms 'Opferaltar', 'Opferstein', 'autel'. Rüppell interpreted the gullies on the stones as 'runnels serving for the collection of the blood'.

Other observers avoided the implied religious purpose, terming them more vaguely 'pedestals' (e.g. Salt). However, since Alvares' time, they have often been recognised as seats. Lefebvre, for example, employs the word *siège*; the *Atlas* volume illustrates, Pl. 4, the King's seat, and includes plans and elevations of others. Rohlfs after his 1881 mission rejected the word 'Opferstein' and suggested that by analogy to the so-called King's Seat, they must be seats for wooden or stone statues. He noted that if the runnels were really intended for blood, they would surely have been extended to allow the blood to flow off. Bent identified them with the pedestals for the metal statues set up by Ezana, and with the thrones set up in Sada (Shado). The DAE prepared an excellent report on these bases, with reconstructions based on the idea that the Aksumite inscriptions formed the back and sides of thrones, slotting into the 'runnels'. It was suggested that a sandstone decorative fragment found built into the front wall of the church was probably the top of the backrest of a throne. The size of the stone inscriptions known to date, with their trimmed bases, fits very well with the runnels cut in the thrones, and this basic reconstruction seems very likely to be correct.

In the outer court of the church, Alvares reported that

> at the gate nearest to the church, there is a large ruin, built in a square [which today is empty], which in other times was a house and has at each corner a big stone pillar, square and worked, very tall with various carvings. Letters can be seen cut in them but they are not understood ... This house is called Ambaçabet, which means house of lions.

Just possibly, this refers to the four-pillared 'King's Seat' in the same court, which is square and has corner pillars. They are not inscribed, nor is the structure very big, although it is prominent enough, and the 'Bishop's Seat' and another pillar beside it may have given a more sizeable impression. Ramusio's translation gives a slightly different description: 'next to the gate which is by the church, is a square field of earth, today empty, but which in other times was full of houses, in which in each corner is a pillar'. Interestingly, the 'House of Lions' at Gondar was identified by Bruce as a part of the royal apartments, where the coronation took place. Perhaps the connection lion/king might explain why the 'King's Seat', also a coronation place, was described to Alvares as the House of Lions. Perhaps, on the other hand, the House of Lions might refer to the place of accommodation of some sort of military grouping. In several copies of charters in the *Book of Aksum*, 'lions' and other persons are specifically excluded from entering certain church fiefs; this seems to refer to members of a corps of soldiers or guards, perhaps distinguished by wearing lion's manes, and not to real lions.

James Bruce had his own ideas about the thrones and pillars: 'Within the outer gate, below the steps, are three small square inclosures, all of granite, with small octagon pillars in the angles, apparently Egiptian; on the top of which formerly were small images of the dog-star, probably of metal.' He further identified, below the king's coronation stone, 'where he naturally places his feet ... a large oblong slab like a hearth, which is not of granite, but of free stone', bearing a damaged inscription. A little ingenuity established that it could 'safely be restored' as reading 'King Ptolemy Euergetes', in Greek. Bruce then added that 'Poncet has mistaken this last word for Basilius; but he did not pretend to be a scholar, and was ignorant of the history of this country.' Poncet nowhere mentions this. Bruce seems to have mistaken the source – or perhaps he simply could not bear to attribute anything at all useful to the Jesuits. It was Jerónimo Lobo who rendered Patriarch Mendez' reading of the word 'Basileus' from the Ezana inscription as 'Basilius' (see above). Bruce mentions the throne, foot-stone and inscription again in describing the career of King Susneyos 'the king ... sits down upon a stone, which, by its remains, apparently was an altar of Anubis, or the dog-star. At his feet there is a large slab of free-stone, on which is the inscription mentioned by Poncet.' The only inscription that could in any way fit Bruce's setting is the brief Ge'ez inscription (DAE 19) of David the Egyptian, found on the throne numbered 7 by the DAE.

Francisco Alvares described the row of thrones further west in the Mannagasha court, noting the 'very new-looking pedestals of masonry well worked', and how they were raised up by the roots of 'Pharaoh's Fig Tree', just as they are today by several of the tree's knobbly-trunked descendants. He also added:

> there are on top of these pedestals twelve stone chairs arranged in order, one after the other, as well made with stone as though they were of wood, with their seats and rests for the feet. They are not made out of a block, but each one from its own stone and separate piece. They say these belong to the twelve judges who at this time serve in the court of the Prester John.

The pedestals alone remain today; conceivably the upper parts were overthrown by the Muslims when the cathedral was burned? If only Alvares had been as addicted to sketching as were his British successors, much valuable evidence about the antiquities of Aksum might have been preserved.

Péro Pais, in a letter of 1612, related how the emperor and patriarch came in procession to take their seats on two stones, covered in silks under an alcove supported by four stone columns. He added that there were twelve others nearby, formerly with stone seats made as well as if of wood, as previous Portuguese (Alvares) who had seen them had said. Barradas and de Almeida also comment briefly on the thrones in the court, the latter writing of:

five or six big pedestals of black stone ... near at hand are four columns of the same stone 10 or 12 spans high. Among them is a seat on which the Emperors sit to be crowned after first having taken his seat on the pedestals I mentioned and after various ceremonies have been performed on them.

Barradas places them rather curiously:

nearby [the Ezana inscription] in the direction of the church, leaning against the foot of the hill on the right-hand side, are some stones which are perfectly square and must measure some four or five span, the thickness at the ends may be a span, but towards their middle the thickness inceases, as in the pedestals of our own columns. They are placed on top of other rough ones with the largest portion being on top. Ancient tradition asserts that these were the seats of the Umbares [from wambar, judge] when they judged.

Barradas seems to conflate the thrones by the rock wall near the Ezana inscription, and the so-called 'judges' seats' in the church compound, which he mentions separately later (Barradas 1996: 120-1). He refers, after describing the straw-roofed church, to a structure outside the door which was the main entrance to the church: 'a small niche-like area made of stone which is open to the air and ill maintained and which is where the Emperor is actually crowned. When the coronation takes place there it must be covered over, likewise always with straw.' He adds also that 'nearby are some large pagoda trees under which there are some stone seats, which must be those used by the important figures during the coronation ceremony' (Barradas 1996: 123–4).

Manoel de Almeida enlarges in his chapter on the coronation:

The first enclosure of the church is the one in which, as I said above, are some seats which were formerly, and still at the time when Father Francisco Alvarez came to this country, twelve very well made stone chairs, as he recounts in his book. Today there are no chairs, and the bases and pedestals on which they stood are not so many. The four columns that I mentioned above seem formerly to have supported a vault. In the centre of them they decorate two pedestals with rich cloths and handsome chairs and the ground at the foot is carpeted. The Emperor sits here on one of the two chairs, the Abuna on the other. At the sides twelve dignitaries, some ecclesiastical, some secular, take their places, six on the right and six on the left.

Almeida was mistaken about the pedestals, as the number has not decreased. Thomas Barneto in 1627 recorded that a large iron throne was placed on the stone base of the royal seat for the coronation rituals.

In Emperor Sarsa Dengel's chronicle, in due recognition of the royal descent, the coronation throne was called the 'Throne of David': 'Then were precious fabrics stretched on the throne of worked stone which the ancients had made; and on this throne was set the King. The throne is called Manbara Dawit, as the fathers had named it of old.' *Manbara Dawit* signifies the throne of David. Among the royal treasures recorded by Abu Salih the Armenian in the early thirteenth century was the throne of David, which, like the Ark of the Covenant, was covered with crosses of gold.

Salt (Valentia 1809, Vol. III) mentions that he was taken to see the king's seat and pillars: 'a small square inclosure surrounded by pillars; on a seat within which the ancient kings used to be crowned'. He provided a romanticised and restored, but very good, drawing of the king's seat, as well as including two single and one double example of the thrones among his illustrations. Salt continued: 'in the inclosure behind the king's seat other remains are scattered about in different directions, but on none of these, after a careful and repeated examination, was I able to perceive the least appearance of any inscription, excepting one, which is very short, in Ethiopic characters'. This was the inscription of David the Egyptian, which he reproduced as well as he could, arriving at the bizarre reading: 'The Aboona David removed and broke to pieces here; he thought within himself that the Lord was pleased that he should do so.' Salt, who considered that this inscription might have relevance to the toppling of the stelae, concluded that Bruce's claimed inscription of Ptolemy Euergetes by the throne was 'altogether fictitious'. Littmann also copied the Ge'ez inscription (throne no. 7 and inscription no. 19 in the DAE numeration). It actually reads: 'It is I, David the Egyptian, who has written this. God have mercy on me.' Oddly enough, another inscription, apparently from Enda Kaleb, exactly the same as this but without the name Dawit, was reported by Rohlfs in 1883; but this only became clear after some ingenious detective work (Gianfranco Fiaccadori 1981). After identifying Mount Am Nelicalos or Qonasel with Abba Liqanos and Debra Qwanasel, and Dachel ebn Negus with Enda Kaleb Negus, Fiaccadori then successfully interpreted a Ge'ez inscription that had been published upside down and backwards, printed in addition in Greek or typographic letters!

The *Book of Aksum* informs us that the thrones were situated at a place called 'Meftaya Hats': 'And again, there are at Meftaya Hats thrones of the Nine Saints; and three (other) thrones, one of King Kaleb, another of Gabra Masqal his son; and the third of Ker Iyefareh (Kir Yefareh); in all, twelve thrones.' I have not been able to identify the last name.

Today, as in 1906 when the DAE made their plans and sketches, there are fifteen throne pedestals in all. Ten pedestals are placed together in a row, the first and ninth with double seats, with an eleventh pedestal a little separated to the northeast – perhaps not counted in the *Book of Aksum* total; it consists only of the seat part, not even having a base block. Rüppell recorded eleven 'altars' here, von Heuglin '11 oder 12'. The six centre pedestals are more elaborate, with corner socles on the bases, clearly for inserting pillars to support some kind of canopy. Four, probably five, of these are still raised on platforms of well-cut stones forming one or two steps below them. In front of this row are two others. To the southeast, quite separate, standing some distance away, are the so-called King's and Bishop's thrones, the former surrounded by its four pillars, with two other pillars, one vestigial, nearer to the inner enclosure gateway. If one day archaeologists – and restorers – could be permitted to investigate these thrones and their surroundings, valuable evidence might be recovered in the vicinity. Fallen and buried inscriptions might very well lie here.

After describing the ceremonies of coronation, Manoel de Almeida notes that when the king's hair had been cut as for clergy at the first tonsure:

> the clergy take up the hairs, the deacons continue to sing at the altar stone with lighted candles and the clergy cense with the thuribles. After going once round the place where the royal chair is, as though in procession, they go towards a stone which stands at the door of the church of Sion, called Meidanita Negue-stat, i.e. protector of the Kings. They put the hairs on it and light them from the thuribles.

A stone called *meidanita negestat* or *memhesana nagast* is noted in the descriptions of the coronation appended to some copies of the *Kebra Nagast* and by Pais around 1620; the king used it in the early part of the coronation ritual.

A relatively modern 'throne' is the one on the east terrace of Maryam Seyon church, made from a large pillar-base apparently originally from Ta'akha Maryam palace, flanked with two chamfered columns. It was already in place when the DAE mission was in Aksum (1906). Possibly it is to be identified with the *meidanita negestat*; it is not, however, 'at the door' of the church. On the west side of the church at the top of the stairs is a large round stone with a pillar capital on top of it, forming another sort of throne. This stone was identified by Monneret de Villard with the *berota 'eben* (see above), but it is called today the *manbara Dawit*, the throne of David.

Church of Arbaat Ensesa

The church of the Four Animals, locally called Arbaat Tensa, also enclosed within the ecclesiastical district, was in 1906 a simple round church with a thatched roof and ostrich egg finial, apparently built by Emperor Iyasu I. It was rebuilt in 1962 as a rectangular structure, ornamented inside with some rather charming modern paintings. During building work, it was found that a number of burials, apparently post-Aksumite, had been made in the area. Under the *maqdas* of the old church were two tombs cut into the rock. Anfray remarked that they resembled the tombs at Yeha, an exciting possibility for pre-Aksumite discoveries, at that time lacking at Aksum itself – although Fattovich and Phillipson have recently found such evidence on top of Beta Giyorgis hill and in Aksum itself. Further investigations, unfortunately, were not possible owing to the sacred nature of the site.

Marilyn Heldman associates a church of the Virgins 'of the *dabtara*' at Aksum, mentioned in the *Book of Aksum*, with a convent near the Church of the Apostles in Jerusalem, just as she associates Maryam Seyon with the Church of the Apostles itself. The present representative at Aksum of the Church of the Virgins she suggests is the church of Arbaat Ensesa, called sometimes the women's church. However, the *Book of Aksum* actually mentions, 'of the *dabtara*', both a Beta Danagel *and* a Beta Arbaat Ensesa, as well as the church of Mary Magdalene (Beta Magdalawit). The church of Arbaat Ensesa was the place in the cathedral compound to which women could come and pray, as the main church was out of bounds to them – Arbaat Ensesa thus became, and still is, a place favoured for the baptism of babies. Perhaps formerly the little church of Mary Magdalene, which lay directly north of the cathedral, just outside the oval inner enclosure, when the DAE were in Aksum in 1906, was also a women's church, as the dedication might hint. Now, of course, the new round church of Maryam Seyon can be used by women. The church of Arbaat Ensesa may also be called Tekla Haymanot, as there is a *debal* with that dedication.

The modern church has a charming multi-storey gatehouse, with a painted baptistery next door to it surmounted by three elaborate metal crosses. The *beta lahm*, where the eucharistic bread is prepared, is to the northeast of the church compound. The terrace surrounding the church is set with several Aksumite cornerstones, column drums and the like, and the south steps, now neglected and overgrown, also contain Aksumite stones. By the northwest corner of the church one short chamfered column is very similar to the four that surround the King's Seat in the Mannagasha Court of the neighbouring cathedral; it shows traces of a coat of plaster. Two others, one with the capital broken, are also placed in front of the church, with a cross reminiscent of the type seen on fifth-century Aksumite coins. At the southeast and northeast corners are granite pillar shafts with palmetto capitals, apparently formerly sculpted on all four sides – these resemble a similar column shaft and capital in the Maryam Seyon enclosure beside the excavations there. Between these on the north side are a small stone cut with several shallow oblong steps, and a marble pillar with sunken oblong panels on the sides and a hole in the top, reminiscent of the columns found at Adulis by Paribeni, which had cone-shaped tops. There are also a small fragment of a round-topped granite stele, and two granite stones with two oblong protrusions, exactly paralleled by those found in a double doorway at the Aksumite mansion ruins called Enda Sem'on, and by one now lying in the inner enclosure of the cathedral. One of these is set into the terrace at ground level in the northwest corner, the other lies under a tree nearby. On the outer walls of the compound are set several Aksumite stones, including one palmetto capital in limestone.

Abba Liqanos

Outside Aksum to the east are two monastic sites dedicated to two of the Nine Saints. The first, the church of Abba Liqanos, is a pilgrimage place set on a hill reached by the path continuing on past Enda Kaleb. From this track there are delightful views of the Adwa mountains, of Abba Pantalewon church on its high hill a little further east, and of the pointed mountain of Damo Galila. From the church hill too the view in all directions is remarkable, as it is also from nearby Enda Kaleb further west. The church is built on a terrace on a rocky outcrop, attained by mounting a rocky stairway. Abba Liqanos of Qwestentenya (Constantinople) was one of the Nine Saints, but no *gadl* or life story of his survives. Little else is related about him except that he is said to have eventually established himself at a place called Debra Qwanasel, presumably the name of this outcrop. A partly battlemented wall surrounded it when the DAE planned the compound in 1906.

The church was an attractive pitched-roofed thatched building, rectangular in shape, with only two component parts, an outer corridor all round and a central sanctuary, on the walls of which were some interesting paintings. It was destroyed in Mengistu's time, 1986/87, when government soldiers bombarded it to dislodge adherents of the Liberation Front. On the terrace are some ancient stone objects, including a pillar socle, a baptismal font with bosses, and another squared stone with a round basin-like top.

The new church stands on a stepped granite base, part of the old church. Three old stone crosses can be seen in the west wall, one in the north, and some of the corner stones may be Aksumite in date.

Abba Pantalewon

The next hill east from Abba Liqanos is named after Abba Pantalewon. On a 40 m.-high cone of rock, visible from afar, stands the small church of Abba Pantalewon (Beta Bendalion on Schimper's map). He was one of the Nine Saints, who came to Ethiopia 'in the reign of Alameda son of Saladoba' probably in the late fifth century AD. At Beta Qatin (a place near Da'ro 'Ela in Aksum, where the Nine Saints installed themselves, legend reports, before going out into the country), the late fifteenth-century *Gadla Pantalewon* relates that the saint constructed a cell in which he remained standing upright for forty-five years, working miracles and healing the sick. He is therefore known as Abba Pantalewon of the Cell. King Kaleb of Aksum is supposed to have consulted him, and eventually, after his successful war with Himyar, to have abdicated his throne to become a monk under Pantalewon's guidance. King Kaleb is also supposed to have been buried at Enda Pantalewon.

Access to Beta Pantalewon is by several routes left from the main road after leaving Aksum. One leads up past the long gully called Mai Shintro (gully), where there is a large round well, Mai Mekan (the well of the barren woman) with deep stepped edges, supplying drinking water and watering for cattle. Another track passes across the fields and winds up through gentler slopes to the foot of the mountain. The church erected on the rock cone seems to have been built over a much more ancient structure, possibly even of pre-Aksumite date. Traces of this remain in the form of fragments of walls built with well-cut blocks of masonry of the type seen at Yeha. But the church has been recently restored, and is now an oblong topped with two finials. According to information from ecclesiastics who have had access to the interior, there is a cavity in the sanctuary, with walls of Aksumite style and provided with a staircase descending inside. One deacon described this as having more than three rooms, and including a tunnel. On my last visit, for the festival day of Pantalewon on 6th Teqemt (16 October) 1997, an elderly monk said that after consultations together they have decided to pierce a door from the outside that will permit access to the graves within without passing through the sanctuary. He described what sounded like a tomb rather of the type of King Bazen's tomb not far away at the entrance to Aksum.

Access to the top of the cone is by a staircase built of stone blocks. There are several architectural remains here, of sculpted stone, including a pierced window (now standing at the north side of the church), an alabaster fragment, an Aksumite water-spout, and some carved foliage on an oblong block. At the top of the steps is part of an Aksumite column with a chamfered edge. On the terrace on the precipitous south side are four large stones each pierced with a central hole; the monks tell that they were used for sacrifice. Built into the west front of the church was a Sabaean inscription, and in the east front a Greek one. These, now in the treasury of the church, situated below the summit on a little terrace near some stone bells and a small towered house, were recorded by the DAE as inscriptions nos. 1 and 2 respectively. No. 1, which was built into the west side between two windows, is a sandstone inscription in Epigraphic South Arabian script, mentioning the kingdom of

D'MT and the deity Dhat-Ba'adan, 'the distant one'; a female aspect of the sun, perhaps the winter sun. Inscription no. 2, which was built into the wall on the east side near the northeast corner, is also sandstone, and is in Greek. It is worn and broken; it mentions the sea, the Aksumites, and possibly Ares, the Greek war god identified by the Aksumites with their royal deity, Mahrem.

The church as it is now is not distinguished by any special features. The south door leads into the *qene mahlet*, from which a roughly carved double doorway in wood enters the *qeddest*, which has a north door to the outside. In the east wall is the door to the sanctuary or *maqdas*, which contains an elaborate canopied *manbara tabot*. It is an extraordinary experience to attend services here at the *qeddest* door, listening to the chants while gazing out from either the north and the south doorways over the countryside far below.

Women are not permitted to ascend to the top, but may visit the church of Mary Magdalawit (Magdalene) at a lower level. This is a modern square construction (1990 or so) inside the compound wall, containing a square *maqdas* preceded by three columns dividing off the *qene mahlet*. From the terrace are superb views of the mountains of Adwa. A graveyard full of cactus plants lies to one side, and the *qolqwal* trees growing on the hillside add to the attractiveness of the place. Under a tree, two large stones are shown, said to have been a favourite seat of the saint in the time of King Kaleb. The priests here have large claims to make for the honour of their church, relating that not only are King Kaleb and his son Gabra Masqal buried here, but also the emperors Baeda Maryam, Zara Yaqob and Naod, as well as three unnamed patriarchs of Alexandria. These are all said to be buried with Pantelewon's own remains in the crypt below the church. In fact, every one of these monarchs has a claimed resting place elsewhere, and in the case of the medieval emperors, their chronicles probably record the truth. Even the translation of the remains of kings from one place to the other, or, in the case of Baeda Maryam, the destruction of his coffin and remains when they were cast into a deep ravine by Oromo invaders, is sometimes recorded. Enda Abba Pantalewon is never mentioned as the destined spot.

The church of St John, mentioned by Walter Plowden, who was in Aksum in 1848, seems in fact to be this one of Abba Pantalewon. Plowden describes it as 'at some distance [from the cathedral] ... perched on a peaked and wooded hill'.

DEBRA DAMO

History

Set on an imposing table mountain in a spectacular setting, this monastery was founded – or so the legends tell us – by a sixth-century saint. Abba Aregawi, or Za-Mikael Aregawi, was one of the famous Nine Saints who came to Ethiopia and spread Christianity in the countryside; indeed, he was the chief of them, the name Aregawi indicating 'the Elder'. The *gadl* or life story of Za-Mikael Aregawi relates – not altogether convincingly – that he was the son of Yeshaq, a Roman prince, and Princess 'Edna. He came with 'Edna to Ethiopia, and eventually settled at Eggala in Tigray on the mountain or *amba* of Damo. A large snake had dwelt there previously, which God instructed to act as a rope to help Za-Mikael up the cliff, with the Archangel Gabriel keeping guard. Later, when the fame of Za-Mikael had spread, King Gabra Masqal had a ramp built to help in the construction of a church on the *amba*, a ramp that was then removed so as to maintain the place's separation from the world. The church was the second to be built in Ethiopia after Aksum cathedral, and was richly endowed by the king. The place was called Debra Damo after the phrase *dahmemo*, 'take it off', uttered by the saint in reference to the ramp. The Debra Damo monastery was apparently also known as Debra Halleluya (Allelujah), according to the *Gadla Tekla Haymanot* and *Gadla Abuna Aregawi*, the name deriving from the triumphant shout of the saint when he arrived at the top.

Debra Damo has been the site of the discovery of a number of interesting objects. In 1940 a hoard of 104 gold coins of the Kushan kings of northern India and Afghanistan was found here. The dating of these has long been uncertain, with the third century AD as one possibility. Now, however, new work seems to be favouring a span between the first century BC and the first century AD for the four kings involved (Bob Senior, personal communication). With these coins was the remains of a gilded casket that had apparently contained them. One might imagine, if the dating is right, that they came to Debra Damo as the result of some of the Indian trade attested in the *Periplus*. Oddly, only one Aksumite coin has been so far reported from the monastery (a coin of Armah, noted by Derek Matthews) but gold and silver Arabic coins (dinars and dirhams) dating from about the eighth to tenth centuries AD, and a number of very old textiles (sixth to twelfth centuries), were also found, probably originating from Egypt and indicating a route for trade goods from the north passing through the region.

Queen Gudit is reported in the *Gadla Abuna Aregawi* to have taken Debra Damo, building a ramp as Gabra Masqal had done. She massacred the princes who were exiled there, as later *amba* Geshen and *amba* Wahni were to be used as places of exile for royal princes. There is no further evidence for this story – except that Miguel de Castanhoso also believed Debra Damo to have been the place of exile of the princes. No historical record exists stating that Aksumite princes, or indeed any others until after the establishment of the 'Solomonic' dynasty in 1270, were separated from the world in this fashion.

It is claimed that Debra Damo was prominent as a monastic and educational centre even before the 1270 restoration. In the *gadl* of Abba Iyasus Mo'a (c. 1211–92), the famous abbot of St Stephen's monastery on an island in Lake Hayq, it is said that he became a monk at Debra Damo after seven years' noviciate. The abbot at the time was Abba Yohanni. St Tekla Haymanot, a pupil of Iyasus Mo'a, later followed him, remaining twelve years at Debra Damo before going on to found Debra Libanos in Shewa. The famous fourteenth-century monk Basalota Mikael is also said to have studied there.

There is more solid evidence for certain later episodes in the history of Debra Damo. The monks of Debra Damo became involved in religious politics in the time of Amda Seyon (1314–44), when the monastery became a centre for the followers of St Ewostatewos (Eustathius), one of two important rival monastic groups – the others followed St Tekla Haymanot, and were centred at Debra Libanos. In Zara Yaqob's time, the superior, Nob, mediated in a dispute between the king and the monks on the question of sabbath observance. Emperor Baeda Maryam's chronicle mentions that in 1468 Abba Mattewos of Debra Damo and other clerics were summoned by the new emperor and told to pray for him and for his recently deceased father Zara Yaqob. The emperor later gave a donation of gold to the monastery.

Miguel de Castanhoso, in his account of the Portuguese journey across Ethiopia to meet Emperor Galawdewos, mentions that Ahmad Grañ had laid siege for an entire year, unsuccessfully, to the *amba* where Lebna Dengel's widow Queen Sabla Wangel was sheltering. From the description, it seems to have been Debra Damo – Tellez in fact refers to it as 'the mountain Damo ... there being no way to get up it, but being hoisted in baskets'. Castanhoso described the mountain:

> The summit is a quarter of a long league in circumference, and on the area on the top there are two large cisterns, in which much water is collected in the winter; so much that it suffices and is more than enough for all those who live above, that is, about five hundred persons. On this summit itself they sow supplies of wheat, barley, millet and other vegetables. They take up goats and fowls; and there are many hives, for there is much space for them; thus this hill cannot be taken by hunger or thirst. Below the summit the hill is of this kind. It is squared and scarped for a height double that of the highest tower in Portugal, and it gets more precipitous near the top, until at the end it makes an umbrella all round, which looks artificial, and spreads out so far that it over-hangs all the foot of the mountain, so that no one at the foot can hide himself from those above; for all round there is no fold or corner, and there is no way up save the one narrow path, like a badly-made winding stair, by which with difficulty one person can ascend as far as a point where he can get no further, for there the path ends. Above this is a gate where the guards are, and this gate is ten or twelve fathoms above the point where the path stops, and no one can ascend or descend the hill save by the basket.

During the collapse of the Ethiopian kingdom in the 1530s the prohibition against women was evidently abrogated in the emergency; or perhaps it had not yet been imposed. Empress Sabla Wangel and one of her sons came here for shelter while the emperor moved about the country, and the empress's women (some thirty of them according to Castanhoso) were also received. On 2 September 1540 Lebna Dengel died. He was buried at Debra Damo. Sabla Wangel received Cristovão da Gama's officers at the *amba* when in 1541 he sent a message to her offering an escort of one hundred men if she would join him in his march to meet her son, the new Emperor Galawdewos. Manuel da Cunha and Francisco Velho attired themselves fittingly, and were hauled up the cliff in a basket. Sabla Wangel was delighted to join them, after four years cooped up on the *amba*, and moved to the Portuguese camp the same day. A store of arms was left at Debra Damo, and collected after da Gama's death in 1542. Marilyn Heldman writes (in Grierson 1993: 193) that Debra Damo was among the monasteries destroyed during this period, but there seems to be no evidence to confirm this, rather the contrary.

However, in 1557/58 the Turks under Özdemir, former governor of Yemen, soon to be *pasha* of Massawa, invaded Ethiopia from Jidda (Jeddah). Seizing Massawa and Arqiqo, he moved inland to Debarwa. Having fortified the town, the Turks moved against the monasteries and towns in the region, including

Debra Damo. It is said that they massacred the monks, defiled the resting places of Lebna Dengel and Abba Aregawi, and ruined the church; David Mathew cites a phrase from the chronicle of Galawdewos that says it was reduced to ruins like a 'shed in a garden of grape vines'. However, as he and later Gerster comment, if this were so there is no trace of such destruction and later restoration apparent, save perhaps the disarrangement of the wooden panels in the narthex ceiling (see below). Debra Damo seems to have been somewhat eclipsed during the time of the Portuguese, not being mentioned in their books by any author after Castanhoso, although many Portuguese ecclesiastics lived relatively close by in their establishment at Fremona beside Adwa.

After the defeat and death of Sabagadis, ruler of Tigray, in early 1831, the inhabitants of Adwa fled the town for safety, among them Samuel Gobat. He was taken for security to 'Debra Damot' but mentions nothing further about it than that to descend from it one had to use a rope, and that some of the monks 'were inclined to listen to the Word of God'. In the next year, as the new ruler of Tigray, Wube, warred with the sons of Sabagadis, Gobat retreated there again on two occasions. This time he does briefly mention that he visited the church, and that there were paintings representing the story of Abba Aregawi. He also went to visit some rock-cut tombs or hermit caves on the *amba*, and heard that next to one in which a hermit was still living there was another in which Abba Aregawi himself was still supposed to occasionally manifest himself. Gobat, however, was not permitted to enter it with a light. Mgr Giustino de Jacobis also lived at Debra Damo for a while in 1843.

Debra Damo Today

The *amba* of Debra Damo is still only accessible – to men and male animals only – by rope (made of plaited leather), lowered from one of the cliffs surrounding the flat-topped, steep-sided mountain or *amba*; this rope once broke when St Tekla Haymanot was leaving the *amba*, but he was saved by the support of six angelic wings. Nowadays those who wish to climb up are assisted by a second rope tied around the waist and hauled up by a monk at the top.

The *amba* is a characteristic geological form in Ethiopia, where many villages with their attached farmland were in the past protected by their position on top of these small and sometimes virtually inaccessible plateaux. The *amba* of Debra Damo is about 1 km. in diameter, and is equipped with wells, cisterns and fields on top.

To reach Debra Damo, one takes the Adwa–Adigrat road past Yeha, turning off it at 60 km. on a smaller road leading to the *amba*. The journey from Yeha is interesting for the scenery, mountainous and magnificent, passing Inticho (Enticcio) on a newly made road and on over crests and through valleys, often with a glimpse of churches, square and white painted in the Tigray style, standing in seemingly inaccessible spots amid their groves of trees. The view grows more and more splendid as the great mass of the *amba* of Debra Damo becomes defined. The rock lies at an odd angle in the nearby hills, so that the stones stand up from the ground like teeth in curious artichoke-like formations. The road, twisting and turning up to the *amba*, leads to a point at the foot of a rocky slope at the base of the *amba* proper, where a mill owned by the monastery grinds grain for the local people. A short climb past the extra-ordinary twisting roots of some trees growing by the *amba* leads to the ropes. The church of Mary, a new structure of the square Tigray type, stands nearby; this can be visited by women. Also visible in the valley nearby is the monument to the freedom fighters who died in the late civil war.

One enters Debra Damo through a low gatehouse built on the cliff over-hang, from which steps mount to a second gatehouse, then up to the plateau. The church is at the east end of the *amba*, with monks' houses scattered in a village consisting of a number of compounds in various places on the flat top of the hill. Many rock-cut cisterns, some situated around the church, others cut into a rocky outcrop further away between groups of substantial stone-built monks' houses, conserve the water supply. There is another small yellow-coloured church of St Mary built on a ledge below the top of the *amba*, on the east, with a small rock-cut grotto hermitage nearby, with a dome and some decoration on the walls. This is supposed to have belonged to Za-Mikael Aregawi himself. The *amba* is a functioning monastery, with, according to the *qese gabaz* in February 1996, more than two hundred monks; although at times in the past there have been as many as a thousand living there, a figure reflected in the many now-ruined houses in the monks' village.

A typical monk's house, in which I was invited to eat a Lenten meal of *injera* made from teff and sorghum and *mitmita* pepper, was entered by a courtyard door with a lock in the form of a wooden bolt housed in a triangular niche beside the doorframe. The bolt slid out from the niche into position to secure the door. Crossing the court, a wooden door in a frame with 'monkey-heads' protruding above gave access to the house. This was surprisingly spacious. A large room formed both living space and bedroom, with bed platforms built in beside the door, and storage niches beneath them. Three large tree-trunk pillars with the broad part forming the 'capitals' supported two cross-beams each, with further layers of smaller branches above making up the ceiling. A rear room acted as a store.

The Enda Abba Aregawi church complex consisted in the days of the DAE visit in 1906 of a walled compound divided into two, the main body of the church being in the eastern part, while in the western part the compound walls divided the church at the level of the porch. A gatehouse with attached bell-tower stood to the west, and a tower-like treasury to the south. This has been much altered now. A low gate enters the compound to the south, with a bell-tower to the left of it. Nearby, a walled cistern is cut into the rock. The church, built of small dark-coloured stones set in a mud mortar, with numerous weathered wooden 'monkey-heads' protruding, stands free, and one can walk right round it. To the north is a substantial treasury (*eqa bet*) with a smaller *beta lahm* (for the preparation of the eucharistic bread) southeast of it. These stand in their own walled compound. A small house completes the buildings in the immediate neighbourhood of the church.

The church was 'discovered' for the modern European scientific world by the Deutsche Aksum-Expedition in 1906. It is a two-storey building of rectangular plan, with two indentations on the longer (20 m.) north and south sides, one on the shorter (9.70 m.) east and west sides. In the north-eastern corner is a projecting two-storey wing (a slightly later addition?), the ground floor windows giving on to to a small walled court with a cistern cut into the rock of the *amba*.

A western addition, the porch, which seems to have been built somewhat later in the same general style, precedes this structure. The corners of the porch consist of masonry pillars, constructed of cut yellow limestone following the Aksumite style of building as seen in the Tomb of the False Door and the Tombs of Kaleb and Gabra Masqal at Aksum. There are two massive door-jambs in the same stone. The base of the double entrance doorway consists of a single stone, which also includes the shaped base for the painted stone central column that divides the two entrances. This low double doorway, with its central column, leads into the porch. Inside, the porch roof is divided into three square sections. Within each section the ceiling is formed by beams running from centre to centre of each square to form a diamond shape, with another square inside that. The sanctuary dome (see below) rests on a similar basis of cross-beams. The immediate impression in this porch, which serves as the *qene mahlet* of the church, is of the richness of the colour of the wood in contrast to the weathered monkey-heads outside. The porch is carpeted, and there is a small window set low in the north wall.

A further double doorway leads from the porch/*qene mahlet* into the narthex, functioning as the *qeddest*. The façade of this, presumably the original façade of the church, is extremely attractive. There are two Aksumite-style doorways, with a long dentilled or ribbed lintel above – exactly the same arrangement as on the (single) doorways depicted on stelae nos. 1–2 at Aksum. The doorways are flanked by light plastered walls, which contrast with the darker wood of the longitudinal beams and monkey-heads. On either side is a single window. The frames are of Aksumite style with square monkey-heads at each corner, the lintel very modestly decorated with some incised vertical lines. The carved wooden window infill is more complex, consisting of a central column flanked by two pilasters supporting arches, over a panel carved with running swastika motifs. The capitals and bases of the columns and pilasters, triple-stepped, and the arch above, form that keyhole-like shape often seen in old Ethiopian window filling, which, if the columns are not distinct (as when seen from within with the light behind), sometimes appears in 'negative' form, not immediately identifiable as an architectural motif.

The narthex has a low and somewhat distorted roof, exhibiting a splendid ceiling composed of carved wooden panels. Three groups of 23 by 23 cm. panels survive carved with various geometrical or animal motifs; for those who cannot see this, either because they cannot travel to Debra Damo, or because they are women, reproductions have been made for the foyer of the Yeha Hotel at Aksum, which give something of an impression. The panels may possibly derive from an earlier structure, perhaps even based on the now vanished ceilings of an Aksumite palace (another collection of such panels, now in Asmara Museum, was found when the old church there was dismantled in 1920, some seemingly coming from an 'Aksumite frieze', others from a similar ceiling). It has been conjectured that the panels may date originally from the seventh to the eleventh centuries.

The ceiling of the narthex is supported by three square columns, the central one of stone, the others wooden, set in a row running north–south, with capitals formed in the shape of four brackets or corbels to support the beams. To the south is a plain doorway surmounted by two wooden arches, leading out into the western part of the compound. To the north, a doorway and small room with a window lead to a staircase-well built around a rectangular masonry pillar. The stairs mount to a light well over part of the narthex, and thence to an open hall also built partly over the narthex and partly over the portico, and to the upper rooms and lofts over the rest of the building. None of these upper rooms is now accessible.

A further twin doorway leads into the nave, and as usual there are two side doors in the north and south walls at the west end (paralleled by windows at the east end). Customarily the women's door of a church is to the south, the men's to the north, but here no women are permitted. In the nave are two rows each of three re-used ancient monolithic columns, some with capitals decorated with a cross motif in various forms, some with square cut bases, some chamfered at the corners. There are pilasters at the east and west ends, altogether forming four bays; the two aisles also have pilasters in the side walls reflecting the columns. The columns and pilasters support wooden beams, the latter by means of corbels.

Over the massive square lintel beams of the nave are panels of wooden 'Aksumite frieze' decoration, consisting of rows of blind Aksumite-style windows with square monkey-heads at each corner. This form of decorative frieze is also continued into the *maqdas*. There is rope-twist decoration along the tops of the frames, and the central panels of the false 'windows' of the frieze are enhanced with cross-based or geometric designs; a veritable 'pattern book' of favourite designs, as Gerster puts it.

The nave walls rise above the frieze, supporting the inner walls of the two lofts above the two flanking aisles, which have lower flat roofs. These walls also show longitudinal beams (but no monkey-heads) and are broken by three Aksumite-style windows with square monkey-heads opening from the lofts. The nave walls also formerly supported a timber roof of trussed construction, based on corbels and cross-beams, which with two rafters supporting the roof formed a high triangle (see also Yimrehana Krestos, Lalibela, above). There was a wooden arch inserted in the central of the three trusses. The nave further supported a rectangular walled central section of the exterior roof, rising above the loft and narthex roofs and the light well, and filled in to cover the 'vault' with a flat roof equipped with water-spouts. Water was thus expelled on to the loft roofs, which sloped slightly, and, also being equipped with water-spouts, drained the whole area effectively. Since the major restoration of 1948 the roof has been flat; regarded by some as a pity, the interest of the trussed roof being lost, and by others as perhaps a more 'Aksumite' form than the complex trussed type. In any case, the 'new' roof already looks old!

Entry to the *maqdas* or sanctuary is by an arch – slightly horseshoe-shaped – of carved wood with a running geometric design. Above it are two square Aksumite-style windows. There is a dome, also of painted wood, over the sanctuary – although panels have now fallen out and been replaced by cloth – and another window at the east end. Two further rooms flank the *maqdas*, the northern one abutting on to the little northeast courtyard with a cistern. It was here that the remains of Emperor Lebna Dengel, who died here in 1540, were preserved. I was informed that these are now kept in a chest in the sanctuary itself.

During the restoration in 1948, Derek Matthews was able to study and record the exact methods by which the walls with their Aksumite-style doors and windows had been constructed. One wall had to be dismantled and rebuilt (the severely dilapidated condition of the church can be seen in the photos in Sergew Hable Sellassie 1972, opp. p. 118, and in Buxton 1949, fig. 81). The system of construction was exactly the same as that shown on the great carved granite stelae at Aksum, employing horizontal timbers surmounted by round cross-members binding the mud-mortared stones together, and similar square cross-members binding the window and door structure. The cross-members are slotted on their lower surfaces to fit over the horizontal beams. Actually at Debra Damo the 'beams' are more like planks, fitted at each corner with blocks giving the effect of squared beams. This system clamps the wall together, the result being a very sturdy structure. Matthews found that the round cross-members do not normally go right through the walls to form monkey-heads on either side, although some do. Larger stones at the corners reinforced the walls, something also frequently found in those Aksumite buildings that have been excavated, and in, for example, the exposed part of the ancient podium at Maryam Seyon cathedral at Aksum. On the northeast, where the church is not built directly on to the rock, there is a stepped podium, another Aksumite reminiscence.

The Aksumite-style doorways even have ribbed moulding over them, as seen on the two largest stelae and on the Tomb of the False Door at Aksum, and some have extra 'rope-twist' design above. Some of the windows, too, have similar decorative carving, and the square monkey-heads may be worked as well.

The dating of the church has always been uncertain. Legend claims that it was founded by Abba Aregawi. There may have been some pagan installation there previously, as the snake legend about Aregawi might hint. King Gabra Masqal, Kaleb's son, is supposed by the author of the *Gadla Aregawi* to have built a church here, around the mid-sixth century – indeed, according to oral tradition his body is supposed to have been buried here, after resting some time at Debra Salem, Asbi (Sergew Hable Sellassie 1972: 164). Gabra Masqal is also supposed to be buried at Beta Pantalewon, Aksum (see above). The church as it survives now was doubtless several times renewed or restored. Buxton suggested that 'much of the existing fabric could be as early as the tenth or eleventh century'. Others have suggested restorations as late as the fourteenth century, or even in the sixteenth century after the Turkish attack.

All in all, the church of Debra Damo, remote and peaceful on its *amba* (one of the few places in Ethiopia where the visitor can escape the eternal requests for pens or money, or itinerant sellers) is a gem of its kind. Perhaps the nearest in atmosphere – and one in which women can share – is the church of Yimrehana Krestos near Lalibela (see above).

13

ROCK CHURCHES IN THE WUQRO REGION

Hidden away in many a valley or mountain, sometimes incredibly difficult to reach unless one has the agility of a mountain goat, the rock-cut churches of Tigray are a characteristic feature of the area. Here I offer only the merest glimpse of a few examples from the enormous number now known. For those who cannot make even the relatively easy journey on the new paved road from Adigrat to Edage Hamus, Sinkata and Wuqro to see these – which are, moreover, fine examples – it is worth trying to see the two rather similar rock churches, the ruined Yekka Mikael and Washate Tekla Haymanot, just outside Addis Ababa, or Adadi Maryam a little further south; although of course Lalibela, on most tourist itineraries, provides the supreme examples of the genre. Nevertheless, single rock churches have a very different atmosphere from the multiple examples crowded together at Lalibela, and in most cases the scenery, too, is well worth the trip. This is true, too, for Abba Mata‘a (Abba Libanos), a rock-cut monastery church near Aksum on the way to Da’erika. It is the only one in the Aksum region, situated halfway up a cliff face in a beautiful tree-filled gorge of red and white-veined rocks; inside it is very simple, with a small two pillared *qene mahlet/qeddest*, and a *maqdas* behind it, with a few late paintings.

From Adigrat, dominated by the Catholic church and campanile of St Mary, and where one can stay in the very simple but pleasant Modern Hotel, the road to Wuqro passes through rich agricultural plains with views of distant mountains. To the left (east) after Sinkat a dirt road weaves among aloes, sisal and cacti towards some rounded rocky 'sugar-loaf' outcrops.

Medhane Alem Addi Qesho

The church of Medhane Alem Addi Qesho, on Saada Amba (White Hill, so-called after the colour of the local rocks), stands high up with a wonderful view down to Addi Qesho in the *woreda* of Wuqro, in the plain called Addi Ihil, land of grain. On the rock slope leading up to the church water-worn holes are shown as the footprints of Christ's horse when he visited the spot. A gatehouse in an enclosure wall gives entrance into an area filled with olive and juniper trees. A second gate admits one to the rock face, with the façade of the church cut into it. The church is claimed as the oldest of the rock churches, constructed by Jesus Christ himself, but modern commentators place it somewhere between the eleventh to twelfth, or late fourteenth to early fifteenth centuries (see Plant 1985). The façade consists of four columns under a heavy cornice. The spaces between the columns have been infilled with walls, leaving a low arched entrance. There are painted crosses near the capitals of the exterior columns.

Inside, through a low arched entrance, there is a long 'narthex' of three bays' width, with two irregular rounded side rooms opening from it. The ceiling is decorated with carving; the southern round room has a circular design on its ceiling. The east wall of the narthex consists of another, inner, façade forming the eastern wall, with four columns cut in the rock. Entrance to the nave and south aisle of the church is by two doors with windows above. The windows are made of wood in Aksumite style, with square monkey-heads at the corners of the frames, and dentilled panels above the doors with decorated lintels below. To the right is an entrance leading to the sanctuary containing a *tabot* (*debal*) dedicated to Mary; the ceiling is ornamented with zigzag patterns, and there is a niche in one wall. To the left, stairs lead to the *beta lahm*, and a tiny entrance leads to a tunnel towards the north aisle of the church.

The church itself is impressive, with nine bays, three east–west and three north–south, divided by columns, and with decorated flat ceilings, different in each bay. The nave has the 'Aksumite frieze' decoration. Beyond the main body of the church is the sanctuary, entered by an arch, and two other flanking rooms. Unfortunately, demands for extra money beyond the official entrance ticket rate, by a greedy *qese gabaz* – a contrast to all other churches seen – mar visits to this church.

Mikael Milahayzengi

This church, nearer the road than Medhane Alem, is attributed, like so many others, to the legendary Aksumite kings Abreha and Asbeha. The church, entered through a small gate in a walled enclosure with *qolqwal* trees, is cut into a large rounded rock outcrop. Broad-built steps lead up to two small rounded holes in the rock with wooden doorways and doors inserted into them. The church is said to have been dedicated to St Qirqos before St Michael came here. The people therefore altered the dedication, and removed the *tabot* of Qirqos elsewhere.

Inside this very simple cave church, two pillars have been left to support the roof in the outer room. Thus there are six bays, the outer three each with a decorated ceiling. The entrance bay has a fine carved dome above it, with 'Aksumite frieze' decoration on three sides. The columns are linked by arches.

Wuqro Cherqos

Directly outside the small town of Wuqro, on a knoll of red rock, is the rock-cut church of Wuqro Cherqos. A modern bell-tower stands in the grounds, and there is a new gatehouse to the compound, as well as some other buildings. On top of the church is a decorative finial.

The church is supposed to have been constructed in AD 254 by the two kings Abreha and Asbeha. It was one of the first of the rock churches of Tigray known. The church was restored outside relatively recently in Haile Sellassie's reign.

Inside, the *qeddest* is rather rough-hewn, but gives a powerful impression with its columns and high ceiling, particularly during services when the readings are done by candlelight, and the chanting of the *dabtara* echoes in the large space. The church is cross-shaped. Four Aksumite-style chamfered columns with bracket capitals and joined by arches support the central part of the roof, high and carved with a cross. Altogether there are five bays north–south and east–west, if one counts the sanctuary bays, and the intermediary columns dividing the aisles and the western bays. The pillars in the aisles have flat architraves, and are reflected in the outer walls by pilasters. In front of the sanctuary arch is a bay with a small cupola carved in the ceiling, and the western bay leading to the porch is barrel vaulted. This and the two bays flanking the central bay exhibit 'Aksumite frieze' decoration. There are apparently two *debalat*, dedicated to Gabriel and Michael, in the side rooms off the *qeddesta qeddusan*.

The *qene mahlet,* here a kind of porch, is cut out of the rock on three sides. It precedes the *qeddest* on the west, the façade, side, with a wooden 'Aksumite' doorway under an arch with two windows leading into the *qeddest* (which can also be entered by two side doors into the western bays). The porch has a central pillar and grille windows. The ceiling, divided into four sections, was carved and painted, but is now much destroyed. Nevertheless, a good impression of the decoration can be gained. The upper part of the walls is also painted, and a number of scenes can be distinguished; cherubim and angels, the Abuna Samuel, the Nine Saints, St Qirqos. The priests tell the story that the church was burned by Gudit, the destructive queen who is supposed also to have toppled the Aksum stelae.

Abreha wa Asbeha

If, instead of going into Wuqro, one turns right at the entrance to the town (where a home-made sign raises hopes by announcing 'Hilton Hotel'), the Hawzien road continues on for 15 km. to one of the best and largest of the rock-hewn churches of Tigray, dedicated to the famous kings of Aksum, the brothers Abreha and Asbeha. They are unknown by that name to history, but they are said in Ethiopian legends to be the kings who adopted Christianity around AD 340. The historical king of Aksum who did adopt Christianity around that time was King Ezana. His name is equally unknown in the Ethiopian legendary accounts. As noted in a previous chapter, the explanation seems to be that, very probably, Abreha/Asbeha and Ezana are the same.

The church is cut into the red rock overlooking a valley, and stands out with its white painted façade sheltering two tall blue doors under arches. This part of the church projects forward, and is flanked on both sides by side wings with smaller Aksumite-style doors to the *qeddest* set further back. To get to the church, one has to climb a substantial new slate staircase, passing through a gatehouse into the enclosure, in which is also an *eqa bet* or treasury.

Inside the *qeddest*, chamfered Aksumite-style columns with stepped capitals, reflected by pilasters in the outer walls, divide the church, which is five bays wide (three bays wide at the west end where the porch is), and five bays deep if one counts the invisible sanctuary. The *maqdas* or sanctuary is beyond, to the east, veiled by curtains; it is said to contain at least four *debalat*. The four central cross-section pillars of the nave only are joined by decorated arches, with a high flat roof decorated with a cross. These pillars have bracket capitals. The roof north and south of this central group is barrel vaulted, completely decorated with cross patterns and with the traditional 'Aksumite frieze' decoration below; rows of typical Aksumite-style blank windows with their characteristic square monkey-heads at the corners. There are windows through the rock at either end of the barrel vault. The bay before the sanctuary has a decorated cupola. The rest of the columns are joined by flat architraves. Many paintings survive at the upper levels, the rest being worn away; they are not necessarily very old, since one depicts *Dejazmach* Gabru and *Ras* Araya, galloping to war led by the late nineteenth-century Emperor Yohannes IV.

The porch is the *qene mahlet*. During the services, the *dabtara* stand in a half-circle here facing in towards the *qeddest*, with their prayer sticks (*maq-wamia*) and sistra (*sanasil*), intoning the chants. A double arched entry of carved and painted wood leads from the porch into the main body of the church. The *qene mahlet* too is painted, and figures of the equestrian saints can be seen to the north, with scenes from Christ's life to the south.

This church, the priests tell one, was destroyed by both Queen Gudit and Ahmad Grañ. However, in the case of a rock-hewn church, such attacks, if they really took place, would affect only the mobile church furniture, unless the enemy really came with the determined intention to obliterate the structure with mallets and the like.

Tomb of Ahmad Negash

Continuing on to Wuqro from the churches noted above, the road passes the new church of Mary Magdalene, impressively perched on a high peak to the left, and enters Nagash. This is a small trading town situated on the top of an immense gorge, the slopes of which are covered with hundreds of stone terraces, and planted with euphorbia candelabra and eucalyptus trees. Here is the white-painted tomb of Ahmad Negash, a simple oblong structure with raised corner finials, and the neat white mosque commemorating the same prominent early Muslim character.

This Ahmad is said to have come with the Muslim exiles to Ethiopia, when they were offered the protection of the *najashi*, the reigning king of Abyssinia, in the 620s, right at the beginning of Islam. In all the Muslim histories, these exiles are mentioned, and even listed by name, and it is fairly certain that there was indeed a large group of the very first followers of Muhammad in Ethiopia. Some died there. Possibly this tomb commemorates one of them. Others (see, for example, Taddesse Tamrat 1972) have suggested that 'Ahmad' is identical with Ashama ibn Abjar, the *najashi* himself (the same word as Nagash), whom some Muslim historians claim as a convert. They record that the prophet honoured him greatly, and mourned his death in 630. He is supposed to have accepted Islam, but concealed this under a subterfuge to keep his throne. The suggestion that a great Christian king might convert seems improbable, but this was not the last time the idea was associated with Ethiopia. It was reiterated, by a later Muslim writer, of Emperor Amda Seyon – a ruler whose chronicle shows him as fiercely anti-Muslim, and also by the Catholics about Emperor Fasiladas.

14

YEHA

The Kingdom of Di'amat: Archaeological Evidence

The beginnings of Ethiopian civilisation are ultimately rooted in the kingdom of Di'amat and Saba. Its history, development and decline remain largely mysterious, but one imprint of its existence is still all-pervading. Almost every newspaper, book and sign in Christian Ethiopia today is written in a script and Semitic language that are direct descendants of those employed millennia ago for the ancient inscriptions of Di'amat.

Despite a certain amount of archaeological investigation, we still know relatively little about this civilisation, which appears to have been fully developed by some two thousand five hundred years ago in the modern-day regions of Tigray and Eritrea on the Ethiopian plateau. Doubtless some aspects derived from local developments in the area since the heyday of the ancient chiefdom of Punt and its successors, which are represented by a number of Sudan–Ethiopia borderland sites. But there was a new impetus, it seems, from abroad. Inscriptions excavated in the ruins of ancient temples and written in the language of Saba across the Red Sea in Yemen appear about this time in several places on the Ethiopian plateau. The main sites associated with south Arabian characteristics, particularly inscriptions, in Ethiopia or Eritrea are Abba Pantalewon, Hawelti-Melazo, Gobochela and Enda Cherqos near Aksum, and Abuna Garima, Matara, Seglamien, Addi Galamo, Feqya, Addi Gramaten, Kaskase and Sabea between Aksum and the eastern escarpment. This spread indicates that the phenomenon of south Arabian influence was quite wide-spread, and therefore presumably not just a transient affair.

The royal title '*mukarrib* of D'MT and Saba' mentioned on a number of these inscriptions seems to suggest a close contact with the south Arabian kingdom of Saba in the Yemen. The linguists who have studied the inscriptions assume the presence of actual Sabaeans in Ethiopia at Matara, Yeha and Hawelti-Melazo. Four rulers are known to date, the earliest apparently the *mlkn* (king) W'RN HYWT, followed by three *mukarrib*s named RD'M, RBH and LMN (the vowels in these names are not written in the ancient south Arabian script, and the exact pronunciation remains uncertain, hence this conventional capitalised form of writing them). Inscriptions from Yeha and Melazo mention MRYB, perhaps the same as Marib, capital of the kingdom of Saba in Arabia. This connection is far from mere fantasy; not only the language and script, but also such elements as the marginally drafted masonry employed, and certain important decorative similarities, link Yeha and the Ethiopia pre-Aksumite sites with Marib, Sirwah and other Arabian sites.

With some of the inscriptions were found stone altars, often marked with the disc and crescent sign so common on southern Arabian objects. Use of this divine symbol continued into Aksumite times – it can be seen on the Matara stele with its Ge'ez inscription, and on the coins of the pre-Christian Aksumite kings. In addition, impressive artwork has come from pre-Aksumite Ethiopian sites; beautifully carved female statues dressed in pleated robes, or in a robe decorated with rosettes, and a canopied stone throne decorated with carved ibex and human figures. Similar figures in pleated robes, and many objects bearing the ibex motif, can be seen also in the San'a Museum in Yemen. The Ethiopian sites have also yielded pottery and those 'small finds' that allow the archaeologist to piece together the more intimate details of the unknown past. Much of this material – though not so much the pottery, which seems to derive from local African traditions – has demonstrable connections with southern Arabia. Some of the statues and altars, as well as pottery, bronze and other items of the pre-Aksumite period are now on exhibit in the National Museum of Addis Ababa. Most impressive of all as a testimony to the capabilities of these pre-Aksumite people, at Yeha near Aksum a temple of finely cut local yellow masonry (variously described as limestone or, more recently, as silicified sandstone) was built during this period. It still stands almost intact, though roofless, high on a knoll surrounded by a circular wall. It is Ethiopia's oldest surviving major building (see below).

It was previously assumed, before closer analysis of the inscriptions, that all this material was the import of settlers from Saba, who brought with them their own civilisation and imposed their political control on the Ethiopian plateau. They were thought to have derived from an Arabian tribe called Habash, which would have been the origin of the designation Habash/Habashat given to them and their new African colonial land by the Arabs of Yemen. In early Arabian inscriptions from Marib and other places the Ethiopian king was entitled '*najashi* of Aksum and of Habashat'.

But more recent studies suggest that there were two groups involved. It seems that the inscriptions written using the epigraphic south Arabian script derive from sources that were related, but not the same. One group wrote in pure Sabaean, the other in a variant 'proto-Ge'ez' language. Together, they reveal the creators of this Ethiopian highland civilisation. There seems to have been a mixture of genuine Sabaeans – perhaps southern Arabian merchants, traders settled in communities such as the Muslim commercial centres attested in Christian Ethiopia later on – with a local Ethiopian people. The latter, including the rulers, were of Ethiopian origin though with a similar cultural development. They shared the script and some of the cultural attributes of their overseas neighbours and trading partners, and established a kingdom named as D'MT in the inscriptions, perhaps to be vocalised something like 'Di'amat'; the first sign of a state-level polity on the plateau. The Ethiopian version of the language would go on to become Ge'ez, the language of Aksum, a Semitic tongue now used only in the Ethiopian church. Its script is the only one in use today – for writing the Amharic language – which is derived, in a cursive version, from the ancient south Arabian writing. The explanation for this closeness of language might be that there was something of a common Red Sea coast cultural heritage that had long contributed to developments on both the Arabian and the Ethiopian sides of the Red Sea, and was cross-fertilised by further contacts at this period – indeed, contacts on an intimate level were maintained on into Aksumite times as well.

As we have seen, the rulers of D'MT were entitled *mukarrib* or *malik*, but although the names of a few rulers using these old south Arabian titles are known their history remains almost completely obscure. The altar inscriptions show that the *mukarrib*s of D'MT worshipped such deities as Ilmuqah, Astar, Hawbas, Dhat-Himyam and Dhat-Ba'adan. The kingdom of Di'amat vanishes from the record by perhaps the third century BC, and nothing more is known of its history – though at any time further archaeological discoveries might reveal more about this very little-known early state. Nevertheless, it seems that the Di'amat phase in Ethiopia gave birth in an indirect way to what may be called, after Egypt and Meroë in the Sudan, the greatest – and still the most mysterious – of all Africa's ancient civilisations: the kingdom of Aksum.

It seems probable that the settlement at Yeha represented a major centre of the kingdom of Di'amat, dating from at least the fourth or fifth century BC to perhaps a few centuries later. With a temple structure of substantial size and evident importance, royal inscriptions, a substantial 'palace' building, and rich tombs (see below), there is a good possibility that it might have been the central place, the capital, of the earliest of the Ethiopian upland kingdoms.

Yeha: Early Visitors

The buildings at Yeha were first noted by Europeans when Francisco Alvares visited the site in the 1520s. He referred to the place as 'Abafaçem', after the church of Abba Afse, one of the Nine Saints, which was built beside the temple. In his 1540 book Alvares noted

> a very good church of Our Lady, well built, with the middle aisle raised above the two sides or edges, with its windows very well constructed, and all the church vaulted ... close to the said church is a very large and handsome tower, both for its height and the good workmanship of its walls, and for its width; it is already getting damaged, and yet it is plain it was a royal affair, all of well-hewn stone; we have not seen such another building. This tower is surrounded by houses, which match it well, with both good walls and flat roofs above, like residences of great lords. They say that these edifices belonged to Queen Candace.

Candace was the 'Ethiopian' queen whose eunuch treasurer was mentioned in the Bible as a convert of the apostle Philip. It is generally believed by Ethiopians – and very likely began to be believed not long after Christianity entered the country in the fourth century, and King Ezana began to refer to part of the Aksumite kingdom as Ethiopia – that such Biblical allusions, actually referring to the Sudanese kingdom of Meroë or Kush, apply to what is today Ethiopia. The Ethiopians who related the tale to Alvares probably identified Candace (a name deriving from the title *kandake*, queen-mother of Meroë) with the Queen of Sheba, also supposed to have been a ruler of Ethiopia. A legend in the *Gadla Afse* (the life story of the saint) kept in the church at Yeha says that two princes called Soba and Noba, sons of Yoktan and Balkis – the name of the Queen of Sheba in Arabic tales – had left Saba in Arabia and came to reign in Ethiopia, building their palace at Yeha.

The chronicle of Sartsa Dengel merely mentions that the king camped at Yaha on his way to defeat the *Bahrnagash* Yeshaq in 1578, but without any further details. Manoel Barradas also noted a church 'not described until now' – he must have missed the 'Abafaçem' reference in Alvares – in the land called Yahâ:

> It is still unfinished, as it has remained since the immemorial time when it was begun, without ever being completed, without ever serving as anything other than a home for cobras and a dwelling place of wild animals, turned into a jungle of weeds and the bushes born within it. This must be the main reason why it is not spoken of, because only the shape testifies to its having been built as a church.

Barradas was completely misled as to the nature of the structure:

> It is square and it is obvious that it was designed to be domed, as shown by the supports it has, which form two rows down the centre, and the curves in its respondence which were begun on one of the two side walls, protruding a bit from them toward the side and sloping as though part of an archway. The walls are rather thick, all of them within and without are of very beautiful quarried stone, grey in colour, well-worked and better set, though without wedges; most of them are seven or eight span in length and some are more, and three or four in breadth, one and a half in width, and it had almost attained its height. It is a bit longer than wide, overall its size is average and not disproportionate.

There was no one who could inform Barradas as to when and by whom it had been built – he was sure, however, that it could not have been Ethiopians who built it, and the old men of Yeha agreed, telling him they 'believed it had been the work of Egyptians, which may well be the case'. The Jesuit, exiled from Ethiopia, imagined some Egyptians in the past, summoned to this land to build a church, and then sent away. He speculated that in the same way in the future people would come to Ethiopia and see the churches of Dancaz, Ennebese (Martula Maryam), Fremona, and the completed domed church of Gorgora, with those at Kollela, Lija Negus, and Sarka; but, because the Portuguese had been driven out, no one would know that it was Patriarch Mendes and the Portuguese who had been the builders (Barradas 1996: 152-3).

James Bruce merely passed by 'the mountain of Yeeha' in 1769, traversing the plain on its top, and leaving the village to the southeast as his party 'began the most rugged and dangerous descent we had met with since Taranta'. He apparently did not notice the temple, prominent though it is; but the very fact that he came so close indicates how the place lay near to the travelled paths, doubtless a point of primary importance in its original choice as the site for so important a temple and settlement.

The British envoy Henry Salt visited 'Yeeha' in 1810, during his mission to Abyssinia. He admired the temple, which, however, he regarded as constituting part of the sixth-century monastery of Abba Afse. Salt briefly describes the building – he writes that it was built of 'a sandstone of a light yellowish cast, covered over with a hard incrustation'. He also noted some fragmentary inscriptions he found 'among some adjoining heaps of stone', which he thought might have come from a 'cincture or frieze which surrounded the upper part of the building'. He illustrated examples of epigraphic south Arabian inscriptions in both sunken and raised relief. This was the first discovery of such inscriptions, and he noted their 'Abyssinian' character, a remark justified in the sense that the cursive Ethiopic script does indeed descend from the square and formal lettering of the monumental south

Arabian type. Salt also related that the priests and some local inhabitants told him various tales about Abba Afse and the buildings, including a story that the Ark of the Covenant had been kept at Yeha for some time before going on to Aksum.

The next visitor to leave a record about Yeha was J. Theodore Bent, an intrepid English traveller who had already visited and written about Great Zimbabwe. He supplied a good description of the ruins of the temple, which he visited with his wife in 1893. His book, *The Sacred City of the Ethiopians*, was published in 1893, with a new edition in 1896. It concentrates on Aksum, but includes a substantial section on Yeha, including some translations by H. D. Müller of a number of the small south Arabian inscriptions found by Bent at the temple site, or built into surrounding houses. One mentioned the name 'WM, which may be the original name of the place, although the name Hawa is also attested from another inscription from the site. Bent thought that the name 'WM might be identified with the Aua or Aue mentioned in an Aksumite inscription – the so-called *Monumentum Adulitanum* – and also by the Byzantine ambassador Nonnosus, who came to Ethiopia in the mid-sixth century. But from the meteorological and geographical data provided by Nonnosus, it seems that Aue must have lain further east, near the escarpment of the Rift Valley (see Munro-Hay 1991: 31)

In 1906 the Deutsche Aksum-Expedition visited Yeha, and following their usual methodical practice surveyed the buildings, preparing excellent plans and elevations of them, as well as taking numerous photographs. These were published in the 1913 report by Enno Littmann and his colleagues.

Francisco Alvares remarked, as did Bent some 370 years later, how fertile the valley of Yeha was, with its irrigation channels and multiplicity of crops. More recently, Joseph Michels, in a survey of agricultural potential in the area published in 1988, put both Yeha and Aksum in his Zone A, with 'low gradient, highly fertile land that is optimal for plow cultivation, requires no fertility intervention other than crop rotation, and relies upon seasonal rain'. Evidently Yeha not only lay on one of the cross-country trade routes, but had water and an ideal environment for the foundation of an important population centre.

Yeha: The Site Today

Yeha lies about thirty miles NNE of Aksum and ten from Adwa, accessible by the main road (unpaved) to Adwa, past the very dramatic scenery of the mountains of Adwa – site of Emperor Menelik II's famous defeat of the Italians over a century ago – then by a smaller road turning right towards Enticcio (Inticho, Entesew). This whole area shows an almost incredible amount of terracing – noted already in the last century but of unknown original date – on the flanking hills. From the secondary road one turns left (north) on to a track for a short way to reach the splendid valley in which, on a knoll backed by the surrounding hills, stands the temple. The imposing structure is visible from some distance, rising above the later church of Enda Abba Afse and its enclosure. The spot is at about 2,130 m. above sea level.

The enclosure of the church and temple is entered by a staircase and a charming two-storey gatehouse. Inside, the area is very attractively planted with euphorbia candelabra (*qolqwal*), mimosa and sycamore trees. Directly facing the entrance gate is the church of Abba Afse, dedicated to one of the Nine Saints who are said to have come from the Roman Empire to Ethiopia in the fifth and sixth centuries. The rectangular church has been rebuilt in the traditional manner, showing many monkey-heads inside and out – it is not that which Alvares referred to as the church of Mary, nor that seen by the DAE, nor even that photographed by Buxton and published in his *Travels in Ethiopia* in 1949, but a more recent replacement (c. 1951, after Doresse, in *Novum Testamentum*, 1, 3, 1956). Some stones from the older churches and from the temple nearby have also been employed in the construction. A block with a frieze of facing ibex in a row, doubtless from the temple, is embedded in the façade of the church. An octagonal marble column lies near the church. Some surviving carved wooden fragments from the previous churches were taken by Doresse to Addis Ababa for preservation in the Section d'Archéologie there. The 'stone bells' or phonoliths formerly noted here – long pieces of stone strung by cords from the branches of a tree, which make a bell-like sound when struck with a wooden stick or another stone – are no longer visible. For photographs of them, see Bent 1896 and Littmann et al. 1913.

To the left (north) of the church is the two-storey treasury, where a considerable collection of ecclesiastical equipment and some manuscripts are kept, as well as one of the old Sabaean inscriptions originally from the temple. To the right is the temple, in front of which stands also a rough stele furnished with a base-plate that has a shallow basin-like circular offering bowl carved into it; there is another such 'bowl' placed at the top of the church steps nearby. Possibly this stele dates to Aksumite times rather than to the earlier south Arabian phase. Formerly, it is recorded, a few other rough stele stood nearby.

The temple itself is a magnificent structure, which has no equal anywhere else in Ethiopia. Extremely well preserved, with up to fifty-two courses of masonry, it dominates the whole valley with its high windowless walls (although there seem to have been two windows in the façade – the west wall – set high up and perhaps related to a second floor?) The lower courses of stone are each set in a little from the one below, in a way reminiscent of the later Aksumite custom of shelving walls, except that the Aksumite style employed the shelving at greater intervals. The longer east–west walls of the temple measure about 61 ft. in length, the shorter north–south walls measure just over 49 ft. The height may have been about 50 ft. The stones, which are marginally drafted and often of substantial size – and very reminiscent of southern Arabian stonework in ancient times – are finely cut and put together without cement. There seem to have been originally two thicknesses of them on the side and back walls, with a certain number of stones set transversely to key the whole together. The wall with the doorway is much thicker, with an exterior set-back for the doors, and two interior niches near the corners away from the doorway.

As already noted, there may originally have been two storeys; the DAE conjectured that a small room in the southeast corner originally contained a staircase. Large square stones in the floor of the temple, with the centres cut out, may indicate pillar emplacements to support an upper floor, and Barradas seems to confirm this with his two rows of 'supports'. In addition, as well as the high windows in the western (façade) wall, in the north wall there is a water-spout passing through the wall about halfway up, which one may suspect was related to a floor at that level. In the south wall there is also a drain pierced through the wall at floor level.

A vestibule to the temple may have existed at the western side, where the entrance is. Bent thought that he saw some original stones still in position, but that the rest of the vestibule in his time – it does not exist now – was of later construction. This vestibule was also indicated in the plans and elevations prepared by the DAE. The DAE publication suggests that it was in fact built over a former entrance staircase, which is indicated in the elevation and reconstruction drawings as a possibility, and which future archaeology might profitably explore. If it seems incredible that such work has not already been done, considering the overwhelming importance of the monument to Ethiopian history, and the excellent possibility that further epigraphic material might be found there, it may be considered a measure of the state of archaeology in the country. The stones Bent noted might, then, have belonged to a landing or platform at the top of the steps, which might still lie below the present ground level. Bent recorded that there were two inscriptions built into the vestibule walls, an indication that it was probably constructed later after the temple had fallen into disuse. Possibly the vestibule was associated with the later construction of a church dedicated to Abba Afse within the temple walls.

At the time of the visits by Bent and the DAE there still remained the ruins of this church built inside the temple structure; from the DAE report it seems to have been complete up to roof level. This building, like the vestibule, included some more ancient decorative fragments built into its walls. The French archaeologist Jean Doresse, who worked here briefly in the 1950s, suggested that the church dated from the time of Abba Afse himself, but, like all the Nine Saints, Afse is in fact known only from much later stories. There is no certainty about anything concerning him, including date and name. Barradas, at any rate, did not mention any such structure when he was there in the first half of the seventeenth century.

By Doresse's time, the building in the centre had already been cleared away. Stone paving was revealed, with a later, coarser type of stone flooring over part of it, doubtless added when earlier alterations were made. In a crypt, 3 m. by 2 m. in size, 1.80 m. deep, which was excavated at the centre rear of the temple, against the east wall, were found fragments of ancient glass, and the remains of lamps or incense burners in bronze to which were attached little bells, and bronze crosses (see the illustration in Doresse 1959: 68). These objects, with the baptistery that was constructed in a former room or staircase-well in the southeast corner of the temple, he dated to the sixth century, regarding them as the oldest preserved relics left by ancient Ethiopian Christianity. The baptistery – which being then unexcavated was marked as a tomb in the DAE plan – was cleared by Doresse in 1955. It is very similar in design to others found subsequently in ancient Ethiopian churches excavated by Paribeni at Adulis and by Anfray at Matara, with two flights of steps leading down into the basin from east and west.

The DAE plan suggests that another room in the northeast corner of the temple balanced that in which the baptistery was later constructed, with, between these two, a deep niche facing east, presumably the sanctuary area. In the interior face of the main walls of the temple, sockets for these lesser internal walls can be clearly seen. The DAE plan also inserts four pillars in the centre. No evidence then existed for this, as not only was the old church inside the temple still standing when the DAE team made their visit, but the temple itself was piled high inside with debris. Nevertheless, some such support must indeed have been required for an upper floor and for the roof, and supports aligned in two rows were noted, as we have seen, by Barradas.

Grat Be'al Guebri and the Yeha Tombs

Bent also noted the giant square stone pillars of the monumental structure now known as Grat Be'al Guebri, standing some three hundred yards away from the temple on the other side of the village. He thought that it would be 'an exceedingly interesting spot to excavate'. The DAE report, too, mentioned this structure and illustrated it with a photograph as well as plans to show the position of the visible features.

The Grat Be'al Guebri edifice was eventually excavated by M. Anfray (a brief account was published in 1972), with the conclusion that it might have been a palace building. It had been destroyed by fire. In many places around the present village of Yeha, and in the area of the temple itself, traces of ancient constructions and the presence of pre-Aksumite pottery indicate that, one day, it might be possible to excavate some of the domestic buildings of the pre-Aksumite population of Yeha.

Finally, a number of tombs at Yeha, dug into the rock below the temple knoll to the southeast and southwest in the Da'ro Mikael area of the village, were excavated. Remains of stelae, which might have originally marked the tombs, were found in the area during the excavations. The tomb shafts cut into the rock were sometimes covered with roughly cut stones. The shafts led to one, two or three small rock-cut chambers, in which were the remains of skeletons, and quantities of grave-goods. The material found included stone incense burners, and some of the curious bronze openwork animal shapes containing south Arabian letters, which may perhaps have acted as some sort of seal or identity mark for the persons named (other similar examples were found at Sabea and Hawelti). There were also numerous red and black pottery vessels of many different forms, bronze tools and ornaments, sickles, chisels, axes, iron swords, chisels, knives and rings, many bead necklaces and some gold rings. Notable among all these objects was the high level of metalwork and the individuality of such elements as the pottery and the 'identity-markers'. Some of this material is on exhibition in the National Museum in Addis Ababa.

Chronological Table and List
of Rulers from Pre-Aksumite Times to
Haile Sellassie and the Revolution

From c. 800 BC (?) Kingdom of Di'amat and Saba

W'RN HYWT
RD'M
RBH
LMN
Rise of Aksum from perhaps 2nd–1st century BC

c. AD 100–650 First Ethiopian Empire, Aksum

		Pliny mentions Adulis
c. AD 100	Zoskales	Periplus of the Erythraean Sea
c. 130		Ptolemy's Geography
c. 200	GDRT, BYGT	South Arabian inscriptions, Addi Galamo bronze
	'ADBH, GRMT	South Arabian inscription
	Sembrouthes	Greek inscription
	ZQRNS, DTWNS	South Arabian inscription
c. 290	Endubis	Aksumite coinage begins
c. 300	Aphilas	
	Wazeba	
	Ousanas	
	'Ezana	356, letter from Constantius II, Ge'ez, and Greek inscriptions
	MHDYS	
	Ouazebas	Last stelae at Aksum (?)

361

c. 400	Eon	
	Ebana	
	Nezool/Nezana	
c. 500	Ousana/Ousana(s) = Tazena (?)	
	Kaleb	
c. 519		Kaleb's expedition to Yemen; Sumuyafaʻ Ashwaʻ viceroy in Yemen
	Alla Amidas = Wazena (?)	
		Abreha becomes king in Yemen
	Ella Gabaz = WʻZB (?)	
c. 550	Ioel	
	Hataz = Iathlia (?)	
c. 570		Persians conquer Yemen
	Israel	
c. 600	Armah	
	Gersem	
		Hasani Danael inscriptions (?)
630		Death of *Najashi* Ashama ibn Abjar
640		Egypt falls to Muslims
		End of Aksum as capital city (?)

c. 650–1137 Post-Aksumite Period

705–15	al-Walid. Picture of *najashi* at Qusayr Amra
	Patriarchate of James of Alexandria. *History of the Patriarchs* notes troubles in Ethiopia
c. 872–91	al-Yaqubi mentions Kuʻbar as *najashi*'s capital
	Patriarchate of Kosmas III of Alexandria. Dispute over Ethiopian succession
c. 950–90	Queen of Bani al-Hamwiyya (Gudit (?)) conquers Ethiopia
969–70	Ethiopian queen sends zebra to king of Yemen
979–1003	Dispute with patriarchate resolved
1073–77	Cyril becomes metropolitan by forged letters
1078–92	Patriarchate of Cyril II of Alexandria. Severus becomes metropolitan
1092–1102	Patriarchate of Michael IV of Alexandria. George becomes metropolitan
1102–28	Patriarchate of Macarius II of Alexandria. Michael becomes metropolitan
1131–45	Michael in dispute with king over consecration of extra bishops

Zagwé Period

1137	Traditional date for beginning of Zagwé period
	Marara Takla Haymanot, first Zagwé king
1152	Metropolitan Michael in dispute with usurping king
	Tantawidim
	Yimrehana-Krestos, Dawit
	Harbay, Gabra Maryam. Queen Markeza?
c. 1210/25	Lalibela, Gabra Masqal. Queen Masqal Kebra
	Na'akuto La'ab. Queen Nesehet Maryam
	Yitbarak

Second Ethiopian Empire, 'Solomonic Restoration'

1270–85	Yekuno Amlak, Tasfa Iyasus
1285–94	Yigba Seyon, Solomon, son of Yekuno Amlak
1294–98	The 'five sons of Yigba Seyon' are said to have reigned a year each:
	Senfa Arad
	Hezba Arad
	Kadema Arad
	Dejen Asgad
	Saba Bahr Asgad
1299–1314	Widim Ra'ad, or Arad, Gabra Masqal, son of Yekuno Amlak. Queen, Jan Mangesha
1314–44	Amda Seyon, Gabra Masqal, son of Widim Ra'ad. Queens, Jan Mangesha, Belen Saba
1344–71	Sayfa Arad, Newaya Krestos, Qwastantinos, son of Amda Seyon
1371–80	Newaya Maryam, Widim Asfare, son of Sayfa Arad
1380–1412	Dawit I, son of Sayfa Arad (often called Dawit II, David of Israel – or Ebna Hakim – being regarded as Dawit I). Queens, Egzi Kebra, Seyon Mogasa, Dengel Sawana
1412–13	Tewodros, son of Dawit I
1413–30	Yeshaq, Gabra Masqal, son of Dawit I
1430	Endreyas, son of Yeshaq (or Endreyas, Hezba Nañ, Tewodoseyos, Widim Ar'ad, brother of Yeshaq), or
1430–33	Hezba Nañ , Takla Maryam, son of Dawit I
1433	Mehrake Nañ , Sarwe Iyasus, son of Hezba Nañ
1434	Badel Nañ , Amda Iyasus, son of Hezba Nañ
1434–68	Zara Yaqob, Qwastantinos, son of Dawit I. Queens, Jan Zela (Bar Zelay?) or Eleni, Jan Hayla or Firé Maryam, Seyon Mogasa
1468–78	Baeda Maryam, Dawit or Kyriakos, son of Zara Yaqob. Queens, Eleni or Admas Mogasa, Jan Sayfa, Baaleta Shehena or Dawit 'Era, Romna, Iresh–Gazet

1478–94	Eskender, Qwastantinos, son of Baeda Maryam. Queen mother, Eleni. Queens (three more)
1494	Amda Seyon II, son of Eskender
1494–1508	Naod, Anbasa Badar, son of Baeda Maryam. Queens, Naod Mogasa, Qafo (or = wife of Lebna Dengel?)
1508–40	Lebna Dengel, Dawit, Wanag Sagad, son of Naod. Queens, Sabla Wangel, Wanag Mogasa, Eleni
1540–59	Galawdewos, Asnaf Sagad, son of Lebna Dengel
1559–63	Minas, Wanag Sagad II, Admas Sagad, brother of Galawdewos. Queen, Admas Mogasa or Selus Hayla or Menchale
1563–97	Sarsa Dengel, Malek Sagad, son of Minas. Queen, Maryam Sena or Malak Mogasa. Concubine, *Emabet* Harago
1597–1603	Yaqob, Malek Sagad II, natural son of Sarsa Dengel. Queen, Nazarena
1603–4	Za Dengel, Asnaf Sagad II, son of Lesana Krestos, son of Minas
1604–7	Yaqob again
1607–32	Susenyos, Sultan Sagad, Malek Sagad III, son of Fasil, son of Yaqob, son of Lebna Dengel. Queen, Wald Sa'ala
1632–67	Fasiladas, Sultan Sagad II, Alam Sagad, son of Susenyos. Queen, Ehta Krestos
1667–82	Yohannes I, Alaf Sagad, son of Fasiladas. Queen, Sabla Wangel or Alaf Mogasa
1682–1706	Iyasu I, the Great, Adyam Sagad, son of Yohannes. Queens, Walatta Seyon or Maryamawit. Concubines, Malakotawit, Maryamawit (Mamit), Qedeste Krestos (and others)
1706–8	Takla Haymanot I, Leul Sagad, Gerum Sagad, Abrak Sagad, son of Iyasu I
1708–11	Tewoflos, Asrar Sagad, son of Yohannes I
1711–16	Yostos, Sehay Sagad, son of Walatta Hawaryat, daughter of Amlakawit, daughter of Yohannes I
1716–21	Dawit II (sometimes called Dawit III or even IV, Lebna Dengel being regarded as Dawit II or III), Adbar Sagad. Son of Iyasu I
1721–30	Bakaffa, Asma Giyorgis, Adbar Sagad II, Masih Sagad, son of Iyasu I. Queens, Berhan Mogasa or Walatta Giyorgis or Mentewab; Awalda Negest. Concubine, Walatta Petros
1730–55	Iyasu II, Adyam Sagad II, Berhane Sagad, son of Bakaffa. Queen, Bersabeh
1755–69	Iyoas, Adyam Sagad III, son of Iyasu II

Zemana mesafint (Era of the Princes/Judges)

1769	Yohannes II, son of Iyasu I
1769–77	Takla Haymanot II, Admas Sagad II, Tebab Sagad, Haile Sagad, son of Yohannes II
1777–79	Solomon II, son of Adigo son of Iyasu II and his first wife

1779–84, 1788–89, 1794–95, 1795–96, 1798–99, 1800 Takla Giyorgis, Fikr
        Sagad, son of Yohannes II
1784–88   Iyasu III, Baala Segab, son of Asegu, son of Iyasu II and his first
        wife
1789–94   Hezqeyas, son of Iyasu II and Bersabeh
1795, 1826   Baeda Maryam II, son of Solomon II
1796–97, 1799 Solomon III, son of Takla Haymanot II
1797–98   Yonas, son of Latsun, son of Fasiladas
1799–1800, 1801 Demetros, son of Arqadewos, son of Afrin, descendant of
        Fasiladas
1800   Takla Haymanot III
1801–18   Egwala Seyon or Gwalu, Newaya Sagad, son of Hezqeyas
1818–21   Iyoas II, son of Hezqeyas
1821–26, 1826–30 Gigar, son of Giyorgis Manfas Qeddus, son of Gabre'el, son
        of Mammo, descendant of Fasilidas
1830–32   Iyasu IV, son of Solomon III
1832   Gabra Krestos, son of Gabre Mesai, son of Walda Amlak, son of
        Aganatheos
1832–40, 1841–42, 1845–50, 1851–55 Sahela Dengel, supposed descendant of
        Fasiladas
1840–41, 1842–45, 1850–51 Yohannes III, son of Takla Giyorgis

Third Ethiopian Empire, the Later Imperial Period

1855–68   Tewodros II (Theodore). Queen, Terunish
1868–72   Takla Giyorgis II
1872–89   Yohannes IV
1889–1913   Menelik II (1865–89, king of Shewa)
1913–16   Lij Iyasu
1916–30   Zawditu
1930–74   Haile Sellassie

Makhzumi Sultans of Shewa

Reputed descendants of Wudd b. Hisham al-Makhzumi, who emigrated from
Arabia in the time of 'Umar b. al-Khattab. They are said to have reigned in Shewa
from AH 283/AD 896 for three hundred and ninety years to 1285–86, but the names
of none of the early sultans have survived. In 1285 Ali b. Wali Asma 'deposed the
kings of Shewa and caused them, to the last one, to descend into the tomb with
their people'. A certain Mhz was installed in Shewa by Ali b. Wali Asma in 1285.

Queen Badit daughter of Maya, d. AD 1063
Harba'ir (Harb Ar'ad?), 1108
Malasma'i, d. 24 August 1183
Husayn, 1180–

Abdallah 1193/94–1235
Muhammad b. Husayn, 1235–
Malzarrah b. Muhammad, 1239, m. Queen Fatima Aydargun, 1245–46
Gbnah, 1252–62
Giram-gazi, abdicated 1263
Dil-gamis, elder brother of Giram-gazi, 1263–
Dil-marrah b. Malzarrah, 1269–78, m. daughter of Wali Asma', 1271
Dil-gamis again, July–August 1278. He was once again deposed briefly in 1279
    by Abdallah ibn Ganah
Ali b. Wali Asma, reigning in Shewa 1280. Dil-marrah taken and killed in 1283

Sultans of the Walasma dynasty, Ifat and Adal (after Cerulli, *RSE*, 1941: 34–5; 1943: after 286).

There is confusion between the dates of these sultans as provided by the different chronicles and historians, but in most cases it is relatively minor.

'Umar Walasma –1275/76
Baziyu b. 'Umar (the 'Ali b. Wali Asma' who conquered Shewa in 1285?), 20
    years
Haqq al-Din I b. 'Umar, 7 years
Huasyn b. 'Umar, 5 years
Nasr al-Din b. 'Umar, 7 years
Mansur b. Baziyu, 5 years
Jamal al-Din b. Baziyu, 7 years
Abut, 2 years
Zubayr, 2 years
Queen Ma'ati-Layla, sister of Zubayr, 2 years
Sabr al-Din I Muhammad (Walkhawy) b. Dalhuy b. Mansur, 1324–29, deposed
    by Amda Seyon?
Ali b. Sabr al-Din, 40 years. Contemporary of Sayfa Arad, 1344–71
Ahmad Harb Ar'ad b. Ali, 2 years (8 years after Maqrizi, then Ali restored)
Haqq al-Din II b. Ahmad, 1376–86 (after Maqrizi, killed in 1374/75)
Muhammad Abu'l-Barakat Sa'ad al-Din b. Ahmad, 1386–1415 (or 1402
    according to Maqrizi)
Sabr al-Din II b. Muhammad, 1415–22. Contemporary of Yeshaq
Mansur II b. Muhammad 1422–25. Captured by Yeshaq
Jamal al-Din b. Muhammad, 1425–33. Contemporary of Yeshaq and Hezba Nañ
Badlay Shihab al-Din Ahmad b. Muhammad, 1433–45. Killed by Zara Yaqob.
Muhammad b. Badlay, 1445–71. Contemporary of Zara Yaqob and Baeda
    Maryam
Ibrahim b. Muhammad, 1471–72 (Ladae Esman of Baeda Maryam's chronicle)
Shams al-Din b. Muhammad, 1472–87
Ibrahim b. qat Nar al-Din, 1487–88
Muhammad b. Azhar al-Din b. Ali b. Abu Bakr b. Muhammad Abu'l

Barakat Saʻad al-Din, 1488–1518?
Ali b. Muhammad, 1518–19?
Fakhr al-Din, 1519
Abu Bakr b. Muhammad, moved sultanate to Harar in 1520
ʻUmar Din b. Muhammad
Muhammad b. Nasir, –1577
Mansur b. Muhammad, 1577
In 1577 *Imam* Muhammad Jassa transferred the sultanate to Aussa, while another
line of *amir*s ruled in Harar until 1887

The succession around 1329 (the date Huntingford prefers to Cerulli's 1332) is
different from Amda Seyon's chronicle, which lists the order as follows:

Haqq al-Din, not expressly cited as a ruler
Sabr al-Din, –1329
Jamal al-Din, 1329
Nasr al-Din, 1329–?

Al-Taghribirdi supplies the genealogy:

Walasma al-Jabarti al-Hanafi
ʻUmar
Mansur
Dalhuy
Nasir al-Din Muhammad
Ali
Ahmad
Saʻad al-Din Abu'l-Barakat Muhammad

Post-revolutionary Ethiopia

President Haile Mengistu Maryam
1991 Flight of Mengistu. Addis Ababa falls to Ethiopian People's Revolutionary
Democratic Front forces

SELECT BIBLIOGRAPHY

For other references, see Munro-Hay 1991 and Munro-Hay and Pankhurst 1995.

Abbadie, Arnauld d' (1868) *Douze ans de séjour dans la haute Ethiopie (Abyssinie)*, Paris, reprinted 1980–83, 3 vols, Vatican.

Almeida, Manoel de (1954) *Some Records of Ethiopia, 1593–1646, Being Extracts from 'The History of High Ethiopia or Abassia'*, trans. and ed. C. F. Beckingham and G. W. B. Huntingford, London.

Alvares, Francisco (1881) *The Prester John of the Indies; A True Relation of the Lands of the Prester John*, rev. and ed. 1961, repr. 1975 Charles Fraser Beckingham and G. W. B. Huntingford, with additional material from *Narrative of the Portuguese Embassy to Abyssinia*, trans. and ed. Lord Stanley of Alderley (London), Cambridge, 2 vols. In Vol. 2 there is a translation into English of the relevant parts of the *Book of Aksum*, pp. 521–5.

Annequin, G. in F. Anfray (1963) 'Chronique archéologique, 1960–1964' with notes by G. Annequin, G. Baillaud and R. Schneider, *Annales d'Ethiopie*, 6: 3–48. The section on Guzara by Annequin is on pp. 22–5.

Annequin, G. (1976) 'De quand datent l'église actuelle de Dabra Berhan Sellasé de Gondar et son ensemble de peintures?', *Annales d'Ethiopie*, 10: 215–26.

Anfray, Francis (1963) 'Une campagne de fouilles à Yeha', *Annales d'Ethiopie*, 5: 173–232.

— (1972) 'Fouilles de Yeha', *Annales d'Ethiopie*, 9: 45–64.

— (1988) 'Les monuments gondariens des XVIIe et XVIIIe siècles', *Proceedings of the Eighth International Conference of Ethiopian Studies*, Vol. I, Addis Ababa, 1984, Addis Ababa: 9–45.

Anfray, Francis and G. Annequin (1965) 'Matara, deuxième, troisième, et quatrième campagnes de fouilles', *Annales d'Ethiopie*, 6.

Arrowsmith-Brown, J. H. (ed.) (1991) *Prutky's Travels to Ethiopia and Other Countries*, London.

Aubin, J. (1996) *Le Latin et l'Astrolabe. Recherches sur le Portugal de la Renaissance, son expansion en Asie et ses relations internationales*, I, Lisbon and Paris.

Barradas, M. (1634) *Tractatus Tres Historico-Geographici (1634), A Seventeenth Century Historical and Geographical Account of Tigray, Ethiopia*, trans. Elizabeth Filleul, ed. Richard Pankhurst 1996, Wiesbaden.

Basset, R. (trans.) (1897–1909) *Histoire de la conquête de l'Abyssinie (XVI Siècle), par Chihab ed-Din Ahmed ben Abd el-Qader surnommé Arab-Faqih*, Paris.

Bent, J. Theodore (1896) *The Sacred City of the Ethiopians*, New York and Bombay.

Berry, LaVerle B. (1989) 'Gondar-style architecture and its royal patrons', *Proceedings of the First International Conference on the History of Ethiopian Art*, London, pp. 123–57.

— (1994) 'The Bahri Gemb and the Genesis of Gondar-style Architecture', in P. Henze (ed.), *Aspects of Ethiopian Art from Ancient Axum to the Twentieth Century*, London, pp. 83–92.

Book of Aksum (Mashafa Aksum, Liber Axumae) see Conti Rossini 1909, de Villard 1938, Alvares 1540.

Bosc-Tiessé, Claire (2000) 'L'histoire et l'art des églises du Lac Tana', *Annales d'Ethiopie*, XVI: 207–70.

Bruce, James (1790) *Journey to Discover the Source of the Nile*, London.

Budge, E. A. Wallis (1928) *The Book of the Saints of the Ethiopian Church*, Cambridge.

— (1928) *History of Ethiopia, Nubia, and Abyssinia*, London.

Burton, Sir Richard (1856) *First Footsteps in East Africa; Or, an Exploration of Harar*, London (several modern reprints).

Buxton, David (1949) *Travels in Ethiopia*, London.

— (1970) *The Abyssinians*, London.

Campbell. I. L. (1999) 'Portuguese influence on the architecture of the Lake Tana region. An enquiry into the rôle of Genetta Iyesus', paper presented to the Fifth International Conference of Ethiopian Art in Lisbon, 28–31 October.

Carta das novas …, see Thomas and Cortesão 1938.

Chojnacki, S. (1983) *Major Themes in Ethiopian Painting, the Influence of Foreign Models and their Adaption from the 13th to the 19th century*, Wiesbaden.

Combes, E. and M. Tamisier (1838) *Voyage en Abyssinie, dans les pays des Galla, de Choa et d'Ifat*, Paris.

Contenson, H. de (1961) 'Les fouilles à Ouchatei Golo près d'Axoum en 1958', *Annales d'Ethiopie*, 4: 3–16.

— (1963) Les fouilles à Axoum en 1958 – Rapport préliminaire', *Annales d'Ethiopie*, 5: 1–40.

Conti Rossini, C. (1909) *Liber Axumae*, Corpus Scriptorum Christianorum Orientalium, Scriptores aethiopici, series altera, T. VIII.

Cosmas Indicopluestes, see Wolska-Conus 1968.

Darkwah, R. H. Kofi (1975) (repr. 1978) *Shewa, Menelik and the Ethiopian Empire 1813–1889*, London, Nairobi, Ibadan, Lusaka.

Dimothéos (1871) *Deux ans de séjour en Abyssinie*, Jerusalem.

Doresse, J. (1956) *Au pays de la reine de Saba. L'Ethiopie antique et moderne*, Paris.

— (1957) *L'empire du Prêtre-Jean*, 2 vols, Paris.

— (1959) (2nd edn 1967) *Ancient Cities and Temples: Ethiopia*, Woking and London.

— (1972) *La vie quotidienne des Ethiopiens chrétiens aux XVIIe et XVIIIe siècles*, Paris.

Fattovich, R. and K. A. Bard (1994) 'The origins of Aksum: a view from Ona Enda Aboi Zague (Tigray)', *New Trends in Ethiopian Studies*, I, papers of the Twelfth International Conference of Ethiopian Studies, Michigan State University, 5–10 September, Trenton, NJ: 16–25.

R. Fattovich, K. A. Bard, L. Petrassi and V. Pisano (2000) *The Aksum Archaeological Area: A Preliminary Assessment*, Naples.

Ferret, P. V. and J. G. Galinier (1847) *Voyage en Abyssinie dans les provinces de Tigré, du Samen et de l'Amhara*, Paris.

— (1844) 'Obelisque d'Axoum', extract from Bulletin de la Société de Géographie, *Revue archéologique*, I: 331 and fig. 3.

Fiaccadori, G. (1981) 'Per una nuova inscrizione Etiopica da Aksum', *Egitto e Vicino Oriente*, IV: 357–67.

Gerster, Georg (1970) *Churches in Rock: Early Christian Art in Ethiopia*, trans. Richard Hosking, London: Phaidon.

Gigar Tesfaye (1987) 'Découverte d'inscriptions guèzes à Lalibela', *Annales d'Ethiopie*, 14: 75–82.

Gobat, S. (1851) *Journal of Three Years' Residence in Abyssinia*, Ashfield, MA, repr. New York 1969; also published as *Journal d'un séjour en Abyssinie pendant les années 1830, 1831, et 1832*, Paris 1853.

Grierson, R. (ed.) (1993) *African Zion. The Sacred Art of Ethiopia*, New Haven, CT and London.

Grierson, R. and S. C. Munro-Hay (1999) *The Ark of the Covenant*, London.

— (2002) *Red Sea, Blue Nile. The Golden Age of Ethiopia*, London.

Guida dell'Africa Orientale Italiana (1938), Consociazione Turistica Italiana, Milan.

Hancock, Graham (1992) *The Sign and the Seal: A Quest for the Lost Ark of the Covenant*, London.

Heldman, Marilyn (1995) 'Legends of Lalibela: the development of an Ethiopian pilgrimage site', *Res*, 27, Spring: 25–38.

Heuglin, T. von (1868) *Reise nach Abessinien*, Jena.

Heuglin, T. von, W. Steudner and H. Schubert (1862) 'Ausflug von Adua nach Aksum', *Peterman's Mittheilungen*, Gotha, cited in Monneret de Villard 1938: 105–8.

Huntingford, G. W. B. (1965) *The Land Charters of Northern Ethiopia*, Addis Ababa.

— (ed.) (1980) *The Periplus of the Erythraean Sea*, London.

Jäger, Otto Arnold and Ivy Pearce (1965) (2nd edn 1974) *Antiquities of North Ethiopia: A Guide*, Stuttgart.

Jesman, C. (1969) 'Early Russian contacts with Ethiopia', *Proceedings of the Third International Conference of Ethiopian Studies, Addis Ababa 1966*, 1, Addis Ababa: 253–67.

Jones, A. H. M. and E. Monroe (1935) *A History of Abyssinia*, Oxford, repr. 1955 as *A History of Ethiopia*.

Kobishchanov, Yuri M. (1979) *Axum*, Philadelphia.

Lefebvre, T. et al. (1845–48) *Voyage en Abyssinie exécuté pendant les années 1839, 1840, 1841, 1842, 1843*, Paris. Vol. 1 is an atlas entitled *Album Historique, ethnologique et archéologique*.

Lejean, G. (1872) *Voyage en Abyssinie exécuté de 1862 à 1864*, Paris.

Leroy, J. (1965) 'Notes d'archéologie et d'iconographie éthiopiennes, *Annales d'Ethiopie*, 6: 229–54.

Lindahl, B. (1970) *Architectural History of Ethiopia in Pictures*, Addis Ababa.

Littmann, Enno et al. (1913) *Deutsche Aksum-Expedition*, 4 vols, Berlin.

Lobo, J. (1984) *The Itinerário of Jerónimo Lobo*, trans. Donald M. Lockhart from the Portuguese text established by M. G. da Costa, London.

Mathew, David (1947) *Ethiopia: The Study of a Polity, 1540–1935*, London.

Matthews, Derek and Antonio Mordini (1959) 'The monastery of Debra Damo, Ethiopia', *Archaeologia*, XCVII: 51–2.

Michels, J. (1988) 'The Axumite kingdom; a settlement archaeology perspective', *Proceedings of the Ninth International Conference of Ethiopian Studies, Moscow 26–29th August 1986*, Moscow, vol. 6: 173–83.

Monti della Corte, Alessandro Augusto (1940) *La chiese ipogee e monolitiche e gli altri monumenti medievali del Lasta*, Rome.

Moreno, M. M. (1942) 'La cronaca di re Teodoro attribuata al dabtara Zanab', *Rassegna di Studi Etiopici*, 2: 143–80.

Munro-Hay, S. C. (1989) *Excavations at Aksum*, London.

— (1991) *Aksum: An African Civilisation of Late Antiquity*, Edinburgh.

— (1984) *The Coinage of Aksum*, New Delhi and Butleigh.

— (1997) *Ethiopia and Alexandria: The Metropolitan Episcopacy of Ethiopia*, Warsaw and Wiesbaden.

Munro-Hay, S. C. and B. Juel-Jensen (1995) *Aksumite Coinage*, London.

Munro-Hay, S. C. and R. K. P. Pankhurst (1995) *Ethiopia*, Oxford.

Murphy, D. (1968) *In Ethiopia with a Mule*, London.

Nersessian, V. and R. Pankhurst (1982) 'The visit to Ethiopia of Yohannes T'ovmacean, an Armenian jeweller, in 1764–66', *Journal of Ethiopian Studies*, 15: 79–104.

Pais (Paez) Péro (1945–46) *História da Etiópia*, 3 vols, Oporto.

Pankhurst, R. K. P. (ed.) (1967) *The Ethiopian Royal Chronicles*, Addis Ababa.

— (1969) 'The Saint Simonians and Ethiopia', *Proceedings of the Third International Conference of Ethiopian Studies, Addis Ababa 1966*, I, Addis Ababa: 169–223.

— (1982) *History of Ethiopian Towns From the Middle Ages to the Early Nineteenth Century*, Wiesbaden.

— (1988) 'Muslim commercial towns, villages and markets of Christian Ethiopia prior to the rise of Tewodros', in S. Uhlig and Bairu Tafla (eds), *Collectanea Aethiopica*, Stuttgart, pp. 111–30.

— (1998) *The Ethiopians*, Oxford.

— (1999) 'Danqaz: an early seventeenth century Ethiopian capital, and its Portuguese, and Portuguese–Indian, architectural connections', paper presented to the Fifth International Conference of Ethiopian Art, Lisbon, 28–31 October.

Pankhurst, R. and D. Gérard (1996) *Ethiopia Photographed: Historic Photographs of the Country and its People Taken between 1867 and 1935*, London.

Pankhurst, R. K. P. and L. Ingrams (1978) *Ethiopia Engraved: An Illustrated Catalogue of Engravings by Foreign Travellers from 1681 to 1900*, London.

Pankhurst, Sylvia (1955) *Ethiopia: A Cultural History*, London.

Parkyns, Mansfield (1853) *Life in Abyssinia*, 2 vols, London.

Pearce, N. (1831) *The Life and Adventures of Nathaniel Pearce Written by Himself During a Residence in Abyssinia from the Years 1810 to 1819*, London.

Perruchon, Jules (1892) *Vie de Lalibela, roi d'Ethiopie*, Paris.

Pétridès, S. P. (1964) *Le Livre d'Or de la Dynastie Salomonienne d'Ethiopie*, Paris.

Phillipson, D. (1977) 'The excavation of Gobedra rock-shelter, Axum', *Azania*, XII: 53–82.

— (1995) 'Excavations at Aksum, Ethiopia, 1993–4', *Journal of the Society of Antiquaries*, 75: 1–41.

— (1998) *Ancient Ethiopia: Aksum, its Antecedents and Successors*, London.

— (2001), *Archaeology at Aksum, Ethiopia, 1993–7*, London.

Plant, R. (1985) *Architecture of the Tigre, Ethiopia*, Worcester.

Plowden W. C. (1868) *Travels in Abyssinia and the Galla Country*, London.

Poissonier, B. (2000) 'Rethinking Aksum?', abstract from a paper delivered at the XVth International Conference of Ethiopian Studies, 6–11 November, printed in the *Abstracts* of the Conference.

Poncet, Charles Jacques (1949) *A Voyage to Ethiopia, 1698–1701*, in *The Red Sea and Adjacent Countries at the Close of the Seventeenth Century*, ed. Sir William Foster, London.

Puglisi, S. (1941) 'Primi risultati delle indagini compiute della missione archeologica di Aksum', *Africa Italiana*, 8: 95–153.

Raffray, A. (1876) *Abyssinie*, Paris.

Rohlfs, G. (1870) *Land und Volk in Afrika. Berichte aus den Jahren 1865–1870*, Bremen.

— (1883) *Meine Mission nach Abessinien*, Leipzig.

Rüppell, E. (1840) *Reise in Abyssinien*, Frankfurt-am-Main.

Salt, Henry (1814) *A Voyage to Abyssinia and Travel into the Interior of that Country, Executed under the Orders of the British Government, in the Years 1809 and 1810*, London.

Sapeto, G. (1845) 'Etudes historiques et géographiques sur l'Abyssinie. Mémoire sue une inscription éthiopienne d'Aksoum', *Nouvelles annales des voyages et des sciences géographiques*, Nouvelle Série, II: 296–301; III: 32–56.

— (1938) 'Gli ultimi cento anni della monarchia abissina', unpublished manuscript, cited in Monneret de Villard 1938, pp. 97–9.

Sergew Hable Sellassie (1972) *Ancient and Medieval Ethiopian History to 1270*, Addis Ababa.

Shiferaw Bekele (1990) 'The state in the Zamana Masafent (1786–1853): an essay in reinterpretation', in *Kasa and Kasa, Papers on the Lives, Times and Images of Téwodros II and Yohannes IV (1855–1889)*, ed. Taddese Beyene, Richard Pankhurst and Shiferaw Bekele, Addis Ababa, pp. 25–68.

Solomon Addis Getahun (1997) 'Addis Alam: the nucleus of Gondar', in K. Fukui, E. Kurimoto and M. Shigeta (eds), *Ethiopia in Broader Perspective: Papers of the 13th International Conference of Ethiopian Studies*, Kyoto, Vol. I: 3–15.

Somigli di S. Detale, T. (1928) *Ethiopia Francescana nei documenti dei secoli XVII e XVIII precedute da cenni storici sulle relazioni con i'Etiopia durante i sec. XIV e XV*, in Bibliotheca Bio-bibliografia della Terra Santa e dell'Oriente Francescano – Documenti, Serie Terza, Tomo I, Parte II, 1643–1681, Florence.

Staude, W. (1959) 'Etude sur la décoration picturale des églises Abba Antonios de Gondar et Dabra Sina de Gorgora', *Annales d'Ethiopie*, 3: 185–250.

Steudner, W. (1862) 'Reise von Keren nach Adoa vom 28. Oktober bis 14. November 1861, sowie Besuch von Axum', *Zeitschrift für allgemeine Erdkunde*, N. F., XII, Berlin, cited in Monneret de Villard 1938, pp. 108–10.

Taddesse Tamrat (1972) *Church and State in Ethiopia, 1270–1527*, Oxford.

Telles (Tellez), Balthasar (1710) *The Travels of the Jesuits in Ethiopia*, London.

Thomas, H., and A. Cortesão (1938) *The Discovery of Abyssinia by the Portuguese in 1520 ...*, London.

Ullendorff, Edward (1960) (2nd edn 1965, 3rd edn 1973) *The Ethiopians: An Introduction to Country and People*, London, Oxford, New York.

Valentia, Lord (George Annesley, Viscount Valentia) (1809) *Voyages and Travels to India, Ceylon, the Red Sea, Abyssinia and Egypt*, 3 vols, London.

Villamont, Jacques Sieur de (1605) *Les Voyages du Sieur de Villamont*, Arras, pp. 341–3.

Van Donzel, E. J. (1979) *Foreign Relations of Ethiopia 1642–1700. Documents Relating to the Journeys of Khodja Murad*, Istanbul.

Villard, Ugo Monneret de (1938) *Aksum, richerche di topografia generale*, Rome.

Walker, C. H. (1933) *The Abyssinian at Home*, London.

Whiteway, R. S. (1902) *Portuguese Expedition to Abyssinia 1541–43*, London.

Wolska-Conus, Wanda (1968) *Cosmas Indicopleustès, La topographie chrétienne*, 3 vols, Paris.

Zagwé Hagiographies and Ethiopian Royal Chronicles

Basset, R. (1881) 'Etudes sur l'histoire d'Ethiopie', *Journal Asiatique*, ser. 6, XVII: 315–434; XVIII: 93–183, 285–389.

Blundell, H. W. (1922) *The Royal Chronicle of Abysinnia, 1769–1840*, Cambridge.

Conti Rossini, C. (1894) 'La storia di Libna Dingil, re d'Etiopia', *Rendiconti della Reale Accademia dei Lincei*, ser. 5, vol. iii: 617–40.

— (1943) 'Gli atti di re Na'akuto La'ab', *Annali*, II, Naples: 105–23.

Conti Rossini, C. and I. Guidi (1907) *Historia regis Sarsa Dengel (Malak Sagad)*, Corpus Scriptorum Christianorum Orientalium, Scriptores Aethiopici, ser. altera III, Paris, pp. 1–191.

Conzelman, W. E. (1895) *La chronique de Galawdewos (Claudius), roi d'Ethiopie*, Paris.

Dombrowsi, F. A. (1903) *Tanasee 106: Ein Chronik der Herrscher Äthiopiens*, Wiesbaden.

Guidi, I. (1903, 1905) *Annales Iohannis I, Iyasu I et Bakaffa*, Corpus Scriptorum Christianorum Orientalium, Scriptores Aethiopici, ser. altera V, parts I–II, Paris.

— (1912) *Annales regum 'Iyasu II et 'Iyo'as*, Corpus Scriptorum Christianorum Orientalium, 61, Scriptores Aethiopici, 28, ser. altera VI, 2 vols, Paris.

— (1926) 'Due nuovi manoscritti della "Cronaca Abbreviata" di Abissinia', *Rendiconti della R. Accademia Nazionale dei Lincei*, serie 6, II: 357–421.

Huntingford, G. W. B. (ed. and trans.) (1965) *The Glorious Victories of Amda Seyon, King of Ethiopia*, Oxford.

Kur, S. (1972) 'Acts of Masqal Kebra, Edition d'un manuscrit Ethiopien de la bibliothèque Vaticane: Cerulli 178', *Memorie della Accademia dei Lincei*, ser. 8, XVI: 383–426.

Marrassini, Pablo (1995) *Il Gadla Yemrehanna Krestos*, Supplemento n. 85 agli Annali (Istituto Universitario Orientale, Napoli), vol. 55, fasc. 4, Naples.

Pereira, F. M. E. (1887–88) *Historia de Minâs, 'Ademâs Sagad, rei de Ethiopia*, Lisbon.

— (1892–1900) *Chronica de Susenyos, rei de Ethiopia*, 2 vols, Lisbon.

Perruchon, J. (1889) 'Histoire des guerres d'Amda Seyon, roi d'Ethiopie', *Journal Asiatique*, ser. 8, t. XIV: 271–363, 381–493.

— (1892) *Vie de Lalibala, roi d'Etiopia*, Publications de l'Ecole des lettres d'Alger, Bulletin de Correspondance Africaine, XLVII, Paris.

— (1893) *Les chroniques de Zar'a Ya'eqob et de Ba'eda Maryam*, Paris.

— (1894) 'Histoire d'Eskender, d'Amda Seyon II et de Na'od, rois d'Ethiopie', *Journal Asiatique*, ser. 9, t. III: 319–66.

INDEX